MW00714283

PEACHTREE®
ACCOUNTING

made Easy

Stephen K. O'Brien
John V. Hedtke
Arnold Berman

Osborne **McGraw-Hill**

Berkeley New York St. Louis San Francisco
Auckland Bogotá Hamburg London Madrid
Mexico City Milan Montreal New Delhi Panama City
Paris São Paulo Singapore Sydney
Tokyo Toronto

Osborne **McGraw-Hill**
2600 Tenth Street
Berkeley, California 94710
U.S.A.

For information on translations and book distributors outside of the U.S.A., write to Osborne **McGraw-Hill** at the above address.

Peachtree Complete® is a registered trademark of Peachtree Software, Inc.

Peachtree® Accounting Made Easy

890 DOC 9987654

ISBN 0-07-881611-4

To Louise Davidove,

　　world traveller, storyteller, first-rate knitter,
　　and the best cookie maker in the world.
　　I am pleased and proud to be her grandson.

—JVH

CONTENTS
AT A GLANCE

CONTENTS

Index **423**

ACKNOWLEDGMENTS

Even under the best of circumstances, writing a book is a major (though very satisfying) undertaking. The following people have all made this book a little easier to complete:

First (and most important), my wife, Patricia Callander Hedtke, who, with reasonably good grace, puts up with my departures into the basement office for months at a time. Without her support and advice, writing wouldn't be nearly as much fun.

Jeff Pepper of Osborne/McGraw-Hill, who supervised this book. Jeff has exhibited patience and calmness throughout the writing of this book, which I'm certain was difficult at times.

Emily Rader, Jeff's Editorial Assistant, a dab hand with paperwork. Thanks, Emily.

Laura Sackerman, Associate Editor, for the time she spent making sure that explanations made sense.

Deborah Craig, freelance copy editor, for having a keen eye.

Peter Hancik, who did an excellent job of setting the book under a tight schedule.

Kathy Krause and Dusty Bernard, for able editing and project management.

Susan Craig and Christel Goese at Peachtree, who provided software, technical advice, and background information.

Martin Kasischke and Craig Nicholls of Professional Management Systems, the Peachtree Complete III support outlet in Seattle, for technical support.

Jay Phillips and the night staff at KEZX FM in Seattle, who have made all my book-writing ventures a little easier over the past year.

Constance Maytum, accountant extraordinaire, for last-minute help and advice.

—John V. Hedtke

INTRODUCTION

Welcome to Peachtree Accounting Made Easy. Peachtree Complete III is the latest version of general accounting software produced by Peachtree Software. Peachtree Complete III offers a number of advantages over other PC accounting packages:

- **It is easy to use and understand.** Peachtree Complete III's modules are clearly defined, and there is extensive online help for every field to show you what you need to enter.

- **It is flexible.** You don't have to tailor your business's accounting practices to fit the shortcomings of your software.

- **It grows with you.** When you buy Peachtree Complete III, you are receiving the complete set of modules. You don't have to buy a number of different modules when you want to add capabilities—they're all part of the basic package.

- **It is inexpensive.** Peachtree Complete III can handle all the accounting requirements for most small businesses. To get the same number of functions and modules, you would have to spend anywhere from two to ten times as much for other PC-based software.

ABOUT THIS BOOK

This book is meant to be a fast introduction to Peachtree Complete III. After giving an introduction to the software, each of the modules is discussed by taking the reader through the menus and explaining what the features accomplish. Screens are plentiful so that you can follow along on your computer. Experienced users will find it quite simple to look up the techniques they will need to run and adapt their system. New users will find instructions on setting up modules and the options available to them.

You don't need to be familiar with Peachtree to use this book, but you should know some basic accounting concepts and understand how to operate your computer. If you are not an accountant yourself and are setting up Peachtree Complete III for your business, you may occasionally want to ask an accountant for advice on setting options and defaults. Most of the information you need to set up and run Peachtree Complete III is already in your company's files. All you will need to do is take some time to plan what you want and then organize the information for entering into Peachtree Complete III.

HOW THIS BOOK IS ORGANIZED

This book is divided into twelve chapters. Each chapter discusses one or two features of Peachtree Complete III in detail. The chapters are organized in the order in which you might set up and use the various features: general accounting concepts, setting up the General Ledger, accounts payable, purchase orders, accounts receivable, and so on.

Chapter 1, "Accounting Basics," describes the differences between accounting and bookkeeping. It also explains the basic accounting process and shows how automating the accounting process with Peachtree Complete III will give you greater control over the accounting process.

In Chapter 2, "General Ledger: Setting Up Your Business," you will see how to set up the General Ledger. This includes setting the general options and defaults for Peachtree Complete III and the General Ledger, as well as setting up account numbers and departments for Big Business, a ficticious sample firm used throughout this book.

Chapter 3, "General Ledger: Setting Up Shop," continues setting up the General Ledger by entering the chart of accounts and account balances for Big Business. You will also learn how to print General Ledger reports such as the transaction register, the trial balance, and a balance sheet.

Chapter 4, "Accounts Payable," introduces you to Peachtree Complete III's Accounts Payable module. In this chapter, you will learn how to add vendors, enter accounts payable invoices, and post credits. You will also see how to print checks for paying outstanding accounts payable invoices and how to post accounts payable to the General Ledger.

Chapter 5, "Purchase Orders," discusses the Purchase Order module. After you install this module, the chapter shows you how to enter and modify purchase order information, how to print, change, and cancel purchase orders, and how to receive shipments. The chapter concludes with information on posting the purchase order information to Accounts Payable.

The receivables side of accounting is dealt with in Chapter 6, "Accounts Receivable and Invoicing." The Accounts Receivable and Invoicing modules are discussed together. You will see how to enter defaults and options for both modules, how to set up and enter transaction types and product codes, sales tax information, and customer information. After this, you will learn about creating and printing invoices and credit memos, entering payments on customer accounts, printing statements, and ageing balances for customers.

Chapter 7, "Setting Up Payroll," is the first of three chapters dealing with the Payroll module. This chapter discusses how to set up Payroll and how to select the account numbers from the General Ledger for pay, taxes, and employee deductions. It also teaches you how to set up miscellaneous deductions and income within Payroll and how to apply garnishments.

Maintaining employee information and taxes are the focus of Chapter 8, "Using Payroll." You will see how to enter and change information about each of your employees, how to deduct taxes, and how to add miscellaneous income such as sick and vacation days.

In Chapter 9, "Generating Payroll," you will see how to enter employee time information from the Job Cost module and time cards and how to enter payroll exceptions. The chapter then shows how to calculate and verify the payroll, print paychecks, and close the pay period.

Chapter 10, "Fixed Assets," describes the various depreciation methods for fixed assets, then demonstrates adding and disposing of fixed assets from your company. The chapter ends by showing you how to print depreciation schedules and lists of assets.

Chapter 11, "Inventory," introduces Peachtree Complete III's Inventory module. Inventory costing methods are discussed, followed by a description of the inventory process. You will then learn how to set up your inventory and create assemblies. The chapter concludes by showing you how to record sales in inventory and run inventory reports.

In Chapter 12, "Job Cost," you will see how to tie Accounts Receivable, Accounts Payable, and Payroll information together for tracking the costs and receipts of a specific job. The chapter discusses tasks such as entering jobs, job phases, and cost codes. The chapter continues with entering estimates, creating change orders, and updating payroll information. It also shows you how to print summaries of the job costs and update the other Peachtree Complete III modules.

CONVENTIONS USED IN THIS BOOK

It may help you to know how various type styles are used to present different kinds of information in this book.

Characters or words you are to type appear in **bold**.

Defined terms are in *italics*.

Keynames appear in "key caps". Keynames are the names appearing on the keys of a standard IBM keyboard, such as (SHIFT), (ENTER), and (INS). If you are supposed to press several keys together, the keys are joined with a plus sign. For example, "Press (CTRL) + (F1)" means to hold down the control key ((CTRL)) and press (F1). "Press (ALT) and type **X, C**" means to hold down (ALT) and type **X**, after which you type **C**.

The screens in this book show you how Peachtree Complete III looks on an IBM computer using an RGB monitor with a standard 80-column display. What you see on your screen may be slightly different, depending on the configuration of your hardware.

ADDITIONAL HELP FROM OSBORNE/McGRAW-HILL

Osborne/McGraw-Hill provides top-quality books for computer users at every level of computing experience. To help you build your skills, we suggest that you look for the books in the following Osborne/McGraw-Hill series that best address your needs.

The " Teach Yourself " series is perfect for people who have never used a computer before or who want to gain confidence in using program basics. These books provide a simple, slow-paced introduction to the fundamentals of popular software packages and programming languages. The "Mastery Skills Check" format ensures that you understand concepts thoroughly before you progress to new material. Plenty of examples and exercises are used throughout the text, and answers are provided at the back of the book.

The "Made Easy" series is also for beginners or users who may need a refresher on the new features of an upgraded product. These in-depth introductions guide users step-by-step from program basics to intermediate use. Every chapter includes plenty of hands-on exercises and examples.

The "Using" series presents fast-paced guides that quickly cover beginning concepts and move on to intermediate techniques and some advanced topics. These books are written for users already familiar with computers and software who want to get up to speed fast with a certain product.

The "Advanced" series assumes that the reader is a user who has reached at least an intermediate skill level and is ready to learn more sophisticated techniques and refinements.

The "Complete Reference" series provides handy desktop references for popular software and programming languages that list every command, feature, and function of a product along with brief but detailed descriptions of their use. These books are fully indexed and often include tear-out command cards. The "Complete Reference" series is ideal for both beginners and pros.

The "Pocket Reference" series is a pocket-sized, shorter version of the "Complete Reference" series. It provides the essential commands, features, and functions of software and programming languages for users of every level who need a quick reminder.

The "Secrets, Solutions, Shortcuts" series is for beginning users who are already somewhat familiar with the software and for experienced users at intermediate and advanced levels. This series provides clever tips, points out shortcuts for using the software to greater advantage, and indicates traps to avoid.

Osborne/McGraw-Hill also publishes many fine books that are not included in the series described here. If you have questions about which Osborne books are right for you, ask the salesperson at your local book or computer store, or write to us at the address found on the copyright page.

OTHER OSBORNE/MCGRAW-HILL BOOKS OF INTEREST TO YOU

We hope that *Peachtree Accounting Made Easy* will assist you in mastering this fine product, and will also pique your interest in learning more about other ways to better use your computer.

If you're interested in expanding your skills so you can be even more "computer efficient," be sure to take advantage of Osborne/M-H's large selection of top-quality computer books that cover all varieties of popular hardware, software, programming languages, and operating systems. While we cannot list every title here that may relate to Peachtree Accounting and to your special computing needs, here are just a few related books that complement *Peachtree Accounting Made Easy*.

DOS Made Easy, by Herbert Schildt, provides a thorough, step-by-step introduction to using both PC-DOS and MS-DOS version 3.3, the popular operating system for the IBM PC and IBM-compatible personal computers. If you are a beginning computer user or want to brush up on your DOS skills, this book provides plenty of exercises and examples that enable you to grow from a beginner into an intermediate DOS user. *DOS 4 Made Easy*, also by Herbert Schildt, provides the same format and covers MS-DOS and PC-DOS version 4.0.

If you're looking for an intermediate-level book, see *Using MS-DOS*, by Kris Jamsa, (covering all versions through 3.3), a fast-paced, hands-on guide organized into 15-minute sessions that quickly cover basics before discussing intermediate techniques and even some advanced topics. If you have DOS version 4, see *Using DOS 4*, by Kris Jamsa.

For all PC-DOS and MS-DOS users (from beginners who are somewhat familiar with the program to veteran users), with any DOS version up to 3.3, see *DOS: The Complete Reference, Second Edition,* by Kris Jamsa. This book provides comprehensive coverage of every DOS command and feature. Whether you need an overview of the disk operating system or a reference for advanced programming and disk management techniques, you'll find it here.

For all Lotus 1-2-3 Release 2.0, 2.01, and 2.2 users, from beginners who are somewhat familiar with the program to veteran users, see *1-2-3 Release 2.2: The Complete Reference*, by Mary Campbell, the ideal desktop resource that lists every command, function, and feature of the program along with brief, in-depth descriptions of how each is used. If you have Lotus 1-2-3 Release 3.0, see *1-2-3 Release 3: The Complete Reference* also by Mary Campbell.

If you are currently using Lotus 1-2-3 Release 2.0, 2.01, or 2.2 and are upgrading to Release 3.0, be sure to look for *1-2-3: From 2 to 3,* by The LeBlond Group. This book quickly helps you make the transition from 2 to 3 while concentrating on business tasks.

Osborne also offers three fine books on Microsoft's Excel. *Excel Made Easy for the Macintosh,* by Edward Jones, takes you step-by-step through a thorough introduction to Microsoft's spreadsheet program. *Using Excel for the PC*, by Edward Jones, quickly covers Excel basics before focusing on intermediate techniques. *Advanced Excel for the PC,* by Amanda C. Hixson, discusses more sophisticated Excel capabilities including charting, built-in auditing, macros, using the Windows interface, and more.

WHY THIS BOOK
IS FOR YOU

Peachtree Accounting Made Easy is for anyone who wants a fast introduction to the many modules of Peachtree Complete III. If you haven't used Peachtree before, the book shows you how to install each module and discusses, in simple terms, each of the options available from the menus. Only minimal accounting experience is required. If you have used Peachtree before, the menu-oriented approach makes this an excellent book for easy reference or a handy guide to a module that you have not used before. Experienced users will also find discussions on how modules can be used together to make a truly integrated accounting system.

Peachtree Accounting Made Easy is the perfect choice for a brief, self-contained introduction to this vast accounting system.

Learn More About Spreadsheet Software

Here is an excellent selection of other Osborne/McGraw-Hill books on spreadsheet software that will help you build your skills and maximize the power of the software you have selected.

If you are a Lotus 1-2-3 beginner, look for *1-2-3 Release 2.2 Made Easy*, by Mary Campbell, a step-by-step, in-depth introduction to 1-2-3 Releases 2.0, 2.01, and 2.2. If you are using Lotus 1-2-3 Release 3.0, see *1-2-3 Release 3 Made Easy,* also by Mary Campbell.

For developing intermediate skills, look for *Using 1-2-3 Release 2.2*, by The LeBlond Group, which covers Lotus 1-2-3 Releases 2.0, 2.01, and 2.2, or *Using 1-2-3 Release 3*, by Martin S. Matthews and Carole Boggs Matthews, which covers Release 3.0.

Borland International's super spreadsheet is explained for all users in *Using Quattro: The Professional Spreadsheet*, by Stephen Cobb. This fast-paced, hands-on guide quickly leads you from fundamentals to intermediate techniques and even some advanced topics.

ACCOUNTING BASICS

Accounting is a fundamental part of running your business. Of course, selling is important. What good is a sale, however, if you can't bill accurately or on time, if your payroll costs are digging you in deeper each day, or if you don't know the cost of the goods you are selling? If you can't measure your business, you can't manage it. Accounting is the yardstick you need to measure, and manage, every aspect of your business.

This chapter is intended for those who know little or nothing about accounting. It covers the basic concepts of accounting in a simple, straightforward way. You don't have to be an accountant to use Peachtree Complete III, but knowing something about accounting helps. If you already know accounting basics, feel free to skim this chapter or go directly to Chapter 2.

ACCOUNTING VERSUS BOOKKEEPING

All businesses do bookkeeping, but not all do accounting. Bookkeeping is the process of recording information on business transactions. If you have a checking account, you do bookkeeping. Accounting requires bookkeeping but encompasses much more, including the design of the bookkeeping system, analysis of accounting data, creating financial reports, and making business decisions. Peachtree Complete III unifies the bookkeeping and accounting processes, providing for journal entries, posting to accounts, financial reporting, and business analysis.

THE IMPORTANCE OF ACCOUNTING

Accounting weaves its way into every aspect of a business. When the salesperson on the road fills out an expense form, that involves accounting. When you cut a payroll check to an employee, that too involves accounting. Even the chair you sit in and the rugs and lamps in your office involve accounting. Accounting plays four major roles in any business: financial control, operations, reporting, and planning.

Financial Control

Financial control is the accounting function that most people are familiar with. TV has popularized the image of a funny little guy with a green eyeshade who keeps track of every pencil and paper clip. While it makes for good television, this character has little to do with accounting in the real world. Managing overhead and production costs can make the difference between profit and loss. You may not care about paper clips, but you probably do care about what your business spends on rent, electricity, personnel, office equipment, and materials.

Controlling costs is a key factor to the success of any business. Consider this example. A business builds a machine at a cost of $50 and sells it for $100. After deducting the cost of sales, advertising, overhead, and other business costs, the company keeps only $10 of the original $100. In other words, the company had to sell $100 to keep $10.

Suppose that the company, by doing things a little differently, finds a way to reduce costs by just $10 per week. While this cost reduction may seem small, it is the equivalent of a $100 sale. Without good accounting practices, however, you won't know where to start cutting costs. Maybe your salespeople are spending too much on their trips, or your production costs are out of line. Perhaps your advertising dollars aren't pulling their weight. A good accounting system helps you identify the problem areas, giving your company the financial control that it needs.

Operations

If you run a business, you know that accounting is a part of your company's day-to-day operations. You are constantly billing customers, generating a payroll, paying bills, and tracking inventory, and each task has a role in the accounting process.

For the operational aspects of accounting, companies have varying approaches. The one-person consulting firm, for example, can simply track billings and expenses. The needs of a dress manufacturer with 50 employees, on the other hand, are far more extensive, involving payroll, inventory, cost estimation, receivables and payables.

Peachtree Complete III is split into modules. This lets your company use only the modules that it needs today, adding the others as the company grows. Peachtree Complete III's menu-driven system also makes learning the system easy. This is a major consideration when you factor in the cost of training personnel.

Reporting

Every business person wants to know periodically how his or her company is doing. Accounting reports, including balance sheets and income statements, provide you with the information you need to assess your company's performance.

Surprisingly, many businesses operate without the benefit of timely accounting reports. It is not uncommon for a company to find itself in a cash crunch months after the problem could have been identified. With Peachtree Complete III, you can have reports on a daily or weekly basis. You never have to be in the dark about where your company stands.

For publicly held companies, financial reporting takes on special significance. Investors and analysts rely on your financial statements to guide them in taking positions and making recommendations. Accurate financial statements are critical to a market economy, which is why the government and the accounting profession spend millions each year to root out fraud and enforce proper accounting methods.

Planning

Accounting has an important role in charting your company's future, which is often reflected in the accounting data that you've accumulated day by day. Yet not enough companies take the time to review their progress over time.

Planning means setting goals and putting together a step-by-step approach for reaching those goals. Setting reasonable goals is a key component of this process. Aiming for the moon won't do you or your business any good. At the same time, setting your sights too low won't produce the results you want. If your business has a good accounting system, you will have the information you need to set attainable goals.

For example, suppose that your inventory system shows that, on average, you have a 60-day supply of parts on hand. Since inventory ties up cash, you want to reduce this unnecessary cost. In reviewing your accounting data, you find that the lowest point your inventory ever fell to was a 30-day supply. With this information, you decide to set a reasonable goal of reducing your average inventory level to 45 days but never letting it fall below 30 days. If you are successful in reaching this goal, you will improve the profitability of your business.

Having set the goal of reducing inventory, you must also define how to achieve that goal. Referring once again to data provided by your accounting system, you find that the fluctuations in inventory are caused by a lack of timely information about current stock levels. Your plan, then, is to computerize the inventory process so that you only order what you really need.

It is clear that a good accounting system is essential to successful business practices. Peachtree Complete III and your personal computer are all that you need to improve your operations, get the information you need, and improve your company's profitability.

ACCOUNTING FUNDAMENTALS

You don't have to be an accountant to use Peachtree Complete III, but it does help if you understand some accounting basics. Fortunately, accounting relies on some fairly simple rules known as generally accepted accounting principles. Learn these rules and you will know all you need to get the most from Peachtree Complete III.

Accounts

The *account* is the basic building block of accounting. In fact, from an accounting point of view, your entire business is little more than many accounts, each one serving a specific purpose. One account tells how much cash you have on hand, another records how much you've paid your employees so far this year, still another tracks your inventory.

All of the accounts belonging to a business, taken together, form the *chart of accounts.* Setting up the chart of accounts is the first step in creating an accounting system. You organize the chart of accounts by major account categories such as assets, liabilities, capital, income, cost of sales, and expenses. Within the categories, you divide accounts further. For example, the asset category might include current assets which, in turn, contains the cash and accounts receivable accounts.

Transactions

While all accounts are used for different purposes, they all have balances that are increased or decreased by *transactions.* A transaction is any business operation that has a monetary impact. Examples include selling merchandise, purchasing inventory, paying bills, and amortizing an asset.

A transaction consists of two parts: *credits* and *debits*. Debits are recorded on the left side of an account and credits are recorded on the right side. Debits increase the balance of the cash account and credits decrease the cash balance. Figure 1-1 shows an account used to record cash transactions. The first item listed in the account is a debit of $5,000. Also listed are two credits for $500 and $200, leaving a net balance of $4,300.

Notice that the credits and debits listed in the cash account do not tell the whole story. The account in Figure 1-1 does not tell you where the $5,000 came from or what the $700 was spent on. In practice, transactions are recorded in a transaction journal before they are posted to their accounts. A transaction journal entry contains all the accounting information for a specific transaction. A typical journal entry might look like this:

Debit Cash $5,000.00

Credit Accounts Receivable $5,000.00

The journal entry indicates that the $5,000 debit to the cash account resulted from a credit to the Accounts Receivable account. In other

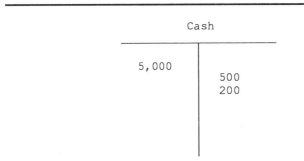

FIGURE 1-1   A typical cash account

s, someone paid their bill. Often an entry in an account will
.ue an identification number indicating which journal entry the
number came from. With Peachtree Complete III, the computer
keeps track of this for you.

The preceding example demonstrates the concept of *double
entry accounting*. The double entry concept is quite simple: Any
transaction contains both credits and debits which, when summed,
are equal. This is true even when the transaction affects more than
one account at a time, as shown here:

Debit Inventory	$5,000.00	
Credit Cash		$3,000.00
Credit Accounts Payable		$2,000.00

In this transaction, the company increases inventory by $5,000,
decreases cash by $3,000, and increases accounts payable by
$2,000. The sum of the credits equals the sum of the debits, and
the accounts are in balance.

If all your entries hold to the rule that debits equal credits, your
books will always balance. Unfortunately, companies that use
manual bookkeeping methods often find their books out of balance
due to clerical errors. These errors can be difficult to track down,
and can waste valuable time and energy. With Peachtree Complete
III, you can ensure that debits will always equal credits.

Assets, Liabilities, and Equity

While all accounts operate in the same fashion, they differ in one
important respect. For some accounts, like the cash account, debits
increase the balance and credits decrease the balance. For other
accounts, debits decrease the balance while credits increase it. The
rule you use depends on whether the account is an asset account,
a liability account, or an equity account.

Assets are the resources a company uses to generate revenue. Examples of assets include buildings, property, equipment, cash, accounts receivable, securities, trademarks, copyrights, patents, and more. When a transaction increases an asset—for example, purchasing a new building—it is recorded as a debit to the asset account.

Whereas assets represent a company's resources, liabilities and equity represent claims on those resources. *Liabilities* represent the economic obligations of a firm to outsiders. *Equity* represents the value allocated to ownership of the firm. These claims can take many forms, including the equity claimed by the owners of the firm, accounts payable, taxes payable, retained earnings, and so on. Liability and equity accounts are increased by credit entries.

For example, if inventory is purchased on credit, the transaction is reflected by a debit to inventory and a credit to accounts payable. Both accounts are increased by the amount of the transaction. Note that some transactions might involve only assets or only liabilities. For example, if inventory is purchased for cash, the transaction consists of a debit to inventory and a credit to cash; one asset account is increased while the other is decreased.

In other words, asset account balances are increased by debits and decreased by credits. Liability and equity account balances, on the other hand, are decreased by debits and increased by credits.

Revenues and Expenses

Two groups of accounts that deserve special attention are *revenue accounts* and *expense accounts*. Revenue is any proceeds from business activities (such as rental or sales income). Expenses are the cost of doing business (such as rent, depreciation expense, professional fees, heat, light, and so on). You determine *income* by subtracting expenses from revenues. To record revenue, you credit a revenue account; to record an expense, you debit an expense account. If revenues exceed expenses, the company makes a profit and equity is increased. If expenses exceed revenues, the company books a loss and equity is decreased.

Accrual Versus Cash Accounting

Accounting methods can be broadly categorized into *accrual accounting* and *cash accounting*. Most people are comfortable with cash accounting because it reflects the way they lead their lives. For example, if you perform work this year but get paid for it next year, that income will go on next year's tax return, not this year's. The rule for cash accounting is that revenues and expenses are recognized *when they are received or paid*.

Many small businesses operate on a cash basis. This works well when revenues and expenses tend to be small or are booked close to the time that they are incurred. For larger companies, however, cash accounting does not adequately reflect their financial situation. These businesses do their accounting on an accrual basis.

In *accrual accounting*, revenues and expenses are recognized in the accounting period in which they are incurred, regardless of when the money comes in or goes out. For example, suppose a company earns $100,000 this year but will not receive payment until next year. The revenue is booked (or accrued) this year through a credit to a revenue account and a debit to accounts receivable. Next year, when the payment is made, accounts receivable is credited and an offsetting debit is made to the cash account. The income is recognized before the money is collected.

The accrual principle also applies to expenses. Your company may incur an expense, for a sales trip perhaps, in one accounting period and pay the expense in another accounting period. Under accrual accounting, the expense is booked in the period in which the sales trip was made by debiting a travel expense account and crediting accounts payable. In the next period, when payment is made, you debit accounts payable and credit the cash account.

Despite its complexities, accrual accounting better reflects your company's financial position. For example, suppose that company A performs some work but will not be paid for it in the current accounting period. The work was done for a reputable client and company A knows that it will collect the revenue. Company B, on the other hand, performed no work during the current accounting period.

Clearly, given the choice you would prefer to be company A. Yet, under the rules of cash accounting, both companies would show the same revenue for the current accounting period. The difference between the two would not appear until the next accounting period, when company A is paid. Using accrual accounting, however, the difference between the two companies would be evident in the current accounting period. For this reason, all companies of significant size use accrual accounting.

Depreciation and Materiality

One aspect of accounting that confuses many people is the distinction between assets and expenses. Both can be increased by expenditures. However, an expense is an expenditure that benefits the company in the current accounting period only, while an asset is a resource that will benefit the company in the current *and* in future accounting periods.

Distinguishing between assets and expenses is important because many assets can be depreciated while expenses cannot. *Depreciation* spreads the cost of an asset over many accounting periods. In the case of a building, each year your company will take a depreciation expense representing the amount of use the building received that year. In other words, assets are turned into expenses over time by means of depreciation.

In some cases, the distinction is obvious. If you spend money to purchase a building, the building should be viewed as an asset since it will provide value to the company over many years. Paying the electric bill, however, is clearly an expense since its benefit is derived only during the current accounting period.

Sometimes the distinction between an asset and an expense is less clear. Strictly speaking, a screwdriver could be viewed as an asset if it is expected to last more than one accounting period. Of course, depreciating something so small as a screwdriver is silly. To deal with these situations, accountants use the rule of *materiality*. An asset is treated as an expense if the financial impact is so small that it will have no material effect on the firm's financial picture.

In practice, the materiality principle requires the accountant to use good judgment to determine when an asset should be treated as an expense. Because expensing an asset reduces current taxes more than depreciating assets, companies have an incentive to expense everything in sight. The best advice is to be prudent: Overindulging in the expensing of assets can leave you open to unhappy audits.

THE ACCOUNTING PROCESS

Peachtree Complete III handles all the details of posting transactions, linking journal entries to account entries, and summarizing account information. Even so, you will get more out of Peachtree Complete III if you understand the manual methods it was designed to replace. The accounting process consists of three elementary steps: journal entry, posting to the ledger, and account summarization.

Journal Entries

The *journal* is a register in which you record every transaction that affects your firm. A typical journal format contains space for a date, the account affected and an explanation, a post reference (used during posting), and spaces for debits and credits. Figure 1-2 shows a typical journal entry for a transaction involving the purchase of supplies for cash.

The journal is an important part of the accounting process for two reasons. First, it provides a chronological history of all transactions affecting your business. If you want to see transactions that occurred on June 15, you can do so easily. Second, the journal puts together all debits and credits associated with a particular transaction. If you just had the chart of accounts, it would be difficult or impossible to match credits and debits from the same transaction.

Posting to the Ledger

Periodically, you must *post* journal transactions to their appropriate accounts. Posting brings your accounts up to date, adding

Date	Account and explanation	PR	Debits	Credits
5/1/90	Supplies		123 34	
	Cash			123 34
	General office supplies			

FIGURE 1-2   A typical journal format

new debits and credits and changing balances. When you post a journal entry, the account number of the posted account is written in the post reference field. This reference simplifies error checking. The transaction in the journal affects two accounts, cash and supplies, both of which are asset accounts. Posting the transaction updates the General Ledger information for these two accounts. Figure 1-3 shows these accounts with the items already posted.

The cash account started the month with a balance of $1,532.32 carried over from the previous month. The posted transaction is a credit of $123.34, which reduces the cash balance. Notice that the post reference field in Figure 1-4 contains J-1. This tells the book-keeper that this transaction originated from page 1 in the journal. This backwards reference completes the link between the account and the journal entry. Also shown in Figure 1-4 is the supplies account. The debit to the supplies account increases the supplies balance.

Entering and posting transactions manually is time consuming and error prone. For many companies, automating this process alone is worth the price of computerizing. With Peachtree Complete III, you simply enter transaction information. The software makes sure that the debits and credits are equal when they are entered and later posts to the correct accounts automatically.

Date	Account and explanation	PR	Debits	Credits
5/1/90	Supplies	10345	123 34	
	Cash	10100		123 34
	General office supplies			

FIGURE 1-3   Using the post reference field

Cash   Account: 10100

Date	Explanation	PR	Debits	Credits	Balance
5/1/90	Balance				1,532 06
5/1/90	Purchase supplies	J-1		123 34	1,408 72

Supplies   Account: 10345

Date	Explanation	PR	Debits	Credits	Balance
5/1/90	Balance				3,221 87
5/1/90	Purchase supplies	J-1	123 34		3,345 21

FIGURE 1-4 A typical ledger format

Account Summarization

After posting, all accounts are up to date. You can now summarize your accounts in the form of financial statements. All financial statements, balance sheets and income statements included, are nothing more than summaries of account balances. In the balance sheet, the accounts are summarized by assets, liabilities, and equity. In the income statement, accounts are summarized by revenues and expenses. These financial statements are discussed in detail in the next section.

Once you know the format of your financial statements, creating them just requires taking account balances and entering them in the right place on the statement. Consider the simplified balance sheet shown in Figure 1-5. The asset, liability, and equity categories are simply the names of the respective accounts. The numbers to the right are the balances in those accounts.

FINANCIAL STATEMENTS

Financial statements are the signposts by which businesses measure their progress. These statements are so important, especially to publicly held corporations, that scores of books have been written on their analysis and interpretation.

While financial statements come in various forms, the two types that most businesspeople recognize are the *balance sheet* and *income statement*. These statements summarize, for a specific period of time, every bit of accounting information available to the firm.

The Balance Sheet

The balance sheet, also known as the *statement of financial condition*, is a snapshot summary of your company's asset, liability,

```
                    XYZ Company
                   Balance Sheet
                 December 31, 1990

         Assets

             Cash                     100
             Inventory                500
             Equipment              1,000

             Total Assets                      1,600

         Liabilities

             Accounts payable         200
             Equity                 1,400

             Total Liabilities               1,600
```

FIGURE 1-5   A simple balance sheet

and equity accounts as of a specific date. The ironclad rule of the balance sheet is

Assets = Liabilities + Equity

If you have entered all of your transactions correctly, so that debits equal credits, this equation will always hold. As a precaution, businesses often run a *trial balance* before generating the balance sheet. A trial balance is simply a sum of all accounts to ensure that credits precisely offset debits. Trial balances were more important when accounting was manual and creating a balance sheet was time consuming. Even with the use of computers, however, trial balances are still widely used as an interim step.

Balance sheets always list assets first, liabilities second, and equity last. Figure 1-6 shows a typical balance sheet. Of course, your balance sheet will contain account categories that make sense for you. Typical asset categories include:

- Cash

- Securities and investments

- Notes receivable

- Accounts receivable

- Accrued receivables

- Merchandise inventory

- Prepaid expenses

- Long-term investments

- Land

- Buildings

- Equipment

- Intangible assets

Typical liabilities include

- Notes payable

- Accounts payable

- Accrued expenses payable

- Income received in advance

- Long-term liabilities

- Long-term debt

- Income tax payable

The balance sheet groups assets, liabilities, and equity into categories, the most common being current assets, prepaid expenses, fixed assets, current liabilities, long-term liabilities, income received in advance, retained earnings, and stock-holders' equity.

- **Current assets**   These include cash and assets that will normally be converted into cash within one year or within the company's normal *operating cycle*, whichever is longer. The operating cycle is the length of time between the purchase of inventory or merchandise and the sale of the finished product. Current assets are also known as liquid assets or working assets.

- **Prepaid expenses**   These are expenses that are paid in advance and provide benefit over a period of time. A common example is insurance or rent paid in advance. Prepaid expenses are also known as deferred expenses or deferred assets.

- **Fixed assets**   These are assets that will provide lasting value to the firm beyond the current accounting period. Because fixed assets "wear out" over a number of years, each year a portion of their cost is taken as a depreciation expense.

```
                        Big Business, Inc.
                          Balance Sheet
                       December 31, 1990

                              ASSETS
Current Assets
  Cash                                           11,200
  Marketable securities                          23,030
  Accounts receivable                    54,000
    Less estimated uncollectible accounts   540  53,460
  Accrued interest receivable                     1,030
  Merchandise inventory                          65,100
  Supplies on hand                                  520
  Prepaid insurance                                 650

  Total current assets                                    154,990

Fixed Assets
  Land                                          54,330
  Building                            150,230
    Less accumulated depreciation      25,340  124,890
  Equipment                            56,300
    Less accumulated depreciation      13,180   43,120

  Total fixed assets                                      222,340
                                                          -------
Total Assets                                              377,330

                    LIABILITIES AND EQUITY

Current Liabilities

  Accounts payable                               34,510
  Accrued wages payable                          13,400
  Taxes payable                                  13,000
  Rent received in advance                       43,220

  Total current liabilities                               104,130

Long-Term Liabilities
  Mortgages payable                              34,200
  Long-term notes payable                        15,000

  Total long-term liabilities                              49,200
                                                          --------
Total Liabilities                                         153,330

Equity
  Common stock                                  201,000
  Retained earnings                              23,000

  Total equity                                            224,000
                                                          -------
Total Liabilities and Equity                              377,330
```

≡ **FIGURE 1-6** A complete balance sheet

- **Current liabilities**   Liabilities that mature (become payable) within one year or one operating cycle are called current liabilities. They typically include accounts payable, wages payable, and taxes payable. In addition, long-term liabilities become current liabilities during the year in which they become due.

- **Long-term liabilities**   Any liability not due within the current accounting period is referred to as a long-term liability. These are sometimes referred to as fixed liabilities or long-term debt, and include mortgages.

- **Income received in advance**   When a customer pays for something in advance, the amount is recorded as income received in advance. A magazine publisher, for example, would include paid subscriptions in this category.

- **Retained earnings**   This amount represents accumulated net income retained by the firm. When a corporation makes a profit, the proceeds can be distributed as dividends or reinvested in the company, in which case they are added to retained earnings.

- **Stockholders' equity**   Owners invest in a company by purchasing capital stock. The amount they pay for the stock is recorded as stockholders' equity. The sum of stockholders' equity and retained earnings represents the owners' value in the company.

The balance sheet is important not just in itself, but as a means of measuring corporate change. Companies often report balance sheets with data for up to five years, making it easy to spot importan changes.

The Income Statement

When people talk about income, they often mean revenue—the amount of money they take in. In accounting, income is very clearly defined as revenue minus expenses. There are even different types of income: income from operations, income before interest and taxes, income before extraordinary items, net income, and so forth. A commonly used term that fits the accounting definition of income is "the bottom line"—what is left over after everything is taken out.

The term "the bottom line" originated from the income statement. An income statement starts out by listing revenues. Expenses are listed next. When expenses are deducted from revenues, the result is income, which appears on the bottom line of the income statement.

The income statement is arguably the most important financial statement because it indicates directly how profitable your company has been over a specific period of time. Most companies are more concerned about profits than about the specific levels of assets, liabilities, and equity. Analysts often use information from both the income statement and balance sheet: Dividing net income by total assets yields *return on assets*, a primary indicator of a company's performance.

A typical income statement (Figure 1-7) begins with revenues. In this case, gross revenues are reduced by returns, allowances for returns, and discounts given, yielding net sales.

After revenue, all expenses are listed. Expenses are often categorized into *cost of goods sold* and *operating expenses*. Cost of goods sold refers to expenses incurred directly in the production of something to be sold. In the example income statement, cost of goods sold is determined by taking beginning inventory, adding all purchases, and deducting the inventory remaining at the end of the accounting period.

Operating expenses are expenses not directly related to the production of something for sale. This category includes selling expense and general administrative expense. By categorizing expenses in this way, you can tell if expenses are out of line in any area.

The bottom of the income statement shows *net income from operations* (net sales less cost of goods sold and operating expenses). Taxes are then deducted, yielding net income—the amount

```
                        Big Business, Inc.
                        Income Statement
                 Year Ending December 31, 1990

Revenue from sales
  Sales                                       215,920
  Sales returns and allowances        2,500
  Discounts                          13,410    15,910
  Net sales                                             200,010

Cost of goods sold
  Beginning inventory (1/1/90)                 45,320
  Purchases                                    73,230
  Less ending inventory (12/31/90)             35,320
  Cost of goods sold                                     83,230
                                                        -------
Gross profit on sales                                  116,780

Operating expenses
  Selling expenses
    Salaries and commissions                   10,000
    Advertising                                23,000
    Insurance                                   4,560
    Supplies                                    1,240
  Total selling expense                                  38,800

  Administrative and general expenses
    Office salaries                            45,000
    Depreciation                               10,450
    Utilities                                   7,660
  Total general expenses                                 63,110
                                                        -------
  Total operating expenses                              101,910

Net income from operations                              14,870
                                                        -------
Taxes                                                    6,690

Net income                                               8,180
```

FIGURE 1-7   A typical income statement

the business retains at the end of the accounting period. Net income can be reinvested in the business by adding it to retained earnings or it can be distributed to the owners as dividends.

AUTOMATING WITH PEACHTREE COMPLETE III

Automating your accounting with Peachtree Complete III can be the most valuable investment you make in your business. Peachtree Complete III not only automates the most tedious aspects of bookkeeping, it completely integrates all accounting functions in one program. You may buy Peachtree Complete III just to do your payroll, but later learn how easily it meets all your business needs. You can use any or all of the modules, depending on your needs.

Many businesses still do their accounting by hand, from journal entries to posting and payroll. If you are among these diehards, Peachtree Complete III can change the way you do business forever. For a modest investment in the Peachtree Complete III software and a personal computer, you will save thousands of dollars lost in manual processing, tracking down errors, producing financial reports, and accounting fees. You'll get a more efficient business, better control over your finances, and the flexibility to expand your accounting system as your business grows.

Increasing Your Efficiency

Do you have any idea how much your present accounting system costs? In addition to the bookkeeper's salary and your accountant's fees, there are hidden costs. For example, consider the cost of losing out on new business because you're tied up writing checks, or the cost of paying overtime or penalties because you can't get your financial statements and tax payments out on time.

Would you hesitate to buy a new piece of equipment that could increase your sales staff's efficiency by 100% or more or increase production by 100%? This is the kind of increase in efficiency you will get from using Peachtree Complete III.

Too many businesspeople hesitate to improve their accounting systems. Sometimes it's a fear of computerization. Sometimes it's a fear of fixing something that is working, or concern about alienating a trusted bookkeeper. There are a hundred reasons not to improve a accounting system, all stemming from one fear or another. As difficult as the transition to computerization may be, however, the rewards are well worth it.

Increased Control

Managing a business means controlling expenses, cash, and corporate assets. When your business was small, you probably had all the control you needed in your checkbook register. But growth means more complex accounting: financial reports, government regulations, payroll, and so on. You simply can't control a growing business if you don't automate.

With Peachtree Complete III, you can get up-to-the-minute reports on a daily basis. Do you want to know who owes you money? The Aged Receivables report will tell you all you need to know, in greater detail than you ever thought possible. Do you need to know how your inventory levels are doing? The Reorder Items report will tell you what items need to be restocked. Do you want to see what you're paying in wages? The Hours/Earnings report will provide the answers. Once you get used to Peachtree Complete III, you'll wonder how you made decisions without it.

Built-in Flexibility

It's easy to start using Peachtree Complete III. The software is completely modular, so you can use just the parts you need. Many businesses start by automating their payroll function, one of the most time-consuming tasks when done manually. From there, you can move easily into accounts receivable and inventory. When you're ready, add accounts payable, invoicing, and job costing. However you use Peachtree Complete III, you'll spend less time on accounting and more time on building your business.

GENERAL LEDGER:
SETTING UP
YOUR BUSINESS

Adding Your Company to Peachtree Complete III
Setting Up the General Ledger
Account Numbers

To computerize your accounting functions with Peachtree Complete III, you must first set up your business on the software. This process can be simple or complicated, depending on the options you select and how involved your chart of accounts is. Peachtree Complete III offers many options that let you customize the software to your needs. This chapter takes you through the setup process step-by-step, so you can start using Peachtree Complete III right away.

ADDING YOUR COMPANY TO PEACHTREE COMPLETE III

To learn about Peachtree Complete III, you will set up the software for Big Business, Inc., a firm that develops coin-operated software for personal computers. Big Business has been growing lately and is going to computerize its accounting using Peachtree Complete III. The software is already installed on the office PC in a subdirectory named PEACH on drive C. To start the program, change to the PEACH subdirectory and enter **PEACH** at the DOS prompt. Immediately, the Peachtree Complete III opening screen pops up (Figure 2-1). The opening screen displays the software's serial number, the name of the user, and the date stored in the computer's memory. If the date is incorrect, type the correct date before you continue. Since the date shown is correct, simply press (ENTER).

Peachtree Complete III first asks you to enter your company's identification code (Figure 2-2). Every business you set up on Peachtree Complete III must have its own unique ID, which consists of two letters or numbers. Once you identify the business,

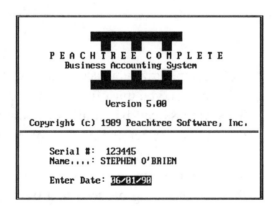

FIGURE 2-1   Peachtree Complete III opening screen

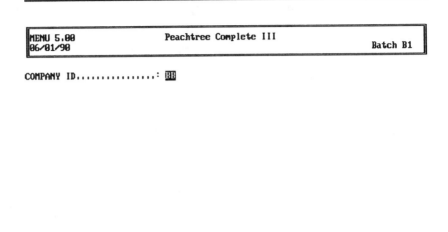

┌──┐
│ MENU 5.00   Peachtree Complete III   │
│ 06/01/90   Batch B1 │
└──┘

COMPANY ID................: ▊▊

Program Directory: C:\PCIII

  F1 Help   F2   Lookup   F5   Printers   F10   DOS

FIGURE 2-2 Enter company's identification code

Peachtree Complete III uses the files it has set up for that particular business. If you want to switch to another business, you can always return to this screen and enter another ID.

At the top of the screen is the Peachtree Complete III information box, which includes the menu you are in and the current date. This information box always keeps tabs on where you are.

At the bottom of the screen, highlighted messages tell you what function keys you can use. At this point, you have the following options:

F1-Help   You can always get help from Peachtree Complete III by pressing the (F1) key

F2 - Lookup   This function lets you select an item from a list instead of typing it or having to remember it. In the current situation, the list would contain all company codes already set up on the system

F5 - Printers   This function sets up Peachtree Complete III
                     to work with your printer or changes the
                     printer you previously selected

F10 - Done   This function tells Peachtree Complete III that
                     you have finished with the current process and
                     want to return to the previous step. If you
                     press (F10) now, you will exit from Peachtree
                     Complete III and go back to DOS

The main task now is to enter an ID code for your business, Big
Business. Since it has not used Peachtree Complete III before, you
need a new ID code. The code is BB; type it into the field and press
(ENTER).

Before continuing, Peachtree Complete III checks to see if the
code just entered already exists. Since BB is a new code, Peachtree
Complete III asks if you want to add the new code (Figure 2-3). In
this case, the answer is clearly yes, so you type **Y** and press (ENTER).
If, on the other hand, you made an error and entered an incorrect
code, you would simply type **N** and press (ENTER).

Since Big Business is using Peachtree Complete III for the first
time, the program asks for some basic information about the
company (Figure 2-4). First, you type in the full company name
and press the (TAB) key to move to the next field. Then enter the
company's address.

```
MENU 5.00                    Peachtree Complete III
06/01/90                                                     Batch B1


COMPANY ID................: BB

   ┌──────────────────────────────────────────────────────────┐
   │ COMPANY ID NOT FOUND.  DO YOU WANT TO ADD IT (Y/N): ▊      │
   └──────────────────────────────────────────────────────────┘
```

═══ **FIGURE 2-3**   Adding a new company name

```
┌──────────────────────────────────────────────────────────────────┐
│MENU 5.00                  Peachtree Complete III                   │
│06/01/90                                                  Batch B1  │
└──────────────────────────────────────────────────────────────────┘

COMPANY ID...............: BB

GENERAL INFORMATION
    Company Name.................: Big Business, Inc.
    Address Line 1...............: 123 Main Street
    Address Line 2...............: Anytown, USA
    Address Line 3...............:
    G/L Account # Size.(5 or 6)..: 5
    Default Backup Drive.........: A
    Default Backup Disk Size.....:   720K

    Accept (Y/N).: Y
```

FIGURE 2-4   Enter company information

The next three fields require some explanation. Peachtree Complete III allows you to use General Ledger account numbers that are either five or six characters long, but not both. You have to decide which to use.

The next field identifies the drive used for backups. Backups are extremely important. If you make a mistake when entering information, you can use backups to restore your original accounts. By maintaining complete sets of backup disks, you can always recover from even the most disastrous errors. To select the drive to use, just type the drive letter. In most cases, you will want to use drive A. You can also use your hard disk for backups, but this will erase old backups every time you make a new one.

The last field identifies the type of drive used for backups. The four common disk drive types are:

- 360 K, 5 1/4-inch

- 1.2 MB, 5 1/4-inch

- 720 K, 3 1/2-inch

- 1.44 MB, 3 1/2-inch

Select the type that matches your drive. When all the information is correct, press (F10) and then type **Y** to continue. Your business is now set up on Peachtree Complete III. The next step is to get your General Ledger going.

SETTING UP THE GENERAL LEDGER

A major step in computerizing your accounting functions is setting up your *General Ledger* — the module that maintains your company's chart of accounts. The General Ledger is the central component of your accounting system. It accepts information from Payroll, Accounts Payable, Accounts Receivable, and Fixed Assets. You can use any of these other modules by themselves, but you need to integrate them with the General Ledger to produce financial statements.

General Ledger is the first selection on the Peachtree Complete III Main Menu (Figure 2-5). To set up the General Ledger for a new business, select this option by either typing **G** or by highlighting the menu option and pressing (ENTER). Since the General Ledger module has not been installed for the new company, Peachtree Complete III asks if you want to install it now (Figure 2-6). Type **Y** and press (ENTER) to continue with the installation.

Before you can install the General Ledger, you must specify which directory you want the files to be stored in. Peachtree Complete III defaults to a subdirectory of the current directory—in this case \PCIII\GLDATA (Figure 2-7). To use this directory, simply press (ENTER). To use another directory, type the directory name and press (ENTER). If the directory does not already exist, Peachtree Complete III will create it for you.

General Ledger setup begins at the Program Options Menu, where you can set the options for General Ledger, automatic file backup, and printer assignments (Figure 2-8). At this point, press (ENTER) to select Set Module Options.

```
┌─────────────────────────────────────────────────────────────┐
│ MENU 5.00             Peachtree Complete III    COMPANY ID: BB │
│ 06/01/90                  Big Business, Inc.                   │
└─────────────────────────────────────────────────────────────┘
        ┌═══════ PCIII Main Menu ═══════┐
        │ ▓G - General Ledger▓          │
        │  A - Accounts Payable         │
        │  R - Accounts Receivable      │
        │  S - Invoicing                │
        │  I - Inventory                │
        │  P - Payroll                  │
        │  F - Fixed Assets             │
        │  J - Job Cost                 │
        │  O - Purchase Order           │
        │  U - Utilities                │
        │  Q - Peachtree Data Query     │
        └───────────────────────────────┘



 ▓F1-Help▓
```

FIGURE 2-5 Peachtree Complete III main menu

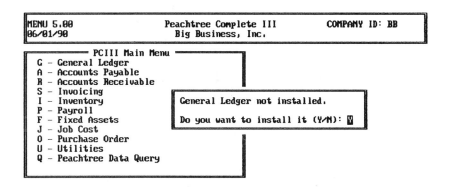

```
┌─────────────────────────────────────────────────────────────┐
│ MENU 5.00             Peachtree Complete III    COMPANY ID: BB │
│ 06/01/90                  Big Business, Inc.                   │
└─────────────────────────────────────────────────────────────┘
        ┌═══════ PCIII Main Menu ═══════┐
        │  G - General Ledger           │
        │  A - Accounts Payable         │
        │  R - Accounts Receivable      │
        │  S - Invoicing             ┌──────────────────────────────┐
        │  I - Inventory             │ General Ledger not installed. │
        │  P - Payroll               │                               │
        │  F - Fixed Assets          │ Do you want to install it (Y/N): ▓ │
        │  J - Job Cost              └──────────────────────────────┘
        │  O - Purchase Order           │
        │  U - Utilities                │
        │  Q - Peachtree Data Query     │
        └───────────────────────────────┘
```

FIGURE 2-6 Installing General Ledger

```
MENU 5.00                 Peachtree Complete III        COMPANY ID: BB
06/01/90                     Big Business, Inc.

┌═══════ PCIII Main Menu ═══════┐
│ G - General Ledger            │
│ A - Accounts Payable          │
│ R - Accounts Receivable       │
│ S - Invoicing                 │
│ I - Inventory                 │
│ P - Payroll                   │
│ F - Fixed Assets              │
│ J - Job Cost                  │
│ O - Purchase Order            │
│ U - Utilities                 │
│ Q - Peachtree Data Query      │
└───────────────────────────────┘

┌───────────────────────────────────────────────────────────┐
│   Enter the subdirectory path where you want your data files to be. │
│              C:\PCIII\GLDATA\                               │
└───────────────────────────────────────────────────────────┘
```

FIGURE 2-7   Selecting the General Ledger directory

```
GLMAINT 5.00            Maintain General Ledger Options    COMPANY ID: BB
06/01/90                     Big Business, Inc.




              ┌═══════ Program Options ═══════┐
              │  O - Set Module Options        │
              │                                │
              │  B - Automatic File Backup     │
              │                                │
              │  P - Set Printer Assignments   │
              └────────────────────────────────┘




 F1-Help                              F10 - Menu    Shft F10 - Home
```

FIGURE 2-8   Options for General Ledger

```
GLMAINT 5.00              Maintain General Ledger Options    COMPANY ID: BB
06/01/90                        Big Business, Inc.

General Module Options                  Fiscal Period Information
   Controller Password......:              Generation Number.....:  0
   Operator Password........:              No. of Fiscal Periods.: 12
   Use Menus................: Y            Current Fiscal Period.:  1
   Allow Changes/Deletions..: Y            Addit. Adj. Period....: N
   Force Control Reports....: Y          Ending Dates for Fiscal Periods (MM/DD)
   Keep Year-to-Date Detail.: Y          Period   Date      Period    Date
   Force Balance Trans......: Y            1.     06/30        8.     01/31
   Use Departments..........: N            2.     07/31        9.     02/28
   Print Account Numbers....: N            3.     08/31       10.     03/31
   Subsidiary Schedules.....: N            4.     09/30       11.     04/30
   Allow Prior Year Adj.....: N            5.     10/31       12.     05/31
   Consolidate Companies....: N            6.     11/30       13.
Update G/L From                           7.     12/31
   Payroll..................:  Y
   Accounts Payable.........:  Y
   Accounts Receivable......:  Y
   Fixed Assets.............:  Y
                                          Accept (Y/N): Y
   F1-Help                                     F8 - Undo
```

═══════ **FIGURE 2-9**   General Ledger options screen

Figure 2-9 contains the first screen you will see when setting the General Ledger program options. As you can see, there are default settings for all the options. You can accept these settings as they stand, but you will probably want to change at least one or two of them. To change options, type **N** and press (**ENTER**).

General Options

General options are selections that affect a variety of General Ledger features. The options you select will affect the way the program runs. Review all the options and set them to values that make sense for your business.

CONTROLLER AND OPERATOR PASSWORDS   Information in the General Ledger is highly sensitive and confidential. If there is any chance of unauthorized people using your computer, you will probably want to protect yourself by assigning a password to the General Ledger module. Peachtree Complete III allows passwords for two levels of access. The *controller password* is the highest level, allowing you to alter any aspect of the General Ledger module. The *operator password* is more restrictive; it lets you use the General Ledger's programs, but does not allow you to change the General Ledger options.

Passwords may contain up to eight letters, numbers, or punctuation marks. Whatever passwords you use, make sure that you will remember them. If you don't, you will lock yourself out. If you don't want password protection, simply leave these fields blank.

USE MENUS   Peachtree Complete III can work in either menu mode or expert mode. *Menu mode* is the default and is the one you should use unless you have difficulties going from menu to menu. In *expert mode,* you make all selections from a single menu, which saves you a few keystrokes.

ALLOW CHANGES/DELETIONS   When you first begin using Peachtree Complete III, you will probably need to make frequent changes to the General Ledger, including changing accounts, deleting accounts, and deleting transactions. Over time, you will want to disallow these types of changes by setting this option to **N**.

FORCE CONTROL REPORTS   Control reports are an important part of your accounting system. They provide an audit trail that you can use to track down every accounting item that has been added or altered. If you set this option to **Y**, control reports will be printed automatically. Otherwise, Peachtree Complete III will ask you each time whether or not you wish to print a control report.

KEEP YEAR-TO-DATE DETAIL   Most business managers use year-to-date information to judge how they've done so far during the year. Peachtree Complete III lets you retain year-to-date data, at the cost of using more disk space and taking more time to make backups. Since year-to-date information is important, you should answer **Y** to this option.

FORCE BALANCE TRANSACTIONS   Whenever you enter transactions into the General Ledger, debits should equal credits. Adhering to this rule ensures that your books will always be in balance. If you select **Y** for this option, Peachtree Complete III will not let you add or delete transactions from the General Ledger *unless* the result leaves the books in balance. If you disable this feature, Peachtree Complete III will not prevent you from entering an out-of-balance transaction. However, computers excel at catching errors such as out-of-balance transactions. Unless you plan to do some sophisticated bookkeeping, you should select **Y** for this option.

USE DEPARTMENTS   If your business is divided into departments, you will want to select the Use Departments option. If you respond **Y**, Peachtree Complete III will keep track of accounts on a department-by-department basis, giving you the detailed information you need to track performance. If you select this option, Peachtree Complete III will later ask you to provide some departmental information.

PRINT ACCOUNT NUMBERS   In Peachtree Complete III, accounts are identified by title and number. Account titles automatically appear on all financial reports. You can select the Print

Account Numbers option to have account numbers printed in addition to the account titles.

SUBSIDIARY SCHEDULES   Businesses often use *master control* accounts or *departmental control* accounts. These are accounts that summarize information in other accounts. For example, a departmental control account for a department store might summarize the men's, women's, and children's departments. Master control accounts work in a similar fashion. (Both departmental and master control accounts will be covered in Chapter 3.) *Subsidiary accounts* are accounts that are summarized by departmental or master control accounts.

Departmental and master control accounts simplify your financial statements by eliminating unnecessary detail. If, however, you want your financial statements to include detailed information on subsidiary accounts, respond with a **Y** to this option.

ALLOW PRIOR YEAR ADJUSTMENTS   After closing the books at the end of a month and the end of a year, a business often needs to adjust those books. Usually, the period of adjustment ends when tax returns are filed. You can use the Allow Prior Year Adj option to allow adjustments to prior periods when necessary. You remove the option when adjustments are completed.

CONSOLIDATE COMPANIES   It's not unusual for someone to own more than one business. Peachtree Complete III allows you to consolidate the financial data of several companies for the purpose of providing consolidated financial reports.

Typing **Y** at the Consolidate Companies option identifies the current company as a *master company*. A master company has no transactions of its own, but is used to summarize the transactions of other companies. If you select this option, Peachtree Complete

III will ask you to identify the companies that are to be consolidated under the current one.

Update Options

One of the crucial features of Peachtree Complete III is its ability to integrate different modules smoothly. An important part of system integration is providing a way to post to the General Ledger transactions from Payroll, Accounts Payable, Accounts Receivable, and Fixed Assets. If you plan to use any of these four modules in conjunction with the General Ledger, simply type **Y** by the appropriate account name.

Fiscal Period Information

Every company divides its year into a number of fiscal periods. In many cases, there is just one fiscal period per year, although it is more common to have 4 or 12 fiscal periods, one for each quarter or month. Peachtree Complete III needs the following information about your company's fiscal period.

GENERATION NUMBER   At the end of each fiscal period, your company closes its books and starts out with a clean slate. Peachtree Complete III does essentially the same thing. Throughout the fiscal period, the program accumulates transaction information in special interim disk files. At the end of the period, when you do your end-of-period processing, these files are assigned a data file generation number and a new file is created for the next period.

Each time work files are closed out, they are assigned a generation number that identifies the period in which they were generated. Peachtree Complete III lets you assign the first generation number. If you don't provide a number, Peachtree Complete III automatically starts with zero.

NUMBER OF FISCAL PERIODS How many fiscal periods does your company have? Enter the answer here. Peachtree Complete III supports six different fiscal periods:

1   Full year fiscal period

2   Six-month fiscal period

4   Quarterly fiscal period

6   Bimonthly fiscal period

12   Monthly fiscal period

13   Four-week fiscal period

You can also add an additional *year-end adjusting period* — an accounting period you use to make end-of-year adjustments to your books — as long as the total number of fiscal periods does not exceed 13.

CURRENT FISCAL PERIOD With the exception of prior period adjustments, Peachtree Complete III allows you to post transactions only to the current fiscal period. In the Current Fiscal Period selection, you must enter the fiscal period in which you will begin posting transactions. For example, suppose your company's fiscal year begins in June and has 12 fiscal periods. If you expect to begin posting transactions in August, you would enter **3** because August is your company's third fiscal period.

ADDITIONAL ADJUSTING PERIOD If you wish to have a special adjusting period added to your fiscal year, enter **Y** here. You can use this period to make any adjustments you need without changing information in any of the real fiscal periods. Note that 13 is the maximum number of fiscal periods Peachtree Complete III supports. In other words, if your company uses 13 fiscal periods per year you cannot have an additional adjusting period.

ENDING DATES FOR FISCAL PERIODS   The last item on the current screen lets you define the ending dates for your company's fiscal periods. Since the default financial period is 12 months, month-end dates are filled in for you. You can easily change the dates to match your fiscal periods.

After you have made all the desired changes to the General Ledger options, press (F10) to return to the confirmation line at the bottom of the screen, type **Y**, and press (ENTER). As you can see in Figure 2-9, Big Business has changed some of the default options, electing not to use departments, and updating the General Ledger from Payroll, Accounts Payable, Accounts Receivable, and Fixed Assets.

ACCOUNT NUMBERS

The next step in setting up your General Ledger is to define your account numbers. Peachtree Complete III allows you complete flexibility in setting up your account numbers, but it is usually a good idea to start out with the standard chart of accounts and modify it as your needs dictate.

Peachtree Complete III recognizes six categories for General Ledger accounts:

- Assets
- Liability & Equity
- Income
- Expenses
- Other Income
- Other Expenses

Each of these categories is assigned a range of account numbers so that Assets, for example, might include any account with an account number between 10000 and 19999. (Note the use of five-digit account numbers consistent with the choice made earlier.) Within these categories, you can have any number of accounts, including master accounts, posting accounts, and accounts used to display titles, totals, and subtotals on reports. Account types are discussed in more detail later in this chapter.

Peachtree Complete III sets up initial account ranges for you, as shown in Figure 2-10. According to these definitions, asset accounts use account numbers from 10000 to 19999, liability and equity accounts use 20000 to 29999, and so on. You can use these numbers if you like. If you decide to modify the default account number ranges, keep the following rules in mind:

- Make sure that the account range you define has ample room for growth.

- Follow the order set by Peachtree Complete III. The Asset account range must be lower than the Liability & Equity range, which must be lower than the Income range.

- The account number you assign to Retained Earnings must be within the range defined for Liability & Equity.

- The Current Earnings account number should be defined as the last posting account in Liability & Equity.

Distributed Earnings

In many cases, especially in limited partnerships, current earnings are distributed among the partners. Usually, the rule for such distribution is a percentage share to which each partner has a claim. Peachtree Complete III lets you define up to five distribution accounts, each defined by an account number and a percentage. If you need this capability, simply type **Y** next to Distribute Current Earnings and press (ENTER).

```
┌─────────────────────────────────────────────────────────────────────────┐
│GLMAINT 5.00          Maintain General Ledger Options      COMPANY ID: BB  │
│06/01/90                    Big Business, Inc.                             │
└─────────────────────────────────────────────────────────────────────────┘

                            Account
                          ..Number..                  ..Description........
   Assets Low #...............:  10000     Source Code 1: CASH RECEIPTS
   Liability & Equity Low #...:  20000     Source Code 2: CASH DISBURSEMENTS
   Income Low #...............:  30000     Source Code 3: JOURNAL ENTRY 1
   Expenses Low #.............:  40000     Source Code 4: JOURNAL ENTRY 2
   Other Income Low #.........:  70000     Source Code 5: JOURNAL ENTRY 3
   Other Expenses Low #.......:  80000     ───────────────────────────────
   Other Expenses High #......:  99999     Source Code 6: REPEATING JE
   Retained Earnings #........:  28000     Source Code 7: REVERSING JE
   Current Earnings #.........:  28500     Source Code 8: REVERSED JE
                                           Source Code 9: PRIOR PERIOD ADJ.
   Distribute Current Earnings: N
   Account #1:      0   Pct #1:    0.00
   Account #2:      0   Pct #2:    0.00
   Account #3:      0   Pct #3:    0.00
   Account #4:      0   Pct #4:    0.00
   Account #5:      0   Pct #5:    0.00     Accept (Y/N): Y
   ■F1-Help                                  ■F8 - Undo■
```

━━━━━
━━━━━ **FIGURE 2-10** Default account ranges and source codes
━━━━━

Next, you must define an account number for the distribution
accounts. These account numbers should be higher in value than
the account number for Current Earnings. For example, if Current
Earnings is account number 28500 (the default value), the first
distribution account should be number 28600. Follow this rule for
up to five distribution accounts.

In addition to account numbers, you need to enter the percentage
share for each distribution account by typing in the number. The
sum of the percentages must be 100%.

Source Codes

As a business manager, you will often want to see a list of
transactions by different categories. You might want to see a list
of just cash receipts, or cash disbursements, or beginning balances.
Peachtree Complete III provides this capability through *source*

codes, codes that tag a transaction as belonging to a particular group. Peachtree Complete III provides 16 different source codes, 11 of which cannot be changed (Table 2-1). While Peachtree Complete III provides default values for codes 1 through 5, you can change these to meet your needs.

Source Code	*Category*
Source codes defined by you (default values shown)	
1	Cash receipts
2	Cash disbursements
3	Journal entry 1
4	Journal entry 2
5	Journal entry 3
Source codes defined by Peachtree Complete III	
0	Prior fiscal period amount
6	Repeating journal entries
7	Reversing journal entries
8	Reversed journal entries
9	Prior period adjustments
A	Transfer balances from Accounts Payable
B	Beginning balances
F	Transfer balances from Fixed Assets
N	Noncurrent transactions
P	Transfer balances from Payroll
R	Transfer balances from Accounts Receivable

TABLE 2-1 Transaction Source Codes

Company Consolidation

If you selected Consolidate Companies from the options screen, Peachtree Complete III will ask you to identify the companies that will be consolidated under the current company. You do this at the screen shown in Figure 2-11. Simply enter up to 32 two-letter company codes, one for each company to be consolidated. Remember that a company used for consolidating other companies has no transactions of its own; it simply reflects the sum of the accounts in the consolidated companies.

Department Information

If your company is large enough to support different lines of business, you may want to keep the books for each department

```
┌─────────────────────────────────────────────────────────────────────────┐
│GLMAINT 5.00           Maintain General Ledger Options   COMPANY ID: BB    │
│06/01/90                    Big Business, Inc.           GENERATION #: 00   │
└─────────────────────────────────────────────────────────────────────────┘
Enter the Company ID'S which will be consolidated into this Chart of Accounts.
      Company           Company               Company              Company
   1.   DD           9.                  17.                    25.

   2.   EE          10.                  18.                    26.

   3.   FF          11.                  19.                    27.

   4.              12.                  20.                    28.

   5.              13.                  21.                    29.

   6.              14.                  22.                    30.

   7.              15.                  23.                    31.

   8.              16.                  24.                    32.

         Enter Number you wish to add/modify.: ▐4▌      Enter Company ID.:

 ▐F1-Help▌                               ▐F8 - Undo▌  ▐F10-Done▌
```

FIGURE 2-11 Companies to consolidate

separate. Among other things, this will help you compare departments to find out where weaknesses are threatening your profitability.

You define accounts with a two-digit number and a short description. You will use the two-digit code to set up *departmental posting accounts*. These accounts are simply subdivisions of General Ledger accounts. For example, suppose that your company has two departments: department 10 (retail sales) and department 20 (trade sales). Assume also that the Accounts Receivable account number is 12000. Department 10's posting account for Accounts Receivable will be 12010 while department 20's will be 12020. Now you can see why General Ledger accounts always end with two zeros—to leave space for department codes.

As you can see, defining departments gives you a handle on your business. You can also define summary departmental accounts, each of which can report the results of up to ten departments. To see how this would work, consider a company that sells three kinds of watches, computers, and calculators. The company has set up the following departments:

Department Number	Description
01	Luxury watches
02	Economy watches
03	Novelty watches
11	Personal Computers
12	Calculators

Summary Departments

0X	Watches
1X	Electronics

The company has also defined two summary departments: Watches, which includes all types of watches, and Electronics, which includes computers and calculators.

In order for you to summarize departments together, the departments must begin with the same number. All three watch departments, for example, begin with the number 0. Therefore, the summary department for watches is defined as 0X. The 0X says "include any account that begins with the number 0." The same logic applies to the electronics department. It is defined as 1X, so it will include computers (department 11) and calculators (department 12).

Whether or not you use departments and summary departments depends on the complexity of your business. Many small businesses will do fine with no departments at all. Larger businesses might need many departments to keep things in order.

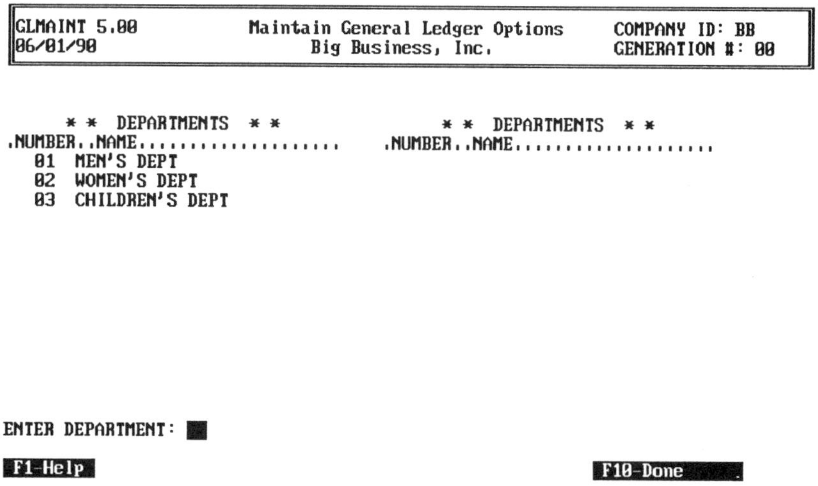

```
GLMAINT 5.00              Maintain General Ledger Options     COMPANY ID: BB
06/01/90                       Big Business, Inc.             GENERATION #: 00


       * *  DEPARTMENTS  * *                * *  DEPARTMENTS  * *
.NUMBER..NAME...................    .NUMBER..NAME...................
    01  MEN'S DEPT
    02  WOMEN'S DEPT
    03  CHILDREN'S DEPT








ENTER DEPARTMENT: █

 F1-Help                                                  F10-Done
```

FIGURE 2-12 Company departments

If you selected the Use Departments option, Peachtree Complete III will ask you to define the departments you want to use. You do this at the screen shown in Figure 2-12. To define a department, simply enter the two-digit code for the department and press (ENTER). If the department code is new, Peachtree Complete III will ask you to confirm its addition. Then type in the name of the department and press (ENTER) again.

Congratulations. You have just set up your company's General Ledger on Peachtree Complete III. Of course, you can make any changes or additions if you need to. The next step is getting your accounting information into the chart of accounts.

GENERAL LEDGER:
SETTING UP
SHOP

Entering Your Account Information
Entering Account Balances
General Ledger Reports

In Chapter 2, you learned how to install the General Ledger module and set up a blank chart of accounts. Now it's time to place information into the chart of accounts so you can start using it. To prepare for this important step, you must bring your chart of accounts up to date. If you are not sure how to do this, ask your accountant for assistance.

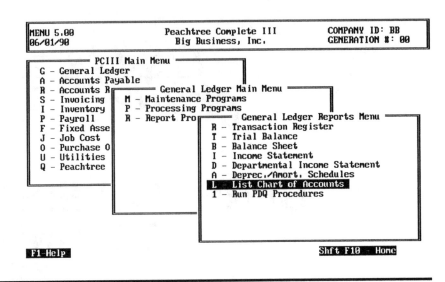

FIGURE 3-1   List Chart of Accounts report option

```
GLRPTS  5.00                List Chart of Accounts      COMPANY ID: BB
06/01/90                      Big Business, Inc.         GENERATION #: 00


                          ┌──── DATA OPTIONS ────┐
                          │ A - ALL DATA FOR ACCOUNTS │
                          │ C - CURRENT YEAR ONLY     │
                          │ N - NO DOLLAR AMOUNTS     │
                          └──────────────────────┘


 F1-Help                        F10 - Done    Shft F10 - Home
```

FIGURE 3-2   Select data options for Chart of Accounts

If it is the middle of an accounting period, you will have to gather account balances as of the beginning of the period as well as all transactions to date. As you can imagine, the farther along in your accounting period you are, the more tedious and time consuming this task becomes. For this reason, most people computerize their accounts at the beginning of a new accounting period, since they have a clean slate to work with.

ENTERING YOUR ACCOUNT INFORMATION

You've just set up your chart of accounts and you need to enter all the account balances and prior period information to bring it up to date. First, however, you should see how the chart of accounts looks right now. You can get this report using the General Ledger Reports Menu.

The Chart of Accounts Report

To view your chart of accounts, select General Ledger from the Peachtree Complete III Main Menu, select Report Programs from the General Ledger Main Menu, and select List Chart of Accounts from the General Ledger Reports Menu (Figure 3-1). Peachtree Complete III asks if you want to see All Data for Accounts, Current Year Only, or No Dollar Amounts (Figure 3-2). In most cases, you will want to select All Data for Accounts. Finally, you need to select the accounts to include in the report. You can select All Accounts or specify a Range of Accounts (Figure 3-3). Simply press (ENTER) to see data on all accounts.

The example company, Big Business, chose to use the standard chart of accounts, which creates an 11-page report. Figure 3-4 shows the beginning of the first page of the report, which lists

```
┌─────────────────────────────────────────────────────────────────────┐
│ GLRPTS  5.00              List Chart of Accounts      COMPANY ID: BB  │
│ 06/01/90                    Big Business, Inc.         GENERATION #: 00│
└─────────────────────────────────────────────────────────────────────┘


ALL DATA FOR ACCOUNTS
                              ┌─── PRINT OPTIONS ───┐
                              │ A - ALL ACCOUNTS    │
                              │ R - RANGE OF ACCOUNTS│
                              └─────────────────────┘




    F1-Help
```

═══ **FIGURE 3-3**   Select print options for Chart of Accounts

accounts in numerical order, beginning with Assets (100), Current
Assets (101), and Cash (105). The report also contains the

- Account number

- Account description

- Account type

- Master/department status

- Group end number

- Report column

ACCOUNT NUMBER AND DESCRIPTION   Account num-
bers and descriptions were discussed in the previous chapter. When
you set up your General Ledger, you had to decide whether to use
five- or six-digit account numbers. Big Business chose to use

```
RUN DATE: 06/01/90                        Big Business, Inc.                                    PAGE    1
RUN TIME: 1:55 PM                           General Ledger
                                           Chart Of Accounts

ACCT    DESCRIPTION          TYP M/D GRP-END COL    CURRENT   NON-CURRENT   PRIOR PD ADJS   BEGIN BAL
====    ===========          === === ======= ===    =======   ===========   =============   =========

100     ASSETS                1                0

101     CURRENT ASSETS        1                1

105     Cash                  2   M   11999    1

110     Cash - Operating      2                1       0.00       0.00           0.00          0.00

PRIOR    1 -   0.00     4 -   0.00     7 -       0.00    10 -   0.00       0.00         0.00
FISCAL   2 -   0.00     5 -   0.00     8 -       0.00    11 -   0.00       0.00    13 -  0.00
PERIODS  3 -   0.00     6 -   0.00     9 -       0.00    12 -   0.00       0.00

115     Cash on Hand          2                1       0.00    5,014.21          0.00          0.00

PRIOR    1 -   0.00     4 -   0.00     7 -       0.00    10 -   0.00       0.00         0.00
FISCAL   2 -   0.00     5 -   0.00     8 -       0.00    11 -   0.00       0.00    13 -  0.00
PERIODS  3 -   0.00     6 -   0.00     9 -       0.00    12 -   0.00       0.00
```

FIGURE 3-4 Chart of Accounts listing

five-digit numbers. On the report, however, account numbers have only three digits—the last two digits are not needed since they report departmental data.

ACCOUNT TYPE   Peachtree Complete III lets you define different account types for different purposes. There are four basic account types: title accounts, posting accounts, subtotal accounts, and income statement total accounts.

Title accounts (type 1) are used to print titles on financial reports. In Figure 3-4, the Assets account (100) is a title account. Its description is printed on financial reports before any others. Current Assets is also a title account. Because title accounts are used only to generate financial reports, you cannot post transactions to them.

Type 2 accounts are generally posting accounts, which receive transactions as they are posted and maintain balances. Actually, not all type 2 accounts are posting accounts—they can also be master control accounts or department control accounts. In Figure 3-4, the Cash account (105) is a master control account and the Cash - Operating account (110) is a posting account. Both are type 2 accounts, but they perform different functions.

You are probably already familiar with posting accounts. They receive financial transactions that are posted from journal entries. Posting accounts are the source of all financial information in the general ledger. The other account types summarize posting accounts or create financial reports. If you are using manual accounting methods, all of your accounts are posting accounts.

Subtotal accounts and income statement total accounts are only for use on financial statements. You do not post transactions to these accounts and they do not contain any financial information of their own.

MASTER/DEPARTMENT STATUS   Even though they are type 2 accounts, master control accounts never receive posted transactions. Instead, they summarize the balances in other accounts. The *group end number* defines the range of accounts that are summarized by a particular master control account. The Cash account in Figure 3-4, for example, has a group end number of 11999, meaning that this account summarizes all accounts numbered from 10500 through 11999. This range includes the Cash - Operating account (11000) and the Cash on Hand account (11500), which are called the subsidiary accounts of the Cash account.

Type 2 accounts can also be departmental control accounts. Like master control accounts, department control accounts never receive posted transactions but instead summarize other accounts. For example, a company with three departments might define three departmental posting accounts under the Cash on Hand account:

Departmental Control Account

       Cash on Hand 115

Departmental Posting Accounts

Cash on Hand (Dept 1)	11501
Cash on Hand (Dept 2)	11502
Cash on Hand (Dept 3)	11503

In this situation, the Cash on Hand account is the departmental account and would report the sum of the three departmental posting accounts. On financial statements, the title of the departmental control account is printed along with the sum of the departmental posting accounts.

REPORT COLUMN   The report column (COL in Figure 3-4) contains the *balance column* code, which controls certain printing options. There are ten different balance column codes that can be grouped into five categories:

0   Centers account titles on financial reports for type 1 accounts

1   Left justifies titles for type 1 accounts

2   Indents the account title on financial reports and places the account balance in the second column for type 2 accounts. This code is used for intermediary totals, such as total current assets and total other assets

3-8   Used with type 2 accounts to compute and print totals and subtotals, indenting the account title and placing the amount in the third through eighth columns. Often used for grand totals such as total assets and total liabilities

9   Applies only to income statement accounts, not to balance sheet accounts. This code is used to print running totals of all previous accounts. The last account in your chart of accounts, which is also the last of your income statement accounts, must be defined using column code 9

ENTERING ACCOUNT BALANCES

Big Business is now ready to enter account data into the empty chart of accounts. In preparation, you have worked with your accountant to get the General Ledger up to date. To start, select Enter Transactions from the General Ledger Processing Menu (Figure 3-5).

The next screen (Figure 3-6) asks you to prepare your printer by setting the paper to the top of the form and pressing (ENTER). You also must enter the number of transactions you intend to enter and the transaction account number hash total. The first item is simple enough, but the others warrant some additional explanation.

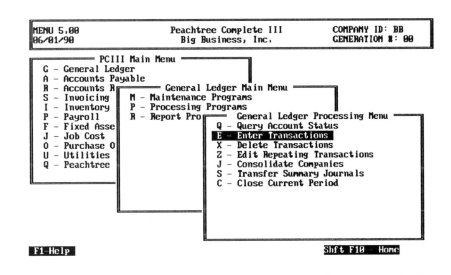

FIGURE 3-5 Select Enter Transactions

```
┌─────────────────────────────────────────────────────────────────┐
│GLPROC 5.00              Enter Transactions       COMPANY ID: BB   │
│06/01/90                 Big Business, Inc.        GENERATION #: 00 │
└─────────────────────────────────────────────────────────────────┘


SET PAPER TO TOP OF FORM - PRESS 'ENTER' TO CONTINUE █

ENTER NUMBER OF TRANSACTIONS:     0

ENTER TRANSACTION ACCOUNT NUMBER HASH TOTAL:            0


ACCEPT (Y/N): Y




F1-Help
```

FIGURE 3-6 Data entry control options

Transaction Count Control

Quality control is an essential part of any accounting process. If you enter an item incorrectly or twice, or if you omit it entirely, the books will contain an error that could be difficult to trace. Peachtree Complete III incorporates some simple control procedures that can alert you to mistakes before they are incorporated into your books.

One control method is *transaction count control,* which is simply the number of transactions you plan to enter. If you tell Peachtree Complete III that you plan to enter two transactions and you actually enter three, the program will alert you to this fact. In many situations, adding the transactions is too much of a bother. You can enter zero in this field to tell Peachtree Complete III not to check the number of transactions entered.

Account Number Hash Total Control

Errors can still slip through while transaction count control is in effect. You might, for example, enter the right number of transactions but post them to the wrong accounts. To check for this type of error, Peachtree Complete III provides *account number hash total control.* A *hash number* is the sum of some other numbers; in this case, the sum of the account numbers to which you will be posting transactions.

To use hash total control, you must add all the account numbers to which you will be posting transactions *before you enter the transactions.* Enter this number when Peachtree Complete III asks for it. As you enter transactions into the General Ledger, Peachtree Complete III keeps a running total of the account numbers used. At the end of the session, Peachtree Complete III compares the computed hash total to the one you entered. If the numbers do not match, an error occurred somewhere along the line.

Clearly, computing a hash total before entering transactions is a time-consuming task. You will want to use this control feature only if you need the utmost security against errors. Otherwise, simply press (ENTER) when Peachtree Complete III asks you for the hash total and no checking will be done.

The final step before entering transactions is to select the source code for the transactions you will be entering. You defined your source codes when you installed the General Ledger. Big Business opted for the default source codes, which include Cash Receipts, Cash Disbursements, Journal Entry 1, Journal Entry 2, Journal Entry 3, Repeating Journal Entry, Reversing Journal Entry, Prior Period Adjustment, Prior Period Amounts, Beginning Balances, and Non-Current Entry. Since you are now entering beginning balances, choose that option from the source code menu (Figure 3-7).

Now you have arrived at the General Ledger transaction entry screen (Figure 3-8). At the top of the screen, Peachtree Complete

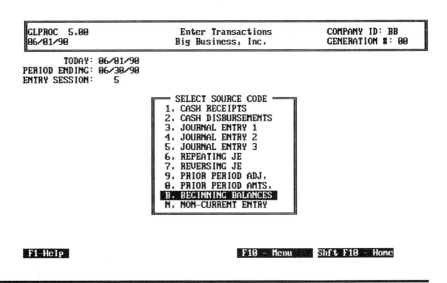

```
GLPROC  5.00                  Enter Transactions          COMPANY ID: BB
06/01/90                      Big Business, Inc.           GENERATION #: 00

       TODAY: 06/01/90
PERIOD ENDING: 06/30/90
ENTRY SESSION:     5
                          ┌─── SELECT SOURCE CODE ───┐
                          │ 1. CASH RECEIPTS         │
                          │ 2. CASH DISBURSEMENTS    │
                          │ 3. JOURNAL ENTRY 1       │
                          │ 4. JOURNAL ENTRY 2       │
                          │ 5. JOURNAL ENTRY 3       │
                          │ 6. REPEATING JE          │
                          │ 7. REVERSING JE          │
                          │ 9. PRIOR PERIOD ADJ.     │
                          │ 0. PRIOR PERIOD AMTS.    │
                          │ B. BEGINNING BALANCES    │
                          │ N. NON-CURRENT ENTRY     │
                          └──────────────────────────┘

 F1-Help                                   F10 - Menu    Shft F10 - Home
```

FIGURE 3-7 The source code menu

FIGURE 3-8 The General Ledger transaction entry screen

III indicates that this is entry session 1 for generation 0 of the General Ledger. That is, this is the first time you are using the General Ledger module to enter transactions. Also on the screen are today's date, the source code for the transactions being entered, the system balance, and the transaction total. The system balance is the sum of all accounts in the chart of accounts, including transactions currently being entered. If you have opted to force accounts to balance, the system balance should always be zero before you enter transactions. The transaction total is simply the total of all transactions currently being entered.

Transaction Entry Fields

The middle portion of the screen is where you enter transactions. The column headings indicate the information you need to enter: a reference number, the transaction date, a description, the account number, the amount of the transaction, and a **Y** to accept the transaction or **N** if you wish to void the entry.

REFERENCE   To provide a complete audit trail, each transaction should be accompanied by a reference number. Usually the reference number will match a journal entry. In the case of beginning balances, however, the reference number should be the account number from the old chart of accounts.

DATE   This date is simply the date on which the transaction took place. When you enter beginning balances, the date should be the cut-over date for the fiscal period.

DESCRIPTION   Each entry must have a description that identifies the transaction that generated it. For beginning balances, the words "Beginning Balance" should suffice.

ACCOUNT   You must enter an account number for a type 2 posting account here. If you cannot remember account numbers, you can press F2 and select the account from a menu, as shown in Figure 3-9.

AMOUNT   The transaction amount goes in this field. In the case of beginning balances, the amount is the closing balance brought forward from the preceding period. To set up the beginning balances for your chart of accounts, simply enter the correct information in each field. Every entry will have the same date and description. You just enter the reference number, the account number, and the amount. Figure 3-10 shows the entries for the first Big Business accounts. As you enter balances, remember that you enter asset balances as positive numbers while you enter liability, equity, and asset contra account balances as negative numbers.

Once you have entered your beginning balances, you can enter any transactions that have accumulated since the beginning of the

```
┌──────────────────────────────────────────────────────────────────┐
│ GLPROC 5.00              Enter Transactions      COMPANY ID: BB    │
│ 06/01/90                 Big Business, Inc.       GENERATION #: 00  │
└──────────────────────────────────────────────────────────────────┘

        TODAY: 06/01/90                      ENTRY SESSION    5
                              ┌──── SELECT ACCOUNT NUMBER ────┐  00
SOURCE CODE  B  BEGINNING BALANCES │ 10000 - ASSETS            │  00
                              │ 10100 - CURRENT ASSETS         │
   LINE.REFERENCE...DATE....DESCRIPTI │ 10500 - Cash           │ EPT
      1 102      06/01/90  Beginning  │ 11000 - Cash - Operating │
                              │ 11500 - Cash on Hand           │
                              │ 12000 - Accounts Receivable    │
                              │ 12500 - Due from Employees     │
                              │ 13000 - Allowance for Bad Debts│
                              │ 13500 - Inventory              │
                              │ 14000 - Total Current Assets   │
                              │ 14500 - FIXED ASSETS           │
                              │ 14700 - Furniture & Fixtures   │
                              └────────────────────────────────┘
```

FIGURE 3-9   Account selection menu

```
┌──────────────────────────────────────────────────────────────────┐
│ GLPROC 5.00              Enter Transactions      COMPANY ID: BB    │
│ 06/01/90                 Big Business, Inc.       GENERATION #: 00  │
└──────────────────────────────────────────────────────────────────┘

        TODAY: 06/01/90                      ENTRY SESSION    5
                                     SYSTEM BALANCE    164457.07
SOURCE CODE  B  BEGINNING BALANCES   TRANS. TOTAL      164457.07

   LINE.REFERENCE...DATE....DESCRIPTION..............ACCOUNT......AMOUNT.ACCEPT
      1 102      06/01/90  Beginning Balance          11000      32515.27  Y
      2 107      06/01/90  Beginning Balance          11500       5014.21  Y
      3 121      06/01/90  Beginning Balance          12000      31001.40  Y
      4 122      06/01/90  Beginning Balance          12500        401.00  Y
      5 130      06/01/90  Beginning Balance          13000      -2510.00  Y
      6 132      06/01/90  Beginning Balance          13500      52331.35  Y
      7 141      06/01/90  Beginning Balance          14700      23881.99  Y
      8 148      06/01/90  Beginning Balance          15000      13001.04  Y
      9 151      06/01/90  Beginning Balance          15500          0.00  Y
     10 153      06/01/90  Beginning Balance          15700      23150.88  Y
     11 158      06/01/90  Beginning Balance          16000     -18342.38  Y
     12 170      06/01/90  Beginning Balance          17500       4012.31  Y
     13 172      06/01/90  Beginning Balance          18000      14000.00  Y
                                              TITLE: Prepaid Advertising

SCREEN FULL - PRESS 'ENTER'  Y
```

FIGURE 3-10   Entering beginning balances

accounting period. When you have correctly entered all transactions, your Peachtree Complete III General Ledger will be completely up to date.

Big Business has only two transactions to enter. To enter the transactions, follow the procedure for entering beginning balances but use a different source code. The first transaction is a payment of an invoice involving a credit to the operating cash account and a debit to accounts payable. First, select the source code for Cash Disbursements (Figure 3-11). The transaction consists of two parts: the credit and the debit. The Peachtree Complete III entries are shown in Figure 3-12. Notice that the credit to the cash account is a negative amount. Both entries have the same reference number and description, so it's easy to match them in the future.

The second transaction occurred when a shipment arrived and was added to inventory. The amount of the transaction was $21,008.34, which represents an increase to inventory (a debit) and

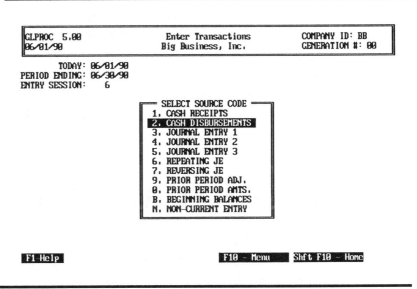

═══ **FIGURE 3-11**   Selecting the source code for Cash Disbursements

```
┌─────────────────────────────────────────────────────────────────┐
│ GLPROC  5.00                Enter Transactions      COMPANY ID: BB │
│ 06/01/90                   Big Business, Inc.        GENERATION #: 00 │
└─────────────────────────────────────────────────────────────────┘
          TODAY: 06/01/90                        ENTRY SESSION    6
                                                 SYSTEM BALANCE    -513.23
    SOURCE CODE  2  CASH DISBURSEMENTS           TRANS, TOTAL      -513.23

    LINE.REFERENCE...DATE....DESCRIPTION..............ACCOUNT......AMOUNT.ACCEPT
       1 90001     06/01/90  Paid Invoice 3102       11000      -513.23  Y
       2 90001     06/01/90  Paid Invoice 3102       20500       513.23  Y
                                              TITLE: Accounts Payable




    ▮F1 Help▮
```

═══════ **FIGURE 3-12**   Cash Disbursements

an increase in accounts payable (a credit). To enter this transaction, Big Business uses the Journal Entry 1 source code for entries involving additions to inventory (Figure 3-13). The actual entries are shown in Figure 3-14; the description notes the shipment number. (Inventory can be handled more efficiently by using the inventory module, decribed later in this book.)

Big Business's books are now up-to-date, reflecting accurate beginning balances and current-period transactions. Now it's time to generate some accounting reports.

GENERAL LEDGER REPORTS

Now that your General Ledger has information in it, you can begin to generate some interesting accounting reports. The most important reports for verifying your accounts are the transaction register, the trial balance, and balance sheet.

```
┌──────────────────────────────────────────────────────────────────┐
│ GLPROC  5.00                Enter Transactions      COMPANY ID: BB │
│ 06/01/90                    Big Business, Inc.       GENERATION #: 00 │
└──────────────────────────────────────────────────────────────────┘

        TODAY: 06/01/90
PERIOD ENDING: 06/30/90
ENTRY SESSION:    6
                         ┌─ SELECT SOURCE CODE ─┐
                         │  1. CASH RECEIPTS      │
                         │  2. CASH DISBURSEMENTS │
                         │ ▐3. JOURNAL ENTRY 1▌   │
                         │  4. JOURNAL ENTRY 2    │
                         │  5. JOURNAL ENTRY 3    │
                         │  6. REPEATING JE       │
                         │  7. REVERSING JE       │
                         │  9. PRIOR PERIOD ADJ.  │
                         │  0. PRIOR PERIOD AMTS. │
                         │  B. BEGINNING BALANCES │
                         │  N. NON-CURRENT ENTRY  │
                         └────────────────────────┘


  ▐F1 Help▌                        ▐F10  Menu▌  ▐Shft F10  Home▌
```

FIGURE 3-13   Selecting the Journal Entry 1 source code

```
┌──────────────────────────────────────────────────────────────────┐
│ GLPROC  5.00                Enter Transactions      COMPANY ID: BB │
│ 06/01/90                    Big Business, Inc.       GENERATION #: 00 │
└──────────────────────────────────────────────────────────────────┘

        TODAY: 06/01/90                      ENTRY SESSION     6
                                             SYSTEM BALANCE   21000.34
SOURCE CODE  3  JOURNAL ENTRY 1              TRANS. TOTAL     21000.34

LINE.REFERENCE...DATE....DESCRIPTION.............ACCOUNT......AMOUNT.ACCEPT
  3 90002      06/01/90  Received Shipment 1020    13500      21000.34  Y
  4 90002      06/01/90  Received Shipment 1020    20500     -21000.34  Y
                                        TITLE: Accounts Payable


  ▐F1 Help▌
```

FIGURE 3-14   Entering the transaction

Transaction Register

A *transaction register* is a listing of all transactions, sorted either by account number or by source code. When you generate a transaction register, Peachtree Complete III asks whether you want the report run by source code or by account number. If you choose source code, Peachtree Complete III also lets you select either a particular source code or all source codes (by entering an asterisk).

Whether sorting by account number or by source code, you must identify the time range to include either the current period, all periods, or a range of periods. In most cases, you will want the current period.

Finally, you may also specify a specific entry session. Each time you enter transactions into the General Ledger, the session number is recorded. You can print a transaction register for any particular session or you can include all sessions by typing 0.

Figure 3-15 contains a sample transaction register for Big Business. This report is sorted by account number. For each account, the report lists the beginning balance, any transactions against that account, and the new balance. Transaction registers have many uses, and are especially good for checking for data entry errors.

Trial Balance

The trial balance is one of the most commonly used accounting statements. You use it primarily to check that accounts are in balance. Because Peachtree Complete III automatically checks for out-of-balance conditions, trial balances are not usually necessary. However, they do provide a clear format for viewing account detail.

```
RUN DATE: 06/02/90      Big Business, Inc.            PAGE   1
RUN TIME:  5:40 PM         General Ledger
                        Transaction Register
------------------------------------------------------------------

ACCT BATCH   DESCRIPTION        REF   S   DATE   PP PE AMOUNT
==================================================================

110    1 Beginning Balance      102   B 06/02/90 01 01 32,515.27
110    4 Paid Invoice 3102      90001 2 06/02/90 01 01    513.23-
                                                       32,002.04*

115    1 Beginning Balance      107   B 06/02/90 01 01  5,014.21

120    1 Beginning Balance      121   B 06/02/90 01 01 31,001.40

135    1 Beginning Balance      132   B 06/02/90 01 01 52,331.35
135    4 Received Shipment 1020 90002 3 06/02/90 01 01 21,008.34
                                                       73,339.69*

147    1 Beginning Balance      141   B 06/02/90 01 01 23,881.99

150    1 Beginning Balance      148   B 06/02/90 01 01 13,001.04

155    1 Beginning Balance      151   B 06/02/90 01 01      0.00

157    1 Beginning Balance      153   B 06/02/90 01 01 23,150.88

205    1 Beginning Balance      201   B 06/02/90 01 01 23,510.03-
205    4 Paid Invoice 3102      90001 2 06/02/90 01 01    513.23
205    4 Received Shipment 1020 90002 3 06/02/90 01 01 21,008.34-
                                                       44,005.14-*
```

FIGURE 3-15   Partial transaction register

Before you print a trial balance, Peachtree Complete III asks if you want a summary report (which contains no transaction detail) or a detailed report. The example report in Figure 3-16 shows transaction details. You also have to select the period you want: the current period, year-to-date, or a range of periods that you specify. You can also view the trial balance on a departmental basis.

```
RUN DATE: 06/02/90                    Big Business, Inc.                                    PAGE   1
RUN TIME: 5:50 PM
                                     DETAIL TRIAL BALANCE
                                    PERIOD ENDING 06/30/90

------ACCOUNT------  -BEGINNING-                ---------- TRANSACTION -----------            --ENDING--
NUMBER  DESCRIPTION   BALANCE   DESCRIPTION      DATE  PP PE S  REFERENCE    AMOUNT            BALANCE
=================================================================================================

110  Cash - Operating    0.00
                   * 32,515.27   Beginning Balance  06/02 01 01 B  102
                                 Paid Invoice 3102  06/02 01 01 2  90001       513.23-
                                                                            32,002.04 *      32,002.04 *

115  Cash on Hand        0.00
                   *  5,014.21   Beginning Balance  06/02 01 01 B  107      5,014.21 *        5,014.21 *

120  Accounts Receivable 0.00
                   * 31,001.40   Beginning Balance  06/02 01 01 B  121     31,001.40 *       31,001.40 *

125  Due from Employees  0.00
                   *    401.00   Beginning Balance  06/02 01 01 B  122        401.00 *          401.00 *

130  Allowance for Bad Debts 0.00
                   *  2,510.00-  Beginning Balance  06/02 01 01 B  130      2,510.00-*        2,510.00-*

135  Inventory           0.00
                   * 52,331.35   Beginning Balance  06/02 01 01 B  132     21,008.34
                                 Received Shipment 1020 06/02 01 01 3 90002 73,339.69        73,339.69 *

147  Furniture & Fixtures 0.00
                   * 23,881.99   Beginning Balance  06/02 01 01 B  141     23,881.99 *       23,881.99 *

150  Machinery & Equipment 0.00
                   * 13,001.04   Beginning Balance  06/02 01 01 B  148     13,001.04 *       13,001.04 *

152  Buildings           0.00
                                                                               0.00 *            0.00 *
```

FIGURE 3-16 Trial balance transaction details

```
RUN DATE: 06/02/90        Big Business, Inc.          PAGE  1
RUN TIME:  5:54 PM
                            Balance Sheet
                            AS OF 06/30/90

                               ASSETS
                               ----------

CURRENT ASSETS
        Cash                   37,016.25
        Accounts Receivable    31,001.40
        Due from Employees        401.00
        Allowance for Bad Debts  2,510.00-
        Inventory              73,339.69
                               -----------
            Total Current Assets           139,248.34

FIXED ASSETS
        Furniture & Fixtures   23,881.99
        Machinery & Equipment  13,001.04
        Vehicles               23,150.88
        Accumulated Depreciation 18,342.38-
                               -----------
            Total Other Assets              41,691.53

OTHER ASSETS
        Prepaid Expenses       18,012.31
        Deposits                5,000.00
                               -----------
            Total Other Assets              23,012.31
                                            -----------
                Total Assets                             203,952.18
                                                        =============


                        LIABILITIES & EQUITY
                        ----------------------

CURRENT LIABILITIES
        Accounts Payable       44,005.14
        Accrued Payroll        40,234.52
        Notes Payable - Bank   10,000.00
        Payroll Taxes Payable  21,507.79
                               -----------
            Total Current Liabilities      115,747.45

LONG TERM LIABILITIES
        Notes Payable - Bank   30,000.00
                               -----------
            Total Long Term. Liab.          30,000.00
                                            -----------
                Total Liabilities                       145,747.45

STOCKHOLDERS EQUITY
        Common Stock                        40,000.00
```

FIGURE 3-17 Balance sheet

```
RUN DATE: 06/02/90          Big Business, Inc.              PAGE  2
RUN TIME:  5:54 PM
                              Balance Sheet
                             AS OF 06/30/90

          Retained Earnings                 18,204.73
          Current Earnings                      0.00-
                                           ------------
               Total Equity                            58,204.73
                                                       -------------
          Total Liab. & Equity                        203,952.18
                                                       =============
```

FIGURE 3-17   Balance sheet *(continued)*

Balance Sheet

You can create a balance sheet easily with Peachtree Complete III
by selecting from several options. First you must specify whether
you want the balance sheet to reflect the current period or a prior
period. You must also indicate whether you want a standard or a
comparative balance sheet. A comparative balance sheet compares
current period figures against either figures from the previous year
or amounts you budgeted for the current period. Finally, you can
specify a header and footer for your balance sheet. The balance
sheet shown in Figure 3-17 is for the current period, has a standard
format, and uses a header (Balance Sheet) but no footer.

Generating financial statements is one of the Peachtree Complete III General Ledger module's finest features. If you've been
doing your accounting manually, you've either gone without financial
statements or have paid a great deal to have them developed. With
Peachtree Complete III, you can generate detailed financial reports
any time and at little cost.

But, as important as it is, the General Ledger is only one of the modules in Peachtree Complete III. The chapters that follow describe how to use Peachtree Complete III's other modules (such as Payroll and Accounts Payable) and how to integrate them into the General Ledger.

ACCOUNTS PAYABLE

Installing Accounts Payable
Selecting Accounts Payable Account Numbers
Adding a Vendor
Entering an Automatic Invoice
Entering an Invoice
Entering a Credit
Issuing Payments to Vendors
Housekeeping

In Chapter 3, you entered beginning balances for your chart of accounts and reviewed some basic General Ledger reports. At this point, the General Ledger is completely set up and you can start entering transactions. This chapter will look at one specific type of transaction: accounts payable.

INSTALLING ACCOUNTS PAYABLE

To install Peachtree Complete III's Accounts Payable module, select Accounts Payable from the PCIII Main Menu (Figure 4-1). Peachtree Complete III asks if you are sure you want to install the Accounts Payable module. Type **Y** and press (ENTER) to continue.

You need to tell Peachtree Complete III where to store your company's Accounts Payable files (Figure 4-2). The default directory is \PEACH\APDATA. You can change this to any directory you like. If the directory you select does not exist, Peachtree Complete III asks if you wish to create it. Type **Y** and press (ENTER).

As with the General Ledger module, you need to set up options for the Accounts Payable module (as shown in Figure 4-3). Select the first option, Set Module Options, and press (ENTER). Peachtree Complete III shows you the Accounts Payable options screen (Figure 4-4). Take a moment to familiarize yourself with the options.

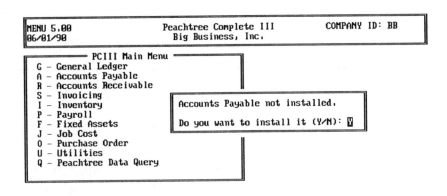

FIGURE 4-1 Installing Accounts Payable

```
╔═══════════════════════════════════════════════════════════════════════╗
║MENU 5.00               Peachtree Complete III        COMPANY ID: BB     ║
║06/01/90                   Big Business, Inc.                            ║
╟──────── PCIII Main Menu ────────────────────────┐                      ║
║ G - General Ledger                              │                      ║
║ A - Accounts Payable                            │                      ║
║ R - Accounts Receivable                         │                      ║
║ S - Invoicing                                   │                      ║
║ I - Inventory                                   │                      ║
║ P - Payroll                                     │                      ║
║ F - Fixed Assets                                │                      ║
║ J - Job Cost                                    │                      ║
║ O - Purchase Order                              │                      ║
║ U - Utilities                                   │                      ║
║ Q - Peachtree Data Query                        │                      ║
║                          └──────────────────────┘                      ║
║        ┌───────────────────────────────────────────────────────────┐   ║
║        │ Enter the subdirectory path where you want your data files to be. │
║        │        C:\PEACH\APDATA\                                    │   ║
║        └───────────────────────────────────────────────────────────┘   ║
╚═══════════════════════════════════════════════════════════════════════╝
```

FIGURE 4-2   Enter the location of your Accounts Payable files

```
╔═══════════════════════════════════════════════════════════════════════╗
║APMAINT 5.00          Maintain Accounts Payable Options   COMPANY ID: BB ║
║06/01/90                   Big Business, Inc.                            ║
╚═══════════════════════════════════════════════════════════════════════╝
```

```
                      ┌──────── Program Options ────────┐
                      │ O - Set Module Options          │
                      │                                 │
                      │ B - Automatic File Backup       │
                      │                                 │
                      │ P - Set Printer Assignments     │
                      └─────────────────────────────────┘
```

`F1-Help`   `F10 - Done`

FIGURE 4-3   Select Set Module Options

```
┌────────────────────────────────────────────────────────────────────┐
│ APMAINT 5.00          Maintain Accounts Payable Options  COMPANY ID: BB │
│ 06/01/90                   Big Business, Inc.            GENERATION #: 00 │
└────────────────────────────────────────────────────────────────────┘

        General Module Options
              Controller Password....:
              Operator Password......:
        Use Menus...................: Y
        Allow Changes/Deletions.....: Y
        Force Control Reports.......: N
        Keep Year-To-Date Detail....: N
        Current A/P Generation #....:  0
        Current Fiscal Period.......:  1
        Report To G/L ..............: Y
        Post To Job Cost............: Y
        Use Pre-Printed Check Stub..: N
        Print Company Name On Check.: Y
        G/L Discount Account........:  43500
        Payer Federal ID Number.....:

            Accept (Y/N): Y
```

FIGURE 4-4   The Accounts Payable options screen

The Controller Password, Operator Password, and Use Menus options work the same for Accounts Payable as for the General Ledger. Refer to Chapter 2 if you need to refresh your memory on how these options work. A brief discussion of the other options on this menu follows.

Allow Changes/Deletions   When you respond **N** to this option, Peachtree Complete III won't let you change or delete transactions in Accounts Payable. However, you can still add new accounts payable transactions and information.

Force Control Reports   Peachtree Complete III can print control reports that produce an audit trail for tracking errors. In Accounts Payable, you can create control reports whenever you add, change, or delete transactions, vendors, or other information. If you respond **Y** to this option, Peachtree Complete III will always print control reports without asking you first. If you respond **N**, Peachtree Complete III will ask before printing control reports.

Keep Year-To-Date Detail   You should always keep your year-to-date information on line whenever possible. If you answer **Y** to this option, more disk space will be taken up but the added information will be useful for tracking errors or inconsistencies in prior accounting periods.

Current A/P Generation #   Accounts Payable makes a copy of the files whenever you close the current period (usually at the end of each month). These file copies are then stored on your disk and are known as a *generation*. Each file has a generation number as part of the file name. You can use files from a previous generation to track specific transactions or changes. Peachtree Complete III lets you assign the first generation number if you want. The default number is 0.

Current Fiscal Period   The current fiscal period tells the General Ledger which period it should post the accounts payable information to. As with the General Ledger, you can enter a fiscal period number between 1 and 13.

Report To G/L   If you respond **Y** and press (ENTER), Accounts Payable collects transaction totals or journal entries in a transfer file. A *transfer file* is a file of information to be transferred from one module to another. Accounts Payable posts the information in the transfer file to the General Ledger when you run Create G/L Journal Entries. You must respond **Y** to this question if you set up the General Ledger to expect accounts payable information (by responding **Y** to the Update from A/P option). Otherwise, you won't be able to post to the General Ledger.

If you respond **N**, Accounts Payable doesn't create a transfer file of information. You can still post accounts payable to the General Ledger yourself if you like, or to a different General Ledger.

Post To Job Cost Enter **Y** in the Post To Job Cost field to post the accounts payable information to the Job Cost module. As with the previous option, Accounts Payable will build a transfer file of the appropriate information. (You will learn about the Job Cost module in Chapter 12.) If you answer **N**, you will have to enter by hand any accounts payable that affects the cost of a job in the Job Cost module.

Use Pre-Printed Check Stub If you have pre-printed check stubs, answer **Y** and press (**ENTER**) here. Otherwise, Peachtree Complete III will print its own headings on the check stubs.

Print Company Name On Check If you don't have custom checks that already have your company name printed on them, answer **Y** and press (**ENTER**) here. Otherwise, Peachtree Complete III will print the company name on the check as it appears in the General Ledger information files.

G/L Discount Account Enter the General Ledger account number for posting discounts taken in Accounts Payable. The account number must already exist in the General Ledger chart of accounts. If you are using the standard chart of accounts, the default is 43500 (for five-digit account numbers) or 435000 (for six-digit account numbers).

Payer Federal ID Number Your company's federal ID number appears on 1099 forms. This can be either the federal employer identification number or a Social Security number. If you are setting up accounts for a sole proprietorship, you will probably use a Social Security number.

SELECTING ACCOUNTS PAYABLE ACCOUNT NUMBERS

After you have entered the Accounts Payable options, Peachtree Complete III asks you to enter the General Ledger account numbers that will be used by the Accounts Payable accounts. Figure 4-5 shows how Peachtree Complete III displays the default account numbers. You can either change these account numbers to suit your needs or use the defaults.

The Accounts Payable account numbers are the General Ledger account numbers that Accounts Payable transactions are posted to. The cash account numbers are General Ledger account numbers for one or more checking accounts. The defaults are 20500 and 11000.

After you select the Accounts Payable account numbers, Peachtree Complete III asks if you want to create the Accounts Payable files, as shown in Figure 4-6. Type **Y** and press (ENTER). Peachtree Complete III will create the Accounts Payable files in the Accounts Payable directory and then return you to the Main Menu.

ADDING A VENDOR

Once you have set your Accounts Payable options, you can start setting up vendors. A *vendor* is anyone from whom the company buys goods or services. You must enter vendor information for each person or company you owe money to.

```
┌─────────────────────────────────────────────────────────────────────┐
│ APMAINT 5.00          Maintain Accounts Payable Options   COMPANY ID: BB │
│ 06/01/90                   Big Business, Inc.                          │
└─────────────────────────────────────────────────────────────────────┘
```

```
                 Accounts Payable              Cash
          Code   Account Number          Account Number
          1          20500                   11000
          2            0                        0
          3            0                        0
          4            0                        0
          5            0                        0
          6            0                        0
          7            0                        0
          8            0                        0
          9            0                        0
```

Accept (Y/N): Y

FIGURE 4-5 Display of default account numbers

```
┌─────────────────────────────────────────────────────────────────────┐
│ APMAINT 5.00          Maintain Accounts Payable Options   COMPANY ID: BB │
│ 06/01/90                   Big Business, Inc.                          │
└─────────────────────────────────────────────────────────────────────┘
```

Ready to Create Accounts Payable Files - Continue (Y/N) Y

FIGURE 4-6 Creating Accounts Payable files

To enter vendor information, start by selecting Maintain Vendors from the Accounts Payable Maintenance Menu shown in Figure 4-7. Tell Peachtree Complete III whether or not you want a control report. You will be prompted for the vendor ID.

A *vendor ID* is a six-character ID code that uniquely identifies each vendor. If you are setting up the accounting system for an established business, you may be able to use their vendor IDs. If you are just starting out on your own, you may need to set up a vendor ID system of your own.

A common vendor ID is the first few letters of the vendor's name followed by a number. For example, if the vendor's name were "Consolidated Amalgamations," the vendor ID would be something like CON001. If there were another company with the same first three letters, such as "Construction Suppliers," their vendor ID would be CON002. Using the first few letters

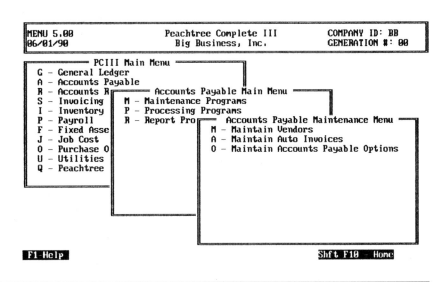

FIGURE 4-7   The Accounts Payable Maintenance Menu

of the company's name gives you a reasonably intuitive way of looking up the company in the vendor file.

Whatever you choose as a vendor ID system, be sure that it can expand with the business. All the accounts payable transactions that you enter for a vendor are keyed to the vendor ID. Once you set up a vendor, you cannot change the vendor ID without deleting the old vendor and setting up a new vendor. Also remember that Peachtree Complete III sorts vendors on reports in order of the vendor code. If you are just using the next available six-digit number for each vendor ID, you may have to look through pages of reports to find a particular vendor.

The vendor ID *is case sensitive*; that is, Peachtree Complete III treats **CON001** and **con001** differently. You may wish to make all letters in vendor IDs uppercase.

After you have entered the vendor ID, Peachtree Complete III asks if you want to add the vendor (Figure 4-8). Type **Y** and press (**ENTER**). The Maintain Vendors screen will appear, as shown in Figure 4-9.

The vendor ID comes from the previous screen. Most of the fields in Figure 4-9 are optional, with the exception of the G/L Account Number, Temporary Vendor (Y/N), and 1099 Vendor (Y/N) fields. The options from Figure 4-9 are discussed here.

Address and Contact Information Enter the vendor's name, address, and postal code as you want it to appear on Accounts Payable reports, checks, and 1099s. The telephone number can be up to 14 characters in any format you wish. The contact is the name of any specific person to contact at the vendor.

G/L Account Number You must make an entry in the G/L Account Number field. This field is the default General Ledger account number for expenses posted for this vendor. If you entered **Y** in the Report to G/L field (shown in Figure 4-4), you can press

```
┌─────────────────────────────────────────────────────────────────────┐
│APMAINT 5.00                    Maintain Vendors        COMPANY ID: BB │
│06/01/90                       Big Business, Inc.       GENERATION #: 00│
└─────────────────────────────────────────────────────────────────────┘

Vendor ID.............: COS001 NOT ON FILE - ADD (Y/N): Y
```

FIGURE 4-8   Adding a vendor

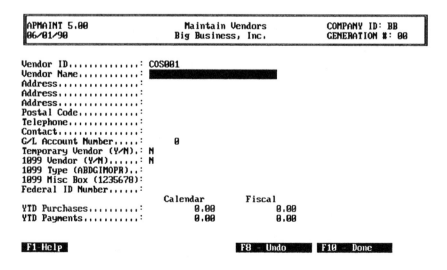

```
┌─────────────────────────────────────────────────────────────────────┐
│APMAINT 5.00                    Maintain Vendors        COMPANY ID: BB │
│06/01/90                       Big Business, Inc.       GENERATION #: 00│
└─────────────────────────────────────────────────────────────────────┘

       Vendor ID.............: COS001
       Vendor Name...........: ▓▓▓▓▓▓▓▓▓▓▓▓▓▓▓▓▓▓▓▓▓▓▓
       Address...............:
       Address...............:
       Address...............:
       Postal Code...........:
       Telephone.............:
       Contact...............:
       G/L Account Number....:        0
       Temporary Vendor (Y/N):  N
       1099 Vendor (Y/N).....:  N
       1099 Type (ABDGIMOPR)..:
       1099 Misc Box (1235678):
       Federal ID Number......:
                                Calendar        Fiscal
       YTD Purchases..........:        0.00          0.00
       YTD Payments...........:        0.00          0.00

   ▊F1-Help▊                        ▊F8 - Undo▊    ▊F10 - Done▊
```

FIGURE 4-9   The Maintain Vendors screen

(F2) in this field to look up the list of valid General Ledger account numbers. The sample information in Figure 4-10 shows this vendor posting to 61500, the office expenses accuont.

Temporary Vendor (Y/N)   You will sometimes make purchases from a vendor with whom you won't be doing business in the future. If you type **Y** in this field, Peachtree Complete III deletes this vendor from the vendor file during end-of-period processing when there is no account activity for the current period. If you type **N**, you must delete the vendor using the Delete Vendor selection, even if there is no account activity for the vendor.

1099 Vendor (Y/N)   If the vendor will need a 1099 form at the end of the year, type **Y** in the 1099 Vendor field; otherwise, type **N**.

1099 Type (ABDGIMOPR)   If you answered **Y** to the previous question, Peachtree Complete III automatically fills in this field

```
APMAINT 5.00                 Maintain Vendors          COMPANY ID: BB
06/01/90                    Big Business, Inc.         GENERATION #: 00


Vendor ID...............: COS001
Vendor Name.............: COSPRO
Address.................: P.O. Box 30606
Address.................: Seattle, WA
Address.................:
Postal Code.............: 98103-0606
Telephone...............: 206-555-7364
Contact.................: Melvin Morsmere
G/L Account Number......: 61500
Temporary Vendor (Y/N).: N
1099 Vendor (Y/N).......: Y
1099 Type (ABDGIMOPR)..: M
1099 Misc Box (1235678): 1
Federal ID Number.......: 999-99-9999
                           Calendar       Fiscal
YTD Purchases...........:      0.00          0.00
YTD Payments............:      0.00          0.00

Accept (Y/N): Y
                                        F8 - Undo
```

───── **FIGURE 4-10**   The sample Maintain Vendors screen

with **M** for "miscellaneous." Although there are nine different 1099 forms, Peachtree Complete III only recognizes the miscellaneous form. Check with the vendor or your accountant if you need help determining the type of 1099 form to file.

1099 Misc Box   Enter the number of the box on the 1099 miscellaneous form where you want the vendor's total payment to be printed (each box on the form is numbered). You can enter box numbers 1-3 or 5-8.

Federal ID Number   Enter the vendor's federal tax ID number. This information will appear on 1099 forms. This information is required if the vendor is listed as a 1099 vendor.

YTD Purchases   These two fields are the calendar and fiscal year total of all the purchases made from this vendor. The calendar total is the total for the calendar year (from January to December). The fiscal total is the total for the 12-month fiscal period (which may be the same as the calendar year). Enter any open invoices or credits with the vendor in these fields.

YTD Payments   These two fields are the calendar and fiscal year total of all the payments made to this vendor. Enter all payments made to the vendor in the calendar and fiscal year. Peachtree Complete III will update the information in all four YTD fields each time you close an accounting period. When you close the year, these fields are reset to 0.

Change Vendor Remit To Address (Y/N)?

After you accept the vendor information, Peachtree Complete III asks if you want to send your payment to the vendor at an address other than the one that you just entered (Figure 4-11). If you type

Y and press (ENTER), a second address screen appears. Enter the new address in these fields. Peachtree Complete III will use this address whenever you print checks. When you accept this information, you return to the Vendor ID screen.

ENTERING AN AUTOMATIC INVOICE

After you have entered your list of current vendors, you can set up automatic invoices. An *automatic invoice* is any invoice amount that repeats regularly. Among other things, you can set up mortgages or leases, auto, health, and business insurance, loans and notes, and licenses as automatic invoices.

When you set up an automatic invoice, you tell Peachtree Complete III to pay a fixed amount to a vendor once a month, every other month, quarterly, semi-annually, or annually. At the

```
APMAINT 5.00                   Maintain Vendors          COMPANY ID: BB
06/01/90                       Big Business, Inc.        GENERATION #: 00

Vendor ID..............: COS001
Vendor Name............: COSPRO
Address................: P.O. Box 30606
Address................: Seattle, WA
Address................:
Postal Code............: 98103-0606
Telephone..............: 206-555-7364
Contact................: Melvin Morsmere
G/L Account Number.....:  61500
Temporary Vendor (Y/N).: N
1099 Vendor (Y/N)......: Y
1099 Type (ABDGIMOPR)..: M
1099 Misc Box (1235678): 1
Federal ID Number......: 999-99-9999
                         Calendar        Fiscal
YTD Purchases..........:        0.00           0.00
YTD Payments...........:        0.00           0.00

Change Vendor Remit To Address (Y/N)? █
```

⟶ **FIGURE 4-11** Send remittances to different address

predetermined time, Peachtree Complete III then automatically generates checks for each of the automatic invoice amounts.

To enter an automatic invoice, select Maintain Auto Invoices from the Accounts Payable Maintenance Menu, as shown in Figure 4-12. After telling Peachtree Complete III whether or not to print a control report, you are prompted for the vendor ID. Enter the appropriate vendor ID.

Peachtree Complete III then asks you for the automatic invoice number. Enter a one- or two-character automatic invoice number. As with vendor IDs, you cannot change automatic invoice numbers once you've accepted them. The first time you enter the automatic invoice, Peachtree Complete III asks if you want to add this number. Type **Y** and press (ENTER). The Maintain Auto Invoices screen appears (shown in Figure 4-13).

You can change the information in any of the following fields whenever you need to.

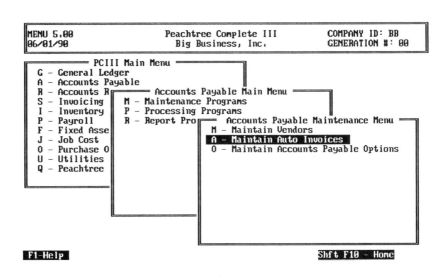

FIGURE 4-12 Select Maintain Auto Invoices

Status (A/I)   The Status (A/I) field tells Peachtree Complete III whether or not to make this invoice active. The default is A (active). If you didn't want to pay the invoice one billing cycle, you would change this field to I.

Amount Due   The Amount Due field contains the amount of the invoice.

Due Day   The Due Day field indicates the day of the month that the invoice is due, from 1 to 31. If the month doesn't have 31 days but you have entered 31, Accounts Payable will pay the invoice on the last day of the month.

Discount Day   Most of the time, you don't get a discount for paying a bill early. Neither credit cards nor the utility companies offer a bonus for early payment. However, many vendors of

```
╔══════════════════════════════════════════════════════════════════╗
║ APMAINT 5.00          Maintain Auto Invoices    COMPANY ID: BB     ║
║ 06/01/90              Big Business, Inc.        GENERATION #: 00    ║
╚══════════════════════════════════════════════════════════════════╝

 Vendor ID..............: COS001    COSPRO
 Auto Invoice Number....: 01

 Status (A/I)...........: A           * * * Distribution * * *
 Amount Due.............:     400.00   ..Account.......Amount..
 Due Day................: 15         1.   61500        400.00
 Discount Day...........: 5          2.       0          0.00
 Discount Percent.......:   2.00     3.       0          0.00
 Number Of Months.......: 12         4.       0          0.00
 Month To Begin.........: 6          5.       0          0.00
 Frequency..............: 1  Monthly  6.      0          0.00
 Last Month Billed......: 0          7.       0          0.00
 # of Months Billed.....:   0        8.       0          0.00
 A/P Account............: 1  20500                 ===========
 Comment................: Retainer - technical svcs
                                                      400.00

 Accept (Y/N): Y
                              ▐ F8 - Undo ▌
```

FIGURE 4-13   The Maintain Auto Invoices screen

business goods and services encourage their customers to pay promptly by offering a small discount off the total bill for payment within the first five or ten days. For example, you might see on the top of a vendor's invoice "2% 10/net 30." This means that you have up to 30 days to pay the balance on the invoice, but if you pay the bill within ten days, you may deduct 2% of the balance.

In the Discount Day field, you enter the last day in the month that you can pay the invoice and still receive a discount for early payment.

Discount Percent   If the vendor offers a discount for early payment, you should enter the percent of the discount in the Discount Percent field. A 2% discount would be 2.00. If you pay the invoice by the discount day entered in the previous field, Accounts Payable subtracts this percent from the total invoice amount.

Number Of Months   The Number Of Months field contains the number of months you want the automatic invoice to continue for. For example, if you are paying off a 36-month installment loan, you would enter 36 in this field.

Month To Begin   In the Month To Begin field, enter the month you want to start paying the automatic invoice.

Frequency   In the Frequency field, enter a code that shows how often to pay on the invoice. The codes are

1   Monthly

2   Bimonthly (every other month)

3   Quarterly (every three months)

4   Semiannually (every six months)

5   Annually

The default frequency is 1, monthly.

Last Month Billed   The Last Month Billed field shows the last month the invoice was billed. If you are just setting up this field, leave it set to 0. Peachtree Complete III will update this field to show the correct month each time you process invoices.

 # Of Months Billed   The # Of Months Billed field shows the number of months (or the number of times) that the invoice has been billed. If you are setting up automatic invoice information for an invoice that has already been billed, enter the appropriate number in this field. If the automatic invoice has not been billed before, leave this field set to 0. When the number in this field equals the number in the Number Of Months field, the billing will stop.

A/P Account   Enter the appropriate Accounts Payable code in the A/P Account field. If you are not sure which code to enter, you can press (F2) to look up the accounts payable codes that you set up earlier.

Comment   You can enter up to 25 characters of descriptive information in the Comment field. This information will appear on the automatic invoice report and the control report.

Distribution   You can specify up to eight different accounts to distribute invoice costs to general ledger accounts.

    Once you have entered and accepted the automatic invoice information, you are asked if you want to maintain the Job Cost distributions. For now, type **N** and press (ENTER). If you type **Y** and press (ENTER), you will see the screen shown in Figure 4-14. You will learn how to use the Job Cost module in Chapter 12.

    Peachtree Complete III returns you to the initial auto invoice screen and prompts for the next automatic invoice number for this vendor. You can continue entering automatic invoices for this

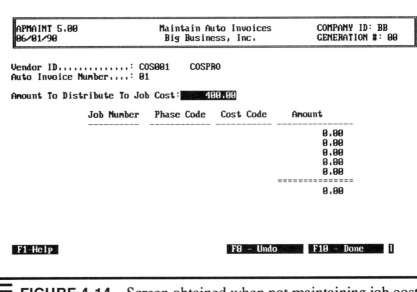

```
┌─────────────────────────────────────────────────────────────────────┐
│APMAINT 5.00              Maintain Auto Invoices        COMPANY ID: BB │
│06/01/90                   Big Business, Inc.           GENERATION #: 00│
└─────────────────────────────────────────────────────────────────────┘

Vendor ID..............: COS001    COSPRO
Auto Invoice Number....: 01

Amount To Distribute To Job Cost:▓▓▓▓    400.00

            Job Number   Phase Code   Cost Code    Amount
            ──────────   ──────────   ──────────   ──────────
                                                       0.00
                                                       0.00
                                                       0.00
                                                       0.00
                                                       0.00
                                                   ==========
                                                       0.00


   F1-Help                        F8 - Undo     F10 - Done    ▯
```

FIGURE 4-14   Screen obtained when not maintaining job cost distribution

vendor, press (ESC) to enter a different vendor ID, or press (ESC) and then (F10) to return to the Main Menu.

ENTERING AN INVOICE

The previous section showed you how to set up an automatic invoice for a client. Although this feature is very useful, most of your vendor invoices will not be fixed amounts and won't repeat on a regular basis. For these invoices, you need to enter specific invoice information that shows the current balance.

To enter an invoice, select Enter Invoices from the Accounts Payable Processing Menu, as shown in Figure 4-15. After telling

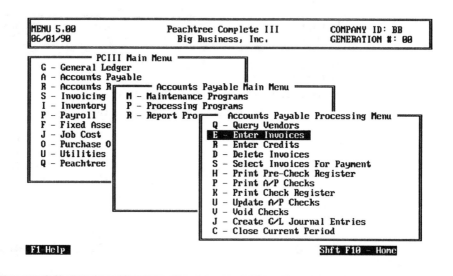

FIGURE 4-15   Select Enter Invoices

Peachtree Complete III whether or not to print a control report, you
see the screen shown in Figure 4-16.

Since you are entering invoices for the first time, type **Y** and
press (**ENTER**) at the Beginning Balances field. Peachtree Complete
III will display a warning. To continue, type **Y** and press (**ENTER**)
again. You are then prompted for the default invoice date. The date
here will be used as the default date for all the invoices you enter.
When you press (**F10**) and accept the information, the Enter Invoices screen appears as shown here:

```
APPROC1 5.00                    Enter Invoices         COMPANY ID: BB
06/01/90                      Big Business, Inc.        GENERATION #: 00
                                              * * Entering Beginning Balances * *

Vendor ID..............: ▮▮▮▮▮▮
```

Enter the vendor ID. If the vendor ID is not on file, you will be taken to the Enter Vendor screen. You can then set up the vendor information before continuing with the invoice procedure. Next you are prompted for the invoice number. This is the vendor's invoice number as it appears on the invoice. On the sample invoice shown in Figure 4-17, the invoice number is 455. You cannot change the invoice number once you have entered it, so make sure that it's correct before you press (ENTER). The remainder of the Enter Invoices screen appears (shown in Figure 4-18). A quick overview of the options on this screen is provided now for easy reference.

Invoice Date In the Invoice Date field, you can use the default date proposed by Peachtree Complete III, or enter a different date.

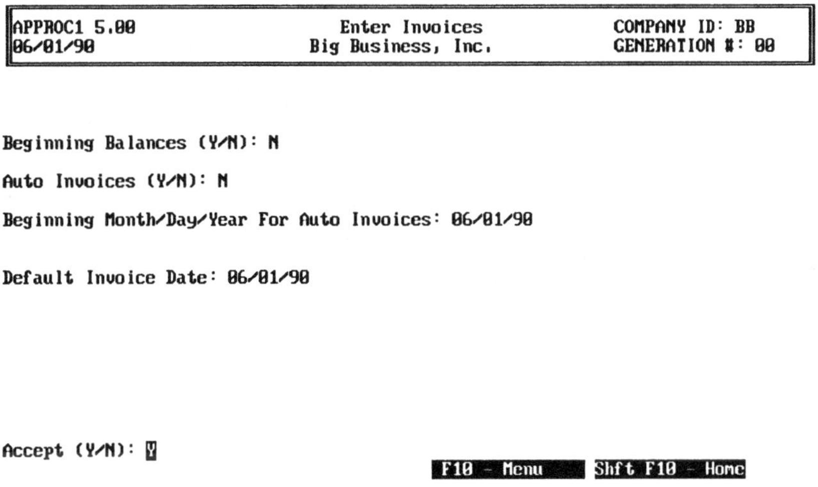

```
APPROC1 5.00                    Enter Invoices              COMPANY ID: BB
06/01/90                       Big Business, Inc.           GENERATION #: 00


Beginning Balances (Y/N): N

Auto Invoices (Y/N): N

Beginning Month/Day/Year For Auto Invoices: 06/01/90

Default Invoice Date: 06/01/90




Accept (Y/N): Y
                                          F10 - Menu     Shft F10 - Home
```

FIGURE 4-16 The Enter Invoices screen

COSPRO
P.O. Box 30606
Seattle, WA 98103
555-7364

Our Invoice No. 455

June 1, 1990

Invoice:

For special writing and editing services on Big Business software documentation
from May 1 through May 31, 1990:

74 hours @ $35/hour $2590

Please pay this amount: **$2590**

Terms: 2% 10/Net 30

≡≡≡ **FIGURE 4-17**   Sample invoice

```
┌──────────────────────────────────────────────────────────────────────┐
│ APPROC1 5.00              Enter Invoices          COMPANY ID: BB       │
│ 06/01/90               Big Business, Inc.         GENERATION #: 00     │
│                                                                        │
│                                      * * Entering Beginning Balances * * │
│ Vendor ID..............: COS001    COSPRO                              │
│ Invoice Number.........: 455                                           │
│                                                                        │
│ Invoice Date...........: 06/01/90         * * * Distribution * * *     │
│ Amount Due.............:        0.00      ..Account......Amount..      │
│ Due Date...............: 01/01/00      1.    61500          0.00       │
│ Discount %.............:        0.00   2.        0          0.00       │
│ Discount Amount........:        0.00   3.        0          0.00       │
│ Discount Date..........: 01/01/00      4.        0          0.00       │
│ A/P Account Code.......: 0              5.        0          0.00       │
│ Comment................:               6.        0          0.00       │
│ Pre-Paid (Y/N).........: N              7.        0          0.00       │
│ Cash Account Code......: 0              8.        0          0.00       │
│ Check Number...........:        0                      ===========     │
│                                                            0.00        │
│                                                                        │
│                                                                        │
│  F1-Help                           F8 - Undo      F10 - Done           │
└──────────────────────────────────────────────────────────────────────┘
```

≡≡≡ **FIGURE 4-18**   The remainder of the Enter Invoices screen

Amount Due   Enter the total dollar amount of the invoice in the Amount Due field. Do not subtract the amounts for early payment discounts (if any).

Due Date   The Due Date field contains the date the amount you entered in the previous field is due. Peachtree Complete III proposes a default due date of 30 days after the invoice date.

Discount %   If there is a discount for early payment, enter the percentage in the Discount % field.

Discount Amount   Peachtree Complete III computes the discount amount by multiplying the invoice amount by the discount percentage you just entered.

Discount Date   The Discount Date field indicates the last date the invoice can be discounted. The default discount date is ten days after the invoice date.

A/P Account Code   Enter the Accounts Payable account code in this field. You can press (F2) to look up the account codes.

Comment   In the Comment field, you can enter up to 25 characters to describe what the invoice is for.

Pre-Paid (Y/N)   Type **Y** and press (ENTER) if this was a prepaid invoice or a C.O.D. Otherwise, type **N** and press (ENTER).

Cash Account Code   If you answered **Y** to the previous question, you need to enter the cash account code the check was written from. You can press (F2) to look up the account codes.

Check Number   If you answered **Y** to Pre-Paid (Y/N), this field contains the number of the check you wrote for the invoice.

Distribution   If you answered **N** to Pre-Paid (Y/N), you need to enter the account codes and the amounts for the distributions in the General Ledger.

Figure 4-19 shows the completed invoice screen for the sample invoice in Figure 4-17. When you accept the information, you are asked if you want to distribute this to Job Cost. If you type **Y** and press (ENTER), you will see the screen shown in Figure 4-14. For now, type **N** and press (ENTER). You will learn how to use the Job Cost module in Chapter 12.

Peachtree Complete III returns you to the invoice number field and prompts for the next invoice number for this vendor. You can continue entering invoices for this vendor, press (ESC) to enter a different vendor ID, or press (ESC) and then (F10) to return to the Main Menu.

```
APPROC1 5.00                    Enter Invoices            COMPANY ID: BB
06/01/90                      Big Business, Inc.          GENERATION #: 00
                                              * * Entering Beginning Balances * *
Vendor ID..............: COS001    COSPRO
Invoice Number.........: 455

Invoice Date...........: 06/01/90            * * * Distribution * * *
Amount Due.............:      2590.00        ..Account.......Amount..
Due Date...............: 07/01/90        1.    61000        2590.00
Discount %.............:      2.00       2.        0           0.00
Discount Amount........:     51.80       3.        0           0.00
Discount Date..........: 06/11/90        4.        0           0.00
A/P Account Code.......: 1  20500        5.        0           0.00
Comment................: Writing & editing - May  6.  0        0.00
Pre-Paid (Y/N).........: N               7.        0           0.00
Cash Account Code......: 0               8.        0           0.00
Check Number...........:        0                           ===========
                                                             2590.00

Accept (Y/N): Y
                                  F8 - Undo
```

FIGURE 4-19   The completed invoice screen

ENTERING A CREDIT

To enter a credit for a vendor, select Enter Credits from the Accounts Payable Processing Menu, as shown in Figure 4-20. After you tell Peachtree Complete III whether or not to print a control report, it asks if you want to enter beginning balances. If you type **Y** and press ⏎(ENTER), you can enter a credit as the beginning balance for a vendor. Otherwise, press ⏎(ENTER) to accept the default. You are then prompted for the default credit date. Like the invoice date, the date in this field will be used as the default date for all the credits you enter. When you press ⏎(ENTER), you are asked if you want to enter open or specific credits, as shown here:

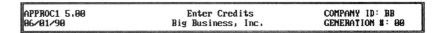

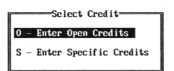

An *open credit* is a credit that does not apply to a specific invoice. For example, you may have prepaid a vendor and not yet ordered merchandise against the credit. A *specific credit* is a credit that applies to a specific invoice. You would enter a specific credit if you had purchased merchandise from a vendor and then returned some of it.

Entering an Open Credit

After you select Enter Open Credits from the Select Credits menu, enter the vendor ID. You are then prompted for the invoice

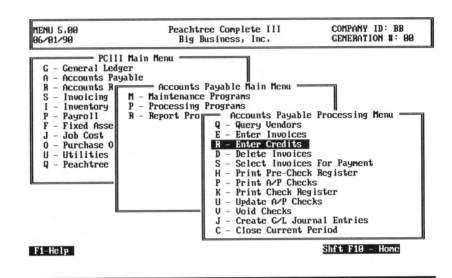

```
MENU 5.00                Peachtree Complete III        COMPANY ID: BB
06/01/90                   Big Business, Inc.           GENERATION #: 00

         ┌─ PCIII Main Menu ─────┐
         │ G - General Ledger    │
         │ A - Accounts Payable  │
         │ R - Accounts R┌─ Accounts Payable Main Menu ─┐
         │ S - Invoicing │ M - Maintenance Programs     │
         │ I - Inventory │ P - Processing Programs      │
         │ P - Payroll   │ R - Report Pro┌─ Accounts Payable Processing Menu ─┐
         │ F - Fixed Asse│               │ Q - Query Vendors                  │
         │ J - Job Cost  │               │ E - Enter Invoices                 │
         │ O - Purchase O│               │ R - Enter Credits                  │
         │ U - Utilities │               │ D - Delete Invoices                │
         │ Q - Peachtree │               │ S - Select Invoices For Payment    │
         │               │               │ H - Print Pre-Check Register       │
         │               │               │ P - Print A/P Checks               │
         │               │               │ K - Print Check Register           │
         │               │               │ U - Update A/P Checks              │
         │               └───────────────│ V - Void Checks                    │
         │                               │ J - Create G/L Journal Entries     │
         │                               │ C - Close Current Period           │
         │                               └────────────────────────────────────┘

  ▐F1-Help▌                                         ▐Shft F10 - Home▌
```

═══════ **FIGURE 4-20**   Select Enter Credits to credit a vendor

number. Because this is an open credit that doesn't apply against
a specific invoice, you can simply type **OPEN CREDIT** in this
field. When you press (ENTER), the screen in Figure 4-21 appears.
A brief description of each of these options follows.

Credit Date   The Credit Date field contains the date of the credit.

Credit Amount   The Credit Amount field is the total dollar
amount of the credit.

A/P Account Code   Enter the Accounts Payable account code in
this field. You can press (F2) to look up the account codes.

Comment   You can enter up to 25 characters to describe what the
credit is for.

```
┌─────────────────────────────────────────────────────────────────────────┐
│APPROC1 5.00                    Enter Credits            COMPANY ID: BB    │
│06/01/90                      Big Business, Inc.         GENERATION #: 00   │
└─────────────────────────────────────────────────────────────────────────┘

      Vendor ID.............: PUG001    Puget Design Shop
      Invoice Number........: OPEN CREDIT

      Credit Date...........: 06/01/90           * * * Distribution * * *
                                                 ..Account......Amount..
      Credit Amount.........:        0.00      1.    61500           0.00
                                               2.        0           0.00
      A/P Account Code......: 0                3.        0           0.00
                                               4.        0           0.00
      Comment...............:                  5.        0           0.00
                                               6.        0           0.00
                                               7.        0           0.00
                                               8.        0           0.00
                                                            ===========

                                                                     0.00


      [F1-Help]                           [F8 - Undo]   [F10 - Done]
```

═══ **FIGURE 4-21** The Enter Credits screen

Distribution   Enter the account codes and the amounts for the distributions in the General Ledger.

Figure 4-22 shows the completed credit screen. When you accept the information, you are asked if you want to distribute this to Job Cost. If you type **Y** and press (**ENTER**), you will see the screen shown in Figure 4-14. For now, type **N** and press (**ENTER**).

Peachtree Complete III returns you to the invoice number field and prompts for the next invoice number for this vendor. You can continue entering credits for this vendor, press (**ESC**) to enter a different vendor ID, or press (**ESC**) and then (**F10**) to return to the Main Menu.

Entering a Specific Credit

After you select Enter Specific Credits from the Select Credits menu, enter the vendor ID. You are then prompted for the invoice

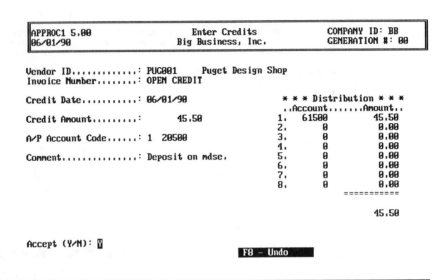

```
┌─────────────────────────────────────────────────────────────────────┐
│ APPROC1 5.00              Enter Credits             COMPANY ID: BB    │
│ 06/01/90                Big Business, Inc.          GENERATION #: 00  │
└─────────────────────────────────────────────────────────────────────┘

  Vendor ID.............: PUG001     Puget Design Shop
  Invoice Number........: OPEN CREDIT

  Credit Date...........: 06/01/90              * * * Distribution * * *
                                                ..Account.......Amount..
  Credit Amount.........:        45.50      1.    61500           45.50
                                            2.        0            0.00
  A/P Account Code......: 1  20500          3.        0            0.00
                                            4.        0            0.00
  Comment...............: Deposit on mdse.   5.        0            0.00
                                            6.        0            0.00
                                            7.        0            0.00
                                            8.        0            0.00
                                                              ===========

                                                                 45.50


  Accept (Y/N): Y
                                        ▐ F8 - Undo ▌
```

FIGURE 4-22   The completed credit screen

number. You can press (F2) to look up the invoice numbers for the vendor. If you try to enter an incorrect invoice number, Peachtree Complete III displays an error message. Figure 4-23 shows the Enter Credits screen for invoice 455 for COSPRO. If this is the correct invoice, type **Y** and press (ENTER); otherwise, press (F8) to enter a different invoice number.

Most of the information on this screen comes from the original invoice. You need to enter the credit amount and a reference code. If you are working from a credit memo, enter the reference code on the credit memo. If you do not have a credit memo, enter **IN-HOUSE** in the Ref. Code field.

When you accept the information, Peachtree Complete III returns you to the invoice number field and prompts for the next invoice number for this vendor.

```
┌──────────────────────────────────────────────────────────────────────────┐
│APPROC1 5.00                    Enter Credits           COMPANY ID: BB      │
│06/01/90                     Big Business, Inc.          GENERATION #: 00    │
└──────────────────────────────────────────────────────────────────────────┘

    Vendor ID....: COS001              COSPRO
    Invoice No...: 455                    Date: 06/01/90

    Entry Date...: 06/01/90  ....Amount...  * * * Distribution * * * * Credit * *
    Due Date.....: 07/01/90     2590.00   ..Account.....Amount... .....Amount...
    Discount Date: 06/11/90       51.80  1.  61000       2590.00
    Credits......:      0          0.00  2.     0           0.00
    Payments.....:      0          0.00  3.     0           0.00
    Net Invoice..:             2590.00   4.     0           0.00
                                         5.     0           0.00
    Comment......: Writing & editing - Ma 6.  0           0.00
                                         7.     0           0.00
    Credit Amount:                       8.     0           0.00
                                                      =========== =============
    Ref. Code....:                                        2590.00

    Correct Invoice (Y/N): Y
                                         ▐ F8 - Undo ▌
```

═══ **FIGURE 4-23**   The Enter Credits screen for invoice number 455

ISSUING PAYMENTS TO VENDORS

The previous sections in this chapter showed how to enter vendors, automatic invoices, and regular invoices. Keeping this information up to date is most of the work involved with Accounts Payable. Once you have your vendors and invoices entered in Peachtree Complete III, you are ready to print checks and make payments.

Issuing payments involves several steps. First, you print a cash requirements report to see how much cash you need to pay all of your open invoices. Next, you select the invoices that you want to pay. After this, you print a pre-check register to verify the invoices that you have selected to pay. When you are satisified with your selections, you print the Accounts Payable checks, followed by a check register. Finally, you update the check information in the

Accounts Payable transaction file to show that the invoices have been paid. The following sections illustrate how to perform each of these steps.

Printing the Cash Requirements Report

The Cash Requirements report gives you a list of all the open invoices sorted by their due dates. You print this report to see how much cash you need to pay all open invoices.

To print the Cash Requirements report, first select Cash Requirements Report from the Accounts Payable Reports Menu, as shown in Figure 4-24. After telling Peachtree Complete III where you want to print the report, you specify the run date. This date appears at the top of the report, but does not affect any of the information in the report. When you press (ENTER), Peachtree Complete III prints the report.

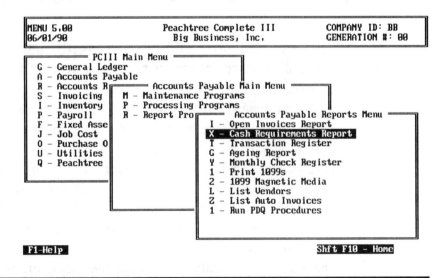

FIGURE 4-24   Select Cash Requirements Report

As you can see from Figure 4-25, Peachtree Complete III gives you a running total of the cash necessary to pay the open invoices. If you need to, you can add, change, or delete invoices, and then print another Cash Requirements report. When you are satisfied that all of the open invoices are on the report, you need to tell Peachtree Complete III which invoices you want to pay.

 If you have a lot of invoices or you need to decide how to divide inadequate cash resources over many vendors, you may want to run an Ageing report before printing the Cash Requirements report. The Ageing report shows aged invoice information for each vendor. You can print the Ageing report by selecting Ageing Report from the Accounts Payable Reports Menu and telling Peachtree Complete III where you want to print the report and how you want it to print.

Selecting Invoices for Payment

To select invoices for payment, choose Select Invoices For Payment from the Accounts Payable Processing Menu (Figure 4-26). You are then asked for the cash account code and if you want to select invoices automatically. If you type **Y** and press (ENTER), you must enter the beginning and ending discount dates. Peachtree Complete III will then select invoices based on the due dates. Otherwise, type **N** and press (ENTER) to select the invoices manually.

After you accept the information on this screen, Peachtree Complete III displays the Select Vendors screen (Figure 4-27). From here, you can tell Peachtree Complete III that you want to select invoices for all vendors or from individual vendors. When you select all vendors (or after you have entered a vendor ID), Peachtree Complete III displays a summary screen showing all the current debits and credits for a single vendor (Figure 4-28).

```
CASH REQUIREMENTS REPORT FOR 6/1/90

RUN DATE: 06/01/90                    Big Business, Inc.                            PAGE  1
RUN TIME: 3:02 PM                     Accounts Payable
                                      Cash Requirements Report

**DATA SORTED BY DUE DATE
DUE DATE/
VENDOR    VENDOR NAME      INVOICE NUMBER  INV.DATE    AMOUNT   DISCOUNT       NET   DAILY TOTAL  REQ.TO DATE
------    -----------      --------------  --------    ------   --------       ---   -----------  -----------
06/17/90
KNO001 Groot Knoovenagle   988             05/18/90    350.00      0.00     350.00      350.00       350.00

06/23/90
PUG001 Puget Design Shop   7628            05/24/90    260.00      0.00     260.00      260.00       610.00

07/01/90
COS001 COSPRO              455             06/01/90  2,590.00     51.80   2,538.20
                                                      129.50-     0.00     129.50-
JOH001 J & P's Kitty City  A324            06/01/90     43.00      0.00      43.00
PUG001 Puget Design Shop   7666            06/01/90    514.67      0.00     514.67
SHA001 Sharma Software     2020            06/01/90  1,200.00      0.00   1,200.00    4,166.37     4,776.37

OPEN CREDITS:
PUG001 Puget Design Shop   OPEN CREDIT     06/01/90     45.50-     0.00      45.50-      45.50-     4,730.87

*** End of Cash Requirements Report ***
```

FIGURE 4-25 The Cash Requirements report

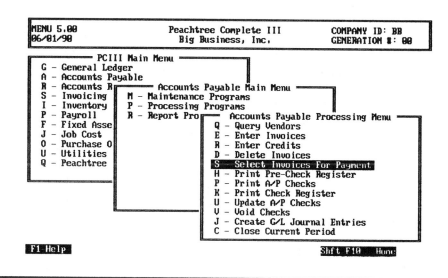

FIGURE 4-26 Select Invoices For Payment

```
APPROC2 5.00              Select Invoices For Payment       COMPANY ID: BB
06/01/90                       Big Business, Inc.           GENERATION #: 00

                        Cash Account: 1 - 11000

Invoices Marked To Pay:        0.00
Discounts Taken.......:        0.00        Available Open Credit:      45.50
Applied Open Credits..:        0.00        Applied Open Credit..:       0.00
                          _____                              _____
Cash Requirements.....:        0.00        Unused Open Credit...:      45.50

                        ┌─Select Vendors─┐
                        │                │
                        │ A   All Vendors│
                        │                │
                        │ S - Selected Vendors │
                        └────────────────┘




   F1-Help                            F10 - Menu    Shft F10 - Home
```

FIGURE 4-27 The Select Vendors screen

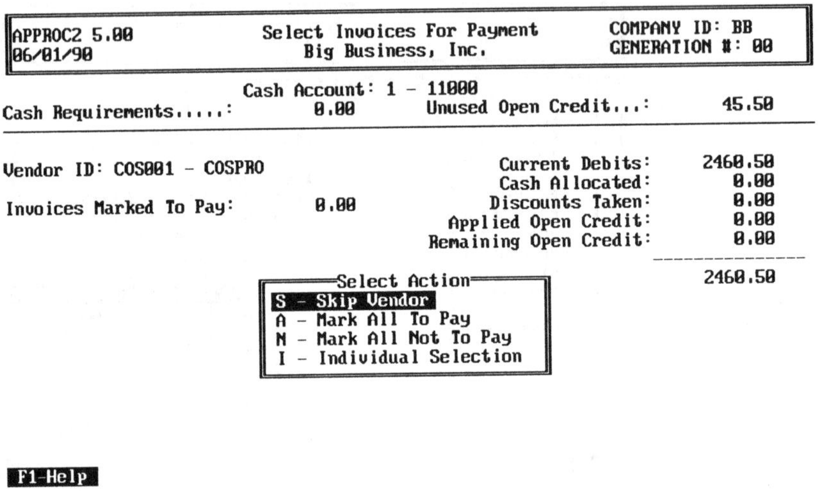

```
┌─────────────────────────────────────────────────────────────────────┐
│ APPROC2 5.00              Select Invoices For Payment      COMPANY ID: BB    │
│ 06/01/90                      Big Business, Inc.           GENERATION #: 00   │
├─────────────────────────────────────────────────────────────────────┤
│                       Cash Account: 1 - 11000                          │
│ Cash Requirements.....:         0.00    Unused Open Credit...:    45.50 │
│─────────────────────────────────────────────────────────────────────│
│ Vendor ID: COS001 - COSPRO                    Current Debits:   2460.50 │
│                                                Cash Allocated:     0.00 │
│ Invoices Marked To Pay:         0.00          Discounts Taken:     0.00 │
│                                            Applied Open Credit:     0.00 │
│                                          Remaining Open Credit:     0.00 │
│                                                               ────────── │
│                          ┌──────Select Action──────┐          2460.50 │
│                          │ S - Skip Vendor          │                   │
│                          │ A - Mark All To Pay      │                   │
│                          │ N - Mark All Not To Pay  │                   │
│                          │ I - Individual Selection │                   │
│                          └──────────────────────────┘                   │
│                                                                         │
│                                                                         │
│ ▐F1-Help▌                                                               │
└─────────────────────────────────────────────────────────────────────┘
```

FIGURE 4-28 Summary screen showing all debits and credits for a vendor

You can skip the vendor entirely and go to the next vendor, mark all the invoices for payment on the next check run (the total for the open invoices appears in the Current Debits field), withhold payment on all the invoices for this vendor, or select invoices for payment individually. If you select **A**, all the invoices are marked for payment. Peachtree Complete III totals the debits, discounts, and credits, and allocates the appropriate amount of cash as shown in Figure 4-29.

You can also select individual invoices for payment. Figure 4-30 shows a single invoice selected for consideration. The invoice information has the same format as the Enter Invoices screen shown earlier in this chapter. From here, you can skip the invoice, mark the invoice for payment, withhold payment, or even issue a partial payment on the invoice. Peachtree Complete III displays helpful information about the invoices for this particular client at the top of the screen.

```
┌─────────────────────────────────────────────────────────────────────┐
│ APPROC2 5.00              Select Invoices For Payment    COMPANY ID: BB │
│ 06/01/90                     Big Business, Inc.          GENERATION #: 00 │
└─────────────────────────────────────────────────────────────────────┘
                        Cash Account: 1 - 11000
  Cash Requirements.....:     2400.70      Unused Open Credit...:      45.50


  Vendor ID: COS001 - COSPRO                      Current Debits:     2460.50
                                                  Cash Allocated:     2400.70
  Invoices Marked To Pay:     2460.50           Discounts Taken:        51.00
                                            Applied Open Credit:         0.00
                                          Remaining Open Credit:         0.00
                                                                 ─────────────
                           ┌─────Select Action─────┐                    0.00
                           │ S - Skip Vendor        │
                           │ A - Mark All To Pay    │
                           │ N - Mark All Not To Pay │
                           │ I - Individual Selection │
                           └────────────────────────┘


  F1-Help
```

FIGURE 4-29   All invoices are paid

```
┌─────────────────────────────────────────────────────────────────────┐
│ APPROC2 5.00              Select Invoices For Payment    COMPANY ID: BB │
│ 06/01/90                     Big Business, Inc.          GENERATION #: 00 │
└─────────────────────────────────────────────────────────────────────┘
  Vendor ID: PUG001 - Puget Design Shop          Current Debits:       774.67
                                            Invoices Marked To Pay:       0.00
                                                                 ─────────────
                                                                      729.17

  Invoice No: 7628                            * * Invoice Not Marked To Pay * *

  Entry Date...: 05/24/90  ....Amount...       * * * Distribution * * *
  Due Date.....: 06/23/90       260.00         ..Account......Amount...
  Discount Date: 01/01/00         0.00      1.  61000          260.00
  Credits......:    0             0.00      2.      0            0.00
  Payments.....:    0             0.00      3.      0            0.00
  Net Invoice..:                260.00      4.      0            0.00
                                                    0            0.00
  A/P Account..: 1  20500  ┌─────Select Action─────┐  0            0.00
  Comment......:           │ S - Skip invoice       │  0            0.00
                           │ M - Mark to pay        │  0            0.00
  Amount To Pay:    0.00   │ N - Mark not to pay    │  ===========
                           │ P - Partially pay      │       260.00
                           └────────────────────────┘

  F1-Help
```

FIGURE 4-30   Selecting a single invoice

You can continue marking invoices in this fashion until you have marked all the invoices you want to pay in this run of checks. By the way, marking an invoice for payment that has a credit balance for payment will reduce the total amount of cash allocated for payments. If you need to, you can add, change, or delete invoices through the Accounts Payable Processing Menu, and print another Cash Requirements report.

You can use Select Invoices For Payment as often as you like. Many people find it easiest to select invoices as soon as they have entered them, then run a Pre-Check register and select any last invoices right before they print their checks. This makes the invoice selection process a daily rather than a monthly task, and makes it easier to determine when and how to pay an invoice while the information is immediately at hand.

Printing the Pre-Check Register

The last thing you need to do before printing the checks is print a Pre-Check register. This gives you one last chance to verify the information before you print the checks themselves. The Pre-Check register is simply a list of the invoices that you have selected for payment.

Select Print Pre-Check Register from the Accounts Payable Processing Menu, as shown in Figure 4-31. After you tell Peachtree Complete III how you want it to print the report, you enter a run date for the report. Peachtree Complete III then prints the Pre-Check register, a sample of which appears in Figure 4-32.

Printing Checks

Having selected your invoices for payment and verified that the information on the check register is complete and correct, you are ready to print checks. Select Print A/P Checks from the Accounts

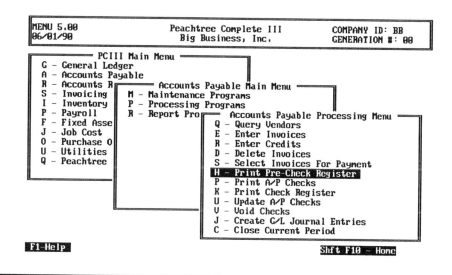

FIGURE 4-31   Select Print Pre-Check Register

Payable Processing Menu. Then tell Peachtree Complete III which printer you want to print the checks on. (You must send the checks to a printer; you cannot print checks to a file or to the screen.)

You then tell Peachtree Complete III what run date you want to appear on the checks, as shown in Figure 4-33. This appears on the checks as the date the check was printed. You also enter the number of the check to be printed as a control mechanism. Peachtree Complete III prints the check number on each check along with the other information. This number should match the preprinted check number. If someone wrote a check manually and didn't record it, the check numbers wouldn't match the next time you printed checks.

A *check mask* is a dummy block of information that Peachtree Complete III will print to help you align your check forms in the printer. Each printing position is filled with the maximum number of characters so that you can adjust the checks precisely. You can

```
PRECHECK REGISTER                                      Big Business, Inc.                                        PAGE   1
RUN DATE: 06/01/90                                      Accounts Payable
RUN TIME:  4:58 PM                                      Pre-Check Register

** CASH ACCOUNT:  1 11000
   ID    INVOICE NUMBER      DATE      GROSS AMOUNT    DISCOUNT    NET AMOUNT    AMOUNT TO PAY    COMMENTS
   --    --------------      ----      ------------    --------    ----------    -------------    --------

COS001 COSPRO
       455               06/01/90        2,460.50       51.80      2,408.70        2,408.70       Writing & editing - May
                                        ----------      ------     ----------      ----------
                            TOTAL:       2,460.50       51.80      2,408.70        2,408.70

JOH001 J & P's Kitty City
       A324              06/01/90           43.00        0.00         43.00           43.00       Office supplies
                                        ----------      ------     ----------      ----------
                            TOTAL:          43.00        0.00         43.00           43.00

KNO001 Groot Knoovenagle
       988              05/18/90          350.00        0.00        350.00          350.00       Research
                                        ----------      ------     ----------      ----------
                            TOTAL:         350.00        0.00        350.00          350.00

PUG001 Puget Design Shop
       7628             05/24/90          260.00        0.00        260.00          260.00       Circuit boards
       7666             06/01/90          514.67        0.00        514.67          514.67
       OPEN CREDIT      06/01/90           45.50-       0.00         45.50-          45.50-      Deposit on mdse.
                                        ----------      ------     ----------      ----------
                            TOTAL:         729.17        0.00        729.17          729.17

SHA001 Sharma Software
       2020             06/01/90        1,200.00        0.00      1,200.00        1,200.00       Contract programming
                                        ----------      ------     ----------      ----------
                            TOTAL:       1,200.00        0.00      1,200.00        1,200.00

                        RUN TOTAL:       4,782.67       51.80      4,730.87        4,730.87
                                        ==========      ======     ==========      ==========

*** End of Pre-Check Register ***
```

FIGURE 4-32 A Pre-Check register

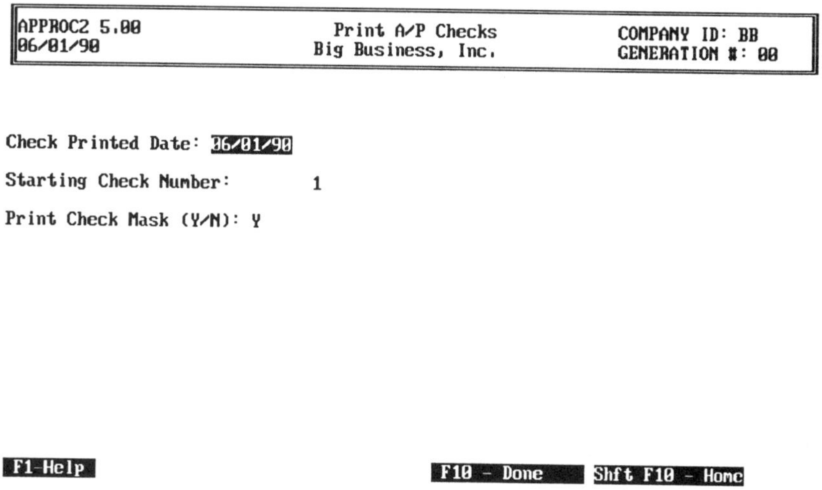

```
┌─────────────────────────────────────────────────────────────────────┐
│ APPROC2 5.00              Print A/P Checks          COMPANY ID: BB    │
│ 06/01/90                 Big Business, Inc.          GENERATION #: 00  │
└─────────────────────────────────────────────────────────────────────┘


     Check Printed Date: ▓06/01/90▓

     Starting Check Number:        1

     Print Check Mask (Y/N): Y




         F1-Help                        F10 - Done      Shft F10 - Home
```

FIGURE 4-33   The date to appear on checks

print the check mask as many times as you like. Peachtree Complete III increments the check number each time it prints the check mask. When you are ready to print the checks, press (F10) and accept the information on the screen. Peachtree Complete III displays the vendor's ID and name as it prints the check for each vendor.

When all the checks are printed, you can print the control report, after which Peachtree Complete III returns you to the Main Menu. If you try to print the same batch of checks again, Peachtree Complete III will warn you that the checks have already been printed and ask you if you want to reprint them. This prevents you from accidentally running the same batch of checks twice.

Printing the Check Register

A check register is very useful for reconciling your checking account with the statements from the bank. You print the Check

Register after you have printed the Accounts Payable checks. Simply select Print Check Register from the Accounts Payable Processing Menu and tell Peachtree Complete III where you want to print the report.

Updating Accounts Payable Checks

To complete the check writing process, you need to update the vendor and transaction information to show that checks have been issued. This is a largely automatic process. You just need to select Update A/P Checks from the Accounts Payable Processing Menu and tell Peachtree Complete III that you want to update the checks. Peachtree Complete III takes the check transaction information and updates the vendor master file and the transaction file. The Transaction register and other reports will now show the check information after each invoice you paid. Invoices paid in full will not appear on the Open Invoice report, and you won't be able to select them again for payment.

Creating G/L Journal Entries

After you have updated the vendor and transaction information, you should also update the General Ledger if you are posting accounts payable information to the General Ledger. Select Create G/L Journal Entries from the Accounts Payable Processing Menu. After specifying the printer and run date, you select one of the options on the Transfer Options screen (shown in Figure 4-34). List G/L Transfers shows you the information that will be transferred to the General Ledger. A sample list appears in Figure 4-35. Consolidate G/L Transfers consolidates the transactions in the Accounts Payable transactions file. Create G/L Transfers transfers the information to the General Ledger and clears the General Ledger entries from the transactions file.

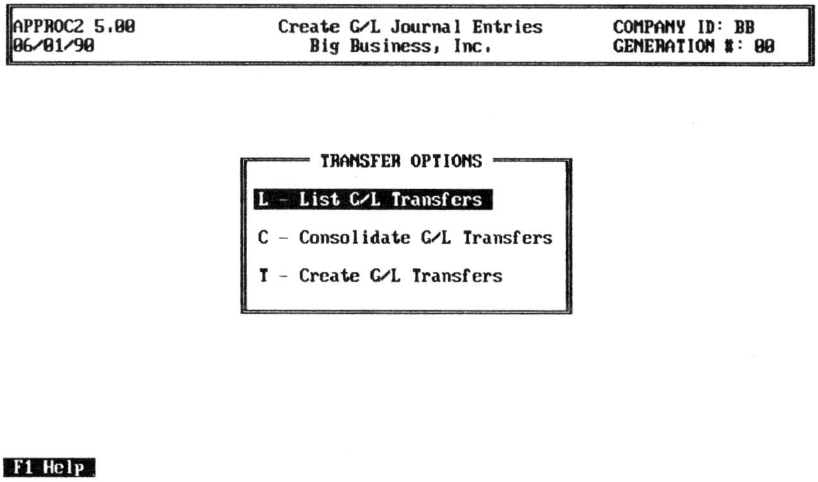

```
┌─────────────────────────────────────────────────────────────────┐
│ APPROC2 5.00          Create G/L Journal Entries   COMPANY ID: BB │
│ 06/01/90                 Big Business, Inc.        GENERATION #: 00│
└─────────────────────────────────────────────────────────────────┘
```

```
        ┌──────── TRANSFER OPTIONS ────────┐
        │                                  │
        │ ▐ L - List G/L Transfers ▌       │
        │                                  │
        │   C - Consolidate G/L Transfers  │
        │                                  │
        │   T - Create G/L Transfers       │
        │                                  │
        └──────────────────────────────────┘
```

▐ F1 Help ▌

FIGURE 4-34   The Transfer Options screen

You should transfer information to the General Ledger at least once a period. If you are paying many invoices, you may want to make it part of the closing process for each check run simply to keep your General Ledger up to date.

HOUSEKEEPING

Most of the work in Accounts Payable involves keeping the vendor and invoice information up to date and printing checks regularly. The housekeeping you must perform is largely a matter of running several reports and closing the accounting period.

Printing the Monthly Check Register   The Monthly Check Register is a list of all the checks you have written in the current period. If you print checks daily or weekly, balancing your check

```
LIST G/L TRANSFERS 6/1/90

RUN DATE: 06/01/90          Big Business, Inc.              PAGE  1
RUN TIME: 12:31 AM            Accounts Payable
                             List G/L Transfers
-----------------------------------------------------------------------------

ACCOUNT SC REFERENCE   DATE         DESCRIPTION       DEBIT        CREDIT
------- -- ---------  --------  ------------------- -----------  -----------
  11000 A  Ck 1003   06/01/90 COS001 Cash                          2408.70
  11000 A  Ck 1004   06/01/90 JOH001 Cash                            43.00
  11000 A  Ck 1005   06/01/90 KNO001 Cash                           350.00
  11000 A  Ck 1006   06/01/90 PUG001 Cash                           260.00
  11000 A  Ck 1006   06/01/90 PUG001 Cash                           514.67
  11000 A  Ck 1006   06/01/90 PUG001 Cash              45.50
  11000 A  Ck 1007   06/01/90 SHA001 Cash                          1200.00
                                                   -----------  -----------
Account    11000 Total:                               45.50      4776.37

  20500 A  OPEN CRE  06/01/90 PUG001 - Open Credit     45.50
  20500 A  IN-HOUSE  06/01/90 COS001 - Entered Invoices 129.50
  20500 A  457       06/01/90 COS001 - Deleted Invoice 1234.00
  20500 A  7628      05/24/89 PUG001 - Deleted Invoice  250.00
  20500 A  Ck 1003   06/01/90 COS001 - Payments       2460.50
  20500 A  Ck 1004   06/01/90 JOH001 - Payments         43.00
  20500 A  Ck 1005   06/01/90 KNO001 - Payments        350.00
  20500 A  Ck 1006   06/01/90 PUG001 - Payments        260.00
  20500 A  Ck 1006   06/01/90 PUG001 - Payments        514.67
  20500 A  Ck 1006   06/01/90 PUG001 - Payments                     45.50
  20500 A  Ck 1007   06/01/90 SHA001 - Payments       1200.00
                                                   -----------  -----------
Account    20500 Total:                             6487.17        45.50

  43500 A  Ck 1003   06/01/90 COS001 - Discounts Taken                51.80

  61000 A  IN-HOUSE  06/01/90 COS001 - Invoice Dist.                 129.50
  61000 A  7628      05/24/89 PUG001 - Deleted Inv. Dis              250.00
                                                   -----------  -----------
Account    61000 Total:                                0.00        379.50

  61500 A  OPEN CRE  06/01/90 PUG001 - Open Credit Dist              45.50
  61500 A  457       06/01/90 COS001 - Deleted Inv. Dis            1234.00
                                                   -----------  -----------
Account    61500 Total:                                0.00       1279.50

                                                   ===========  ===========
                                       Total:       6532.67       6532.67


*** End of List G/L Transfers ***
```

FIGURE 4-35 The information to be transferred to the General Ledger

statement from the individual check registers may be difficult. The Monthly Check Register gives you all the check information in a single report.

Printing 1099s   At the end of the year, you will need to print 1099 forms for all contract and qualifying vendors. If you select Print 1099s from the Accounts Payable Reports Menu, you must print the 1099s to a printer (like checks). If you want to print 1099s to a disk file (for reporting 1099 information to the government on magnetic media), you should select 1099 Magnetic Media instead.

Closing the Period   Closing the current fiscal period eliminates the paid invoices from the current period and carries any open invoices and credits forward to the next month. Closing the current period also increments the generation number and creates a copy of the Accounts Payable files for the new generation.

Select Close Current Period from the Accounts Payable Processing Menu. If you are closing the period for the end of the calendar or the fiscal year, type **Y** and press (ENTER) at the appropriate prompt to tell Peachtree Complete III to clear the year-to-date purchases and payments fields for the vendors. Peachtree Complete III then updates the files and returns you to the Main Menu.

You should be sure to update your Accounts Payable checks and create General Ledger journal entries before closing the period. If you do not, checks and journal entries for the current period will be posted in the next accounting period.

chapter **5**

PURCHASE ORDERS

Installing Purchase Order
Entering Purchase Orders
Printing Purchase Orders
Creating and Printing Change Orders
Cancelling Purchase Orders
Receiving Shipments
Update Inventory
Enter A/P Invoices
Purchasing Closed and Cancelled Purchase Orders
Other Helpful Purchase Order Reports

Chapter 4 explained how to set up the Accounts Payable module, enter vendors and invoices, and generate checks for paying bills. This chapter will demonstrate how to install Peachtree Complete III's Purchase Order module. A *purchase order* is a form that a business sends to a vendor. This form describes the services or merchandise that the business wants to buy. Purchase orders include the name and address of the buyer and the vendor, a description of the items being purchased, a cost for each item, and a total cost. In addition, purchase orders may list the terms and conditions for delivery, shipping charges, and other information about the purchase. You can track and control business expenditures by allowing no orders to be placed without an approved purchase order.

INSTALLING PURCHASE ORDER

You must have installed Accounts Payable before you can install Purchase Order. However, you don't have to wait until the start of a period to install Purchase Order; you can start using it at any time. You can enter all open purchase orders into the Purchase Order module and then use it to issue all new orders. You can also maintain your existing purchase order system and switch over to the Purchase Order module with all new purchase orders from a given date.

To install Peachtree Complete III's Purchase Order module, select Purchase Order from the PCIII Main Menu (Figure 5-1). Peachtree Complete III asks if you are sure you want to install the Purchase Order module. Type **Y** and press (ENTER) to continue.

You need to tell Peachtree Complete III where to store your company's purchase order files (Figure 5-2). The default directory is \PEACH\PODATA. You can change this to any directory you like. If the directory you select does not exist, Peachtree Complete III asks if you wish to create it. Type **Y** and press (ENTER).

As with General Ledger and Accounts Payable, you need to set up options for the Purchase Order module (as shown in Figure 5-3). Select the first option, Set Module Options, and press (ENTER). Peachtree Complete III shows you the first Maintain Purchase Order Options screen (Figure 5-4).

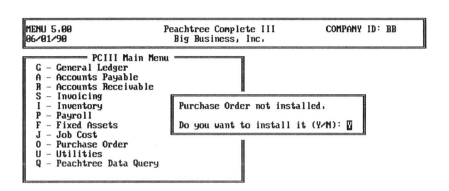

FIGURE 5-1   Installing Purchase Order

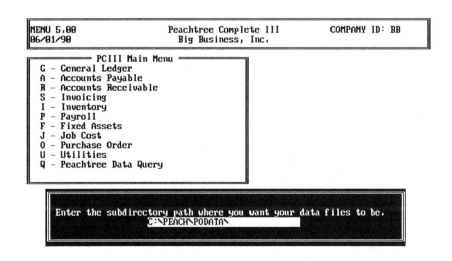

FIGURE 5-2   Selecting the Purchase Order directory

```
┌──────────────────────────────────────────────────────────────────┐
│ POMAINT 5.00        Maintain Purchase Order Options   COMPANY ID: BB│
│ 06/01/90                 Big Business, Inc.                         │
└──────────────────────────────────────────────────────────────────┘

                    ┌─────── Program Options ───────┐
                    │                               │
                    │  O - Set Module Options       │
                    │                               │
                    │  B - Automatic File Backup    │
                    │                               │
                    │  P - Set Printer Assignments  │
                    │                               │
                    └───────────────────────────────┘


        ▐F1-Help▌                        ▐F10 - Menu▌ ▐Shft F10 - Home▌
```

FIGURE 5-3   Options for Purchase Order

```
┌──────────────────────────────────────────────────────────────────┐
│ POMAINT 5.00        Maintain Purchase Order Options   COMPANY ID: BB│
│ 06/01/90                 Big Business, Inc.                         │
└──────────────────────────────────────────────────────────────────┘

PURCHASE ORDER MODULE OPTIONS :          AUTOMATIC NUMBERING OPTIONS:

Controller Password..........:           Current P/O Number...:        1
Operator Password............:           Ending P/O Number....:   999999
Use Menus....................: Y         P/O Reset Number.....:        1
Allow Changes/Deletions......: Y
Force Control Reports........: N
Grand Totals Page............: N
Preprinted Forms.............: N
Print Company Name On P/O....: Y
Interface With Inventory.....: N
Add New Items To Inventory...: N
Add New Vendors To A/P.......: N
Enter Costs At Receipt.......: Y
Enter New Items At Receipt...: Y
Automatic P/O Numbering......: Y

ACCEPT? (Y/N)...: ▐Y▌
```

FIGURE 5-4   Maintain Purchase Order Options screen

Entering Purchase Order Module Options

There are numerous options available. A brief description of each option should help you tailor Purchase Order to your needs. The Controller Password, Operator Password, and Use Menus options work the same for Purchase Order as for the General Ledger. Refer to Chapter 2 if you need to refresh your memory on how these options work.

Allow Changes/Deletions   When you respond **N** to the Allow Changes/Deletions option, Peachtree Complete III will not let you change or delete transactions in Purchase Order. However, you can still add new purchase order transactions and information.

Force Control Reports   Peachtree Complete III can print control reports that produce an audit trail for tracking errors. In Purchase Order, you can create control reports whenever you add, change, or delete receipts or accounts payable invoices, or update the inventory. If you respond **Y** to the Force Control Reports option, Peachtree Complete III will always print control reports without asking you first. If you respond **N**, Peachtree Complete III will ask before printing control reports.

Grand Totals Page   The grand totals will help you determine your outstanding purchase requests and create short-term budgets. If you respond **Y** to the Grand Totals Page option, Peachtree Complete III will print the grand totals for the Purchase Order Status report, the Open Purchase Order report, and the On-Order report on a separate page. If you respond **N**, Peachtree Complete III will not print the grand totals on a separate page.

Preprinted Forms   If you enter **Y** at the Preprinted Forms option, Peachtree Complete III will print purchase orders formatted for its preprinted purchase order forms. If you enter **N**, Peachtree Complete III will print the purchase orders formatted for blank paper.

Print Company Name On P/O   If you enter **Y** at the Print Company Name On P/O option, Peachtree Complete III prints your company name and address on the purchase order. You would use this option if you were printing purchase orders on blank paper or on forms from Peachtree that did not include your company name and address. If you select **N** here and are not using preprinted forms, Peachtree Complete III asks you to confirm that you don't want the company name and address printed on the purchase order.

Interface With Inventory   Enter **Y** to interface the Purchase Order module with the Inventory module. This will enable you to look up an inventory item's stock number directly when you are creating a purchase order. You will also be able to order inventory automatically when it falls below the predetermined reorder level, and add new items to inventory from the Purchase Order module. If you enter **N** for this option, you can use the Purchase Order and Inventory modules without interfacing them, or just use the Purchase Order module.

 If you want to use the Inventory module and the Purchase Order module together, you should install the Inventory module first. If you install the Purchase Order module first, you will have to close or cancel all outstanding purchase orders before you can connect the two modules. See Chapter 11 for information on setting up and using the Inventory module.

Add New Items To Inventory   If you answered **Y** to the previous option, entering **Y** at the Add New Items To Inventory option lets you add new inventory items to the Inventory module through the Purchase Order module. Enter **N** if you don't want to update the

Inventory module through the Purchase Order module or you aren't using the Inventory module.

Add New Vendors To A/P   Entering **Y** for the Add New Vendors To A/P option lets you add new vendors to the Accounts Payable module directly from Purchase Order. This feature is useful when you are first setting up a business. When you first set up Accounts Payable, you probably entered only vendors to whom you owe money or for whom you have open invoices. As you proceed with normal business operations, there will be many vendors that you have not entered yet. Enter **N** if you don't want to enter vendors through Purchase Order.

Enter Costs At Receipt   Entering **Y** at the Enter Costs At Receipt option allows you to enter or change the cost of an item when you receive a shipment through the Enter Receipts option. You should use this feature if you are interfacing Purchase Order with Inventory. Enter **N** to suppress the item unit cost.

Enter New Items At Receipt   Entering **Y** for the Enter New Items At Receipt option lets you receive items that you didn't order. This could happen if the item you order is out of stock and the vendor ships you an acceptable substitute, or if the vendor ships you items that you didn't order but can use anyway. Enter **N** here if you don't want to accept receipt of items that you didn't order.

Automatic P/O Numbering   Enter **Y** in the Automatic P/O Numbering field to let Purchase Order number your purchase orders for you, starting with the number entered in Current P/O Number. Enter **N** to enter your own purchase order numbers manually or to use purchase order numbers that contain letters.

note If you enter **N** for Automatic P/O Numbering, you cannot make entries for the Current P/O Number, Ending P/O Number, and P/O Reset Number options.

Current P/O Number   If you entered **Y** in the Automatic P/O Numbering field, enter the current purchase order number in the Current P/O Number field. This will be the number of the first purchase order you will print with Peachtree Complete III. If you are using preprinted purchase order forms, enter the purchase order number on the first form.

Ending P/O Number   If you entered **Y** in the Automatic P/O Numbering field, enter the highest purchase order number in the sequence in the Ending P/O Number field. After this number, Peachtree Complete III will renumber the purchase orders, starting with the number in the next field.

P/O Reset Number   If you entered **Y** in the Automatic P/O Numbering field, enter the number to start renumbering purchase orders within the P/O Reset Number field.

Entering Purchase Order Default Values

After you have accepted the Purchase Order module options, Peachtree Complete III displays the second Maintain Purchase Order Options screen, shown in Figure 5-5. Now you set up the defaults for purchase orders. All of these options, reviewed here, can be changed for a specific purchase order as necessary.

Cert. Of Compliance Default   Enter **Y** in the Cert. Of Compliance Default field if your vendors should send you a certificate of compliance before shipping your order. A *certificate of compliance* is a statement that the vendor can completely fill your

```
┌──────────────────────────────────────────────────────────────────┐
│POMAINT 5.00          Maintain Purchase Order Options  COMPANY ID: BB│
│06/01/90                    Big Business, Inc.                        │
└──────────────────────────────────────────────────────────────────┘

                    PURCHASE ORDER DEFAULT VALUES:

      Cert. Of Compliance Default..: N
      Confirm To Default...........:
      Default Purchaser............:
      Purchaser's Phone Number.....:
      Freight On Board Default.....:
      Ship Via Default.............:
      Credit Terms Default.........:
      Misc. Cost #1 Description....:
      Misc. Cost #2 Description....:
      Misc. Cost #3 Description....:
      Misc. Cost #4 Description....:


      ─────────────────────────────────────────────────────────

      ACCEPT? (Y/N)...: Y
```

FIGURE 5-5   Purchase Order Default Values screen

order. City and state organizations or businesses that must comply with government purchasing regulations may require vendors to file certificates of compliance. Enter **N** here if you do not need certificates from vendors prior to shipment.

Confirm To Default   Enter the name of the person or department a vendor should contact for more information or to confirm an order. You may leave this field blank if you wish.

Default Purchaser   Enter the name of the purchaser. This will probably be the company name and the department name (if any) for whom you are setting up Purchase Order. You may leave this field blank if you wish.

Purchaser's Phone Number   Enter the phone number the vendor should use to obtain more information or to confirm a purchase order. You may leave this field blank if you wish.

Freight On Board Default   Enter the default information about who will pay for shipping merchandise to your company. If you enter **Shipping point** in this field, you agree to pay for shipping from the place the merchandise was shipped. If you enter **Destination** in this field, the vendor pays for shipping the merchandise to you. You may leave this field blank if you wish.

Ship Via Default   Enter the name of a preferred shipping company or method in this field, such as **Post Office, UPS, Cospro Trucking, BEST WAY** (to let the vendor decide), or **WILL CALL** (if you will pick up the merchandise yourself). You may leave this field blank if you wish.

Credit Terms Default   Enter the default credit terms for your vendors, such as **Net 30** for payment due within 30 days from receipt, or **1/10 Net 30** to designate a one percent discount if the invoice is paid within 10 days or the whole invoice amount due within 30 days from receipt. You may leave this field blank if you wish.

Misc. Cost #1- #4 Description Fields   In these fields, enter any additional information about costs, such as applicable tax rates, or storage and handling. This information will appear on the purchase order after the items you are ordering and before the total. You may leave any or all of these fields blank if you wish.

Figure 5-6 shows the defaults for Big Business. When you accept these defaults, Peachtree Complete III returns you to the Program Options screen. After you press (F10), Peachtree Complete III asks if you want to create the purchase order files. Type

```
┌─────────────────────────────────────────────────────────────────────────┐
│POMAINT 5.00           Maintain Purchase Order Options    COMPANY ID: BB   │
│06/01/90                     Big Business, Inc.                            │
└─────────────────────────────────────────────────────────────────────────┘

                       PURCHASE ORDER DEFAULT VALUES:

     Cert. Of Compliance Default..: N
     Confirm To Default...........: James K. Habakkuk
     Default Purchaser............: Big Business, Inc.
     Purchaser's Phone Number.....: 1-206-555-7364
     Freight On Board Default.....: Destination
     Ship Via Default.............: UPS or best way
     Credit Terms Default.........: Net 30
     Misc. Cost #1 Description....: 8.1% tax
     Misc. Cost #2 Description....: Rush chgs
     Misc. Cost #3 Description....:
     Misc. Cost #4 Description....:


     ACCEPT? (Y/N)...: Y
```

FIGURE 5-6   Purchase Order defaults for Big Business, Inc.

Y and press (ENTER). Peachtree Complete III will create the purchase order files and return you to the menu.

ENTERING PURCHASE ORDERS

Once you have set up the Purchase Order module, you are ready to enter purchase orders. If you have not set up Purchase Order to let you enter new vendors to Accounts Payable as necessary, you should make sure that the vendor information in Accounts Payable is as up to date as possible.

To enter a purchase order, select Enter/Change Purchase Orders from the Purchase Order Processing Menu as shown in Figure 5-7. Peachtree Complete III then asks you if you want to add, edit, cancel, or close a purchase order (Figure 5-8). Select Add A

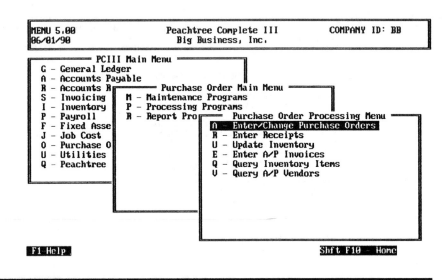

FIGURE 5-7 Select Enter/Change Purchase Orders

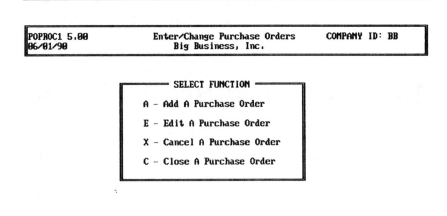

FIGURE 5-8 Select Function screen

Purchase Order. Peachtree Complete III then prompts you for the vendor ID and the purchase order date.

You can enter a vendor ID in the VENDOR ID field, or press (F2) to look up the available vendors. Peachtree Complete III lets you enter the vendor information if you enter a vendor ID that is not already entered in Accounts Payable and you entered **Y** in the Add New Vendors To A/P field in the Purchase Order module options. When the vendor ID has been entered, Peachtree Complete III displays the current system date as the default purchase order date. You can use this date or enter a different date.

Entering Purchase Order Header Information

When you press (ENTER) in the Purchase Order Date field, Peachtree Complete III displays the header information for the purchase order. As you can see in Figure 5-9, the information in these fields is determined by the information in the purchase order default fields. You can change this information if you wish.

Entering Purchase Order Line Items

After you accept the header information, you enter the specific line items for the purchase order. Figure 5-10 shows a blank line item screen. The options in Figure 5-10 are addressed in the following discussion.

Type   Enter **P** if the item you are purchasing is a product or **S** if it is a service.

Dept/Item #   Enter 3 characters for the department number and up to 15 characters for the item number. If you aren't using departments, enter **0** followed by two spaces. You can press (F2)

```
┌─────────────────────────────────────────────────────────────────────┐
│ POPROC1 5.00              Enter/Change Purchase Orders    COMPANY ID: BB │
│ 06/01/90                     Big Business, Inc.                          │
├─────────────────────────────────────────────────────────────────────┤
│     Add Purchase Order                 Add Header Information            │
│ PURCHASE ORDER #.....:      1      AMOUNT ORDERED.......:          0.00  │
│ VENDOR ID............: COS001      AMOUNT RECEIVED......:          0.00  │
│ PURCHASE ORDER DATE..: 06/01/90    AMOUNT BACK-ORDERED..:          0.00  │
├─────────────────────────────────────────────────────────────────────┤
│ VENDOR:                           SHIP TO:                              │
│    NAME........: COSPRO            ▓Big Business, Inc.▓                  │
│    ADDRESS.....: P.O. Box 30606    123 Main Street                     │
│                  Seattle, WA       Anytown, USA                        │
│                                                                         │
│    POSTAL CODE.: 98103-0606                                            │
│                                                                         │
│ CONFIRM TO...........: James K. Habakkuk                               │
│ PURCHASER............: Big Business, Inc.                              │
│ PURCHASER'S PHONE #..: 1-206-555-7364    STATUS........: NEW           │
│ F.O.B................: Destination                                     │
│ SHIP VIA.............: UPS or best way    TERMS.........: Net 30        │
│ CERT COMP REQUIRED...: N                  RECEIVE BY....:   /  /        │
├─────────────────────────────────────────────────────────────────────┤
│  F1-Help                            F10 - Done                          │
└─────────────────────────────────────────────────────────────────────┘
```

FIGURE 5-9   Purchase Order header information

```
┌─────────────────────────────────────────────────────────────────────┐
│ POPROC1 5.00              Enter/Change Purchase Orders    COMPANY ID: BB │
│ 06/01/90                     Big Business, Inc.                          │
├─────────────────────────────────────────────────────────────────────┤
│     Add Purchase Order                 Add Line Items Information        │
│ PURCHASE ORDER #.....:      1      AMOUNT ORDERED.......:          0.00  │
│ VENDOR ID............: COS001      AMOUNT RECEIVED......:          0.00  │
│ PURCHASE ORDER DATE..: 06/01/90    AMOUNT BACK-ORDERED..:          0.00  │
├─────────────────────────────────────────────────────────────────────┤
│  TYPE  — DEPT/ITEM # ——        QUANTITY      UNIT COST     TOTAL COST    │
│                                                                         │
│ P                                                                       │
│ DESC:                      REC UNIT:      SELL UNIT:     RATIO:         │
│ VND ITEM #:                COMMENT.:                                    │
├─────────────────────────────────────────────────────────────────────┤
│  F1-Help                            F10 - Done                          │
└─────────────────────────────────────────────────────────────────────┘
```

FIGURE 5-10   Purchase Order Line Item screen

to look up inventory items already purchased from this vendor. You can also press (SHIFT) + (F2) to list all the items in Inventory. This is useful if you are purchasing from a new vendor an item already in Inventory.

Desc Enter an optional item description of up to 20 characters in this field. If you are purchasing an item already entered in the Inventory module, the description will appear automatically in this field.

Vnd Item # Enter an item number of up to ten characters that your vendor uses to identify the item. If you are purchasing an item already entered in Inventory, the vendor item number will appear automatically in this field.

Quantity Enter the number of units of the item you want to buy, less any units you have already received as a partial shipment on a purchase order and for which you have been invoiced by the vendor, or any change in the number of units resulting from a change order notice.

Unit Cost Enter the unit cost. This is the amount that you expect to pay for the item. Purchase Order will multiply this number by the quantity you just entered and fill in the total cost for this item. If you are purchasing an item already entered in Inventory, the unit cost will appear automatically in this field.

Rec Unit Enter up to four characters to denote the unit in which you will be receiving the item, such as **Case**, **Each**, **Box**, or **Gr**. If you are entering a line item for a service, you may skip this field. If you are purchasing an item already entered in Inventory, the receiving unit will appear automatically in the field.

Sell Unit Enter up to four characters to denote the unit in which you will be selling the item. This unit may be different from the receiving unit you entered previously. For example, you may purchase units by the gross and sell them by the dozen or individually. If you are entering a line item for a service, enter an appropriate selling unit for reports. For example, if you are selling technical writing services billed per hour, you might enter **Hour** in this field. If you are purchasing an item already entered in Inventory, the selling unit will appear automatically in the field.

Ratio Enter a number denoting the ratio between the receiving unit and the selling unit. For example, if both units are the same, the ratio will be 1. If you receive units by the gross and sell them by the dozen, the ratio is 12 to 1, so you would enter **12**. If you are purchasing an item already entered in Inventory, the ratio will appear automatically in the field.

Comment Enter up to 20 characters of optional information for the line item. The comment will appear after the line item information on the printed purchase order.

 If you are setting up Purchase Order and are entering purchase orders that have already been issued manually, enter **DUPLI-CATE-DON'T SEND** or **PCIII DUPLICATE** in the Comment field to prevent sending this purchase order to the vendor.

When you accept the line item (Figure 5-11), Purchase Order adds the amount ordered with this line item to totals at the top of the screen. You may now enter another line item.

```
┌─────────────────────────────────────────────────────────────────────┐
│POPROC1 5.00           Enter/Change Purchase Orders     COMPANY ID: BB │
│06/01/90                    Big Business, Inc.                         │
└─────────────────────────────────────────────────────────────────────┘
      Add Purchase Order                  Add Line Items Information
PURCHASE ORDER #......:     1        AMOUNT ORDERED.......:        171.00
VENDOR ID............: COS001        AMOUNT RECEIVED......:          0.00
PURCHASE ORDER DATE..: 06/01/90      AMOUNT BACK-ORDERED..:          0.00

   TYPE  — DEPT/ITEM # —         QUANTITY      UNIT COST      TOTAL COST

    P    0   12034                    5.00     34.2000000         171.00
DESC: PC KEYBOARD             REC UNIT: EACH  SELL UNIT: EACH RATIO:  1.00
VND ITEM #:  PC84KEYBD        COMMENT.: No substitutes, pls.

     P
DESC:                         REC UNIT:       SELL UNIT:     RATIO:
VND ITEM #:                   COMMENT.:



ACCEPT? (Y/N): Y
 F1-Help              F5 - List                    F10 - Done
```

FIGURE 5-11   Entering a line item

If you have already entered several line items, you can press (F5)
to see those line items. If you want to change information for a
specific line item, press (F7) and tell Purchase Order which line
item you want to edit. You can delete a line item by pressing
(F8) and indicating which line item you want to delete. If you
want to add more line items to the purchase order, press (F6).

When you are done entering line items, press (F10). Purchase
Order asks you if you want to enter any miscellaneous costs. If you
answer **Y**, Purchase Order displays the Miscellaneous Costs
screen, as shown in Figure 5-12. The descriptions for the items are
those you entered in the Miscellaneous Costs fields in the Purchase
Order Defaults screen. After you enter the costs (if any) and accept
the information, Purchase Order prompts for the next purchase
order number and vendor ID. You can continue to enter purchase
orders or return to the menu.

```
┌──────────────────────────────────────────────────────────────────┐
│POPROC1 5.00            Enter/Change Purchase Orders    COMPANY ID: BB │
│06/01/90                     Big Business, Inc.                      │
└──────────────────────────────────────────────────────────────────┘
      Add Purchase Order                    Add Misc, Costs Information
PURCHASE ORDER #.....:      1           AMOUNT ORDERED......:      1794.40
VENDOR ID...........: COS001            AMOUNT RECEIVED.....:         0.00
PURCHASE ORDER DATE..: 06/01/90         AMOUNT BACK-ORDERED..:        0.00

                         MISCELLANEOUS COSTS

      DESCRIPTION       COST AMOUNT     AMOUNT APPLIED    AMOUNT POSTED

  1.  ▓3.1% tax▓               0.00            0.00             0.00

  2.  Rush chgs               0.00            0.00             0.00

  3.                          0.00            0.00             0.00

  4.                          0.00            0.00             0.00


    ▓F1-Help▓                         ▓F10 - Done▓
```

═══════ **FIGURE 5-12**   Entering miscellaneous costs

PRINTING PURCHASE ORDERS

When you have entered your purchase order information, you can print purchase orders. Start by selecting Print Purchase Orders from the Purchase Order Reports Menu, as shown in Figure 5-13. After you tell Purchase Order where you want to print the purchase orders, you are asked which document you want to print (Figure 5-14). Select Purchase Order from the Select Document to Print Menu.

You can now select which purchase orders you want to print from the Select Orders to Print Menu. When you have selected the purchase orders, Purchase Order asks you for the number of copies to print. It also asks if you want certificate of compliance copies and if you want a document mask. A *document mask* is similar to a check mask—you can use it to align your purchase order forms in the printer. Each printing position is filled with the maximum number of characters so you can adjust the forms precisely. You

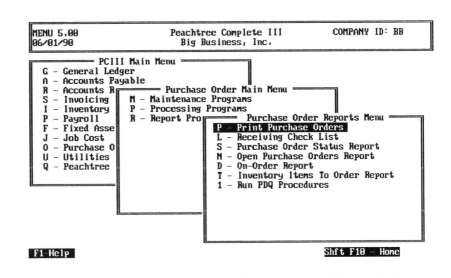

FIGURE 5-13   Select Print Purchase Orders

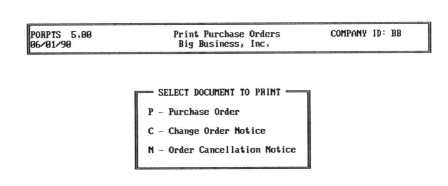

FIGURE 5-14   Select Document To Print screen

can print the document mask as many times as you like. When you
are ready to print the purchase orders, answer **N** to the prompt "Do
you want to print another document mask?" Figure 5-15 shows a
printed document mask. When the purchase orders have been
printed, Purchase Order returns you to the menu.

Before you send purchase orders to your vendors, it is a good
idea to review them. You may have asked your vendor for 1000
of an item instead of 100, for example, or you may have omitted
several line items from a purchase order.

You can change a purchase order by selecting Edit A Purchase
Order from the menu shown earlier. You can then change header

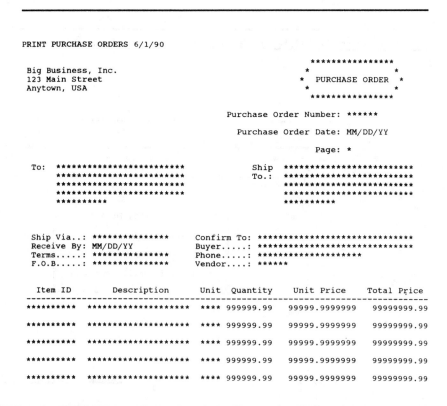

FIGURE 5-15 Printed Purchase Order document mask

information and add, change, or delete line items. When you are done, press (F10) to accept the information. You can also edit the miscellaneous costs for the purchase order if you wish.

CREATING AND PRINTING CHANGE ORDERS

Suppose that you send a purchase order to a vendor but discover that you need twice as many of an item as you ordered. You could always phone the vendor directly, but this wouldn't leave a paper trail for shipping and accounts payable. In a case like this, it is best to issue a change order. A *change order* is simply a purchase order that has been amended. You send the change order to the vendor to supersede the original purchase order.

You can use the Enter/Change Purchase Orders option on the Purchase Order Processing Menu to change to a purchase order. When you are done, select Print Purchase Orders from the Purchase Order Reports Menu as if you were going to print purchase orders. After you select the device you want to print the purchase orders on, select Change Order Notice on the Select Document to Print screen shown in Figure 5-14.

Select the notices you want to print from the Select Notices to Print Menu. Then specify the Change Order Notice Date and whether or not you want certificate of compliance copies and a document mask. A sample change order appears in Figure 5-16. As you can see, it is similar to a purchase order, but Peachtree Complete III has added a large change order heading. Next you would send this form to the vendor and to your shipping clerks, who would use it to replace the original purchase order.

If you change a purchase order after you have printed it, and then reprint the purchase order, Peachtree Complete III asks if you want

```
CHNG
                                        ****************
Big Business, Inc.                      *              *
123 Main Street                         *  PURCHASE ORDER  *
Anytown, USA                            *              *
                                        ****************

------------------------------------    Purchase Order Number:    1
    * CHANGE ORDER NOTICE *
                                        Purchase Order Date: 06/01/90
Change Order Notice Date: 06/01/09
------------------------------------             Page:  1

  To:  COSPRO                           Ship  Big Business, Inc.
       P.O. Box 30606                   To.:  123 Main Street
       Seattle, WA                            Anytown, USA
       98103-0606



  Ship Via..: UPS or best way    Confirm To: James K. Habakkuk
  Receive By:   /  /             Buyer.....: Big Business, Inc.
  Terms.....: Net 30             Phone.....: 1-206-555-7364
  F.O.B.....: Destination        Vendor....: COS001


   Item ID       Description      Unit  Quantity    Unit Price    Total Price
  --------------------------------------------------------------------------
  PC84KEYBD   PC KEYBOARD         EACH     5.00    34.2000000        171.00
      No substitutes, pls.

  PSAT230W    230W Power Supply   EACH    10.00    61.5400000        615.40

  4256-10DIP  256-10 RAM chip     TUBE    20.00    50.4000000       1008.00

  HG1521 Mon  MONOCHROME MONITOR  EACH    20.00    54.7200000       1094.40

              Misc Cost                           8.1% tax........    145.31
              Misc Cost                           Delivery........     20.00
```

FIGURE 5-16   Printed Change Order Notice

to treat the changed purchase order as a change notice. If you answer **Y**, the Change Notice heading will appear on the printed purchase order.

CANCELLING PURCHASE ORDERS

You may occasionally need to cancel a purchase order because you are dissatisfied with a vendor or you have decided not to purchase any of the items on the purchase order. To cancel a purchase order, select Enter/Change Purchase Orders on the Purchase Order

Processing Menu, then select Cancel A Purchase Order from the Select Function menu, and then specify the purchase order number. Peachtree Complete III will display the purchase order's header information (as shown in Figure 5-17) and ask if you want to cancel this purchase order. Type **Y** and press (ENTER) to cancel the purchase order.

You now need to print a copy of the cancelled purchase order to send to the vendor and to shipping. Select Print Purchase Orders from the Purchase Order Reports Menu as if you were going to print purchase orders. After you select the device you want to print on, select Order Cancellation Notice from the Select Document to Print screen.

Select the range of notices you want to print as you did with purchase and change orders. After you specify the number of copies and whether or not you want a document mask, Peachtree Complete III prints the cancellation notices. A sample cancellation notice appears in Figure 5-18.

```
┌─────────────────────────────────────────────────────────────────────────┐
│POPROC1 5.00              Enter/Change Purchase Orders     COMPANY ID: BB  │
│06/01/09                      Big Business, Inc.                           │
├─────────────────────────────────────────────────────────────────────────┤
│      Cancel Purchase Order                  Cancel Header Information      │
│PURCHASE ORDER #......:       3          AMOUNT ORDERED.......:    1050.00  │
│VENDOR ID.............: SHA001           AMOUNT RECEIVED......:       0.00  │
│PURCHASE ORDER DATE..: 06/01/90          AMOUNT BACK-ORDERED..:       0.00  │
│                                                                           │
│VENDOR:                               SHIP TO:                             │
│    NAME........: Sharma Software        Big Business, Inc.                │
│    ADDRESS.....: 517 Marlinspike Lane   123 Main Street                   │
│                  Tonasket, WA           Anytown, USA                      │
│                                                                           │
│    POSTAL CODE.: 98993                                                    │
│                                                                           │
│CONFIRM TO...........: James K. Habakkuk                                   │
│PURCHASER............: Big Business, Inc.                                  │
│PURCHASER'S PHONE #..: 1-206-555-7364    STATUS.........: MODIFIED (PRINTED)│
│F.O.B................: Destination                                         │
│SHIP VIA.............: UPS or best way   TERMS.........: Net 30            │
│CERT COMP REQUIRED...: N                 RECEIVE BY....:   /  /            │
│                                                                           │
│CANCEL THIS PURCHASE ORDER? (Y/N): Y                                       │
│ F1-Help                                                                   │
└─────────────────────────────────────────────────────────────────────────┘
```

══ **FIGURE 5-17** Cancelling the purchase order

Be sure that you are cancelling the correct purchase order. You cannot edit or reactivate a purchase order that has been cancelled.

```
CANCELLED PO

                                             ****************
Big Business, Inc.                           *              *
123 Main Street                              *  PURCHASE ORDER  *
Anytown, USA                                 *              *
                                             ****************

---------------------------------      Purchase Order Number:      3
  * ORDER CANCELLATION NOTICE *
                                       Purchase Order Date: 06/01/90
---------------------------------
                                                    Page:  1

   To:  Sharma Software             Ship  Big Business, Inc.
        517 Marlinspike Lane        To.:  123 Main Street
        Tonasket, WA                      Anytown, USA
        98993


   Ship Via..: UPS or best way     Confirm To: James K. Habakkuk
   Receive By:   /  /              Buyer.....: Big Business, Inc.
   Terms.....: Net 30              Phone.....: 1-206-555-7364
   F.O.B.....: Destination         Vendor....: SHA001


   Item ID       Description      Unit  Quantity   Unit Price    Total Price
-----------------------------------------------------------------------------
Production   Production design    HRS     30.00    35.0000000       1050.00
    Marketing design



                                            Subtotal:           1050.00
                                            Total...:           1050.00

                          Authorized Signature: _____.
```

FIGURE 5-18   Cancellation notice

RECEIVING SHIPMENTS

So far, you have learned how to enter, correct, and print purchase orders. However, this is only the first half of the process. After you have sent the purchase orders to your vendors, you need to prepare for the merchandise that will arrive. This section will demonstrate how to receive merchandise and post the information.

Printing the Receiving Check List

You can print a receiving check list for your shipping clerks that lists each item on the purchase orders and the quantity ordered. To print the receiving check list, select Receiving Check List from the Purchase Order Reports Menu. Figure 5-19 is a portion of a receiving check list. As you can see, all the information on the purchase order has been put on this report. Blanks are added at the right of the page for each item so the clerk can enter the quantities received of each item.

Entering Receipts

When a shipment comes in, the clerk will mark the receiving check list to show what has and has not arrived. You can then use the marked report to enter actual receipts of items against the purchase order. Start by selecting Enter Receipts from the Purchase Order Processing Menu as shown in Figure 5-20. After telling Peachtree Complete III whether you want a control report, enter a purchase order number.

ENTERING FULL RECEIPT OF ITEMS If you have received all the items in an order, select Full Receipt Of This Order from the Select Function menu (Figure 5-21). Purchase Order will

```
RECEIVING CHECK LIST                                                     Page:  1

                         --------------------
                         RECEIVING CHECK LIST
                         --------------------

Purchase Order Number:        1    Ship To: Big Business, Inc.      Vendor:  COSPRO
Purchase Order Date..: 06/01/90             123 Main Street                  P.O. Box 30606
Receive By Date......:   /  /               Anytown, USA                     Seattle, WA
Vendor ID............: COS001                                                       98103-0606


Vendor       Our                                    Quantity   Already   Received    Partial    Qty. Received
Item #       Inventory ID    Item Description   Stk  Ordered   Received  All Units   Receipt     (If Partial)
--------     ------------    ----------------   ---  --------  --------  ---------   --------    -------------

PC84KEYBD    PO  12034       PC KEYBOARD        Yes    5.00      0.00    _____   _____    _____

PSAT230W     PO  10115       230W Power Supply  Yes   10.00      0.00    _____   _____    _____

4256-10DIP   PO  24800       256-10 RAM chip    Yes   20.00      0.00    _____   _____    _____

HG1521 Mon   PO  32143       MONOCHROME MONITOR Yes   20.00      0.00    _____   _____    _____


Number of items on this page:      4.00    Total number of items:      4.00       Signature: _____
```

FIGURE 5-19 Receiving Check List

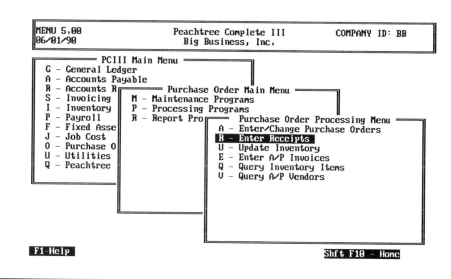

```
┌─────────────────────────────────────────────────────────────────────┐
│MENU 5.00              Peachtree Complete III        COMPANY ID: BB   │
│06/01/90                 Big Business, Inc.                           │
├─────────────────────────────────────────────────────────────────────┤
│ ┌──── PCIII Main Menu ────┐                                          │
│ │  G - General Ledger     │                                          │
│ │  A - Accounts Payable   │                                          │
│ │  R - Accounts R┌──────── Purchase Order Main Menu ───────┐         │
│ │  S - Invoicing │ M - Maintenance Programs                │         │
│ │  I - Inventory │ P - Processing Programs                 │         │
│ │  P - Payroll   │ R - Report Pro┌─── Purchase Order Processing Menu ──┐│
│ │  F - Fixed Asse│               │ A - Enter/Change Purchase Orders   ││
│ │  J - Job Cost  │               │ R - Enter Receipts                 ││
│ │  O - Purchase O│               │ U - Update Inventory               ││
│ │  U - Utilities │               │ E - Enter A/P Invoices             ││
│ │  Q - Peachtree │               │ Q - Query Inventory Items          ││
│ └────────────────┘               │ V - Query A/P Vendors              ││
│                                  └────────────────────────────────────┘│
│ F1-Help                                            Shft F10 - Home     │
└─────────────────────────────────────────────────────────────────────┘
```

════ **FIGURE 5-20**   Select Enter Receipts

```
┌─────────────────────────────────────────────────────────────────────┐
│POPROC1 5.00                  Enter Receipts         COMPANY ID: BB    │
│06/01/90                    Big Business, Inc.                         │
├─────────────────────────────────────────────────────────────────────┤
│                                                                       │
│ PURCHASE ORDER #.....:      1        AMOUNT ORDERED......:    2000.00  │
│ VENDOR ID............: COS001        AMOUNT RECEIVED.....:       0.00  │
│ PURCHASE ORDER DATE..: 06/01/90      AMOUNT BACK-ORDERED.:       0.00  │
│                                                                       │
│             ┌──────── SELECT FUNCTION ────────┐                       │
│             │                                 │                       │
│             │ P - Partial Receipt Of This Order                       │
│             │                                 │                       │
│             │ R - Receive Remainder Of This Order                     │
│             │                                 │                       │
│             │ F - Full Receipt Of This Order  │                       │
│             └─────────────────────────────────┘                       │
│                                                                       │
│                                                                       │
│ F1-Help   F2 - View P/O                                               │
└─────────────────────────────────────────────────────────────────────┘
```

════ **FIGURE 5-21**   Select Full Receipt Of This Order

ask if you want to record receipt of all outstanding line items for the purchase order. Type **Y** and press (**ENTER**). Purchase Order will make the appropriate entries for each item on the purchase order. As it does so, it adds the amount for each item to the Amount Received field in the upper-right corner of the screen.

Suppose that you answered **Y** at the Enter New Items At Receipt in the Purchase Order options. After the purchase order has been processed, Purchase Order will ask if you want to record the receipt of items not on the original purchase order. If you received items that you didn't order and you want to keep them, type **Y** and press (**ENTER**). You will see a screen like the one in Figure 5-22. You can add a line item to the purchase order on this screen. When you have accepted the information, Purchase Order displays the Enter Receipts screen (Figure 5-23). Enter the number of units received on this purchase order. You can also adjust the unit cost and the comment before you accept the information. From here, you can

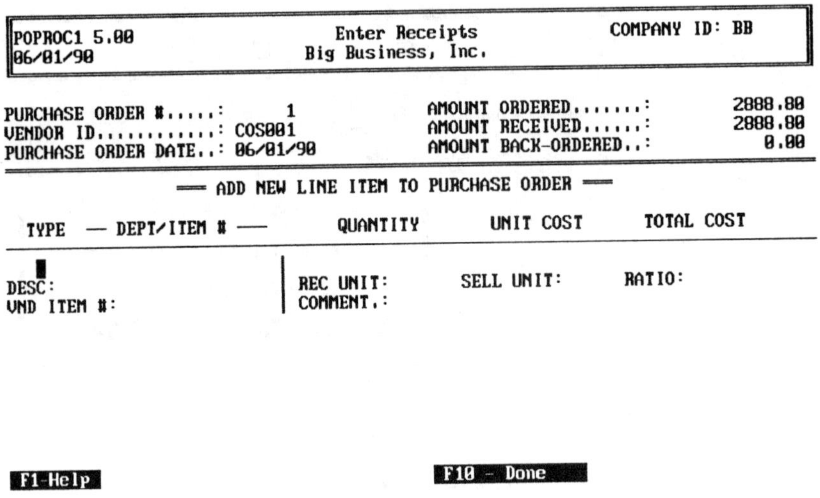

FIGURE 5-22   Adding a line item

```
┌─────────────────────────────────────────────────────────────────────┐
│ POPROC1 5.00                  Enter Receipts          COMPANY ID: BB  │
│ 06/01/90                    Big Business, Inc.                        │
└─────────────────────────────────────────────────────────────────────┘

 PURCHASE ORDER #.....:    1        AMOUNT ORDERED.......:     2000.00
 VENDOR ID...........: COS001       AMOUNT RECEIVED......:     2000.00
 PURCHASE ORDER DATE..: 06/01/90    AMOUNT BACK-ORDERED..:        0.00
─────────────────────────────────────────────────────────────────────
                        UNITS        TOTAL      CURRENT     ITEM'S
        ITEM ID         ORDERED     RECEIVED    RECEIPT    UNIT COST
─────────────────────────────────────────────────────────────────────

 PO  32143               10.00        0.00      ▓▓▓▓10.00▓

 COMMENT: Not on original PO




  ▐F1-Help▌  ▐F2 - Detail▌
```

FIGURE 5-23   Enter Receipts screen

continue adding line items received as part of this shipment, or you can return to the Enter Receipts screen and enter another purchase order number.

 If you have miscellaneous costs as part of the purchase order, Purchase Order asks if you want to apply these. If you type **Y** and press (ENTER), Purchase Order asks how you want to apply the costs in Accounts Payable. Then you enter distributions for the various amounts of the miscellaneous costs. If you type **N** and press (ENTER), Purchase Order will not apply the miscellaneous costs to the invoiced amount.

ENTERING PARTIAL RECEIPT   Sometimes a vendor will be temporarily out of stock on an item. You will usually receive a partial shipment and a notice that the missing item is on back order.

To enter receipt of only part of a purchase order, select Partial Receipt Of This Order from the Select Function menu shown in Figure 5-21. Purchase Order then shows you a list of the items on the purchase order (a sample appears in Figure 5-24). Select the first item you have received. Purchase Order displays the Enter Receipts screen and positions the cursor at the number of units received (Figure 5-25). Enter the number of units you received with this order.

You can then adjust the unit cost if you wish. You must have pressed **Y** in the Enter Costs At Receipt field in the Maintain Purchase Order Options screen. For example, if the item changed its price between the time you ordered and the time you received the shipment, you can change the amount on the purchase order to reflect this. Finally, you can add or edit the comment for this line item. After you accept the information on the screen, Purchase Order shows you the list of line items from Figure 5-24. You can

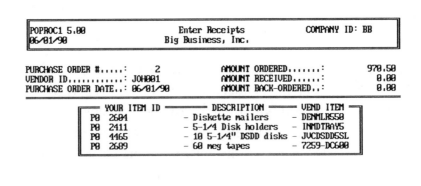

FIGURE 5-24 Entering a partial receipt

```
┌─────────────────────────────────────────────────────────────────┐
│ POPROC1 5.00                  Enter Receipts        COMPANY ID: BB │
│ 06/01/90                      Big Business, Inc.                   │
└─────────────────────────────────────────────────────────────────┘

  PURCHASE ORDER #.....:     2        AMOUNT ORDERED.......:     970.50
  VENDOR ID............: JOH001       AMOUNT RECEIVED......:       0.00
  PURCHASE ORDER DATE..: 06/01/90     AMOUNT BACK-ORDERED..:       0.00
                           UNITS       TOTAL      CURRENT      ITEM'S
        ITEM ID          ORDERED     RECEIVED     RECEIPT    UNIT COST
  ─────────────────────────────────────────────────────────────────

  PO  2604                200.00        0.00    ▒▒▒200.00▒▒

  COMMENT: Anti-static mailers



  ▐F1-Help▌ ▐F2 - Detail▌
```

FIGURE 5-25   Entering partial receipt of an item

select another line item, add line items by pressing (F6) (if you answered **Y** at Enter New Items At Receipt in the Purchase Order options), or press (F10) to finish working with this purchase order.

RECEIVING THE REMAINDER OF A SHIPMENT   One of the most common reasons for receiving a partial shipment is having your merchandise arrive on two different days. Since you should always post receipts of merchandise as soon as possible, you should have already entered the first partial shipment on the purchase order. Now that the rest of the order is here, you need to complete the receipt.

To enter receipt of the remainder of a purchase order, select Receive Remainder Of This Order from the Select Function menu shown in Figure 5-21. Purchase Order will ask if you want to record receipt of all outstanding line items for the purchase order, as it did when you entered full receipt of an order. Type **Y** and press (ENTER).

Purchase Order will make the appropriate entries for each item on the purchase order. As it does so, it adds the amount for each item to the Amount Received field in the upper-right corner of the screen. You can also add line items to the purchase order if you wish.

UPDATE INVENTORY

If you are using Peachtree Complete III's Inventory module with Purchase Order, you need to update the inventory before you can process the Accounts Payable invoice information. Select Update Inventory from the Purchase Order Processing Menu. After you tell Purchase Order whether you want a control report, Purchase Order asks you which items you want to post (as shown in Figure 5-26). After you select the purchase orders you want to post, Purchase Order tells you that it is going to post all outstanding

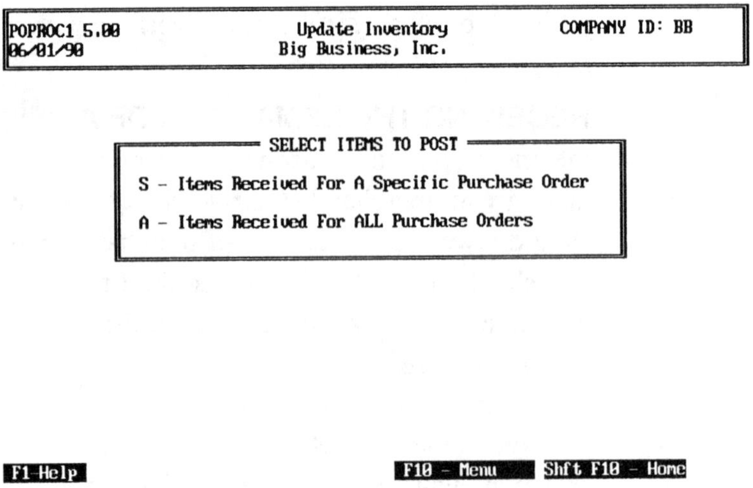

```
POPROC1 5.00              Update Inventory        COMPANY ID: BB
06/01/90               Big Business, Inc.


                ═══ SELECT ITEMS TO POST ═══
     S - Items Received For A Specific Purchase Order

     A - Items Received For ALL Purchase Orders



    F1-Help                          F10 - Menu    Shft F10 - Home
```

FIGURE 5-26   Select Items To Post to inventory

(received but not yet posted to inventory supply levels) items to
Inventory.

ENTER A/P INVOICES

Your vendors will send you invoices for the merchandise that you
have purchased. When you receive an invoice billing you for the
merchandise ordered on a purchase order, you can post it to
Accounts Payable. Select Enter A/P Invoices from the Purchase
Order Processing Menu and tell Purchase Order if you want a
control report.

Purchase Order will ask you for the purchase order number, the
vendor ID, and the invoice number, as shown in Figure 5-27. The
invoice number is the number that appears on the vendor's invoice.
When you enter the invoice number, Purchase Order displays a

```
┌─────────────────────────────────────────────────────────────────┐
│POPROC2 5.00              Enter A/P Invoices      COMPANY ID: BB   │
│06/01/90                  Big Business, Inc.                       │
└─────────────────────────────────────────────────────────────────┘
 Purchase Order #........:      1
 Vendor ID...............: COS001    COSPRO
 Invoice Number..........: 190
```

FIGURE 5-27   Initial A/P screen

standard accounts payable entry screen (shown in Figure 5-28). Enter the information in the fields. See Chapter 4, "Accounts Payable," if you need more information on entering accounts payable information.

If the purchase order has no open line items—that is, if all the merchandise has been received—Purchase Order asks if you want to close the purchase order. Closing a purchase order tells Peachtree Complete III that there will be no further activity on that purchase order. Type **Y** and press (ENTER) if you want Purchase Order to close the invoice now. Remember, however, that once you close a purchase order, you can't edit it any more. If for some reason you expect further activity on this purchase order, you may want to keep it open. You can close it later via Enter/Change Purchase Orders on the Purchase Order Processing Menu, much as you cancelled a purchase order.

```
┌──────────────────────────────────────────────────────────────────┐
│ POPROC2 5.00              Enter A/P Invoices     COMPANY ID: BB    │
│ 06/01/90                  Big Business, Inc.                       │
└──────────────────────────────────────────────────────────────────┘
 Purchase Order #........:      1
 Vendor ID...............: COS001    COSPRO
 Invoice Number..........: 490

 Invoice Date............: 06/01/90          * * * Distribution * * *
 Amount Due..............:      3479.11      ..Account.......Amount..
 Due Date................: 01/01/00      1.   61500        0.00
 Discount %..............:      0.00      2.       0        0.00
 Discount Amount.........:         0.00   3.       0        0.00
 Discount Date...........: 01/01/00      4.       0        0.00
 A/P Account Code........: 0             5.       0        0.00
 Comment.................:               6.       0        0.00
 Pre-Paid (Y/N)..........: N             7.       0        0.00
 Cash Account Code.......: 0             8.       0        0.00
 Check Number............:         0                   ===========
                                                              0.00

 ▐ F1-Help ▌                       ▐ F8 - Undo ▌  ▐ F10 - Done ▌
```

FIGURE 5-28 Entering A/P Invoices

PURGING CLOSED AND CANCELLED PURCHASE ORDERS

Since you can't edit any of the information, closed and cancelled purchase orders take up space in your files. Once you have posted the information to Accounts Payable and Inventory, you should clear out any closed or cancelled orders from the files. To purge closed and cancelled orders, select Purge Closed/Cancelled Orders from the Purchase Order Maintenance Menu. Purchase Order asks if you want to review each purchase order before it is deleted from the files. If you type **N** and press (ENTER), Purchase Order will delete the closed and cancelled orders and then return you to the menu. If you type **Y** and press (ENTER), Purchase Order will display each closed or cancelled order, asking if you want to delete it from the files. When you have finished reviewing and deleting purchase orders, Purchase Order will delete the information from the purchase order data files so that they contain no extraneous information.

OTHER HELPFUL PURCHASE ORDER REPORTS

The Purchase Order Reports Menu includes several reports that you may find helpful for tracking purchase orders:

- The Purchase Order Status Report tells you the status of each purchase order, either by purchase order number or by vendor ID. You should check the status of your purchase order files frequently. If you have many closed or cancelled purchase orders, you should purge them. The report may also pinpoint ordering problems, such as an excessive number of items back ordered with one vendor. This report is a summary report, and shows only the total for each purchase order.

- The Open Purchase Orders Report shows all purchase orders for which you have not received all the items you ordered. This report is a detail report. It shows the purchase order number and the vendor ID, followed by the information for each line item including the quantity received to date. You can use this report to check with the shipping clerks to see if specific items have been received.

- The On-Order Report is a list of everything that is currently on order. It shows the inventory ID, the item description, the purchase order number, whether the item is in stock, how many you have on hand and on order, how many have been received, and the dollar amount on order. You can use this report to identify specific items that are on order but have not yet come in, so you don't order too many. By sorting the report by vendor ID instead of purchase order, you can also see how many and what kind of items are on order with any particular vendor.

- The Inventory Items to Order Report is useful for keeping track of your inventory stocks. It shows the item ID and description, the vendor ID and vendor item ID, the reorder level for the item, the minimum reorder quantity, the number currently in inventory, the number on order, and the number you need to order. Run this report frequently. If your business turns its stock of merchandise once a month and it takes you at least two weeks to reorder some of your inventory items, you should run this report at least once a week.

chapter **6**

ACCOUNTS RECEIVABLE AND INVOICING

Installing Accounts Receivable and Invoicing
Entering Transaction Types and Production Codes
Entering Sales Tax Information
Setting Up and Maintaining Customer Information
Creating Automatic Transactions
Creating Invoices and Credit Memos
Entering Payments
Housekeeping

The last few chapters have described how to process accounts payable and how to purchase things from vendors, both of which increase your liabilities. In this chapter, you will now learn how to use Peachtree Complete III's Accounts Receivable and Invoicing modules, which increase your company's assets.

Accounts Receivable, along with General Ledger and Accounts Payable, is the third and final component of the basic accounting cycle. Accounts Receivable is simply the money owed to you by your customers. Each time you sell a product or service to a customer on credit, the amount the customer owes you is charged to the Accounts Receivable account in the General Ledger. The Invoicing module is closely related to the Accounts Receivable module. Its primary purpose is to create and post *invoices,* detailed bills that you send to your customers that describe the exact terms, quantities, prices, and freight information relating to a transaction.

You could use the Accounts Receivable module by itself to produce all of your customers' bills as statements. Statements are a summary of invoiced amounts over time. They are particularly useful for billing your customers for services and other charges that don't have a tangible product associated with them. Furthermore, some activities, such as writing off bad debts, can only be done through Accounts Receivable.

Why then should you use the Invoicing module? Invoicing lets you connect Accounts Receivable information directly to the Inventory module. If you interface Invoicing with Inventory, you can check customer requests for products against available stock. If you set up both Accounts Receivable and Invoicing, you can enter either invoices or print statements, depending on what you are billing your customers for.

The Accounts Receivable and Invoicing modules require that you set up a great deal of information before you enter actual transactions and invoices. The setup process will be much easier if you spend some extra time organizing your information with the forms for Accounts Receivable and Invoicing in the back of the Peachtree Complete III manual.

INSTALLING ACCOUNTS RECEIVABLE AND INVOICING

If you haven't done so already, you should install the General Ledger module (see Chapters 2 and 3). You use Accounts Receivable to post information about receivables to the General Ledger automatically. You can use the Create G/L Journal Entries options to summarize your transactions from Accounts Receivable, and transfer them to the appropriate General Ledger accounts with the Transfer Summary Journals option. You can also connect Accounts Receivable to Job Cost to show how much money a given job is making. The Job Cost module is discussed in Chapter 12.

You can connect Invoicing to the Inventory module (discussed in Chapter 11) to track your available inventory and keep from selling items that are out of stock. You can also determine how well each item is selling and how much profit you are making.

Installing Accounts Receivable

You start installing Accounts Receivable by selecting Accounts Receivable from the PCIII Main Menu. Peachtree Complete III will display a message that Accounts Receivable is not installed, and will ask if you want to install it (Figure 6-1). Type **Y** and press (**ENTER**). Peachtree Complete III will then prompt you for the subdirectory for the Accounts Receivable data, as shown in Figure 6-2. Type a new directory or press (**ENTER**) to accept the default directory. If the directory you select does not exist, Peachtree Complete III will ask if you wish to create it. Type **Y** and press (**ENTER**).

As with the previous modules, you must enter the options for the Accounts Receivable module. Select Set Module Options

```
MENU 5.00                  Peachtree Complete III          COMPANY ID: BB
06/01/90                      Big Business, Inc.

         ======= PCIII Main Menu =======
     G - General Ledger
     A - Accounts Payable
     R - Accounts Receivable
     S - Invoicing              ┌──────────────────────────────────────┐
     I - Inventory             │ Accounts Receivable not installed.     │
     P - Payroll               │                                        │
     F - Fixed Assets          │ Do you want to install it (Y/N): Y     │
     J - Job Cost              └──────────────────────────────────────┘
     O - Purchase Order
     U - Utilities
     Q - Peachtree Data Query
```

FIGURE 6-1   Installing Accounts Receivable

```
MENU 5.00                  Peachtree Complete III          COMPANY ID: BB
06/01/90                      Big Business, Inc.

         ======= PCIII Main Menu =======
     G - General Ledger
     A - Accounts Payable
     R - Accounts Receivable
     S - Invoicing
     I - Inventory
     P - Payroll
     F - Fixed Assets
     J - Job Cost
     O - Purchase Order
     U - Utilities
     Q - Peachtree Data Query


     ┌──────────────────────────────────────────────────────────┐
     │ Enter the subdirectory path where you want your data files to be. │
     │            C:\PEACH\ARDATA\                                │
     └──────────────────────────────────────────────────────────┘
```

FIGURE 6-2   Selecting the Accounts Receivable and
Invoicing directory

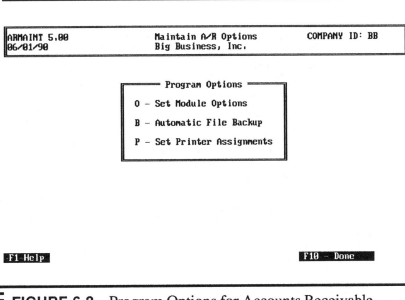

```
ARMAINT 5.00              Maintain A/R Options          COMPANY ID: BB
06/01/90                  Big Business, Inc.

                      ┌───── Program Options ─────┐
                      │                           │
                      │  O - Set Module Options   │
                      │                           │
                      │  B - Automatic File Backup│
                      │                           │
                      │  P - Set Printer Assignments│
                      │                           │
                      └───────────────────────────┘



 F1-Help                                          F10 - Done
```

══════ **FIGURE 6-3**   Program Options for Accounts Receivable

from the Program Options menu (Figure 6-3) and press (ENTER).
Peachtree Complete III shows you the first Accounts Receivable
Options screen (Figure 6-4). The first Accounts Receivable Op-
tions screen actually has four different sets of options: General
Module, Invoice Numbering, Service Charge, and Age Analysis.

ENTERING GENERAL MODULE OPTIONS   General module options set general information for using Accounts Receivable for your company. The Controller Password, Operator Password,
and Use Menus options work the same for Accounts Receivable
as for the General Ledger. Refer to Chapter 2 if you need to
refresh your memory on how these options work. The other menu
options are reviewed here.

Allow Changes/Deletions   When you respond **N** to the Allow
Changes/Deletions option, Peachtree Complete III won't let you

```
┌─────────────────────────────────────────────────────────────────────┐
│ ARMAINT 5.00              Maintain A/R Options       COMPANY ID: BB   │
│ 06/01/90                  Big Business, Inc.                          │
└─────────────────────────────────────────────────────────────────────┘
  General Module Options               Service Charge Options
      Controller Password.....:            Customer Types........: 0
      Operator Password.......:            Amount or Percentage..: P
      Use Menus...............: Y          Min Amount............:        0.00
      Allow Changes/Deletions.: Y          Include Past Charges..: N
      Force Control Reports...: Y          Avg Daily/Ending Bal..: E
      Keep YTD Detail.........: Y          Service Chg Amts/Pcts
      Current G/L Period......:  1             Code 1.............:        0.00
      Post to General Ledger..: Y             Code 2.............:        0.00
      Consolidate A/R Trans...: N             Code 3.............:        0.00
      Check Credit Limit......: Y             Code 4.............:        0.00
      Generation Number.......:  0
      Print Company Name......: Y
      Print Titles............: Y         Age Analysis Options
  Invoice Numbering Options                 Age Period Length....:  030
      Auto Numbering......:     Y           Dunning Messages
      Start Number........:           1         Period 1:
      End Number..........:      999999         Period 2:
      Reset Number........:           1         Period 3:
                              Accept (Y/N)..:  Y
  ┌─────────┐                              ┌───────────┐
  │ F1-Help │                              │ F8 - Undo │
  └─────────┘                              └───────────┘
```

───── **FIGURE 6-4**   First Accounts Receivable default values screen

change or delete transactions in Accounts Receivable. However, you can still add new Accounts Receivable transactions and information.

Force Control Reports   Peachtree Complete III can print control reports that produce an audit trail for tracking errors. In Accounts Receivable, you can create control reports whenever you add, change, or delete invoices, or update the inventory. If you respond **Y** to the Force Control Reports option, Peachtree Complete III will always print control reports without asking you first. If you respond **N**, Peachtree Complete III will ask before printing control reports.

Keep YTD Detail   If you enter **Y** at the Keep YTD Detail option, Accounts Receivable will keep all transaction detail for customers until you purge it with the Purge Transaction utility. If you enter **N**, Accounts Receivable saves the information on all invoices until you close the current period. Accounts Receivable will then purge all the transaction detail for closed invoices. Both choices will give you the information on all transactions in the current period.

 Saving transaction detail may be a problem if your hard disk does not have a lot of room for transaction data, or if you expect to have a lot of accounts receivable transactions. If you are not sure, select **N**. You can change this option later if you need to, although you will not be able to restore deleted transaction data from previous periods.

Current G/L Period   Enter a period from 1 to 13 for the Current G/L Period option. The data you post from Accounts Receivable to the General Ledger will post into this period. Once you enter the period to post to, Accounts Receivable will update this automatically when you close the current period and transfer the summary journals to the General Ledger. If you are not posting information to the General Ledger, simply press (**ENTER**) to accept the default.

Post to General Ledger   Enter **Y** in the Post to General Ledger field if you want to post information from Accounts Receivable to the General Ledger. Accounts Receivable will then build a summary accounts receivable journal that you can post to the General Ledger with the Transfer Summary Journals option. If you enter **N**, Accounts Receivable will not build a summary accounts receivable journal automatically. You can, however, use the Create G/L Journal Entries option to create a list of the transactions in the current period that you can manually post to your own General Ledger.

Consolidate A/R Trans   Enter **Y** in the Consolidate A/R Trans field if you want to list on customer statements the current transactions and a combined transaction showing the balance for any transactions from prior periods. (Most credit card statements list the current transactions and carry the previous balance forward in this fashion.) Enter **N** if you want the customer statements to list all transactions on current and open invoices for current and prior periods.

Check Credit Limit   If you enter **Y** in the Check Credit Limit field, Accounts Receivable will check the customer's credit limit (set with the Maintain Customers option) each time you enter a transaction that would increase the customer's balance. If the transaction would exceed the customer's credit limit, Accounts Receivable will display a warning message. (You can still enter the transaction if you wish.) If you enter **N** in this field, Accounts Receivable won't check credit limits for customers.

Generation Number   Accounts Receivable makes a copy of the files whenever you close the current period (usually at the end of each month). These copies, known as a generation, are then stored on your disk. Each file has a generation number as part of the file name. You can use files from a previous generation to track specific transactions or changes. Peachtree Complete III lets you assign the first generation number if you want. The default number is 0.

Print Company Name   If you don't have custom invoice or statement forms that already have your company name printed on them, answer **Y** and press (ENTER) in the Print Company Name field. Accounts Receivable will print the company name on the invoice as it appears in the General Ledger information files.

Print Titles   If you don't have custom invoice or statement forms with preprinted column headings, answer **Y** and press (ENTER) in the

Print Titles field. Accounts Receivable will print the standard column headings on the invoice and statement.

ENTERING INVOICE NUMBERING OPTIONS The second section on the first Accounts Receivable Options screen lets you determine how to number your accounts receivable invoices.

Auto Numbering Enter **Y** in the Auto Numbering field to let Accounts Receivable number your invoices for you, starting with the number entered in Start Number. Enter **N** to enter your own invoice numbers manually or to use invoice numbers that contain letters.

Start Number If you entered **Y** in the Auto Numbering field, enter the current invoice number in the Start Number field. This will be the number of the first invoice you print with Accounts Receivable. If you are using preprinted invoice forms, enter the invoice number on the first form.

End Number If you entered **Y** in the Auto Numbering field, enter the highest invoice number in the sequence in the End Number field. After this number, Accounts Receivable will renumber the invoices, starting with the number in the next field.

Reset Number If you entered **Y** in the Auto Numbering field, enter the invoice number to start renumbering invoices with the Reset Number field.

ENTERING SERVICE CHARGE OPTIONS The service charge options tell Accounts Receivable what kind of service charges you want to apply and how you want to apply them.

Customer Types In the Customer Types field, enter a code for the type of customers to whom you want to apply Accounts Receivable service charges. Service charges are applied to all accounts with a past due balance for customers of the type specified here. If you enter **O**, Accounts Receivable will not apply service charges to any customer. If you enter **1**, Accounts Receivable will apply service charges only to Balance Forward customers. If you enter **2**, Accounts Receivable will apply service charges only to Regular customers. If you enter **3**, Accounts Receivable will apply service charges to Regular and Balance Forward customers.

Amount or Percentage   If you enter **A** in the Amount or Percentage field, Accounts Receivable will apply a set amount for a past due service charge. If you enter **P** in this field, Accounts Receivable will use a percentage of the past due amount as the service charge.

Min Amount   Enter the minimum amount for the service charge in this field. If you don't want to have a minimum amount, enter **0**.

Include Past Charges   If you enter **Y**, Accounts Receivable will add any past due service charges to the total due to calculate new service charges. If you enter **N**, Accounts Receivable will exclude overdue service charges when calculating new service charges.

Avg Daily/Ending Bal   Enter **A** in the Avg Daily/Ending Bal field to calculate a customer's service charge based on his or her average daily balance. Enter **E** to use the customer's ending balance.

Codes 1 - 4   You use the service charge codes to determine the service charges levied against past due invoices. If you are using a flat fee calculation, these codes are the amounts that will be charged. If you are calculating service charges as a percentage of the invoice, the codes are the percentages to charge. You can enter amounts or percentages from 0 to 99.99 in each of these fields. For example, entering 12.00 can represent either 12% or $12.00, depending on your choice in the Amount or Percentage field.

When you set up a customer, you will assign a service charge code. Having one code at 0.00 makes it easy to set up a "preferred" customer who is never charged a service fee by Accounts Receivable.

ENTERING AGE ANALYSIS OPTIONS

Age analysis options let you set the period for ageing. You can also specify the type of dunning message for overdue clients.

Age Period Length   Enter the length of your ageing period. The default is 30 days. Accounts Receivable uses this information to determine the length of the four ageing periods.

Dunning Messages (Periods 1 - 3)   Enter three dunning messages of up to 20 characters. These messages will appear on the statements of customers with balances one, two, or three periods overdue.

 Dunning messages appear only on the statements of those customers so selected in Maintain Customers.

ENTERING PAYMENT TERMS OPTIONS

Once you have accepted the information on the first Accounts Receivable Options screen, the second Accounts Receivable Options screen appears (Figure 6-5). You enter the payment terms options on this screen. Payment terms are the terms that you give to your customers. You can define up to five different types of payment terms.

The first four sets of terms codes set up terms based on the number of days after the purchase. The fifth term code is based on a specific date rather than a number of days.

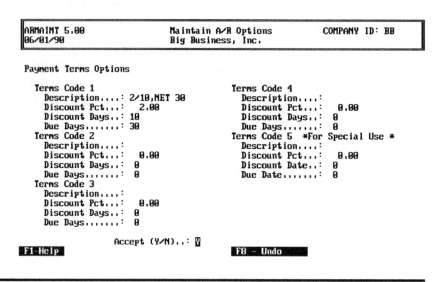

```
ARMAINT 5.00                 Maintain A/R Options          COMPANY ID: BB
06/01/90                     Big Business, Inc.

Payment Terms Options

    Terms Code 1                           Terms Code 4
       Description....: 2/10,NET 30            Description....:
       Discount Pct...:   2.00                 Discount Pct...:   0.00
       Discount Days..: 10                     Discount Days..: 0
       Due Days.......: 30                     Due Days.......: 0
    Terms Code 2                           Terms Code 5  *For Special Use *
       Description....:                        Description....:
       Discount Pct...:   0.00                 Discount Pct...:   0.00
       Discount Days..: 0                      Discount Date..: 0
       Due Days.......: 0                      Due Date.......: 0
    Terms Code 3
       Description....:
       Discount Pct...:   0.00
       Discount Days..: 0
       Due Days.......: 0

                      Accept (Y/N)..: Y
  F1-Help                                    F8 - Undo
```

═══ **FIGURE 6-5**   Second Accounts Receivable default values screen

Description (Term Codes 1 through 5)   In the Description field, enter up to 11 characters that describe the type of terms for each code. The default for term code 1 is 2/10,NET 30. Other descriptions you might use are 1/15,NET 30 and NO DISCOUNT.

Discount Pct (Term Codes 1 through 5)   In the Discount Pct field, enter a percentage from 0 to 99.99 discounted from the invoice for early payment. For example, the default discount percent in term code 1 is 2%, entered as 2.00.

Discount Days (Term Codes 1 Through 5)   In the Discount Days field, enter the number of days from the date of the invoice in which the customer may use a discount.

Due Days (Term Codes 1 through 4)   In the Due Days field, enter the number of days in which an invoice is due. The default entry for term code 1 is 30.

Due Date (Term Code 5 only)   In the Due Date field, enter the date in the month the invoice is due. For example, if invoices must be paid by the 10th, enter 10. Enter 30 to specify the last day of the month.

After you accept the information on this screen, Accounts Receivable returns you to the Program Options screen (shown in Figure 6-3). When you press (F10), Accounts Receivable asks if you want to create the Accounts Receivable files. Press (ENTER). Accounts Receivable will create the various files and return you to the Main Menu.

Installing Invoicing

The previous section showed you how to install Accounts Receivable and set options. This section will demonstrate how to install and set options for the Invoicing module. Invoicing is an integral part of Accounts Receivable. If you don't want to use Invoicing, you can skip this section.

Start installing the Invoicing module by selecting Invoicing from the Main Menu. Peachtree Complete III tells you that Invoicing is not installed, and asks if you want to install it (Figure 6-6). Type **Y** and press (ENTER). You will not need to specify a subdirectory for the Invoicing data—Peachtree Complete III uses the same subdirectory for Accounts Receivable and for Invoicing. Select Set Module Options from the Program Options menu, and press (ENTER) to bring up the Invoicing Options screen (Figure 6-7).

The Use Menus option works the same for Invoicing as for the General Ledger. Refer to Chapter 2 for details.

```
MENU 5.00                Peachtree Complete III        COMPANY ID: BB
06/01/90                    Big Business, Inc.

═════════════ PCIII Main Menu ═════════════
 G - General Ledger
 A - Accounts Payable
 R - Accounts Receivable
 S - Invoicing
 I - Inventory              ┌──────────────────────────────────────┐
 P - Payroll                │ Invoicing not installed.             │
 F - Fixed Assets           │                                      │
 J - Job Cost               │ Do you want to install it (Y/N): Y   │
 O - Purchase Order         │                                      │
 U - Utilities              └──────────────────────────────────────┘
 Q - Peachtree Data Query
```

══════ **FIGURE 6-6**   Installing Invoicing

```
SIMAINT 5.00             Maintain Invoicing Options     COMPANY ID: BB
06/01/90                    Big Business, Inc.




              Use Menus......................: Y
              Use Inventory in Invoicing....: N
              Automatic Invoice Numbering...: Y
              Starting Invoice Number.......:      1
              Ending Invoice Number.........: 999999
              Reset Invoice Number..........:      1
              Print Company Name On Invoice: Y
              Print Field Titles On Invoice: Y

              ACCEPT (Y/N): Y
```

`F1-Help`   `F8 - Undo`

══════ **FIGURE 6-7**   Invoicing Options screen

Use Inventory in Invoicing   Enter **Y** if you want to use Inventory with Invoicing (see Chapter 11 for more on the Inventory module). This will let you check your product inventory when you sell merchandise. Invoicing also lets you do a nonstock return and a nonstock sale, for returning or selling items that are not part of your regular inventory. Enter **N** if you aren't using Inventory or don't want to use it with Invoicing.

Automatic Invoice Numbering   Enter **Y** to let Invoicing number invoices for you, starting with the number entered in Starting Invoice Number. Enter **N** to enter invoice numbers manually or to use invoice numbers that contain letters.

Starting Invoice Number   If you entered **Y** in the Automatic Invoice Numbering field, enter the current invoice number in the Starting Invoice Number field. If you are using preprinted invoice forms, enter the invoice number on the first form.

Ending Invoice Number   If you entered **Y** in the Automatic Invoice Numbering field, enter the highest invoice number in the sequence in the Ending Invoice Number field. After this number, Invoicing will renumber the invoices, starting with the number in the next field.

Reset Invoice Number   If you entered **Y** in the Automatic Invoice Numbering field, enter the invoice number with which to start renumbering invoices in the Reset Invoice Number field.

Print Company Name On Invoice   If you don't have custom invoice forms that include your company name, answer **Y** and press (ENTER) in the Print Company Name On Invoice field. Invoicing will print the company name on the invoice as it appears in the company file.

Print Field Titles On Invoice If you don't have custom invoice forms with preprinted column headings, answer **Y** and press (ENTER) in the Print Field Titles On Invoice field. Invoicing will print the standard column headings on the invoice.

After you accept the information on this screen, Invoicing returns you to the Program Options screen. When you press (F10), Invoicing asks if you want to create the Invoicing files. Press (ENTER). Invoicing will create the invoicing header and detail files, and return you to the Main Menu.

ENTERING TRANSACTION TYPES AND PRODUCTION CODES

Once you have entered your Accounts Receivable and Invoicing options, you need to set up the transaction types and product codes. Each time you enter a transaction, you need to enter a two-character transaction type that tells Accounts Receivable what kind of transaction it is, such as a sale, a credit, an adjustment, and so on. Table 6-1 lists the available transaction types.

You use product codes to group your transactions. Product codes are a single character and can be a number from 0 to 9, a letter from A to Z, or a blank. You need to set up a product code for each type of activity. For example, Big Business might set up some of its product codes as follows:

Product Code	Product or Department
A	Assembled computer
B	Kit for computer
C	Parts
D	Software

E	Repair service
F	Miscellaneous
G	Support

Give some thought to how you want to group transactions and information on reports. For example, you might want to show all

Transaction Type	Transaction
AD	Adjustment
BD	Bad debt write-offs
CI	City tax
CO	County tax
CP	Cost of product
CS	Cost of service
EP	Early payment discount
FR	Freight
MC	Miscellaneous credit
MD	Miscellaneous debit
PA	Payment
RE	Return
RS	Return of service
SA	Sale
SC	Service charge
SS	Sale of service
ST	State tax

TABLE 6-1   Accounts Receivable Transaction Types

computer game sales as one type of transaction. Allow yourself as much flexibility and as much room to grow as possible. If you have already set up your Inventory module, use your product Inventory codes in Accounts Receivable and Invoicing.

Five transaction types—CI, CO, FR, SC, and ST—will only take a blank for the product code.

To set up transaction types and product codes, select Maintain G/L Accounts Dist File from the Accounts Receivable Maintenance Menu (as shown in Figure 6-8). After telling Accounts Receivable whether you want to print the General Ledger account file and a control report, you will see the screen shown in Figure 6-9.

Enter a transaction type in the Trans. Type column. Next enter the product code for the transaction. If this is the first time you have entered this product code for this transaction type, Accounts

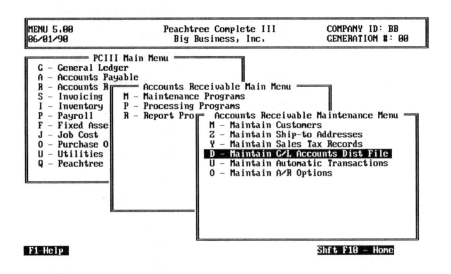

FIGURE 6-8   Select Maintain G/L Accounts Dist File

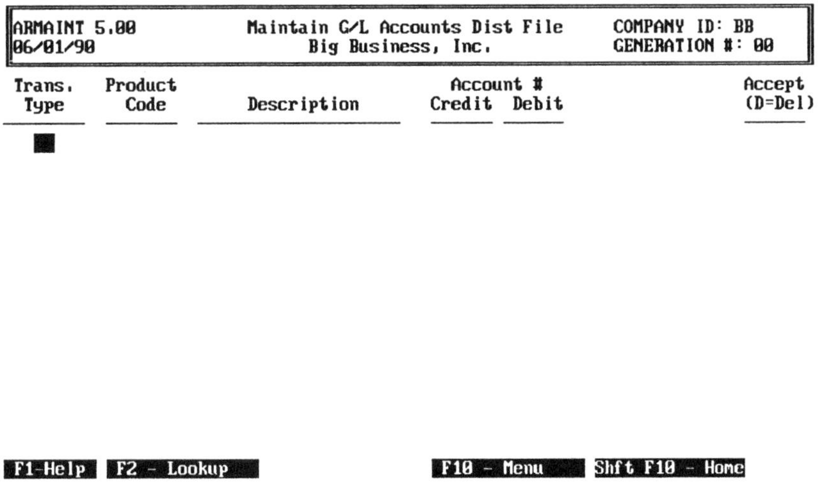

```
┌─────────────────────────────────────────────────────────────────────┐
│ ARMAINT 5.00        Maintain G/L Accounts Dist File    COMPANY ID: BB │
│ 06/01/90                 Big Business, Inc.            GENERATION #: 00 │
│ Trans.    Product                        Account #              Accept │
│ Type       Code        Description      Credit  Debit           (D=Del) │
│  ▆                                                                      │
│                                                                         │
│                                                                         │
│                                                                         │
│                                                                         │
│                                                                         │
│  F1-Help   F2 - Lookup              F10 - Menu    Shft F10 - Home       │
└─────────────────────────────────────────────────────────────────────┘
```

FIGURE 6-9   Enter Transaction Type screen

Receivable will ask if you want to add this product code. Type **Y** and press (**ENTER**). You can now enter the description and the credit and debit General Ledger account numbers.

Figure 6-10 shows the screen with some of the transaction types and product codes set up for Big Business. Continue entering the transaction types and associated product codes for all transaction types your company uses now, has used in the past, or is likely to use in the future. At the very least, you must set up the CI, CO, and ST transaction types to use Accounts Receivable and Invoicing. You can change the information for a transaction type and product code combination by entering the type and product code on the screen. Accounts Receivable will display the current information and then you can edit it.

When you have set up all the transaction types, press (**F10**). Accounts Receivable will return you to the Maintenance Menu.

```
┌──────────────────────────────────────────────────────────────────────────┐
│ARMAINT 5.00          Maintain G/L Accounts Dist File    COMPANY ID: BB    │
│06/01/90                   Big Business, Inc.            GENERATION #: 00   │
│                                                                            │
│ Trans.   Product                          Account #              Accept   │
│ Type      Code      Description        Credit  Debit             (D=Del)  │
│ ─────────────────────────────────────────────────────────                │
│  PA                 Payment            12000  11000                 Y      │
│  SA        A        Assembled computer 30500  12000                 Y      │
│  SA        B        Kit for computers  30500  12000                 Y      │
│  SA        C        Replacement parts  30500  12000                 Y      │
│  SA        D        Software           30500  12000                 Y      │
│  SA        E        Repair service     30500  12000                 Y      │
│  SA        F        Miscellaneous      30500  12000                 Y      │
│  RE        A        Assembled computer 12000  30500                 Y      │
│  RE        B        Kit for computers  12000  30500                 Y      │
│  RE        C        Replacement parts  12000  30500                 Y      │
│  RE        D        Software           12000  30500                 Y      │
│  RE        E        Repair service     12000  30500                 Y      │
│                                                                            │
│   F1-Help                            F8 - Undo                             │
└──────────────────────────────────────────────────────────────────────────┘
```

FIGURE 6-10   Sample transaction types

ENTERING SALES TAX INFORMATION

The next step in setting up Accounts Receivable and Invoicing involves setting up sales tax information.

Accounts Receivable will calculate sales tax for any of the following transaction types:

FR	Freight
MC	Miscellaneous credit
MD	Miscellaneous debit
RE	Return
RS	Return of service
SA	Sale
SS	Sale of service

You can set up Accounts Receivable to calculate separate state, county, and city taxes for each of these categories. You must have at least one sales tax code to use Accounts Receivable and Invoicing.

To enter sales tax codes, select Maintain Sales Tax Records from the Accounts Receivable Maintenance Menu (Figure 6-11). After you tell Accounts Receivable whether you want a control report, you are prompted for a sales tax code. Enter up to three characters for the sales tax code. If you will have many sales tax options, make sure that they are easily distinguishable.

When you enter a sales tax code for the first time, you must tell Accounts Receivable that you want to add it, as shown in Figure 6-12. Accounts Receivable then displays the screen shown in Figure 6-13.

Sales Taxable/Exempt Enter **T** (for taxable) if this sales tax code will calculate taxes for transaction types MC, MD, RE, RS, SA,

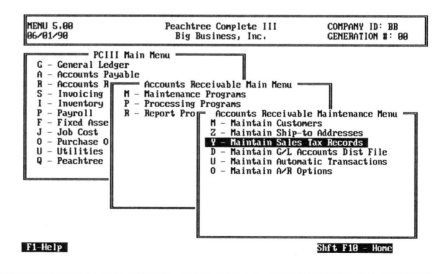

FIGURE 6-11 Select Maintain Sales Tax Records

```
┌──────────────────────────────────────────────────────────────────────┐
│ ARMAINT 5.00          Maintain Sales Tax Records    COMPANY ID: BB     │
│ 06/01/90                 Big Business, Inc.         GENERATION #: 00    │
└──────────────────────────────────────────────────────────────────────┘
  SALES TAX CODE: C01       ┌─────────────────────────────────────┐
                            │ Tax Code Not Found. Add (Y/N).: Y   │
                            └─────────────────────────────────────┘




  ▌F1-Help▐
```

FIGURE 6-12 Adding a tax code

```
┌──────────────────────────────────────────────────────────────────────┐
│ ARMAINT 5.00          Maintain Sales Tax Records    COMPANY ID: BB     │
│ 06/01/90                 Big Business, Inc.         GENERATION #: 00    │
└──────────────────────────────────────────────────────────────────────┘
  SALES TAX CODE: C01                  STATUS: Active

  Sales   Taxable/Exempt...: T           ┌──── ***** TAX BRACKETS ***** ────┐
  Freight Taxable/Exempt...: T           │          State  County   City   │
  State─────────────────────────         │                                 │
    Name...................:             │   .00      0       0       0    │
    Tax Percentage........:    0.000     │   .01      0       0       0    │
    Use Tax Brackets......: N            │   .02      0       0       0    │
  County────────────────────────         │   .03      0       0       0    │
    Name...................:             │   .04      0       0       0    │
    Tax Percentage........:    0.000     │   .05      0       0       0    │
    Maximum Taxable.......:   0.00       │   .06      0       0       0    │
    Use Tax Brackets......: N            │   .07      0       0       0    │
  City──────────────────────────         │   .08      0       0       0    │
    Name...................:             │   .09      0       0       0    │
    Tax Percentage........:    0.000     │   .10      0       0       0    │
    Maximum Taxable.......:   0.00       │                                 │
    Use Tax Brackets......: N            └─────────────────────────────────┘
  ▌F1-Help▐              ▌F8 - Undo▐    ▌F10 - Done▐
```

FIGURE 6-13 Maintain Sales Tax Records screen

and SS. Enter **E** (for exempt) if you don't want Accounts Receivable to calculate taxes on these transaction types.

 If you are selling to both wholesale and retail customers, you may have cases where one customer transaction is taxable and the next is exempt. For this situation, you should establish a sales tax code that is exempt, but also has all the appropriate sales tax information. When you enter a transaction for a wholesale customer (usually untaxed), you can leave the sales tax code as exempt. When you enter a transaction for a retail customer, you can change the exempt status to taxable.

Freight Taxable/Exempt Enter **T** (for taxable) if this sales tax code will calculate taxes for freight (transaction type FR). Enter **E** (for exempt) if you don't want Accounts Receivable to calculate taxes on freight.

Name (State, County, City) Enter up to 20 characters to identify this sales tax code in the appropriate field.

Tax Percentage (State, County, City) Enter the tax percentage with up to three decimal places. For example, to enter a sales tax of 7.8%, enter **7.800**.

Maximum Taxable (County, City) Enter the maximum amount for which Accounts Receivable will calculate this tax. If there is no maximum amount, accept the default of 0.00.

Use Tax Brackets (State, County, City) Enter **Y** if you want Accounts Receivable to calculate taxes below a dollar using tax brackets. Enter **N** if you want Accounts Receivable to calculate taxes as a straight percentage.

Tax Brackets (State, County, City)   If you entered **Y** in the Use Tax Brackets field, you need to enter the amounts in the Tax Brackets fields. Enter the amount in the appropriate column for each breakpoint. When Accounts Receivable calculates taxes using this tax code, it will compute the percentage on the whole dollar amount and add this to the tax computed for any partial dollar amount using the tax bracket information.

When you have entered the information, press (F10). You will then be able to accept the information on the screen. You can also enter **A** or **D** to activate or deactivate the sales tax code. This is a handy feature: If you know that you will need a sales tax code in the near future, you can enter it now and set the status to inactive.

When you accept the information, Accounts Receivable returns you to the Sales Tax Code field. You can enter another sales tax code, or press (F10) to return to the Maintenance Menu.

SETTING UP AND MAINTAINING CUSTOMER INFORMATION

The last step in setting up Accounts Receivable is to set up your customers. Each customer will have a file of information, much like the vendor information stored in Accounts Payable. Once you have entered general customer information, you can enter customer beginning balances.

Entering Customer Information

To enter customer information, select Maintain Customers from the Accounts Receivable Maintenance Menu, as shown in Figure 6-14. After telling Accounts Receivable whether you want a control report, enter a customer ID.

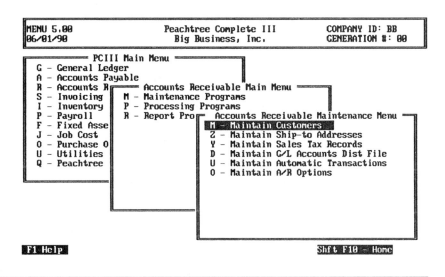

FIGURE 6-14 Select Maintain Customers

A customer ID is a six-character ID code that uniquely identifies each customer. A common way to create a customer ID involves taking the first few letters of the customer's name and following them with a number. For example, if the customer's name was "Oberon Computers," the customer ID would be something like OBE001. If there were another company with the same first three letters, such as "Oberto & Callander," their vendor ID would be OBE002. Using the first few letters of the customer's name gives you a reasonably intuitive way of looking up the customer in the file.

The customer ID is case sensitive; that is, Accounts Receivable treats OBE001 and obe001 differently. You may wish to set a policy that all letters in customer IDs be entered as capital letters.

Whatever you choose as a customer ID system, be sure that it can expand with the business. All the accounts receivable transactions that you enter for a customer are keyed to the customer ID. Once you set up a customer, you cannot change the customer ID without deleting the old customer and setting up a new customer. Also remember that Accounts Receivable sorts customers on reports in order of the customer code. If you are just using the next available six-digit number for each customer ID, you may have to look through many pages to find a particular customer.

After you have entered the customer ID, Accounts Receivable asks if you want to add the customer. Type **Y** and press (ENTER). The Maintain Customers screen appears, as shown in Figure 6-15.

Customer Name   Enter a customer name of up to 25 characters in the Customer Name field. This information is required. Accounts Receivable will list the customer name as you have entered it on customer invoices and statements and on the Aged Receivables report and the Invoice Register.

```
┌─────────────────────────────────────────────────────────────────────┐
│ ARMAINT 5.00                  Maintain Customers        COMPANY ID: BB│
│ 06/01/90                      Big Business, Inc.         GENERATION #: 00│
├─────────────────────────────────────────────────────────────────────┤
│ Customer   ID: LIL001                   Debit────                     │
│ Customer Name: ██████████████████         Last Date        01/01/00   │
│ Address......:                            Last Amt            0.00     │
│ Address......:                            YTD  Amt            0.00     │
│ City, ST.....:                          Credit────                    │
│ ZIP Code.....:                            Last Date        01/01/00   │
│ Telephone....:                            Last Amt            0.00     │
│ Contact......:                            YTD  Amt            0.00     │
│ Salesperson..:                          Payments────                  │
│ ─────────────────────────────             Last Date        01/01/00   │
│ Customer Class..: A                       Last Amt            0.00     │
│ Account Type....: R                       YTD  Amt            0.00     │
│ Service Chg Code: 1                      Service Charges────           │
│ Terms Code    : 1                         Last Date        01/01/00   │
│ Sales Tax Code : C01                      Last Amt            0.00     │
│ Discount Percent:    0.00                 YTD  Amt            0.00     │
│ Ship Addresses..: N                                                   │
│ Dunning Notices.: Y                     Balance              0.00     │
│ Credit Limit....:         0.00                                        │
│                                                                       │
│  F1-Help                        F8 - Undo       F10 - Done            │
└─────────────────────────────────────────────────────────────────────┘
```

FIGURE 6-15   Customer information screen

Address   Enter up to 25 characters in one or both of the two Address fields. If you only have one line of address information, enter it on the the first line and leave the second line blank.

City, ST   Enter up to 25 characters for the city and state.

ZIP Code   Enter up to 10 characters in the ZIP Code field.

Telephone   Enter up to 12 characters in the Telephone field.

Contact   Enter up to 25 characters in the Contact field. Accounts Receivable includes the customer contact name on the Customer List.

Salesperson   Enter up to 8 characters in the Salesperson field. Accounts Receivable prints the salesperson's name on invoices.

Customer Class   Enter a single letter or number in the Customer Class field. This field allows you to group customers in order to print statements for a class of customers. For example, you might set up a coding system to group customers by salesperson, geographic region, sales territory, type of business, type of purchase, or amount of money the customer is likely to spend in the future.

Account Type   Enter **R** for a Regular customer, **B** for a Balance Forward customer, or **T** for a Temporary customer. What you enter in the Account Type field determines how Accounts Receivable computes service charges for this customer and how much transaction detail Accounts Receivable stores. If you entered **N** in the Keep YTD Detail field, Accounts Receivable stores transaction detail for Regular customers for as long as the invoice is open (still has a nonzero balance), regardless of the period in which the transactions may have occurred. Accounts Receivable will only store the current period transaction information for Balance Forward and Temporary customers, and will not store the transaction detail for any of the previous periods.

On the other hand, if you entered **Y** in the Keep YTD Detail field, Accounts Receivable stores transaction detail for Regular customers until you purge it with the Purge Transaction utility. Accounts Receivable also keeps the transaction detail for Balance Forward and Temporary customers until you purge it, but you must print a Transaction Register for all accounting generations in order to examine it. All payments are applied to the Balance Forward and Temporary customers' ageing period balances rather than to a specific transaction detail.

 When you close the period, Accounts Receivable purges all Temporary customers whose account balance is zero along with the associated account information. You should only establish customers as Temporary if you are sure that they will not make further purchases from you after you close the current batch of invoices. Accounts Receivable does not automatically purge Balance Forward or Regular customers, but you can delete them through the Maintain Customers program.

Service Chg Code   Enter the service charge code for this customer. You learned earlier how to set up service charges. Pressing (F2) will display the service charge codes and the associated percentages or amounts.

Terms Code   Enter the terms code for this customer. The terms code tells Accounts Receivable what discounts and payment terms you are assigning to the customer. Pressing (F2) will display the terms codes and the associated percentages or amounts.

Sales Tax Code   Enter the sales tax code for this customer. Pressing (F2) will display the tax codes you have defined.

Discount Percent Enter the discount percentage for all transactions for this customer. This is not the same as the discount for early payment. For example, if your wholesale customers get a 5% discount on all transactions, you would enter **5.00** in this field. If the customer receives no special discount, press (**ENTER**) to accept the default of 0.00.

Ship Addresses Enter **Y** to use a different shipping address than the one shown at the top of the screen. You can then enter separate shipping addresses with the Maintain Ship-to Addresses selection on the Accounts Receivable Maintenance Menu. When you prepare a customer's invoice, the Invoicing module will ask you which mailing address to print on the invoice. Enter **N** if you want Accounts Receivable to use the mailing address at the top of the screen.

Dunning Notices Enter **Y** if you want to print a dunning notice on the customer's account statement when the balance is past due. The dunning messages correspond to the messages you entered as part of the Accounts Receivable options. Enter **N** to prevent Accounts Receivable from printing dunning notices.

Credit Limit Enter the customer's credit limit in this field. If a customer invoice would cause the outstanding balance to exceed this amount, Accounts Receivable will give you a warning notice. You can enter the invoice if you wish. If you don't use or don't want to assign a credit limit, press (**ENTER**) to accept the default of 0.00.

 You must have answered **Y** to Check Credit Limit in the Accounts Receivable options for Accounts Receivable to check the outstanding balance against the credit limit. If you answered **N**, Accounts Receivable will never check the credit limit, regardless of your entry in the Credit Limit field.

For the following three sets of fields—Last Date, Late Amt, and YTD Amt—you just need to make initial entries in these fields when you set up a customer. Subsequently, Accounts Receivable updates these fields each time there is a transaction.

Last Date (Debit, Credit, Payments, Service Charges) Enter the most recent date the customer made a transaction. For example, if the customer last made a payment on 5/24/90, enter **5/24/90** in the Payment Last Date field.

Last Amt (Debit, Credit, Payments, Service Charges) Enter the amount of the last transaction.

YTD Amt (Debit, Credit, Payments, Service Charges) Enter the year to date transaction amounts.

Balance You don't need to make an entry in this field. Accounts Receivable will maintain the current customer balance in this field.

If you specified different shipping addresses, Accounts Receivable will ask if you want to edit the shipping addresses after you accept the information on this screen. When you type **Y** and press (**ENTER**), you see the shipping address screen shown in Figure 6-16

You need to enter a shipping ID of up to six characters in the Shipping ID field. This ID is different from the customer ID. You will use it to select which address you want to print on the invoice. Enter the appropriate shipping information in the fields. Once you have accepted this information, you can enter another shipping ID and address, or you can press (**F10**) to return to the Customer ID field. From here, you can enter another customer, or press (**F10**) again to return to the Maintenance Menu.

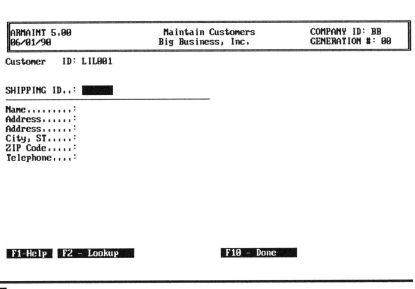

```
ARMAINT 5.00              Maintain Customers        COMPANY ID: BB
06/01/90                  Big Business, Inc.         GENERATION #: 00

Customer   ID: LIL001

SHIPPING ID..: ████████

Name.........:
Address......:
Address......:
City, ST.....:
ZIP Code.....:
Telephone....:




    F1-Help   F2 - Lookup                F10 - Done
```

═══════ **FIGURE 6-16**   Shipping address screen

If you want to add, change, or delete shipping addresses, select Maintain Ship-to Addresses from the Accounts Receivable Maintenance Menu. You can then view the primary customer address as well as any of the other shipping addresses on file for the customer. You must use this program if you want to delete a shipping address.

Printing a Customer List

A customer list is the easiest way to check that you have entered all of your customers and that the information is correct. Printing a customer list is very simple. Select List Customers from the Accounts Receivable Reports Menu, as shown in Figure 6-17. Tell Accounts Receivable where you want to print the report, and then

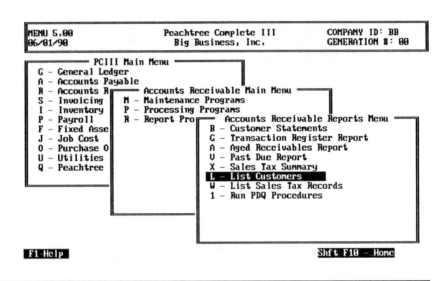

FIGURE 6-17 Select List Customers

enter the report date. Accounts Receivable lets you sort the report by customer ID or by customer name, and also lets you select a range of customers. Figure 6-18 shows a sample customer list.

If you spot any errors in the information on the customer list, you can use the Maintain Customers selection to make corrections.

Entering Customer's Beginning Balances

The last part of setting up customer information involves entering beginning balances for each of your customers. For Regular customers, the beginning balance is the invoice balance as of the date you started using Accounts Receivable and Invoicing. For Balance Forward customers, the beginning balance is the account balance.

Select Enter Transactions from the Accounts Receivable Processing Menu, as shown in Figure 6-19. Accounts Receivable

CUSTOMER LIST AS OF 6/1/90

RUN DATE: 06/01/90
RUN TIME: 1:38 AM

Big Business, Inc.
Accounts Receivable
List Customer Accounts

PAGE 1

CUST ID.	NAME-ADDRESS	TYPE	S.C. CODE	TERMS CODE	TAX CODE	DISC. %	CREDIT LIMIT	YTD DEBITS	YTD CREDITS	BALANCE
GILMAN	Joel Gilman, Attorney / 2200 Sixth Ave. / Penthouse / Seattle, WA 98121 / CONTACT..: Donna / PHONE....: 206-514-2636 / SALESMAN.: JVH	BAL. FWD	1	1	001	0.00	5000.00	0.00	0.00	0.00
KRELL	Krell Office Systems / 100 Main Street / Suite 2A / Edmonds, WA 98020 / CONTACT..: Missy Krell / PHONE....: 206-555-9046 / SALESMAN.: JVH	REGULAR	1	1	001	0.00	4000.00	0.00	0.00	0.00
LIL001	Lily Pod Systems / 1523 Carnelian / Tulalip, WA 98454-0203 / CONTACT..: Mr. Wan / PHONE....: 206-808-7635 / SALESMAN.: SO	REGULAR	1	1	001	0.00	0.00	0.00	0.00	0.00
SANTOS	Santos, Harley, and Jones / Arctic Building / Suite 202 / Seattle, WA 98104-4520 / CONTACT..: Ms. Marjie Peterson / PHONE....: 206-312-6294 / SALESMAN.: JVH	BAL. FWD	1	1	001	0.00	3500.00	0.00	0.00	0.00
GRAND TOTALS	4 CUSTOMERS LISTED							0.00	0.00	0.00

*** END OF List Customer Accounts ***

FIGURE 6-18 Sample customer list

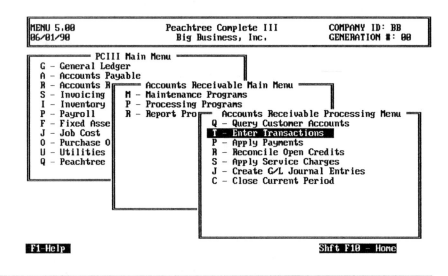

```
MENU 5.00                 Peachtree Complete III        COMPANY ID: BB
06/01/90                     Big Business, Inc.          GENERATION #: 00
        ┌───────── PCIII Main Menu ─────────┐
        │ G - General Ledger                │
        │ A - Accounts Payable              │
        │ R - Accounts R┌──── Accounts Receivable Main Menu ────┐
        │ S - Invoicing │ M - Maintenance Programs             │
        │ I - Inventory │ P - Processing Programs              │
        │ P - Payroll   │ R - Report Pro┌── Accounts Receivable Processing Menu ──┐
        │ F - Fixed Asse│               │ Q - Query Customer Accounts            │
        │ J - Job Cost  │               │▐T - Enter Transactions               ▌│
        │ O - Purchase O│               │ P - Apply Payments                     │
        │ U - Utilities │               │ R - Reconcile Open Credits             │
        │ Q - Peachtree │               │ S - Apply Service Charges              │
        │               │               │ J - Create G/L Journal Entries         │
        │               │               │ C - Close Current Period               │
        │               │               │                                        │
        └───────────────┘               │                                        │
                        └───────────────┤                                        │
                                        └────────────────────────────────────────┘
 ▐F1-Help▌                                              ▐Shft F10 - Home▌
```

═══════ **FIGURE 6-19**   Select Enter Transactions

requires that you print a control report when you enter beginning balances. Next enter the transaction date (this is the cutoff date after which your transactions for this customer are handled by Accounts Receivable).

Enter a customer ID. Accounts Receivable displays transaction header information (Figure 6-20). This information includes the customer's name, outstanding balance, and credit limit. In the Transaction Type field, enter **BB** (beginning balance). Accounts Receivable skips the Product Code field and shows you the screen in Figure 6-21. Enter the information on the screen as described next.

Invoice Number   Enter an invoice number. If you are using automatic invoice numbering, Accounts Receivable will not supply the invoice number for you. You cannot change an invoice number once you have accepted it, so be careful.

```
┌──────────────────────────────────────────────────────────────────┐
│ ARPROC  5.00            Enter Transactions        COMPANY ID: BB   │
│ 06/01/90               Big Business, Inc.         GENERATION #: 00  │
└──────────────────────────────────────────────────────────────────┘
Customer ID.: GILMAN    Joel Gilman, Attorney       Balance:      0.00
Trans. Type.: █                                 Credit Limit:  5000.00
Product Code:
```

F1-Help   F2 - Lookup

═══════ **FIGURE 6-20**   Transaction header

```
┌──────────────────────────────────────────────────────────────────┐
│ ARPROC  5.00            Enter Transactions        COMPANY ID: BB   │
│ 06/01/90               Big Business, Inc.         GENERATION #: 00  │
└──────────────────────────────────────────────────────────────────┘
Customer ID.: GILMAN    Joel Gilman, Attorney       Balance:      0.00
Trans. Type.: BB  Begin. Bal.                   Credit Limit:  5000.00
Product Code:

Invoice Terms    Terms      Trans.   Due    Discount  Trans.            T
Number  Code  Description   Date     Date   Date      Amount   Comment  E
██████

                                     State Tax.:        0.00
                                     County Tax:        0.00
                                     City Tax..:        0.00
                                                    ─────────
                                     Invoice Total:     0.00
```

F1-Help   F10 - Done

═══════ **FIGURE 6-21**   Entering a beginning balance

Terms Code Enter the appropriate terms code. Accounts Receivable will fill in the Terms Description based on this information. You cannot change the terms code once you accept an invoice's beginning balance.

Trans. Date Enter the transaction date. With this date and the terms code information, Accounts Receivable will calculate the due date and the discount date. If you are entering information for a Regular customer, enter the date of the actual invoice. If this is a Balance Forward customer, this date should be the cutoff date.

Due Date and Discount Date Accounts Receivable will compute these dates for you. You can change them if you wish, or press (ENTER) to accept the defaults. Accounts Receivable uses the due date to create the Ageing Report.

Trans. Amount Enter the invoice balance. If you are setting up the beginning balance for a Balance Forward customer, this amount is the account balance.

Comment Enter up to ten characters of optional information about the transaction. Accounts Receivable will print this information on the Enter Transactions Control Report and the Transaction Register.

T/E Enter **T** if this is a taxable transaction or **E** if the transaction is exempt.

State Tax, County Tax, and City Tax Accounts Receivable will enter default taxes in these three fields based on the tax rates you have established earlier. You can change the amounts or press (ENTER) to accept the defaults.

The finished transaction screen looks like the one shown in Figure 6-22. After you enter a transaction, Accounts Receivable will automatically update the customer's balance information. The Maintain Customer screen will display an updated account balance and a debit amount entry reflecting this transaction.

If you are working on a Balance Forward customer, you also need to distribute his or her account balances across the four ageing periods. To do this, select Maintain Customers from the Accounts Receivable Maintenance Menu. Enter the customer ID and press (ENTER) to accept the information shown on the screen. Accounts Receivable will ask if you want to edit the balance forward ageing. Type **Y** and press (ENTER). You will see the screen shown in Figure 6-23.

Since you just entered a beginning balance transaction in the Enter Transactions screen, Accounts Receivable has updated the balance for the current period and the total balance forward to

```
┌─────────────────────────────────────────────────────────────────────┐
│ARPROC  5.00                Enter Transactions        COMPANY ID: BB   │
│06/01/90                    Big Business, Inc.         GENERATION #: 00 │
└─────────────────────────────────────────────────────────────────────┘
Customer ID.: GILMAN    Joel Gilman, Attorney      Balance:          0.00
Trans. Type.: BB  Begin. Bal.                       Credit Limit:   5000.00
Product Code:

Invoice Terms     Terms      Trans.   Due      Discount    Trans.              T
Number  Code  Description    Date     Date     Date        Amount    Comment   E

000001   1    2/10,NET 30 06/01/90 07/01/90 06/11/90      254.66 Begin Bal  T

                                     State Tax.:          0.00
                                     County Tax:         20.63
                                     City Tax..:          0.00
                                                       ────────
                                     Invoice Total:     275.29


                                            Accept (Y/N)  Y

                                          ▐ F8 - Cancel ▌
```

FIGURE 6-22 Sample beginning balance

```
┌─────────────────────────────────────────────────────────────────────────┐
│ ARMAINT 5.00              Maintain Customers         COMPANY ID: BB       │
│ 06/01/90                  Big Business, Inc.          GENERATION #: 00     │
└─────────────────────────────────────────────────────────────────────────┘
 Customer   ID: GILMAN

     Balance Forward Ageing
   ┌─────────────────────────
          Current:    ███275.23█
    1-  30  Days:          0.00
   31-  60  Days:          0.00
  Over  60  Days:          0.00

  Balance Forward:       275.23
  Balance Current:       275.23




    ▐ F1-Help ▌                      ▐ F8 - Undo ▌  ▐ F10 - Done ▌
```

FIGURE 6-23 Distributing balances

reflect the amount of the transaction. You now need to distribute
this amount across the ageing periods for the Ageing Report to be
accurate. The sum of the subsidiary amounts must equal the total
balance forward. When you are done distributing the amounts,
press (F10) and then (ENTER) to accept the information. You can
then enter another customer ID, or press (F10) to return to the
Maintenance Menu.

Printing an Aged Receivables Report

You can check your balance forward distributions quickly and easily
by printing an Aged Receivables report. Select Aged Receivables
Report from the Accounts Receivable Reports Menu and tell
Accounts Receivable where you want to print the report. Then

specify the report date and whether you want Regular, Balance Forward, or both types of customer.

Accounts Receivable next asks if you want to update the balance forward ageing. Type **N** and press (ENTER). This prevents Accounts Receivable from ageing the account information for your balance forward customers. Press (ENTER) to accept the default ageing date, and select detailed or summary ageing and the customers you want a report on. As you can see from the report in Figure 6-24, the Balance Forward customers have aged information. The beginning balances for the Regular customers appear in the current column.

CREATING AUTOMATIC TRANSACTIONS

Accounts Receivable and Invoicing require more setup than the modules you have worked with so far. However, now that you have entered the Accounts Receivable and Invoicing options, transaction types, sales tax information, and customer information, you can start entering transactions. First you need to learn about automatic transactions.

Automatic transactions are transactions that Accounts Receivable posts to a customer's account on a regular basis. If any of your customers pay you rents or leases, a fixed royalty amount for a given period, or a credit balance on a fixed contract, you can set up an automatic transaction. Automatic transactions are very much like the automatic invoices for accounts payable (see Chapter 4).

When you set up an automatic transaction, you tell Accounts Receivable to bill a customer a fixed amount once a month, every other month, quarterly, semiannually, or annually. At the predetermined time, Accounts Receivable automatically generates these transactions. Setting up automatic transactions can free you from a considerable amount of repetitive work. The following example

CHECK ON DISTRIBUTIONS

RUN DATE: 06/01/90
RUN TIME: 1:12 PM

Big Business, Inc.
Accounts Receivable
Detailed Aged Receivables Report

PAGE   1

Ageing Date: 06/01/90

CUST. ID	CUSTOMER NAME	INVOICE NUMBER	DUE DATE	CURRENT	1 - 30 PAST DUE	31 - PAST DUE	60 PAST DUE	OVER 60 OPEN CR	TOTAL
GILMAN	Joel Gilman, Attorney 206-514-9815	----	----	0.00	154.13	121.16	0.00	0.00	275.29
KRELL	Krell Office Systems	004309	07/01/90	1611.61	0.00	0.00	0.00	0.00	1611.61
LIL001	Lily Pod Systems	004310	07/01/90	1015.48	0.00	0.00	0.00	0.00	1015.48
SANTOS	Santos, Harley, and Jone 206-312-6294	----	----	0.00	2317.82	0.00	0.00	0.00	2317.82
	TOTALS:			2627.09	2471.95	121.16	0.00	0.00	5220.20

*** END OF Detailed Aged Receivables Report ***

≡ **FIGURE 6-24** Aged Receivables report

shows how to set up an automatic transaction for a customer of Big Business, Inc. who pays a monthly fee for on-site service and support.

To enter an automatic transaction, select Maintain Automatic Transactions from the Accounts Receivable Maintenance Menu (shown in Figure 6-25). Once you have entered some automatic transactions, Accounts Receivable will ask if you want to print a list of automatic transactions. After telling Accounts Receivable where to print a control report, you see the screen shown in Figure 6-26. Most of the information you enter in the fields described next is the standard transaction information you entered before.

Customer ID   Enter a customer ID. If you enter a customer ID not already on file, you can add it now.

Auto Trans. ID   Enter one or two characters in the Auto Trans. ID field. This field uniquely identifies the automatic transaction

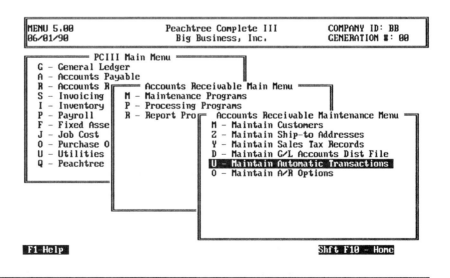

FIGURE 6-25   Select Maintain Automatic Transactions

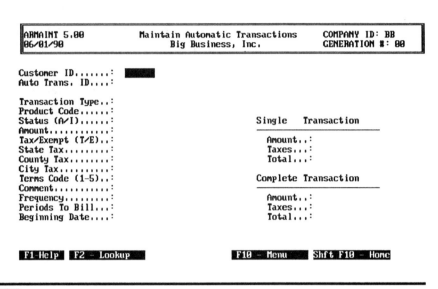

```
ARMAINT 5.00              Maintain Automatic Transactions      COMPANY ID: BB
06/01/90                        Big Business, Inc.             GENERATION #: 00

   Customer ID.......:    ▮▮▮▮▮▮
   Auto Trans. ID....:

   Transaction Type..:
   Product Code......:
   Status (A/I)......:                     Single   Transaction
   Amount............:                   ─────────────────────────
   Tax/Exempt (T/E)..:                      Amount..:
   State Tax.........:                      Taxes...:
   County Tax........:                      Total...:
   City Tax..........:
   Terms Code (1-5)..:                     Complete Transaction
   Comment...........:                   ─────────────────────────
   Frequency.........:                      Amount..:
   Periods To Bill...:                      Taxes...:
   Beginning Date....:                      Total...:


     F1-Help   F2 - Lookup                 F10 - Menu    Shft F10 - Home
```

FIGURE 6-26 Maintain Automatic Transactions screen

for this customer. You cannot change this number once you have entered and accepted it.

If this automatic transaction is not on file, Accounts Receivable will ask if you want to add it. Type **Y** and press (ENTER). Accounts Receivable will fill in a number of the fields for you, as shown in Figure 6-27. You can change any or all of the default information.

Transaction Type Enter the appropriate transaction type for this transaction. Table 6-1 listed all possible transaction types.

Product Code Enter the product code for this transaction. You must have set up the product code for the transaction type through the Maintain G/L Accounts Dist option.

```
┌──────────────────────────────────────────────────────────────────────────┐
│ARMAINT 5.00          Maintain Automatic Transactions    COMPANY ID: BB     │
│06/01/90                   Big Business, Inc.            GENERATION #: 00    │
└──────────────────────────────────────────────────────────────────────────┘

     Customer ID.......:  KRELL    Krell Office Systems
     Auto Trans. ID....:  01

     Transaction Type..:  SA
     Product Code......:
     Status (A/I)......:  A                    Single    Transaction
     Amount............:         0.00         ─────────────────────────
     Tax/Exempt (T/E)..:  T                     Amount..:        0.00
     State Tax.........:         0.00           Taxes...:        0.00
     County Tax........:         0.00           Total...:        0.00
     City Tax..........:         0.00
     Terms Code (1-5)..:  1  2/10,NET 30       Complete Transaction
     Comment...........:
     Frequency.........:  M                     Amount..:        0.00
     Periods To Bill...:  1                     Taxes...:        0.00
     Beginning Date....:  06/01/90              Total...:        0.00


     ▐ F1-Help ▌  ▐ F2 - Lookup ▌          ▐ F8 - Undo ▌   ▐ F10 - Done ▌
```

═══════ **FIGURE 6-27**   Default values for Automatic Transactions

Status (A/I)   Enter **A** if you want this transaction to be active. When you run Generate Auto Transactions as part of the Enter Transactions option, Accounts Receivable creates a transaction based on the information you entered here. Enter **I** if you want this transaction to be inactive. You can activate a transaction at any time by changing this field to **A**.

Amount   Enter the amount of the transaction. Each invoice created from an automatic transaction will have only one transaction amount on it.

Tax/Exempt (T/E)   Enter **T** if the transaction is taxable, or **E** if it is exempt.

State Tax, County Tax, and City Tax   Enter tax amounts in each of these fields, or press (**ENTER**) to accept the defaults calculated by Accounts Receivable. If you change any of the tax rates, Accounts Receivable will recalculate the taxes the next time you generate the transaction.

Terms Code (1 - 5)   Enter the terms code, or press (**ENTER**) to accept the default.

Comment   Enter up to ten characters in the Comment field. Accounts Receivable will print this text on the control report and the Transaction Register.

Frequency   Enter one of the following codes for the frequency of the transaction:

Code	Frequency
M	Monthly
B	Bimonthly
Q	Quarterly
S	Semiannually
A	Annually

Periods to Bill   Enter the number of periods you want Accounts Receivable to bill the customer for this transaction.

Beginning Date   Enter the date you want the automatic transaction to begin. Accounts Receivable will not generate a transaction before this date.

Figure 6-28 shows the Maintain Automatic Transactions screen right before you accept it. The single amounts show the

```
┌─────────────────────────────────────────────────────────────────────────┐
│ARMAINT 5.00            Maintain Automatic Transactions    COMPANY ID: BB  │
│06/01/90                      Big Business, Inc.           GENERATION #: 00 │
└─────────────────────────────────────────────────────────────────────────┘

  Customer ID.......:  KRELL    Krell Office Systems
  Auto Trans. ID....:  01

  Transaction Type..:  SA
  Product Code......:  G
  Status (A/I)......:  A                    Single    Transaction
  Amount............:       240.00          ─────────────────────────
  Tax/Exempt (T/E)..:  T                      Amount..:     240.00
  State Tax.........:         0.00            Taxes...:      18.72
  County Tax........:        18.72            Total...:     258.72
  City Tax..........:         0.00
  Terms Code (1-5)..:  1  2/10,NET 30       Complete Transaction
  Comment...........:                       ─────────────────────────
  Frequency.........:  M                      Amount..:    5760.00
  Periods To Bill...:  24                     Taxes...:     449.28
  Beginning Date....:  06/01/90              Total...:    6209.28


  Accept (Y/N/D):  Y
   F1-Help                              F8 - Undo
```

FIGURE 6-28   Sample Automatic Transaction

transaction amount and the taxes Accounts Receivable will bill to the client on each invoice. The complete amounts are the total amounts billed to the client over the life of the automatic transaction.

When you accept the transaction, you can enter another automatic transaction ID for this customer or press (ESC) to enter another customer ID. Press (F10) at the customer ID to return to the Maintenance Menu.

When you select Enter Transaction after you have set up an automatic transaction, you are asked if you want to generate automatic transactions. If you enter **Y**, Accounts Receivable will create transactions for each of the active automatic transactions that apply to this period. The transaction information will appear on the customer's next statement.

CREATING INVOICES AND CREDIT MEMOS

This section describes how to enter and print invoices and credit memos. (Credit memos are the same as invoices—anything here about entering and printing invoices applies to credit memos as well.) If you prefer to create statements rather than invoices, you can enter information through the Enter Transactions screen you used to set up beginning balances for customers. The next section also describes how to use the Enter Transactions screen to write off bad debts.

Entering Invoices and Credit Memos

To enter invoices or credit memos, select the Enter Invoices option from the Invoicing Processing Menu (Figure 6-29). Invoicing first asks if you want to process repeating invoices (much the same as the automatic transactions you saw earlier). Type **N** and press (ENTER). You'll learn how to enter repeating invoices later in this section.

Invoicing asks if you want to enter current or repeating invoices (Figure 6-30). Select Current Invoices. Invoicing opens the invoicing data files, and then asks if you want to print an invoice alignment guide. Press (ENTER). The invoice alignment guide will print Xs in the print positions for the invoice so you can align it in the printer. Once forms are properly aligned, enter **N**.

Enter **I** if you are entering invoices or **C** if you are entering credit memos. Then enter the invoice date—the date the invoice transaction occurred. The default is the system date, but you can enter any date you like. After you accept the information, select Add Invoice from the Process Options menu to bring up the first Enter Invoices screen.

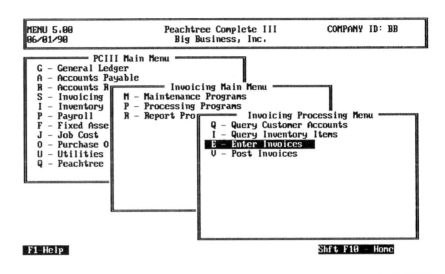

```
┌─────────────────────────────────────────────────────────────────────┐
│MENU 5.00                  Peachtree Complete III      COMPANY ID: BB  │
│06/01/90                     Big Business, Inc.                        │
├──────── PCIII Main Menu ──────────────────────────────────────────────┤
│  G - General Ledger                                                   │
│  A - Accounts Payable                                                 │
│  R - Accounts R┌───────── Invoicing Main Menu ──────────┐             │
│  S - Invoicing │ M - Maintenance Programs               │             │
│  I - Inventory │ P - Processing Programs                │             │
│  P - Payroll   │ R - Report Pro┌───── Invoicing Processing Menu ──────┤
│  F - Fixed Asse│               │ Q - Query Customer Accounts          │
│  J - Job Cost  │               │ I - Query Inventory Items            │
│  O - Purchase O│               │ E - Enter Invoices                   │
│  U - Utilities │               │ V - Post Invoices                    │
│  Q - Peachtree │                                                      │
│                                                                       │
└───────────────────────────────────────────────────────────────────────┘
  F1-Help                                           Shft F10 - Home
```

FIGURE 6-29   Select Enter Invoices

```
┌─────────────────────────────────────────────────────────────────────┐
│SIPROC1 5.00                   Enter Invoices          COMPANY ID: BB  │
│06/01/90                     Big Business, Inc.                        │
│                                                                       │
│                     ┌───── INVOICE OPTIONS ─────┐                     │
│                     │ C - Current Invoices      │                     │
│                     │ R - Repeating Invoices    │                     │
│                     └───────────────────────────┘                     │
│                                                                       │
└───────────────────────────────────────────────────────────────────────┘
  F1-Help
```

FIGURE 6-30   Invoice Options Menu

The information on the first Enter Invoices screen is invoice header information. As soon as you enter the customer ID, Invoicing fills in most of the fields by using the customer's file. You need to supply the customer's purchase order number if one is available, as well as additional shipment information in the Shipped Via field. If you use sales orders, you may want to enter the number in the Our Order No. field. Figure 6-31 shows the first Enter Invoices screen just before you accept the information.

When you accept the information, the second Enter Invoices screen appears (Figure 6-32). This screen is similar to the Enter Transactions screen shown earlier. Enter information on each transaction for this invoice, as described next.

Transaction Type Enter the transaction type in this field. Invoice transaction types are listed in Table 6-2. Although this list is similar to Table 6-1, it includes a few additional transaction types. There

```
┌─────────────────────────────────────────────────────────────────┐
│ SIPROC1 5.00                 Enter Invoices          COMPANY ID: BB │
│ 06/01/90                  Big Business, Inc.                       │
└─────────────────────────────────────────────────────────────────┘

INVOICE NUMBER.....: 000002   Current Invoices              Add Inv.

CUSTOMER ID: LIL001

SOLD TO: Lily Pod Systems        SHIP TO:  Lily Pod Systems
         1523 Carnelian                    1523 Carnelian

         Tulalip, WA                       Tulalip, WA
                       98454-0203                      98454-0203
P.O. NUMBER.: B2648-1            SALES
P.O. DATE...: 06/01/90          TAX: C01                      0.000
SALESMAN....: SO                          King County Sales   7.800
TERMS CODE..: 1    2/10,NET 30                               0.000
SHIP DATE...: 06/01/90
SHIPPED VIA.: Customer will call
OUR ORDER NO: SO-141


ACCEPT (Y/N): Y
 F1-Help
```

FIGURE 6-31 Sample invoice header screen

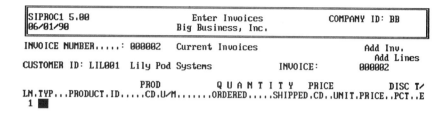

```
SIPROC1 5.00                     Enter Invoices              COMPANY ID: BB
06/01/90                        Big Business, Inc.

INVOICE NUMBER.....: 000002   Current Invoices                   Add Inv.
                                                                 Add Lines
CUSTOMER ID: LIL001  Lily Pod Systems            INVOICE:        000002

                        PROD           Q U A N T I T Y   PRICE        DISC T/
LN.TYP...PRODUCT.ID.....CD.U/M.......ORDERED.....SHIPPED.CD..UNIT.PRICE..PCT..E
  1 ▪
```

```
F1-Help   F2 - Lookup                      F10 - Done
```

═══ **FIGURE 6-32**   Invoice Transaction screen

are two new codes for sales and returns of items not normally stocked in Inventory: SN and RN. You can also enter a comment by entering a special transaction type: CM. If you are entering transactions for a credit memo, you should restrict the transactions to crediting transactions (AD, CR, MC, RN, RE, and RS) to avoid confusing your customers.

 If you want to enter early payment discounts, bad debt write-offs, or service charges, you must use the Enter Transactions screen in Accounts Receivable.

Product ID   Enter the product code (as set up in the Inventory module) in this field. If you are directly interfacing Invoicing to Inventory, you can press (F2) to look up the product codes already on file. If you enter a product code not on file for any transaction type other than a nonstock sale or return (SN or RN), you must add the item to Inventory. See Chapter 11 for more on the Inventory module.

Transaction Type	Transaction
AD	Adjustment
BD	Bad debt write-offs
CI	City tax
CM	Comment
CO	County tax
CP	Cost of product
CS	Cost of service
EP	Early payment discount
FR	Freight
MC	Miscellaneous credit
MD	Miscellaneous debit
PA	Payment
RE	Return (stock item)
RN	Return (nonstock item)
RS	Return of service
SA	Sale (stock item)
SC	Service charge
SN	Sale (nonstock item)
SS	Sale of service
ST	State tax

TABLE 6-2   Invoice Transaction Types

The description related to the product ID appears below the Product ID field. You can change this information if you like.

Product Code   Enter a product code in this field. You can press (F2) to look up the product codes for this transaction type.

Unit of Measurement   Enter up to four characters in this field to indicate the units the product is sold in. For example, enter Each, Case, or Doz; to represent a service, use units such as Hour or Mnth.

Quantity Ordered   Enter the quantity ordered of this product. If this is a credit adjustment (transaction type AD), enter a negative quantity, for example, **−4.00**. If you are using Invoicing with Inventory, merchandise that is being returned is automatically entered as a negative. Returns will increase the quantity of items available in Inventory.

Quantity Shipped   Enter the quantity of the product to be shipped on this order. If the quantity to be shipped exceeds the number of items available in Inventory, Invoicing displays a warning message and tells you how many items are available. You must then adjust the number to be shipped to be equal to or less than the number in Inventory. You cannot ship more items than are ordered.

Price Code   Enter the inventory price code (inventory items can have up to three different prices to accommodate different classes of customer—for instance, retail, wholesale, and supplier). Press (F2) to see the choices for this item.

Unit Price   Enter the unit price in this field. If the item is an Inventory item and you are interfacing Invoicing with Inventory, Invoicing will enter a default based on the price code you just entered.

Discount Percent   Enter the discount percentage for the customer on this transaction. Invoicing will use the customer's standard discount percentage from the customer file as the default.

T/E   Enter **T** if this is a taxable transaction or **E** if the transaction
is exempt.

When you have entered all the information for a single transaction,
Invoicing will display the net amount for the transaction and ask if you
want to accept the transaction. After accepting the transaction, you can
enter another transaction. You can also edit or delete transaction items
by pressing (F7) to edit or (F8) to delete a line. Figure 6-33 shows a
completed invoice right before you accept it. When you have accepted
the invoice information, you can print the invoice or go to the first
Enter Invoices screen and enter another invoice.

If you want to change an invoice, select Edit Invoice from the
Processing Options menu. You can change the header information
or add, change, or delete transactions. You cannot change an
invoice that has been posted.

Cancelling Invoices and Credit Memos

To cancel an invoice or a credit memo, select Cancel Invoices from
the Processing Options Menu. Invoicing will display the header information for the invoices and the total invoice amount. It will then ask
if you want to cancel this invoice. Type **Y** and press (ENTER) to do so.

Entering Repeating Invoices

It's easy to enter a repeating invoice. Start by selecting the Enter Invoices
option from the Invoicing Processing Menu. Type **N** and press (ENTER)
to skip processing repeating invoices (if you entered **Y** now, Invoicing

```
┌─────────────────────────────────────────────────────────────────────────┐
│SIPROC1 5.00                     Enter Invoices            COMPANY ID: BB  │
│06/01/90                       Big Business, Inc.                          │
└─────────────────────────────────────────────────────────────────────────┘
  INVOICE NUMBER.....: 000002    Current Invoices                  Add Inv.
                                                                   Del Lines
  CUSTOMER ID: LIL001  Lily Pod Systems          INVOICE:          000002

                         PROD          Q U A N T I T Y   PRICE         DISC T⁄
  LN.TYP...PRODUCT.ID.....CD,U⁄M,......ORDERED.....SHIPPED.CD,.UNIT.PRICE,.PCT,.E
   1 SA 0  10101          C EACH        1.00       1.00     331.1000  0.00 T
   2 SA 0  10115          C EACH        1.00       1.00      99.9500  0.00 T
   3 SA 0  100            B EACH        3.00       0.00     954.5000  2.00 T
   4 RE 0  32143          C EACH       -4.00      -4.00      53.0400  0.00 T




                                                   NET AMOUNT:     218.89
                                                         TAX:      17.07
                                                    PAYMENTS:       0.00
  INVOICE COMPLETE (Y⁄N): Y                            TOTAL:     235.96
  █F1-Help█  █F5 - List█     █F6 - Add█     █F7 - Edit█    █F8 - Undo█
```

FIGURE 6-33 Sample completed invoice

would look for repeating invoices already on file and try to create customer invoices from them). Select Repeating Invoices at the Invoice Options screen. Invoicing will open the data files.

Now select Enter Repeating Invoices from the Repeating Invoice Options Menu. (You can list the repeating invoices on file by selecting List Repeating Invoices.) Enter **I** if you are entering a repeating invoice or **C** if you are entering a repeating credit memo. Then enter the invoice date as you did for a normal invoice. After accepting the information, select Add Invoice from the Process Options Menu to bring up the first Enter Invoices screen.

The first Enter Invoices screen for repeating invoices is almost identical to the screen shown in Figure 6-31, except that the invoice ID is not entered automatically by Invoicing. Enter an invoice ID that will identify this repeating invoice for this customer. Invoicing will fill in the header information on the rest of the screen, as shown in Figure 6-34.

In addition to the standard header information, you need to enter the frequency, the beginning date, the number of periods to invoice, the last invoice date, and the invoice status. The last invoice date is the date the invoice was last processed. You can leave this blank and let Invoicing make an entry for you when it processes the repeating invoice. The rest of these fields are the same as for entering an automatic transaction. Accept the header information and enter transaction items on the second Enter Invoices screen, as you did before.

Once you have set up information for a repeating invoice, you can create the invoice each period by entering **Y** at the "Processing repeating invoices" prompt at the start of the Enter Invoices procedure. Invoicing will examine the file of repeating invoices and create an invoice for each repeating invoice that is active, eligible to be created, and has not been processed this period.

You can change and cancel repeating invoices and credit memos, like any other invoice or credit memo.

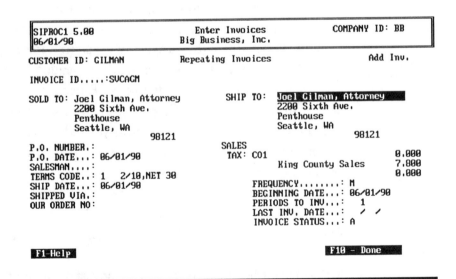

FIGURE 6-34 Entering a Repeating Invoice

Printing Invoices and Credit Memos

You should print invoices and credit memos as soon as possible after you have entered them so that you can distribute them to your customers quickly. The due dates for invoices and credit memos are based on the date you enter the information rather than when the invoices and credit memos are printed.

To print invoices and credit memos, select Print Invoices from the Invoicing Reports Menu, as shown in Figure 6-35. After specifying where to print, select the invoices you want to print from the Program Options Menu: current invoices, backorder invoices, or posted invoices. Current invoices are unposted invoices. Backorder invoices are invoices written for a backordered item (you specify backordered items from the Inventory module). Posted invoices are invoices that have already been posted to Accounts Receivable. Next select the range of invoices you want to print. When Invoicing is done printing the invoices, it returns you to the Main Menu.

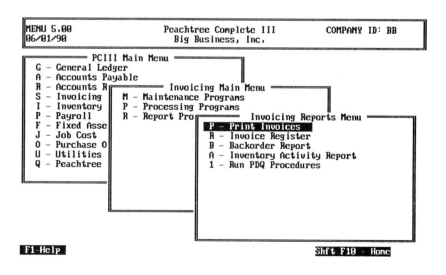

FIGURE 6-35   Select Print Invoices

You can print a report of invoiced sales that couldn't be shipped because merchandise in Inventory was listed as backordered. Select Backorder Report from the Invoicing Reports Menu. Tell Invoicing where to print the report, and enter the report date.

Printing the Invoice Register

The Invoice Register is a summary report of all the invoices and credit memos entered in Invoicing but not yet posted. You should print an Invoice Register each time you print invoices and credit memos.

To print an Invoice Register, select Invoice Register from the Invoicing Reports Menu. Tell Invoicing where to print the report and what the report date should be. A sample Invoice Register appears in Figure 6-36.

Printing the Inventory Activity Report

If you are using Invoicing with Inventory, you should print an Inventory Activity report whenever you print invoices. This report lists the inventory activity on any item sold or returned, as well as cost of goods sold and profit information. To print the Inventory Activity report, select Inventory Activity Report from the Invoicing Reports Menu. Tell Invoicing where to print the report and what the report date should be. A sample Inventory Activity report appears in Figure 6-37.

Posting Invoices

Once you have printed the invoices and credit memos and run an Invoice Register, you are ready to post the invoices to your

```
INVOICE REGISTER FOR 6/1/90

RUN DATE: 06/01/90                          Big Business, Inc.                                            PAGE  1
RUN TIME: 5:23 AM                            Sales Invoicing
                                             Invoice Register

INVOICE  INVOICE  CUST.                                         MERCHANDISE   OTHER                SALES    INVOICE
NUMBER   DATE     ID     CUSTOMER NAME          TERMS           /SERVICES     CHARGES   FREIGHT    TAX      TOTAL
-------  -------  -----  -----------------------  -----------   -----------   -------   -------   -------   -------
000002   06/01/90 LIL001 Lily Pod Systems        2/10,NET 30        218.89      0.00      0.00     17.07    235.96
000003   06/01/90 GILMAN Joel Gilman, Attorney   2/10,NET 30        447.63      0.00      0.00     34.92    482.55
000004   06/01/90 KRELL  Krell Office Systems     2/10,NET 30        600.00      0.00      0.00     46.80    646.80
000005   06/01/90 SANTOS Santos, Harley, and Jones 2/10,NET 30      1131.50      0.00      0.00     88.26   1219.76
000006   06/01/90 LIL001 Lily Pod Systems        2/10,NET 30        200.00      0.00      0.00     15.60    215.60
000007   06/01/90 GILMAN Joel Gilman, Attorney   2/10,NET 30        300.00      0.00      0.00     23.40    323.40
000008   06/01/90 SANTOS Santos, Harley, and Jones 2/10,NET 30         0.00      0.00      0.00      0.00      0.00
                                                                -----------   -------   -------   -------   -------
NO. OF ITEMS LISTED:  7                                             2898.02      0.00      0.00    226.05   3124.07

              REPORT SUMMARY TOTALS

                   TAXABLE    NON-TAXABLE     GROSS
                  ---------   -----------   ---------
Sales.........:    3335.18        0.00       3335.18
Misc. Debits..:       0.00        0.00          0.00
Returns.......:     437.16-       0.00        437.16-
Misc. Credits.:       0.00        0.00          0.00
Freight.......:       0.00        0.00          0.00
                  ---------   -----------   ---------
Sub-Totals....:    2898.02        0.00       2898.02

Credits.......:       0.00        0.00          0.00
Payments......:       0.00        0.00          0.00
Adjustments...:       0.00        0.00          0.00
Service Charges:      0.00        0.00          0.00
                  ---------   -----------   ---------
Sub-Totals....:       0.00        0.00          0.00

                 SALES TAXES  TAX REFUNDS     GROSS
                  ---------   -----------   ---------
State.........:       0.00        0.00          0.00
County........:     226.05        0.00        226.05
City..........:       0.00        0.00          0.00
                  ---------   -----------   ---------
Tax Sub-Total.:     226.05        0.00        226.05
                                            ==========
Report Total..:                              3124.07

*** End Of - Invoice Register ***
```

FIGURE 6-36 Sample Invoice Register

INVENTORY ACTIVITY FOR 6/1/90

RUN DATE: 06/01/90
RUN TIME: 5:34 AM

Big Business, Inc.
Sales Invoicing
Inventory Activity Report

PAGE   1

PRODUCT ID	P C	INVOICE NUMBER	ITEM DESCRIPTION	UNIT MEAS	N S	QUANTITY ORDERED	QUANTITY SHIPPED	TOTAL COST	TOTAL SALES	PROFIT	PCT OF PROFIT
Multisync monitor	C	000005	Color multisync moni	EACH	*	2.00	2.00	0.00	1356.50	1356.50	100.00
On-site training	G	000006		HOUR	*	8.00	8.00	0.00	200.00	200.00	100.00
Service retainer	F	000007	Retainer for extende	MNTH	*	1.00	1.00	0.00	300.00	300.00	100.00
VGA monitor	C	000005	Exchange VGA for mul	EACH		1.00-	1.00-	0.00	225.00-	225.00-	100.00-
consulting	F	000003	Consulting services	HOUR	*	16.00	16.00	6400.00	400.00	6000.00-	1500.00-
consulting	F	000003	Install chips.	HOUR	*	2.00	0.00	0.00	0.00	0.00	0.00
Items Listed: 2						18.00	16.00	6400.00	400.00	6000.00-	1500.00-
onsite training	F	000004		EACH	*	24.00	24.00	0.00	600.00	600.00	100.00
PO 100	B	000002	PC KIT	EACH		3.00	0.00	0.00	0.00	0.00	0.00
PO 100	B	000003	PC KIT	EACH		4.00	0.00	0.00	0.00	0.00	0.00
PO 100	B	000008	PC KIT	EACH		1.00	0.00	0.00	0.00	0.00	0.00
Items Listed: 3						8.00	0.00	0.00	0.00	0.00	0.00
PO 10101	C	000002	286 Motherboard	EACH		1.00	1.00	150.00	331.10	181.10	54.70
PO 10115	C	000002	230W Power Supply	EACH		1.00	1.00	61.54	99.95	38.41	38.43
PO 24800	C	000003	256-10 RAM chip	EACH		144.00	0.00	0.00	0.00	0.00	0.00
PO 32143	C	000002	MONOCHROME MONITOR	EACH		4.00-	4.00-	0.00	212.16-	212.16-	100.00-
PO 32143	C	000003	MONOCHROME MONITOR	EACH		1.00	1.00	0.00	47.63	47.63	100.00
Items Listed: 2						3.00-	3.00-	0.00	164.53-	164.53-	100.00-
Total Items Listed: 15						203.00	49.00	6611.54	2898.02	3713.52-	128.14-

FIGURE 6-37 Sample Inventory Activity report

```
RUN DATE: 06/01/90                                Big Business, Inc.                                          PAGE  2
RUN TIME: 5:34 AM                                  Sales Invoicing
                                                Inventory Activity Report

                   P INVOICE                      UNIT N  QUANTITY  QUANTITY                                  PCT OF
PRODUCT ID         C NUMBER   ITEM DESCRIPTION     MEAS S  ORDERED   SHIPPED   TOTAL COST  TOTAL SALES  PROFIT  PROFIT
---------          --------   ---------------      ------  --------  --------  ----------  -----------  ------  ------

Sales:             UNITS      SALES         COST          PROFIT    % PROFIT
                   -----      -----         ----          ------    --------

Stocked....:        3.00      478.68      211.54          267.14      55.81
Non-Stocked:       51.00     2856.50     6400.00         3543.50-    124.05-
Services...:        0.00        0.00        0.00            0.00       0.00
                   -----      -------     -------         -------    -------
Total......:       54.00     3335.18     6611.54         3276.36-     98.24-

Returns:

Stocked....:       4.00-     212.16-       0.00          212.16-     100.00-
Non-Stocked:       1.00-     225.00-       0.00          225.00-     100.00-
Services...:       0.00        0.00        0.00            0.00       0.00
                   -----     -------      -------        -------     -------
Total......:       5.00-     437.16-       0.00          437.16-     200.00-

Totals:

Stocked....:       1.00-     266.52      211.54           54.98       20.63
Non-Stocked:      50.00     2631.50     6400.00         3768.50-     143.21-
Services...:       0.00        0.00        0.00            0.00       0.00
                  ======     =======     =======        =======     =======
Total......:      49.00     2898.02     6611.54         3713.52-     128.14-


*** End Of - Inventory Activity Report ***
```

FIGURE 6-37 Sample Inventory Activity report (*continued*)

customers' accounts. The posting process clears the Invoice Register of outstanding invoices, updates the inventory information based on the sales and returns, and updates customer account and invoice balances. Because you cannot edit or delete invoices and credit memos after you have posted them, make sure that all the invoices and credit memos are correct before you start the posting process.

To post invoices, select Post Invoices from the Invoicing Processing Menu. Invoicing will back up your invoice files as a safety measure before continuing, depending upon how your Backup options are set up. Next, select Post Current Invoices from the Program Options Menu. (You would select Delete Previously Posted Invoices if you wanted to back out the posted invoices and restore the backed up invoice files.)

Invoicing warns you (shown in Figure 6-38) that you are about to post the invoices and gives you another chance to stop the

```
SIPROC2 5.00                    Post Invoices              COMPANY ID: BB
06/01/90                      Big Business, Inc.
```

```
This program option will post all unposted invoices.  Once this
option is run you will not be able to edit the invoices.



Post Invoices (Y/N): N
```

≡≡≡ **FIGURE 6-38** Post Invoices warning

process. Type **Y** and press (**ENTER**), and then tell Invoicing where to print the control report. As each invoice is posted, the invoice number is displayed on the screen. When all the invoices have been posted, Invoicing returns you to the Processing Menu.

ENTERING PAYMENTS

The most agreeable part of Accounts Receivable and Invoicing is receiving payments from your customers. You should post payments to customer accounts as soon as you receive a payment from a customer. First check the status of the customer's account, then enter the payment, and finally print a transaction register for a permanent record of the activity.

Checking a Customer's Account

Suppose that you have received a payment on account from Joel Gilman, attorney. To check the status of his account, select Query Customer Accounts from the Accounts Receivable Processing Menu (Figure 6-39). At the customer ID prompt, enter Joel Gilman's customer ID: **GILMAN**. The Query Customer Accounts screen appears (Figure 6-40).

The information shown here tells you that Joel Gilman is a Balance Forward customer, and that he currently owes you a total of $1,081.24. When you press (**ENTER**), you see a list of the current open invoices on his account (Figure 6-41). The Comment field shows that these have been posted from Invoicing. Press (**ENTER**) to return to the customer ID field, and (**F10**) to return to the Main Menu.

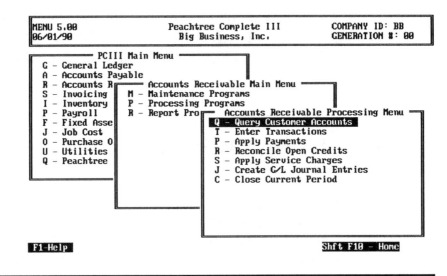

FIGURE 6-39   Select Query Customer Accounts

```
ARPROC  5.00                 Query Customer Accounts        COMPANY ID: BB
06/01/90                      Big Business, Inc.            GENERATION #: 00

Customer ID.....: GILMAN Joel Gilman, Attorney
                         2200 Sixth Ave.
                         Penthouse
                         Seattle, WA        98121
Telephone #.....: 206-514-9815      ──LAST──  ──DATE──   ──AMOUNT──
Customer Class..: A                 Debit     06/01/90      323.40
Account Type....: B                 Credit    01/01/00        0.00
Service Chg Code: 1                 Payment   01/01/00        0.00
Terms Code......: 1    2/10,NET 30  Service Charge 01/01/00  0.00
Sales Tax Code..: CO1               ──YTD──              ──AMOUNT──
                                    Debit                  1631.82
Credit Limit....:     5000.00       Credit                    0.00
Balance Forward.:      275.29       Payment                   0.00
                                    Service Charge             0.00
Ship Addresses..: N
Dunning Notices.: Y                 Pending Invoices:          0.00
Discount Percent:     0.00          Adjusted Balance:       1081.24


PRESS ⏎ TO CONTINUE     'P' TO PRINT A COPY ▮
```

FIGURE 6-40   Query Customer Accounts screen

```
┌──────────────────────────────────────────────────────────────────────────┐
│ ARPROC  5.00              Query Customer Accounts        COMPANY ID: BB    │
│ 06/01/90                    Big Business, Inc.           GENERATION #: 00   │
└──────────────────────────────────────────────────────────────────────────┘
 Customer ID.....: GILMAN Joel Gilman, Attorney
                          2200 Sixth Ave.
                          Penthouse
                          Seattle, WA          98121

         ┌───────────┬──┬───────┬───────┬────────┬──────┬─────────┬─────────┐
         │           │  │Trans. │ Due   │Discount│ Disc.│         │         │
    Inv# │Transaction│PC│ Date  │ Date  │  Date  │ Rate │ Amount  │ Comment │
   ──────┼───────────┼──┼───────┼───────┼────────┼──────┼─────────┼─────────┤
   000003│Sale       │  │06/01/90│07/01/90│06/11/90│ 2.00│   482.55│Invoicing│
   000007│Sale       │  │06/01/90│07/01/90│06/11/90│ 2.00│   323.40│Invoicing│
         │           │  │       │       │        │      │         │         │
         │           │  │       │       │        │      │         │         │
         │           │  │       │       │        │      │         │         │
         │           │  │       │       │        │      │         │         │

 END OF TRANSACTIONS LIST -- PRESS ◄─┘ TO CONTINUE   'P' TO PRINT A COPY █
```

FIGURE 6-41   Open invoices for customer

Entering a Payment for a
Balance Forward Customer

Since Joel Gilman is a Balance Forward customer, you will be
applying his payment to the ageing periods instead of to a specific
invoice. You have just received a check, number 5784, for $500
from Joel Gilman. To apply this to his account, select Apply
Payments from the Accounts Receivable Processing Menu (Figure
6-42). Tell Accounts Receivable where to print the control report,
and then enter the transaction date and the customer ID. Figure
6-43 shows the initial Apply Payments screen.

Enter the customer's check number (or a comment, such as
CASH PMT) in the Reference field, and the amount of the
payment in the Amount field. The remainder of the screen appears,

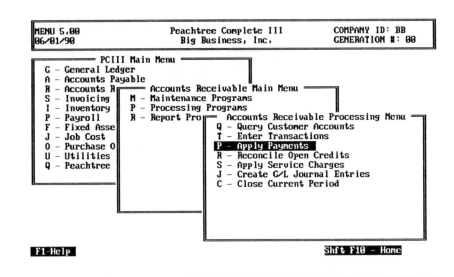

```
MENU 5.00                 Peachtree Complete III      COMPANY ID: BB
06/01/90                    Big Business, Inc.         GENERATION #: 00

        ┌─── PCIII Main Menu ───┐
        G - General Ledger
        A - Accounts Payable
        R - Accounts R┌─ Accounts Receivable Main Menu ─┐
        S - Invoicing │ M - Maintenance Programs
        I - Inventory │ P - Processing Programs
        P - Payroll   │ R - Report Pro┌─ Accounts Receivable Processing Menu ─┐
        F - Fixed Asse│               │ Q - Query Customer Accounts
        J - Job Cost   │               │ T - Enter Transactions
        O - Purchase O │               │ P - Apply Payments
        U - Utilities  │               │ R - Reconcile Open Credits
        Q - Peachtree  │               │ S - Apply Service Charges
                       │               │ J - Create G/L Journal Entries
                       │               │ C - Close Current Period

 F1-Help                                      Shft F10 - Home
```

FIGURE 6-42   Select Apply Payments

```
ARPROC 5.00                  Apply Payments          COMPANY ID: BB
06/01/90                    Big Business, Inc.        GENERATION #: 00

Customer ID: GILMAN      Joel Gilman, Attorney


Reference..: CK          Amount:             Balance:        1081.24




 F1-Help
```

FIGURE 6-43   Initial Apply Payments screen

as shown in Figure 6-44. You can see the amounts in each of the four ageing periods as well as the remaining undistributed amount.

For Balance Forward customers, you should usually apply payments towards the oldest period's balance, then the next oldest balance, and so on. Enter **PA**, the payment transaction type, in the Trans. Type column, followed by the appropriate product code. Accounts Receivable will automatically apply the payment to the oldest balance. You can adjust this amount if you like. If there are any undistributed funds remaining, Accounts Receivable will apply them to the next oldest balance, and so on until all of the payment has been distributed. Figure 6-45 shows the finished Apply Payments screen. You can enter another customer ID or press (**F10**) to return to the Accounts Receivable Processing Menu.

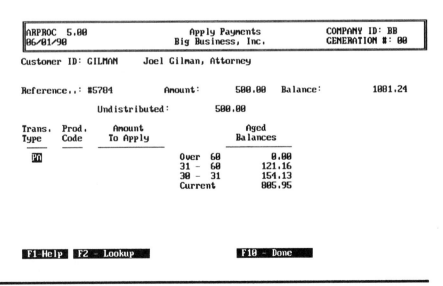

FIGURE 6-44   Complete Apply Payments screen

```
┌────────────────────────────────────────────────────────────────────────┐
│ARPROC  5.00                    Apply Payments          COMPANY ID: BB    │
│06/01/90                       Big Business, Inc.        GENERATION #: 00  │
└────────────────────────────────────────────────────────────────────────┘
 Customer ID: GILMAN      Joel Gilman, Attorney

 Reference..: #5704          Amount:       500.00   Balance:       1001.24

             Undistributed:        500.00

 Trans.  Prod.    Amount                    Aged
 Type    Code    To Apply                Balances
 ────    ────    ────────               ─────────
  PA                              Over  60        0.00
                      121.16      31 -  60      121.16
                      154.13      30 -  31      154.13
                      224.71      Current       805.95


 Accept (Y/N) Y

 █F1-Help█
```

FIGURE 6-45   Payments applied to invoices

Entering a Payment for a Regular Customer

Suppose that you have also received a payment from Missy Krell at Krell Office Systems. Missy Krell is a Regular customer, so her payment will be applied to specific invoices.

Again, go to the customer ID field of the Apply Payments screen. Enter **KRELL**, the customer ID for Krell Office Systems, and enter the check number and the amount. A slightly different screen appears (Figure 6-46).

The earliest invoice with the lowest number will appear in the Invoice Number field. You can press (F2) to look up the outstanding invoices, their due dates, and their balances (Figure 6-47). Select an invoice to apply a payment to. If the payment is before the discount date, Accounts Receivable will enter EP as the transaction type, and will automatically calculate the discount for you. When you accept this item, it then prepares to enter a PA transac-

```
┌─────────────────────────────────────────────────────────────────────────┐
│ ARPROC  5.00                   Apply Payments          COMPANY ID: BB     │
│ 06/01/90                      Big Business, Inc.        GENERATION #: 00   │
└─────────────────────────────────────────────────────────────────────────┘
Customer ID: KRELL      Krell Office Systems


Reference..: #1411            Amount:      2517.13  Balance:        2517.13

              Undistributed:            2517.13

Invoice    Due     Trans. Prod.   Invoice        Amount
Number     Date    Type   Code    Amount         To Apply

█000001█
```

F1-Help   F2 - Lookup

FIGURE 6-46   Applying Payments for a regular customer

```
┌─────────────────────────────────────────────────────────────────────────┐
│ ARPROC  5.00                   Apply Payments          COMPANY ID: BB     │
│ 06/01/90                      Big Business, Inc.        GENERATION #: 00   │
└─────────────────────────────────────────────────────────────────────────┘
Customer ID: KRELL      Krell Office Systems


Reference..: #1411            Amount:      2517.13  Balance:        2517.13

              Undistributed:            2517.13

Invoice    Due     Trans. Prod.   Invoice        Amount
Number     Date    Type   Code    Amount         To Apply
          ══════ Select Invoice ══════
         │ 000001 - 07/01/90 -       258.72*│
         │ 000004 - 07/01/90 -       646.80*│
         │ 004309 - 07/01/90 -      1611.61*│
          ─────────────────────────────────
```

FIGURE 6-47   Selecting an Invoice

tion for the balance. Accounts Receivable will apply undistributed funds to the balance until the balance is zero or it runs out of undistributed funds. Repeat this process to apply payments to other invoices.

If you have undistributed funds remaining, you can enter an invoice number of **0** and apply a payment to it equal to the remaining funds (Figure 6-48). This will leave an open credit for that customer. You can continue entering payments for customers, or press (F10) to return to the Accounts Receivable Processing Menu.

Entering Transactions

There are a few transaction types that you cannot enter through the Invoicing module, such as writing off bad debts (BD), early payment discounts (EP), and service charges (SC). You may also

```
┌──────────────────────────────────────────────────────────────────────┐
│ARPROC  5.00               Apply Payments          COMPANY ID: BB       │
│06/01/90                 Big Business, Inc.         GENERATION #: 00     │
└──────────────────────────────────────────────────────────────────────┘
Customer ID: KRELL       Krell Office Systems


Reference..: #1411         Amount:      2517.13  Balance:        -0.00

    0               Undistributed:        18.11

Invoice   Due      Trans. Prod.   Invoice      Amount
Number    Date     Type   Code    Amount       To Apply

000001   07/01/90  EP              258.72          5.17
000001   07/01/90  PA              253.55        253.55
000004   07/01/90  EP              646.80         12.94
000004   07/01/90  PA              633.86        633.86
004309   07/01/90  PA             1611.61       1611.61
0                  PA                             18.11


Accept (Y/N) Y

 F1-Help
```

FIGURE 6-48   Applying an open credit

wish to make an entry to a customer's account without generating an invoice. For this, you would use the Enter Transactions screen.

To enter a transaction through the Enter Transactions screen, follow the general procedure described earlier in "Entering a Customer's Beginning Balance." Instead of entering **BB** as the transaction type, enter whatever transaction type you want. Fill in the rest of the fields as you did before.

 You can enter bad debts and service charges through the Apply Payments screen. You can also enter service charges through the Apply Service Charges screen.

Reconciling Open Credits

Some of your customers will undoubtedly build up open credits. Before you print customer statements showing the account balances, you may want to apply the open credits to outstanding customer balances. This will give you and your customers a more accurate picture of their account balance.

To reconcile the open credits, select Reconcile Open Credits from the Accounts Receivable Processing Menu. Tell Accounts Receivable if you want to reconcile open credits for all customers or for selected customers. Then tell Accounts Receivable whether you want to review each customer or have Accounts Receivable apply open credits automatically. If you tell Accounts Receivable to apply open credits automatically, it will apply open credits to the lowest numbered invoice with an unpaid balance. It will continue to apply the credits to open invoices in this fashion until the credits have been used up.

If you tell Accounts Receivable that you want to review the customers, you can apply the credits to specific invoices. Figure 6-49 shows a sample screen for a customer. You can tell Accounts Receivable which invoice to apply the credit to, or you can simply

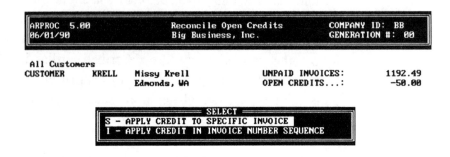

```
ARPROC  5.00                  Reconcile Open Credits         COMPANY ID: BB
06/01/90                      Big Business, Inc.             GENERATION #: 00

All Customers
CUSTOMER     KRELL    Missy Krell              UNPAID INVOICES:    1192.49
                      Edmonds, WA              OPEN CREDITS...:     -50.00

                        ═════ SELECT ═════
                        S - APPLY CREDIT TO SPECIFIC INVOICE
                        I - APPLY CREDIT IN INVOICE NUMBER SEQUENCE


              F1-Help
```

FIGURE 6-49   Reconciling Open Credits screen

have Accounts Receivable apply the credit starting with the lowest numbered invoice. If you want to apply the credits yourself, Accounts Receivable will ask you for the invoice number. Press (F2) to look up the outstanding invoices and their balances.

When you have processed all the customers in the file, Accounts Receivable returns you to the Accounts Receivable Processing Menu.

Applying Service Charges

If you set up Accounts Receivable to allow service charges, you will need to apply them before printing customer statements. Service charges can be for almost anything: miscellaneous order handling, charge for credit account, membership fee, late payment, and so on. Accounts Receivable creates separate invoices for service charges. This makes them easier to track and allows the charges to appear on the customer statements.

To enter service charges, first select Apply Service Charges from the Accounts Receivable Processing Menu. Tell Accounts Receivable where to print the control report. Next, tell Accounts Receivable the ending and starting dates for the period for which you are applying service charges. Accounts Receivable will ask if this is a trial or a final run. If you enter **T**, you can review only the customer accounts and associated service charges. You cannot change the service charge amounts or create invoices on a trial run.

When you enter **F** for a final run of service charges, Accounts Receivable asks if you also want to create invoices for service charges, if you want to do this for all customers, Balance Forward customers, or Regular customers, and if you want to review each customer. Figure 6-50 shows the Apply Service Charges screen. If you accept the information, Accounts Receivable will create a service charge transaction and, optionally, an

```
┌────────────────────────────────────────────────────────────────────┐
│ ARPROC  5.00            Apply Service Charges      COMPANY ID: BB    │
│ 06/01/90                  Big Business, Inc.       GENERATION #: 01  │
└────────────────────────────────────────────────────────────────────┘

Customer Account No.....: SANTOS
Customer Name...........: Santos, Harley, and Jones
Account Type............: BAL FWD
Annual S. C. Rate.......:  10.00
Amount Subject To S. C..:    3537.58
Service Charge Amount...:    10.00

Accept? (Y/N): Y
```

```
███ F10 - Quit ███
```

FIGURE 6-50 Apply Service Charges screen

invoice. You can print service charge invoices like any other customer invoice. You must post service charge invoices before they will appear on customer statements.

Printing Customer Statements

At the beginning of every accounting period, you may want to send statements to all customers with active accounts. These statements show the customers a summary of their account activity along with their current account balance. You can create customer statements at any time in the accounting period.

To print statements, select Customer Statements from the Accounts Receivable Reports Menu. After you tell Accounts Receivable where you want to print the statements, enter the statement date (the date the statements are being printed) and the statement ageing date (the "as of" date; the date Accounts Receivable will use to age the statement information). You can also add a customized message of up to 75 characters to the statements. Accounts Receivable then asks if you want to print dunning messages. Type **Y** and press (**ENTER**) to allow dunning messages for overdue clients, or type **N** and press (**ENTER**) to suppress dunning messages for all statements you are printing.

Then tell Accounts Receivable if you want to print statements for customers with zero balances. Next, specify whether to sort the statements by customer ID or customer class. (The customer class is a classification you set up as part of the customer information. If you are doing cycled billing and statements, you will want to use this option.) Finally, tell Accounts Receivable to print statements for all customers or just a range. A completed screen appears in Figure 6-51.

Accounts Receivable is now ready to print the customer statements. You can print an alignment guide before the statements if you like. An alignment guide is a document mask that lets you line up your statements exactly in the printer. A sample customer statement appears in Figure 6-52.

You can print customer statements as often as you like.

Printing the Transaction Register

The Transaction Register lists all the transactions you have entered through the Enter Transactions, Enter Invoices, Apply Service Charges, and Apply Payments screens. You should print the Transaction Register frequently during a period to check that all the Accounts Receivable and Invoicing transactions are complete and correct. You should also print a final Transaction Register immediately before you close a period as a permanent record of transactions.

```
┌────────────────────────────────────────────────────────────────────────┐
│ ARRPTS  5.00              Customer Statements         COMPANY ID: BB     │
│ 06/01/90                  Big Business, Inc.          GENERATION #: 00    │
└────────────────────────────────────────────────────────────────────────┘
Statement Date:            06/01/90

Statement Ageing Date:     06/01/90

Statement Message (Y/N): Y
Message:
 Account as of 6/1/90.  Call J. Hedtke or S. O'Brien if you have questions.

Print Dunning Messages (Y/N):  Y

Print Zero Balance Statements (Y/N):  Y

Sort By Customer........: ID
Customer List Selection: ALL



Print Alignment Guide (Y/N): Y
 F1-Help
```

═══ **FIGURE 6-51**   Selecting Customer Statements options

```
CUSTOMER STATEMENTS FOR 6/1/90
                         ****************
Big Business, Inc.       ***          ***
123 Main Street          ***  STATEMENT  ***
Anytown, USA             ***          ***
                         ****************

                         STATEMENT DATE:  06/01/90

                         CUSTOMER ID.:  GILMAN

                              PAGE 1
=========================
Joel Gilman, Attorney
2200 Sixth Ave.
Penthouse
Seattle, WA             98121
=========================

Account as of 6/1/90. Call J. Hedtke or S. O'Brien if you have questions.

INVOICE   DATE     TERMS OR REF   CODE   DEBITS    CREDITS    BALANCE
-------   --------  --------------  ----  ---------  ----------  ----------
                    BALANCE FWD.                                275.29
0         06/01/90  #5784          PA                500.00-    500.00-
000003    06/01/90  Invoicing      SA    482.55                 482.55
000007    06/01/90  Invoicing      SA    323.40                 323.40
                                         ---------  ----------  ----------
                                         805.95     500.00-     581.24


              1 -  30    31 -  60
 CURRENT    PAST DUE    PAST DUE                              ==========
---------   ----------   ----------
  581.24        0.00        0.00          TOTAL DUE     581.24
OVER 60                                                      ==========
PAST DUE      TOTAL     OPEN CR
----------   ---------   ----------
    0.00      581.24        0.00
```

FIGURE 6-52 Sample Customer Statement

To print a Transaction Register, select Transaction Register Report from the Accounts Receivable Reports Menu and tell Accounts Receivable where you want to print the report. After you enter the report date, specify either a transaction register (all transactions) or an open items register (only those items that are still open on the books).

Accounts Receivable lets you select all transactions, a range of transactions, or all debit or all credit transactions. You can also print transactions from the current generation, all generations, or a range of generations. Figure 6-53 shows a sample transaction register.

HOUSEKEEPING

You have seen how to perform the routine daily and monthly Accounts Receivable and Invoicing tasks. You now need to find out about special tasks that occur irregularly or only once a period. These tasks include such things as ageing the Balance Forward customers, creating the journal entries for General Ledger, and closing the period.

Ageing the Balance Forward Customers

The beginning of this chapter discussed how to print an Aged Receivables Report. Accounts Receivable asked if you wanted to update the balance forward ageing. You previously answered **N** so that Accounts Receivable didn't change the ageing on the report. When you answer **Y** to this question, Accounts Receivable asks you for the ageing date. This is the "as-of" date, the date that Accounts Receivable will use to age the information. You then select detailed or summary ageing, and the range of customers you want to report on and age. When Accounts Receivable runs the report, it ages the balances for all Balance Forward customers. This information is also aged throughout Accounts Receivable. A sample Aged Receivables report appeared in Figure 6-24.

TRANSACTION REGISTER FOR 6/1/90

RUN DATE: 06/01/90
RUN TIME: 3:38 AM

Big Business, Inc.
Accounts Receivable
Transaction Register

PAGE 1

Generation: 00

CUST. ID	TRANSACTION TYPE	INVOICE NO.	P C	TRANS. DATE	DUE DATE	DISCOUNT DATE	E.P. DISC%	COMMENT	CREDIT AMOUNT	DEBIT AMOUNT	NET AMOUNT
GILMAN	Credit	0	A	06/01/90	/ /	/ /	0.00	credit	200.00-		200.00-
GILMAN	Payment	0		06/01/90	/ /	/ /	0.00	#5784	500.00-		500.00-
GILMAN	Sale	000003		06/01/90	07/01/90	06/11/90	2.00	Invoicing		482.55	482.55
GILMAN	Sale	000007		06/01/90	07/01/90	06/11/90	2.00	Invoicing		323.40	323.40

CUSTOMER TOTALS: 700.00- 805.95 105.95

Generation: 00

CUST. ID	TRANSACTION TYPE	INVOICE NO.	P C	TRANS. DATE	DUE DATE	DISCOUNT DATE	E.P. DISC%	COMMENT	CREDIT AMOUNT	DEBIT AMOUNT	NET AMOUNT
KRELL	Credit	0	A	06/01/90	/ /	/ /	0.00		316.24-		316.24-
KRELL	Payment	0		06/01/90	/ /	/ /	0.00		18.11-		18.11-
KRELL	EP Discount	000001		06/01/90	/ /	/ /	0.00	#1411	5.17-		5.17-
KRELL	OCR. Debit	000001		06/01/90	/ /	/ /	0.00				0.00
KRELL	OCR. Debit	000001		06/01/90	/ /	/ /	0.00				0.00
KRELL	OCR. Debit	000001		06/01/90	/ /	/ /	0.00				0.00
KRELL	OCR. Debit	000001		06/01/90	/ /	/ /	0.00				0.00
KRELL	Payment	000001		06/01/90	/ /	/ /	0.00	#1411	253.55-		253.55-
KRELL	Sale	000001	G	06/01/90	07/01/90	06/11/90	2.00			258.72	258.72
KRELL	EP Discount	000004		06/01/90	/ /	/ /	0.00	#1411	12.94-		12.94-
KRELL	Payment	000004		06/01/90	/ /	/ /	0.00	#1411	633.86-		633.86-
KRELL	Sale	000004		06/01/90	07/01/90	06/11/90	2.00	Invoicing		646.80	646.80
KRELL	Sale	000009	A	06/01/90	07/01/90	06/11/90	2.00			1,611.61	1,611.61
KRELL	Beg. Balance	004309		06/01/90	07/01/90	06/11/90	2.00			1,611.61	1,611.61
KRELL	Payment	004309		06/01/90	/ /	/ /	2.00	#1411	1,611.61-		1,611.61-

CUSTOMER TOTALS: 2,851.48- 4,128.74 1,277.26

Generation: 00

CUST. ID	TRANSACTION TYPE	INVOICE NO.	P C	TRANS. DATE	DUE DATE	DISCOUNT DATE	E.P. DISC%	COMMENT	CREDIT AMOUNT	DEBIT AMOUNT	NET AMOUNT
LIL001	Credit	0	C	06/01/90	/ /	/ /	0.00	1411	50.00-		50.00-
LIL001	Payment	0		06/01/90	/ /	/ /	0.00	1411	9.03-		9.03-
LIL001	EP Discount	000002		06/01/90	/ /	/ /	0.00	1411	4.72-		4.72-
LIL001	Payment	000002		06/01/90	/ /	/ /	0.00	1411	231.24-		231.24-
LIL001	Sale	000006		06/01/90	07/01/90	06/11/90	2.00	Invoicing		235.96	235.96
LIL001	EP Discount	000006		06/01/90	/ /	/ /	0.00	1411	4.31-		4.31-
LIL001	Payment	000006		06/01/90	/ /	/ /	0.00	1411	211.29-		211.29-
LIL001	Sale	000006		06/01/90	07/01/90	06/11/90	2.00	1411		215.60	215.60
LIL001	Beg. Balance	004310		06/01/90	07/01/90	06/11/90	2.00	Invoicing		1,015.48	1,015.48
LIL001	Payment	004310		06/01/90	/ /	/ /	0.00	1411	1,015.48-		1,015.48-

CUSTOMER TOTALS: 1,526.07- 1,467.04 59.03-

```
RUN DATE: 06/01/90                        Big Business, Inc.                                    PAGE  2
RUN TIME: 3:38 AM                        Accounts Receivable
                                         Transaction Register
-------------------------------------------------------------------------------------------------------
CUST. TRANSACTION  INVOICE  P  TRANS.              DISCOUNT  E. P.                CREDIT    DEBIT    NET
 ID     TYPE        NO.     C  DATE    DUE DATE     DATE     DISC%  COMMENT       AMOUNT   AMOUNT  AMOUNT
-----  -----------  -------  -  -----  --------    --------  -----  ----------    ------   ------  ------
GSANTOS  Sale       000005     06/01/90 07/01/90  06/11/90   2.00  Invoicing             1,219.76  1,219.76

                   GRAND TOTAL TRANSACTIONS=  31                                5,077.55- 7,621.49  2,543.94
                                                                               ========= ======== ========

*** END OF Transaction Register ***
```

FIGURE 6-53 Sample Transaction Register

You must run an Aged Receivables report at least once each accounting period to age the balance forward customers. You can run it more often if you like.

Printing the Sales Tax Summary

The Sales Tax Summary is a report that lists the totals accumulated for the tax codes that you have set up. You can use this information to send payments to the various state, county, and city tax agencies.

To print a Sales Tax Summary, select Sales Tax Summary from the Accounts Receivable Reports Menu. Tell Accounts Receivable where you want to print the report and enter the report date. Accounts Receivable will then print the Sales Tax Summary (shown in Figure 6-54).

If this is the end of a period, you can also clear the sales tax accumulators. This zeros the balances for the sales tax codes in preparation for the next period. You can select state, county, city, or all totals, or press (F10) to return to the Accounts Receivable Reports Menu without clearing sales tax totals. You can also delete any sales tax records that have been deactivated through the Maintain Sales Tax Records option. After accepting the information, Accounts Receivable will clear the totals. Press (F10) to return to the Accounts Receivable Reports Menu.

Printing the Past Due Report

The Past Due Report is simply an Aged Receivables report for customers with past due balances. Select Past Due Report from the Accounts Receivable Reports Menu. Tell Accounts Receivable where you want to print the report, the report date, and the date you last aged the customer information. You can specify a detailed or summary report. Accounts Receivable returns you to the Accounts Receivable Menu automatically when the report is printed.

SALES TAX AS OF 6/1/90

RUN DATE: 06/01/90
RUN TIME: 9:39 AM

Big Business, Inc.
Accounts Receivable
Sales Tax Summary

PAGE 1

CODE	STATE NAME	COUNTY NAME	CITY NAME	SALES TAX	TAXABLE SALES	NON-TAXABLE SALES	TOTAL SALES
CI1			Seattle City Sales	0.00	0.00	0.00	0.00
				0.00	0.00	0.00	0.00
				0.00	0.00	0.00	0.00
			CITY TOTALS:	0.00	0.00	0.00	0.00
			COUNTY TOTALS:	0.00	0.00	0.00	0.00
CO1		King County Sales		0.00	0.00	1735.00	1735.00
				342.66	1495.00	3138.02	4633.02
				0.00	0.00	1735.00	1735.00
co1		King County Sales		0.00	0.00	0.00	0.00
				0.00	0.00	0.00	0.00
				0.00	0.00	0.00	0.00
			CITY TOTALS:	0.00	0.00	1735.00	1735.00
			COUNTY TOTALS:	342.66	1495.00	3138.02	4633.02
			STATE TOTALS:	0.00	0.00	1735.00	1735.00
ST1	Wash State Sales			0.00	0.00	0.00	0.00
			CITY TOTALS:	0.00	0.00	0.00	0.00
			COUNTY TOTALS:	0.00	0.00	0.00	0.00
			STATE TOTALS:	0.00	0.00	0.00	0.00

*** REPORT TOTALS ***

	SALES TAX	TAXABLE SALES	NON-TAXABLE SALES	TOTAL SALES
STATES:	0.00	0.00	1735.00	1735.00
COUNTIES:	342.66	1495.00	3138.02	4633.02
CITIES:	0.00	0.00	1735.00	1735.00
TOTAL TAX:	342.66			

*** END OF Sales Tax Summary ***

FIGURE 6-54 Sales Tax Summary

Creating the G/L Journal Entries

Just before you close the period, you need to prepare the information to transfer to the General Ledger. If you are directly interfacing Accounts Receivable with the General Ledger, you will create a file of transactions to transfer to the General Ledger. You can also print a list of transactions for transferring manually to another General Ledger.

Start by selecting Create G/L Journal Entries as shown in Figure 6-55, and tell Accounts Receivable where to print the control report. You are then given three choices on the Transfer Options menu:

- List G/L Transfers will give you a detailed list of the General Ledger transactions. This report is similar to the Transaction Register, except that it is sorted by General Ledger account number rather than by customer ID. Use this report as a final check of your transactions before closing the period.

- Consolidate G/L Transactions consolidates by account number all the transactions for the current period. When it finishes, you will have a single debit or credit transaction for each General Ledger account number. This option also prints the Consolidate G/L Transfers List, which contains the same information as the G/L Transfers List produced by the previous option.

- Create G/L Transfers creates the Accounts Receivable summary journal that the General Ledger module uses to post accounts receivable transactions to the General Ledger accounts. This option also prints a transfer list. Be sure that you have backed up your Accounts Receivable and Invoicing files before using this option.

If you are not sure what you need in the way of reports, select all three options in order. This will give you a detailed report, a summary report, and the transfer file for the General Ledger module.

Closing the Period or the Year

Once you have created the Accounts Receivable summary journal with the Create G/L Journal Entries option, you are ready to close the current period. Select Close Current Period from the Accounts Receivable Processing Menu and enter the period ending date. If this is also the end of the year, type **Y** and press (ENTER) at the "End Of Year" prompt; otherwise, press (ENTER). When you accept the information, Accounts Receivable will close the current period. Be sure that you have backed up your Accounts Receivable and Invoicing files before closing the period.

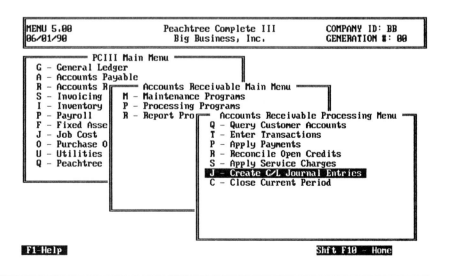

FIGURE 6-55   Select Create G/L Journal Entries

When you close the current period, Accounts Receivable purges all closed invoices (those with a zero balance) for your Regular customers. It also calculates the customer's net balance and purges all invoice information for all Balance Forward customers. When you examine transactions from a previous period, notice that Accounts Receivable has replaced the product code with an asterisk to signify that this is not a current transaction. Temporary customers with account balances of zero and no current activity are purged from the customer file.

SETTING UP
PAYROLL

Installing Payroll
Selecting Payroll General Ledger Account Numbers
Defining Miscellaneous Deductions and Income
Garnishments
Creating the Payroll Files

Generating a weekly payroll is one of the most time-consuming tasks in any business. There are many details to keep track of—employee information, time sheets, state and federal government regulations and requirements. There is also the time-consuming task of writing out the checks. Nevertheless, you must do this job right or you'll risk complaints from employees and penalties from the government.

For all of these reasons, payroll is a main motive for companies to switch to computerized accounting systems. Peachtree Complete III's Payroll module will simplify your payroll processing tremendously, while reducing errors and automatically integrating all the payroll information into the General Ledger.

INSTALLING PAYROLL

To install Peachtree Complete III's Payroll module, select Payroll from the PCIII Main Menu (Figure 7-1). Peachtree Complete III will ask if you are sure you want to install the payroll module. Type **Y** and press (**ENTER**) to continue.

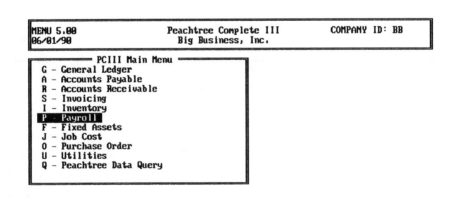

```
MENU 5.00                  Peachtree Complete III        COMPANY ID: BB
06/01/90                      Big Business, Inc.
         ┌──────────── PCIII Main Menu ────────────┐
         │ G - General Ledger                      │
         │ A - Accounts Payable                    │
         │ R - Accounts Receivable                 │
         │ S - Invoicing                           │
         │ I - Inventory                           │
         │ P - Payroll                             │
         │ F - Fixed Assets                        │
         │ J - Job Cost                            │
         │ O - Purchase Order                      │
         │ U - Utilities                           │
         │ Q - Peachtree Data Query                │
         └─────────────────────────────────────────┘


   F1 Help
```

═══ **FIGURE 7-1** Selecting the Payroll option

Peachtree Complete III needs to know where to store your company's payroll files. The default directory is \PEACH\PRDATA (Figure 7-2), but you can change this to any directory that you choose. If the directory you select does not exist, Peachtree Complete III asks if you wish to create it. If you do, type **Y** and press (ENTER).

Peachtree Complete III now presents the Program Options Menu (Figure 7-3). You need to select Set Module Options in order to tailor the Payroll module to your needs.

The payroll options screen, shown in Figure 7-4, contains a whole host of options from which you can choose to make the Payroll module work best for your company. Before going any further, you should familiarize yourself with every one of these options.

The Controller Password, Operator Password, and Use Menus options work the same here as they do in the General Ledger module. Refer back to Chapter 2 for more information.

```
MENU 5.00                    Peachtree Complete III         COMPANY ID: BB
06/01/90                        Big Business, Inc.

┌═════════ PCIII Main Menu ═════════┐
│  G - General Ledger               │
│  A - Accounts Payable             │
│  R - Accounts Receivable          │
│  S - Invoicing                    │
│  I - Inventory                    │
│  P - Payroll                      │
│  F - Fixed Assets                 │
│  J - Job Cost                     │
│  O - Purchase Order               │
│  U - Utilities                    │
│  Q - Peachtree Data Query         │
└───────────────────────────────────┘

     ┌─────────────────────────────────────────────────────────────┐
     │ Enter the subdirectory path where you want your data files to be. │
     │              C:\PCIII\PRDATA                                   │
     └─────────────────────────────────────────────────────────────┘
```

FIGURE 7-2   Entering the Payroll directory

```
┌──────────────────────────────────────────────────────────────────┐
│ PRMAINT 5.00              Maintain Payroll Options    COMPANY ID: BB │
│ 06/01/90                    Big Business, Inc.                      │
└──────────────────────────────────────────────────────────────────┘


              ┌──────────── Program Options ────────────┐
              │                                         │
              │  ▐ 0 - Set Module Options ▌              │
              │                                         │
              │   B - Automatic File Backup             │
              │                                         │
              │   P - Set Printer Assignments           │
              │                                         │
              └─────────────────────────────────────────┘




   ▐ F1-Help ▌                    ▐ F10 - Menu ▌  ▐ Shft F10 - Home ▌
```

───────────
═══════════ **FIGURE 7-3**   Program options


```
┌──────────────────────────────────────────────────────────────────┐
│ PRMAINT 5.00              Maintain Payroll Options    COMPANY ID: BB │
│ 06/01/90                    Big Business, Inc.                      │
└──────────────────────────────────────────────────────────────────┘

General Module Options              Accrual Options
  Controller Password........:        Automatic Sick Hours....: Y
  Operator Password..........:        Automatic Vacation Hours: Y
  Use Menus..................: Y      Annual Sick Hours.......:    40.00
  Allow Changes/Deletions....: Y      Annual Vacation Hours...:    80.00
  Force Control Reports......: N
  Current Fiscal Period......: 1    Overtime Rates
  Payroll Generation Number..: 0      Rate 1..................:     1.50
  Post to General Ledger.....: Y      Rate 2..................:     2.00
  Use Pre-Printed Checks.....: N
  Use Accounts Payable Forms.: N    Differential Information
  Use 24 Hour Time Clock.....: Y      Amount or Percentage....: P
  Min/Decimal Time Entry.....: D      Shift 2.................:    10.00
  Disburse Tips..............: Y      Shift 3.................:    20.00
  Departmentalize Payroll....: N
  State/Local Tax by Dept....: N

                       Accept (Y/N)...: ▐Y▌
```

───────────
═══════════ **FIGURE 7-4**   Payroll options

Allow Changes/Deletions

If you respond **N** to the Allow Changes/Deletions option, Peachtree Complete III won't allow you to change employee information, terminate an employee, or reactivate an employee. However, you can still add employees and change tax information.

Force Control Reports

In certain processes, Peachtree Complete III can print control reports that serve as an audit trail for tracking errors. In payroll, control reports can be created when printing checks, posting the current period, closing the current year, or updating from the Job Cost module. If you respond **Y** to the Force Control Reports option, Peachtree Complete III always prints control reports without asking you first. If you respond **N**, Peachtree Complete III asks before printing control reports.

Current Fiscal Period

You only need the Current Fiscal Period option if you post payroll transactions to the General Ledger. When you transfer payroll transactions to the General Ledger, you must identify the period to which the transactions should be applied. Here, you enter the first fiscal period in which transactions will be posted. Because Big Business is starting at the beginning of the fiscal year, fiscal period 1 is selected, but you should select whatever period is correct for you.

Once you enter the current fiscal period, you should never need to change this value again—Peachtree Complete III automatically updates the number for you. When you post transactions to the General Ledger in Post Current Period, the program asks, "Is this the last posting for the month?" If it is the last posting, respond with Y and Peachtree Complete III will increment the current fiscal period counter for you.

Payroll Generation Number

When you run the Post Current Period program, Peachtree Complete III automatically makes a backup copy of the employee data file. The backup file is called a *generation* and is identified by a generation number. Generation numbers range from 0 to 99, and are automatically updated each time you post the current period transactions. (After 99, the generation goes back to 0.) Peachtree Complete III lets you specify the generation number to use for the first generation of employee data. While you can use any number between 0 and 99, it makes sense to use the default value of 0.

Once you set this number, don't change it. Peachtree Complete III uses this number to keep track of transactions. If you change it, the software will accidentally try to process transactions for the new generation number.

Post to General Ledger

Peachtree Complete III can integrate all the accounting modules. If you want to take advantage of this and automatically post payroll transactions to the General Ledger, type **Y** at the Post to General Ledger option. However, if you prefer to post payroll transactions manually to the General Ledger, type **N** at this option. To help those doing manual entry, the Post Current Period program can be used to print a listing of current period payroll transactions.

Use Pre-Printed Checks

When Peachtree Complete III prints checks, it can include or omit your company's name. If you are using checks that have the company name preprinted on them, respond **Y** to this prompt. If you are using generic checks, respond **N** to this prompt and Peachtree Complete III will print your company name and address on the check.

Use Accounts Payable Form

The Use Accounts Payable Form option controls how your check stubs are printed. Check stubs come in two types: multipurpose and custom. Multipurpose check stubs are blank, so that the software doesn't have to align the print with the rows and columns on the stub. Custom stubs have preprinted rows and columns. If you use custom stubs, the software must know exactly where to print information so that it appears correctly on the stub.

Peachtree Complete III prints checks in both the Payroll and Accounts Payable modules. If you want to use the same blank checks for both modules, the checks must be printed on multipurpose forms. On the other hand, if you want to use customized stubs, you need to have separate checks printed for Payroll and Accounts Payable. If you want to use multipurpose forms, type a **Y** at this option. To use a customized stub, type an **N**.

Use 24-Hour Time Clock

Before you enter employee time sheets into the Payroll module, Peachtree Complete III must know what format you are using for time entries: military or standard. Military format uses a 24-hour time clock. For example, instead of entering 3 P.M. you would enter 15.00. Type **Y** to select military time or **N** to select standard time.

Min/Decimal Time Entry

Time values have decimal portions that indicate the number of minutes past the hour. This decimal portion can either represent minutes or fractions of an hour. If the decimal portion represents minutes, the entry 5.15 means 15 minutes after 5 o'clock. If, on the other hand, the decimal portion represents fractions of an hour, 5.15 means 0.15 of an hour, or 9 minutes after 5 o'clock. (Most businesses record time in fractions of an hour.) Type **M** to select decimal portions as minutes; type **D** to select decimal portions as fractions of an hour.

Disburse Tips

If your employees receive tips, you must let Peachtree Complete III know whether or not they keep their tips or turn them in for reimbursement through their payroll check. If your employees turn in tips, type **Y** for the Disburse Tips option; if they keep their tips, type **N**. Note that you must enter all tips by using the Enter Exceptions option, regardless of disbursement.

Departmentalize Payroll

If your company is organized into departments, you will probably want to departmentalize your payroll by typing a **Y** at the Departmentalize Payroll option. Selecting this option lets you view payroll information by department. This is important if you are trying to manage payroll costs in a large organization. If you decide to departmentalize payroll, you must assign each employee to a department.

State/Local Tax by Department

Companies that are organized into departments will benefit from generating tax journal entries by department. If you select the State/Local Tax by Department option, Peachtree Complete III will generate departmentalized journal entries for tax withheld, unemployment tax expense, and unemployment tax liability. Type **Y** to select this option.

Accrual Options

Most businesses offer their employees time off for sickness and vacation. Peachtree Complete III gives you some flexibility in how these benefits are accrued to employees.

AUTOMATIC SICK HOURS AND AUTOMATIC VACATION HOURS If you want your employees to accrue sick hours or vacation hours with each pay period, type **Y** for the Automatic Sick Hours and Automatic Vacation Hours options. Sick hours and vacation hours are accrued based on the total number of days and hours allotted to the employee per year. (Time is accrued every time you run Calculate Pay.) You can select accrual for both sick hours and vacation hours or for either one individually.

ANNUAL SICK HOURS AND ANNUAL VACATION HOURS In order to accurately accrue sick hours and vacation hours, Peachtree Complete III needs to know the total number of hours employees can have each year. Standard amounts are 40 hours of sick leave and 80 hours of vacation time. Enter the appropriate amounts here. If your employees do not accrue sick leave or vacation, enter zeros here.

Note that the amounts you enter for these options are merely default values that should apply to the majority of your employees. If some employees get more or fewer sick and vacation hours, you can set different amounts for these employees by using the Maintain Employees option discussed in Chapter 8, "Using Payroll."

Overtime Rates

Peachtree Complete III lets you define two different overtime rates, known as Rate 1 and Rate 2. The values you enter are used as multipliers that are applied to the employee's standard pay rate. You can enter any number from 0 to 99.99, but the most common selections are 1.5 (time and a half) and 2.0 (double time).

Differential Information

Many companies operate in shifts, with shift employees earning a differential above that earned by employees working regular hours. Usually, the third shift (also known as the graveyard shift) earns more than the second shift (also known as the swing shift) and the second shift earns more than the standard shift. In order to compute shift differential pay, Peachtree Complete III needs to know whether the differential is a percent or an amount and how much to add each time.

AMOUNT OR PERCENTAGE Shift differential can be computed either as a flat amount above standard pay or as a percentage increase in standard pay. The default is P for percentage, but you can change this to A for a flat amount if that is what your company uses. When you select **P** for percentage, Peachtree Complete III increases the employee's standard rate of pay by a set percentage. If you select amount, the program adds a flat amount to the employee's hourly earnings.

SHIFT 2 AND SHIFT 3 Once you have selected amount or percentage, you must give Peachtree Complete III the numbers it needs to compute the shift pay. If you selected percentage, you need to enter a percentage for both the second and the third shifts. The percentage can be any number from 0 to 99.99.

If you select amount, you must specify the dollar amount that Peachtree Complete III adds to the hourly pay of shift workers. You can enter any dollar amount up to $9,999.99.

SELECTING PAYROLL GENERAL LEDGER ACCOUNT NUMBERS

After you have entered the payroll options, Peachtree Complete III asks you to enter the General Ledger account numbers that will be used by payroll accounts. Figure 7-5 shows how Peachtree Complete III displays the default account numbers. You can either change these account numbers to suit your needs or use the defaults. For readers who know little about payroll processing, the accounts are described next.

```
PRMAINT 5.00             Maintain Payroll Options       COMPANY ID: BB
06/01/90                  Big Business, Inc,            GENERATION #: 00

                        Payroll G/L Account Numbers

                    Depts                                          Depts

Net Pay .................:  11000  N    Earned Income Credit.......:  23000  N
Employee's FICA..........:  22400  N    Draw Exceeds Commission....:  50100  N
Employer FICA Accounts                  Gross Pay...................:  50100  N
    Expense .............:  51400  N    Misc. Income Accounts
    Liability ...........:  22400  N        Tips.....................:  50100  N
Federal Withholding......:  22100  N        MISC. #1.................:  50100  N
Misc. Deduction Accounts                    MISC. #2.................:  50100  N
INSUR. ................:   61000  N        MISC. #3.................:  50100  N
401k  ................:    61000  N    Federal Unemployment Accounts
EMP LOAN...............:   61000  N        Expense..................:  51600  N
SAVINGS ...............:   61000  N        Liability................:  22600  N
FIVE   ...............:    61000  N    Industrial Ins. Expense....:  50000  N
SIX    ...............:    61000  N    Industrial Ins. Liability..:  23000  N
                                        Suspense Account...........:  24000  N

                        Accept (Y/N)..: Y
```

FIGURE 7-5 Payroll General Ledger account numbers

Net Pay

Net pay is the amount paid to your employees: that is, it's the total pay less all deductions.

Employee's FICA, Employer FICA Expense, and Employer FICA Liability

FICA stands for Federal Insurance Contributions Act and is more commonly referred to as social security. These accounts contain, respectively, the amount deducted from employees' paychecks for FICA, and your company's total FICA expense and FICA liability.

Federal Withholding

Federal withholding indicates the amount deducted from employees' paychecks for federal income tax.

Miscellaneous Deduction Accounts

The miscellaneous deduction accounts contain the amount withheld from employees' pay for any of up to six accounts that you define. Peachtree Complete III provides default values for the first four accounts—insurance, 401k, employee loans, and savings—but you can change these to meet your needs. (Also see the section "Defining Miscellaneous Deductions and Income.")

Earned Income Credit

This category indicates the earned income credits earned by employees.

Draw Exceeds Commission

Salespeople are often allowed to draw against commission income. Usually, commission income exceeds the amount drawn out, and the employee is paid the difference. If, however, the commission income does not exceed the amount drawn, the employee owes the company the difference. This account contains the amount by which an employee's draw exceeds his or her commissions.

Gross Pay

The Gross Pay account contains the total amount, before taxes or deductions, paid to employees.

Miscellaneous Income Accounts

The miscellaneous income accounts keep track of income other than wages (tips, for example) that your employees earn. (Also see the section "Defining Miscellaneous Deductions and Income.")

Federal Unemployment Expense

This category indicates the company's federal unemployment tax expense.

Federal Unemployment Liability

This selection notes the company's federal unemployment tax liability.

Industrial Insurance Expense

The Industrial Insurance Expense account contains the expense the company has incurred by the state's industrial insurance tax.

Industrial Insurance Liability

The Industrial Insurance Liability account contains the company's industrial insurance tax liability.

Suspense Account

The Suspense account is a catchall for a variety of transactions, including those that do not fall into any of the other General Ledger accounts, and employee deductions that could not be made because the net pay was too little to cover them.

DEFINING MISCELLANEOUS DEDUCTIONS AND INCOME

After defining your company's payroll account numbers, you need to define any accounts that will be used for miscellaneous deductions and income. Any business can have many reasons for deductions and many sources of income other than wages. To help companies tailor the Payroll module to their needs, Peachtree Complete III provides six accounts for miscellaneous deductions and three accounts for miscellaneous income. The screen shown in Figure 7-6 displays the options you can select for each miscellaneous account.

```
┌──────────────────────────────────────────────────────────────────────┐
│PRMAINT 5.00              Maintain Payroll Options       COMPANY ID: BB │
│06/01/90                    Big Business, Inc.           GENERATION #: 00│
└──────────────────────────────────────────────────────────────────────┘
```

```
                                             TAXABLE
                      NAME.......A/P...B/A...FED...FICA...FUTA.......CEILING
Misc. Deduction #1:   INSUR.      A     A     Y     Y     Y            0.00
Misc. Deduction #2:   401k        A     A     Y     Y     Y            0.00
Misc. Deduction #3:   EMP LOAN    A     A     Y     Y     Y            0.00
Misc. Deduction #4:   SAVINGS     P     A     Y     Y     Y            0.00
Misc. Deduction #5:   FIVE        P     A     Y     Y     Y            0.00
Misc. Deduction #6:   SIX         P     A     Y     Y     Y            0.00


                      NAME......DISBURSE...AMT/PCT........CEILING
   Misc. Income #1:   MISC. #1       Y       P            0.00
   Misc. Income #2:   MISC. #2       Y       A            0.00
   Misc. Income #3:   MISC. #3       Y       A            0.00


Accept (Y/N).: ▓
```

FIGURE 7-6   Miscellaneous deductions and income

Miscellaneous Deductions

An account used for miscellaneous deductions is defined by the following characteristics: its name, whether deductions are made as an amount or a percentage, whether deductions are made before or after taxes have been deducted, whether federal, FICA, and FUTA (Federal Unemployment) taxes are deducted before or after the miscellaneous deduction, and a ceiling for the deduction.

NAME   In this category, you provide the name for the account to be used for miscellaneous deductions. These names will appear on screen and in reports. Select a name that meaningfully describes the type of transactions contained in the account.

A/P: AMOUNTS OR PERCENTAGES Peachtree Complete III payroll can make deductions as either fixed amounts or as percentages of employees' gross pay. If the miscellaneous deduction is a fixed amount that is deducted each pay period, enter an **A** in the A/P column. You must specify the amount of the deduction by using the Maintain Employees function.

If you select **P**, Peachtree Complete III deducts an amount equal to a percentage of the employee's gross pay. You must specify the percentage used to compute the deduction by using the Maintain Employees function.

B/A: BEFORE TAXES OR AFTER TAXES Some deductions are taxable while others are not. If a deduction is taxable, you must include it in taxable income when making tax computations. If, on the other hand, the deduction is not taxable, you must subtract the amount of the deduction from gross pay before computing taxes.

If you set the B/A option to **A**, Peachtree Complete III includes the amount of the deduction in taxable income for federal, FICA, and FUTA taxes. If you set this option to **B**, Peachtree Complete III makes the deduction before computing taxes.

In rare instances, a deduction may be made both on a before and after basis. When you specify the **B** option, you must indicate, one by one, whether or not the deduction is taxable for federal taxes, FICA, and FUTA. If it is not taxable at all, simply enter **N** for all three. If it is taxable for some but not others, specify **Y** where the deduction is taxable and **N** where it is not. Note that when you select **A**, all taxable categories are automatically set to **Y**, and you cannot change them individually.

TAXABLE: FED, FICA, AND FUTA If you select **B** for before taxes, you must indicate, for each tax category, whether the deduction is taxable or not. Entering a **Y** means that the deduction is taxable for the purposes of this type of tax.

CEILING   Peachtree Complete III lets you restrict the amount deducted from an employee's pay to some maximum, known as a *ceiling*. The ceiling is an annual figure and protects the employee from making total deductions beyond the ceiling amount. The ceiling can be any amount up to $9,999,999.99. If the deduction has no ceiling, enter a zero in this field.

Miscellaneous Income

An account used for miscellaneous income is defined by just three characteristics: its name, whether disburse income is calculated as an amount or a percent, and the ceiling on the income.

NAME   As with miscellaneous deductions, you can name miscellaneous income accounts as you like, but you should choose a mean-ingful name. This name will appear both on the screen and in reports.

DISBURSE   In some cases, miscellaneous income is not paid out through an employee's paycheck. In such cases, the income must be included in gross pay for the purposes of tax computations, but the amount is not made part of the paycheck. If miscellaneous income is disbursed through the paycheck, set this option to **Y**; otherwise, set it to **N**.

AMT/PCT   Like miscellaneous deductions, miscellaneous income can take the form of a fixed amount or a fixed percentage. Enter **A** in this field if the income is a fixed amount or **P** if it is a percentage of pay. Use the Maintain Employees function to enter the amount or the percentage to be used in the calculations.

CEILING   If the miscellaneous income is subject to ceiling (a maximum amount the employee is entitled to earn), enter the ceiling in this field. As with miscellaneous deductions, the maximum allowable ceiling is $9,999,999.99. If no ceiling applies, enter a zero in this field.

GARNISHMENTS

A *garnishment* is a deduction, mandated by a court of law, that is used primarily to ensure payment of debts incurred by the employee. Garnishments are calculated as a percentage of an employee's disposable pay. (Use the Maintain Tax File function discussed in Chapter 8, "Using Payroll," to set the percentage amount of the garnishment.) There can be some flexibility in determining how miscellaneous deductions and income affect disposable pay.

In some cases, miscellaneous income is considered part of disposable pay, while in other cases it is not. Likewise, some types of miscellaneous income may be deducted from disposable pay while others are not. The screen shown in Figure 7-7 allows you to specify whether or not each miscellaneous deduction and income account is deducted from or added to gross income prior to calculating disposable pay. If you select **Y**, the deductions or the income is included in gross pay to calculate the garnishment. If you select **N**, the deductions and income are not included.

CREATING THE PAYROLL FILES

At this point, you have entered all the information Peachtree Complete III needs to set up the payroll files. The program asks if you are ready to set up the files (Figure 7-8) and asks you to enter

```
╔══════════════════════════════════════════════════════════════════╗
║ PRMAINT 5.00              Maintain Payroll Options    COMPANY ID: BB║
║ 06/01/90                     Big Business, Inc.       GENERATION #: 00║
╚══════════════════════════════════════════════════════════════════╝

Disposable Income Calculation for Garnishments

INCOME
  Tips   ..: N
  MISC. #1..: N
  MISC. #2..: N
  MISC. #3..: N

DEDUCTIONS
  INSUR. ..: N
  401k   ..: N
  EMP LOAN..: N
  SAVINGS ..: N
  FIVE   ..: N
  SIX    ..: N


Accept (Y/N)..: Y
```

═══ **FIGURE 7-7**   Disposable income calculations for garnishments

```
╔══════════════════════════════════════════════════════════════════╗
║ PRMAINT 5.00              Maintain Payroll Options    COMPANY ID: BB║
║ 06/01/90                     Big Business, Inc.       GENERATION #: 00║
╚══════════════════════════════════════════════════════════════════╝




            Ready to Create Payroll Files - Continue (Y/N)..: Y

            Month Ending Date of First Payroll..: 06/01/90
```

```
F1-Help
```

═══ **FIGURE 7-8**   Setting up payroll files

the month ending date of the first payroll (the last day in the month in which you will first run a payroll). After you enter the date, Peachtree Complete III creates the payroll files and you are ready to begin entering your employee data.

chapter 8

USING PAYROLL

Maintaining the Tax File
Maintaining Employee Records
Miscellaneous Income Screen
Quarter-to-Date and Year-to-Date

MAINTAINING THE TAX FILE

To operate correctly, Peachtree Complete III Payroll must have accurate information about your company's federal, state, and local tax requirements. The program comes configured with the most recent information for both federal and state taxes. You should check the default information to make sure that it is up to date.

Payroll Tax Codes

Peachtree Complete III organizes payroll tax information by tax codes—two-letter abbreviations that identify a type of tax. The program comes with the following three tax codes:

- US for federal income tax withholding, employer's FICA, and FUTA (federal unemployment tax)

- SS for employee's FICA

- EI for earned income credits

For state taxes, Peachtree Complete III uses standard postal abbreviations (including the District of Columbia and Puerto Rico). State tax information comes with Peachtree Complete III, and is accurate as of the date the software was shipped. Even so, you should make sure the defaults are correct.

In addition to federal and state taxes, your company may be subject to payroll taxes at the county or city level. For these and other taxes (including garnishments), you must set up customized tax codes. Customized payroll tax codes consist of two-digit numbers, from 50 to 94.

It is easy to set up a customized tax code. First, enter the code you want to use for the special tax category. Next, select the predefined form tax code you want to use. (Peachtree Complete III defines several form tax codes that you can use as templates when setting up customized tax codes.) Finally, enter your information into the tax code. To find out which form tax code you should use, refer to Appendix B in the "Using Payroll" manual accompanying your software.

Maintaining Payroll Tax Information

To begin maintaining your company's payroll tax information, select Maintain Tax File from the Payroll Maintenance Menu

(Figure 8-1). Peachtree Complete III will ask you to enter the tax code for the payroll tax you want to maintain. To select federal taxes, type **US** and press (**ENTER**).

The first Federal Tax Maintenance screen is shown in Figure 8-2, and includes the employer federal tax ID, information on FIT, FICA, FUTA, and EIC, and the hourly minimum wage.

EMPLOYER ID   The Employer ID is the code that the federal government uses to identify your company. The number, which the Internal Revenue Service assigns to your company, is printed on various reports, including the Tax File List, the 941 Worksheet, the FUTA Report, and on W-2 statements.

TAXATION ON MISCELLANEOUS INCOME   If your employees earn tips or other types of miscellaneous income, you must

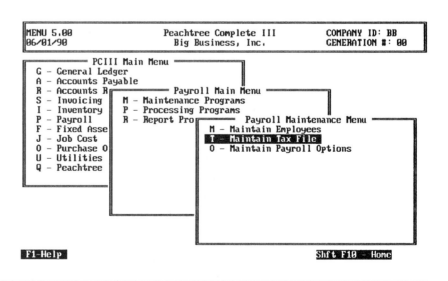

FIGURE 8-1   Selecting the Maintain Tax File option

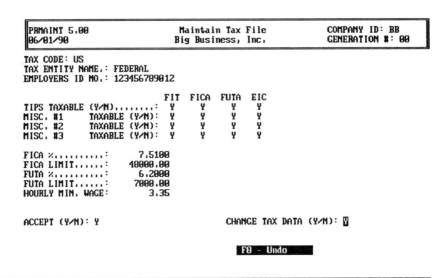

```
┌──────────────────────────────────────────────────────────────────┐
│PRMAINT 5.00              Maintain Tax File        COMPANY ID: BB   │
│06/01/90                  Big Business, Inc.       GENERATION #: 00 │
└──────────────────────────────────────────────────────────────────┘
TAX CODE: US
TAX ENTITY NAME.: FEDERAL
EMPLOYERS ID NO.: 123456789012

                             FIT  FICA  FUTA  EIC
TIPS TAXABLE (Y/N)........:   Y    Y     Y    Y
MISC. #1    TAXABLE (Y/N):    Y    Y     Y    Y
MISC. #2    TAXABLE (Y/N):    Y    Y     Y    Y
MISC. #3    TAXABLE (Y/N):    Y    Y     Y    Y

FICA %...........:       7.5100
FICA LIMIT......:     48000.00
FUTA %...........:       6.2000
FUTA LIMIT......:      7000.00
HOURLY MIN. WAGE:         3.35

ACCEPT (Y/N): Y                      CHANGE TAX DATA (Y/N): Y


                            ▌F8 - Undo▐
```

FIGURE 8-2   The Federal Tax Maintenance screen

specify whether or not these incomes are included when computing federal income tax (FIT), FICA, FUTA, and earned income credit (EIC). In each case, a **Y** tells Peachtree Complete III to include the tips or miscellaneous income in the calculations.

FICA AND FUTA PERCENTAGES AND LIMITS   Both the FICA and FUTA taxes are computed as a percentage of employee income. Likewise, both are subject to a maximum amount, over which taxes are not computed. The default percentage for FICA is 7.51% with a limit of $48,000 per year. This means that, for each pay period, the employer incurs a tax liability of 7.51% of an employee's pay. However, when the employee's pay exceeds $48,000, FICA is no longer computed for that employee. In these fields, you must enter the percentages and income ceilings that apply to your company.

HOURLY MINIMUM WAGE The last field on this screen is the Hourly Minimum Wage. This will be the federal minimum wage. Enter the correct value in this field.

Filing Status

Federal tax computations are affected by the employee's filing status (married or single) and the number of exemptions that the employee is claiming. The screen shown in Figure 8-3 indicates that code A is used for single and code B for married employees. In addition, you can specify the amount to be deducted from taxable pay for each exemption claimed. In this case, the amount is $2,000. This screen also tells you that the applicable tax rate is graduated depending on the filing status. At the bottom of the screen, Peachtree Complete III asks if you want to change the rate tables. Enter **Y** if you want to review or modify these tables.

```
PRMAINT 5.00                 Maintain Tax File          COMPANY ID: BB
06/01/90                     Big Business, Inc.         GENERATION #: 00

TAX ENTITY NAME: FEDERAL

FILING STATUS
     A single
     B married

STARTING WITH ANNUALIZED TAXABLE WAGES

DEDUCT    2000.00 PER EXEMPTION

APPLY GRADUATED RATE TABLE BY FILING STATUS




ACCEPT (Y/N): Y                 RATE TABLE(S) EXIST, CHANGE (Y/N): Y
                                           F8 - Undo
```

FIGURE 8-3 The filing status

FEDERAL TAX BRACKETS Peachtree Complete III maintains graduated tax tables that are used to compute federal income tax withholding for employees. Figure 8-4 shows the tax table for single employees. Another tax table is maintained for married employees.

The amount withheld from an employee's pay is determined by the entries in the table and consists of a percentage of pay plus an additional flat amount. For example, if you use the values in Figure 8-4, the amount withheld from an employee with an income of \$50,000 per year after exemptions would be 33% of \$4,000 (50,000 – 46,000) plus \$10,160.50. Ask your accountant if the withholding tables need to be changed for your employees.

FICA WITHHOLDING Tax code SS controls the way Peachtree Complete III computes FICA for employees. The screen in Figure 8-5 shows a sample entry. You just need to enter the per-

```
PRMAINT 5.00                 Maintain Tax File              COMPANY ID: BB
06/01/90                     Big Business, Inc.             GENERATION #: 00
TAX ENTITY NAME: FEDERAL

single
                  PERCENT OF (WAGES - BRACKET) + AMOUNT
                BRACKET           PERCENT              AMOUNT
                   0.00            0.0000                0.00
                1100.00           15.0000                0.00
               19650.00           28.0000             2782.50
               46000.00           33.0000            10160.50
              105430.00           28.0000            29772.40

ACCEPT (Y/N): Y
                                  F8 - Undo
```

FIGURE 8-4 The federal tax withholding table

```
PRMAINT 5.00              Maintain Tax File        COMPANY ID: BB
06/01/90                  Big Business, Inc.        GENERATION #: 00

TAX ENTITY NAME: FICA

STARTING WITH TAXABLE WAGES

WITHHOLD   7.5100 PERCENT OF THE FIRST    48000.00




ACCEPT (Y/N): Y
                                              F8 - Undo
```

FIGURE 8-5   The FICA withholding screen

centage to be deducted for FICA (the default is 7.51%) and the ceiling amount over which FICA is not deducted (the default is $48,000).

MAINTAINING EMPLOYEE RECORDS

Keeping employee records up to date, and using that information to generate payroll checks, is one of the most time-consuming bookkeeping tasks. Peachtree Complete III simplifies this job and automatically uses the information that you enter to produce accurate payrolls. To maintain employee payroll information, select Maintain Employees from the Payroll Maintenance Menu (Figure 8-6).

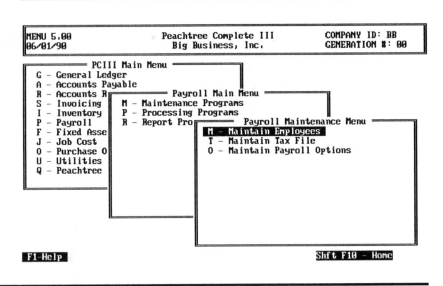

FIGURE 8-6 Selecting the Maintain Employees option

Employee Code

Peachtree Complete III will ask you to enter the code for the employee you wish to maintain (Figure 8-7). If you are entering information for a new employee, you can enter any code that is not being used. A valid employee code consists of any combination of up to four characters. You can use any combination of numbers and letters.

If you are just starting out, you might want to set up an employee coding system. Peachtree Complete III uses the employee code to sort employee payroll information, so the code system you use should take this into account. For example, your code might consist of the first two letters of the employee's last name followed by the year that the employee was hired. It's unlikely that your company will employ two people with the same code.

```
PRMAINT 5.00                Maintain Employees        COMPANY ID: BB
06/01/90                    Big Business, Inc.        GENERATION #: 00


DEPARTMENT..:  0    EMPLOYEE CODE..: 106




 F1-Help  F2 - Lookup
```

─── **FIGURE 8-7**   The Maintain Employees option

Personal Information

The first screen you come to (Figure 8-8) maintains personal information about an employee, including name, address, and important dates.

NAME AND ADDRESS   In the first seven fields, simply enter the employee's name, address, city, state, social security number, and telephone number.

COMMENT   The Comment field is for your information only— Peachtree Complete III does not use it in any way. You can enter anything you like or leave this field blank.

```
┌──────────────────────────────────────────────────────────────────────┐
│ PRMAINT 5.00              Maintain Employees       COMPANY ID: BB      │
│ 06/01/90                  Big Business, Inc.        GENERATION #: 00    │
└──────────────────────────────────────────────────────────────────────┘

   DEPARTMENT..: 0      EMPLOYEE CODE..: 106      TITLE..: PERSONAL INFORMATION
                                                  PROCESSING STATUS...: NW
   NAME............: Bill T. Jones
   ADDRESS.........: 4 Cherry Lane
   ADDRESS.........:
   CITY,STATE......: Endwell, NY
   ZIP CODE........: 13760
   SOC. SEC. NO....: 111-22-3333
   PHONE...........: 555-1212
   COMMENT.........:
   STATUS (A/I)....: A
   DATE EMPLOYED...: 06/01/90
   DATE TERMINATED.: 01/01/00
   LAST CHECK DATE.: 01/01/00
   LAST CHECK NO...:      0
   LAST CHECK AMOUNT:     0.00

                           ACCEPT (Y/N): Y
                           ▐ F8 - Undo ▌
```

FIGURE 8-8   The Personal Information screen

ACTIVE/INACTIVE STATUS   Peachtree Complete III processes payroll for active employees only. Note that you cannot change the status of an employee directly. If you wish to change an employee's status to inactive, you must terminate that employee. Peachtree Complete III will then change her or his status for you.

DATE EMPLOYED/TERMINATED   The Date Employed field shows the date on which the employee was first hired for work. Peachtree Complete III reports this date on the 941A State Wage Report for the first quarter of employment. The date also appears on the Employee File List. While an employee is active, the date in the Date Terminated field should be 01/01/00. If the employee is currently terminated, enter the date now.

LAST CHECK DATE, NUMBER, AMOUNT   In the Last Check Date, Last Check No, and Last Check Amount fields, enter the date, number, and amount of the last paycheck issued to this employee. If the employee is new, you can accept the default dates supplied by Peachtree Complete III. In either case, the values in these fields will be automatically updated every time you generate a payroll.

Rates and Flags

The Rates and Flags screen (Figure 8-9) contains a broad variety of information required when generating a payroll. Among other things, it includes the status of the employee, the shift worked, and deferred deductions.

STATUTORY EMPLOYEE   The pay of a statutory employee is subject to FICA withholding but not to federal income tax withholding. This status will be indicated on the employee's W-2 form.

```
┌─────────────────────────────────────────────────────────────────────────┐
│PRMAINT 5.00                   Maintain Employees         COMPANY ID: BB   │
│06/01/90                       Big Business, Inc.         GENERATION #: 00  │
└─────────────────────────────────────────────────────────────────────────┘

DEPARTMENT..:  0      EMPLOYEE CODE..: 106       TITLE..: RATES & FLAGS
                                                 PROCESSING STATUS...: NW
STATUTORY EMPLOYEE..: N              CUR. DEFER. DEDUCTIONS.:        0.00
DECEASED............: N              YTD. DEFER. DEDUCTIONS.:        0.00
TIPPED EMPLOYEE.....: N              CUR. ALLOC. DEDUCTIONS.:        0.00
LEGAL REP...........: N              COST OF GROUP TERM LIFE
942 EMPLOYEE........: N                         OVER $50000:        0.00
EIC STATUS..........: N              FICA TAKEN ON TERM LIFE:  N
SHIFT CODE..........: 1              STANDARD WORK WEEK.....:       40.00
PAY PERIOD..........: M              STANDARD OUT. 1 HOURS..:        0.00
PAY TYPE............: S              STANDARD OUT. 2 HOURS..:        0.00
PAY RATE/SALARY/DRAW:      0.000     PENSION................:  N
COMMISSION RATE %...:    0.00        DEFERRED COMPENSATION..:  N
MAXIMUM CHECK AMOUNT:      0.00      SUTA TAXABLE...........:  Y
FED. FILING STATUS..: M              INDUSTRIAL INSURANCE %.:        0.00
FED. EXEMPTIONS.....:  1
ADDL. FED. TAX......:      0.00

                          ACCEPT (Y/N): Y
                          ▀▀▀▀▀▀▀▀▀▀▀▀▀▀
                           F8 - Undo
```

FIGURE 8-9   The Rates and Flags screen

DECEASED The IRS requires businesses to indicate an employee's death on the W-2 form. When an employee dies, change this field from N to Y.

TIPPED EMPLOYEE If this employee receives tips, you must inform the IRS. In such cases, you have to report the amount of allocated tips—the difference between the amount of tips reported by the employee and the IRS's minimum of 8% of gross sales.

LEGAL REP Enter a **Y** in the Legal Rep field if the employee is a minor. This information is reported on the W-2 form.

942 EMPLOYEE Household workers, among others, are classified as 942 status. If an employee falls into this category, you must report the status on her or his W-2 form. Earnings from 942 employees are not included in the 941 worksheet or on the 941A report.

EIC STATUS Some employees qualify for an earned income credit (EIC). You can enter one of three codes here: Enter **N** if the employee is not eligible for EIC payment; enter **U** if the employee is eligible and files one W-5 form; or enter **T** if the employee is eligible and files two W-5 forms.

SHIFT CODE In the Shift Code field enter the shift this employee will be working—1, 2, or 3. Employees who work shift 2 or 3 earn a differential over their base pay.

PAY PERIOD The Pay Period field indicates how frequently an employee is paid. Enter **W** for weekly, **B** for biweekly, **S** for semimonthly, or **M** for monthly.

PAY TYPE   An employee falls into one of four pay categories: H stands for hourly, S stands for salary, D stands for draw, and C stands for commission. An employee who earns a commission may also earn a salary.

PAY RATE/SALARY/DRAW   In the Pay Rate/Salary/Draw field, enter either the employee's annual salary (for salaried or commissioned employees), the employee's hourly pay (for hourly employees), or the employee's annual total draw (for those being paid by draw). If the employee earns a straight commission, enter a zero here. Peachtree Complete III uses this number to calculate an employee's pay.

COMMISSION RATE %   If the employee is paid by commission or draw, enter the percentage of sales that the employee receives in the Commission Rate % field.

MAXIMUM CHECK AMOUNT   If you enter an amount in the Maximum Check Amount field, Payroll will notify you if the employee's check exceeds this amount. If you do not want to be warned, enter a zero.

FEDERAL FILING STATUS   Peachtree Complete III provides the following codes to indicate the employee's federal filing status:

M   Married

S   Single

*   Statutory or no federal withholding

!   No FICA or federal withholding

Married with federal withholding but not FICA withholding

@   Single with federal withholding but not FICA withholding

&   No withholding for federal income tax, FICA, or FUTA

In the Fed. Filing Status field, enter the correct code for this employee.

FEDERAL EXEMPTIONS   An employee can declare from 0 to 99 exemptions from withholding. In the Fed. Exemptions field, enter the number claimed by this employee.

ADDITIONAL FEDERAL TAX   In the Add. Fed. Tax field, enter the additional amount, if any, to be withheld from an employee's pay.

DEFERRED AND ALLOCATED DEDUCTIONS   Under certain circumstances, an employee's pay may be insufficient to cover all deductions. The Peachtree Complete III Payroll module allows you to defer these deductions. The Current Deferred Deduction field contains the amount of deferred deductions from the most recent pay period. The YTD Deferred Deductions field contains the sum of deferred deductions for the current year. The Current Allocated Deductions field contains the amount that will be taken out of the employee's next paycheck, reducing the employee's year-to-date deferred deductions.

COST OF GROUP TERM LIFE OVER $50,000   The Internal Revenue Service requires companies to report the cost of company-paid group term life insurance in excess of $50,000 per year. In this field, enter the amount in excess of $50,000 that your company will pay for this employee's life insurance.

FICA TAKEN ON TERM LIFE   At some point in the year, you must use the Enter Exceptions program to calculate the FICA on the amount you paid for group term life over $50,000 for individual employees. When you do this, Peachtree Complete III changes the value in this field from N to Y.

STANDARD WORK WEEK AND OVERTIME   The Standard Work Week field and the two overtime fields let you enter the standard hours you expect this employee to work from week to week. Hours worked in the standard work week are paid at the employee's base rate. Hours worked in Ovt.1 or Ovt. 2 (overtime) are paid at the rates you set using the Maintain Payroll option.

PENSION AND DEFERRED COMPENSATION   If this employee participates in a pension plan or receives deferred compensation, note this by entering a **Y** in the appropriate field. This information will be reported to the IRS on the W-2 form.

SUTA TAXABLE   If this employee's income is subject to SUTA, (state unemployment tax) enter a **Y** in the SUTA Taxable field. If this field contains a Y and you assigned a SUTA tax rate for this employee's state tax code, Peachtree Complete III will compute SUTA when you generate a payroll.

INDUSTRIAL INSURANCE %   If your state requires your company to pay an industrial insurance tax, enter in the Industrial Insurance % field the percentage required to compute the correct amount of this tax. The percentage you enter in this field is multiplied by the number of hours worked by the employee.

Tax Code Screen

In addition to federal taxes, you must set up your payroll for state and local taxes. You do this at the Tax Code screen (Figure 8-10). In this screen, you can specify up to four tax codes for an employee. These can include tax codes for state, county, and city taxes as well as garnishments.

TAX CODE   In the Tax Code field, enter a two-letter state tax code or any of the special tax codes that you set up for local taxes and garnishments. If you will use a tax code for garnishment, be sure to enter that code last.

FILING STATUS   To compute state taxes correctly, Peachtree Complete III must know the employee's filing status. Unfortu-

```
┌─────────────────────────────────────────────────────────────────────┐
│ PRMAINT 5.00              Maintain Employees          COMPANY ID: BB  │
│ 06/01/90                  Big Business, Inc.          GENERATION #: 00 │
└─────────────────────────────────────────────────────────────────────┘

  DEPARTMENT..:  0    EMPLOYEE CODE..: 106      TITLE..: TAX CODE
                                                PROCESSING STATUS...: NW
    TAX          FILING                MISC. TAX   ADDIT.    MISC.
    CODE.........STATUS.....EXEMPTIONS.....FACTOR.......TAX........TAX AMOUNT
  1. 0                      0             0.00        0.00        0.00
  2. 0                      0             0.00        0.00        0.00
  3. 0                      0             0.00        0.00        0.00
  4. 0                      0             0.00        0.00        0.00

                                          TAXABLE (Y/N)
                                      WITHHOLDING  UNEMPLOYMENT

  DEDUCTIONS............AMOUNT......CEILING.
    1.INSUR.   DED. A      0.00
    2.401k     DED. A      0.00
    3.EMP LOAN DED. A      0.00
    4.SAVINGS  DED. P      0.00
    5.FIVE     DED. P      0.00
    6.SIX      DED. P      0.00
                                   ACCEPT (Y/N): Y
                                   ███ F8 – Undo ███
```

═══ **FIGURE 8-10**   The Tax Code screen

nately, filing status codes differ from state to state. For example, in Wisconsin (tax code WI) the filing statuses are A for single and B for married. In Oklahoma (tax code OK), however, the filing statuses are A for single, D for married or head of household, and P for married both working (optional). Some states do not have filing statuses, in which case you will leave this field blank. To determine the correct code for your employee, check Appendix B in the "Using Payroll" manual accompanying your software.

EXEMPTIONS   For each tax code, you must enter the number of exemptions claimed by the employee. When calculating amounts to withhold from pay, Peachtree Complete III multiplies the number of exemptions by the amount per exemption that you entered earlier.

MISCELLANEOUS TAX FACTOR   Certain states allow for a special calculation, called a *miscellaneous tax factor,* that affects an employee's withholding. For example, if your company is in Maryland and you wish to compute state and local taxes simultaneously, you simply take the percentage used for local taxes, for example 30%, add 100, and enter the total (130) as a miscellaneous tax factor. In short, local taxes are computed as 30% of state taxes. Only a few states have a miscellaneous tax factor; check your manual's Appendix B to see if your state has one.

ADDITIONAL TAX   For each tax code, you can specify an amount to be withheld from an employee's pay. Enter that amount, if any, in the Addit. Tax field.

MISCELLANEOUS TAX AMOUNT   In some states, the employer must withhold an amount from an employee's pay as a miscellaneous item. For example, in Missouri, the employer must withhold the amount found on line 6 of the Missouri W-4 statement. You would enter the amount on line 6 into the Misc. Tax

Amount field and Peachtree Complete III would deduct it from the employee's pay every pay period.

DEDUCTIONS Peachtree Complete III allows you to specify up to six automatic deductions from an employee's pay. There are many reasons for deductions, including insurance, payment on employee loans, 401k plans, and savings plans. You already defined your company's miscellaneous deductions using Maintain Payroll Options. Now, as you add and update employees, you must specify the amount to deduct and the maximum annual amount for each type of deduction.

TAXABILITY OF WITHHOLDING AND UNEMPLOYMENT
Peachtree Complete III needs to know whether to take deductions before or after it computes withholding and unemployment tax. For example, if deductions are taken on an after-tax basis, you should enter a **Y** under Withholding, and Peachtree Complete III will compute the amount to withhold before subtracting deductions. Likewise, if you set Unemployment to Y, the program computes the unemployment tax liability before making deductions.

MISCELLANEOUS INCOME SCREEN

Figure 8-11 contains information about miscellaneous income, sick hours, and vacation hours.

Miscellaneous Income: Amount and Ceiling

When you set up your payroll, you were allowed to define a number of miscellaneous income categories. For each employee, you must identify the amount (either in dollars or in a percentage) of the miscellaneous income she or he will receive as well as any

```
╔══════════════════════════════════════════════════════════════════════════╗
║ PRMAINT 5.00               Maintain Employees        COMPANY ID: BB        ║
║ 06/01/90                   Big Business, Inc.        GENERATION #: 00      ║
╚══════════════════════════════════════════════════════════════════════════╝

DEPARTMENT..: 0       EMPLOYEE CODE..: 106      TITLE..: MISC. INCOME
                                                PROCESSING STATUS...: NW
MISC. INCOME........AMOUNT......CEILING.
  1. MISC. #1 P          0.00 CO. DEFAULT
  2. MISC. #2 A          0.00 CO. DEFAULT
  3. MISC. #3 A          0.00 CO. DEFAULT

ACCRUE SICK HOURS BY HOURS WORKED...: N
SICK HOURS PER YEAR.................:      40.00
HOURS REQUIRED TO ACCRUE 1 SICK HOUR:
YTD SICK HOURS ACCRUED..............:       0.00
YTD SICK HOURS USED.................:       0.00
ACCRUE VAC. HOURS BY HOURS WORKED...: N
VACATION HOURS PER YEAR.............:      80.00
HOURS REQUIRED TO ACCRUE 1 VAC. HOUR:
YTD VACATION HOURS ACCRUED..........:       0.00
YTD VACATION HOURS USED.............:       0.00
UNION CONTRACT ENDING DATE..........: 01/01/00
                                     ACCEPT (Y/N): Y
                                     [ F8 - Undo ]
```

FIGURE 8-11   The Miscellaneous Income screen

applicable ceiling on each type of income. Note that the amounts you enter here are default amounts—you can change these amounts each pay period by using Enter Exceptions.

If the miscellaneous income is paid as a flat amount per year, you must enter the total annual amount and Peachtree Complete III will compute the correct fraction of that amount each pay period.

Accrue Sick Hours/Vacation Hours by Hours Worked

Hourly employees can accrue sick hours and vacation hours based on either the number of hours they work each pay period or a fixed number of hours per year. If you select a fixed number of hours, you must also define the number of hours that the employee has to work in order to earn one sick or vacation hour. Note that only hourly workers can earn sick hours and vacation hours by the number of hours they work.

Sick Hours/Vacation Hours per Year

If the employee earns a set number of sick hours and vacation hours per year, you must define the total number of hours that she or he can accrue in one year. The defaults are 80 hours of vacation and 40 hours of sick leave. Whatever numbers you use, Peachtree Complete III will divide them by the number of pay periods and accrue the correct amount.

Hours Required to Accrue
1 Sick Hour/Vacation Hour

If the employee earns sick hours and vacation hours by the number of hours worked, you must define the number of hours that the employee has to work to earn one sick hour and one vacation hour.

YTD Sick Hours/Vacation Hours Accrued

The YTD Sick Hours Accrued and YTD Vacation Hours Accrued fields contain the number of sick hours and vacation hours the employee has accrued during the year. For new employees, you don't need to enter a number in this field, since they will have accrued no hours at the time you set them up. If you are adding an existing employee, however, you should enter the number of hours he or she has accrued so far.

YTD Sick Hours/Vacation Hours Used

The YTD Sick Hours Used and YTD Vacation Hours Used fields contain the number of sick hours and vacation hours the employee has used during the current year. If an employee uses sick hours or vacation hours during a pay period, use Enter Exceptions to record the number of hours used. Peachtree Complete III will then automatically update the contents of these fields with the additional hours.

Union Contract Ending Date

Often, a company's contract with a union will stipulate that, on the date that the union's contract expires, union employees will lose any accrued sick hours or vacation hours they have accrued but

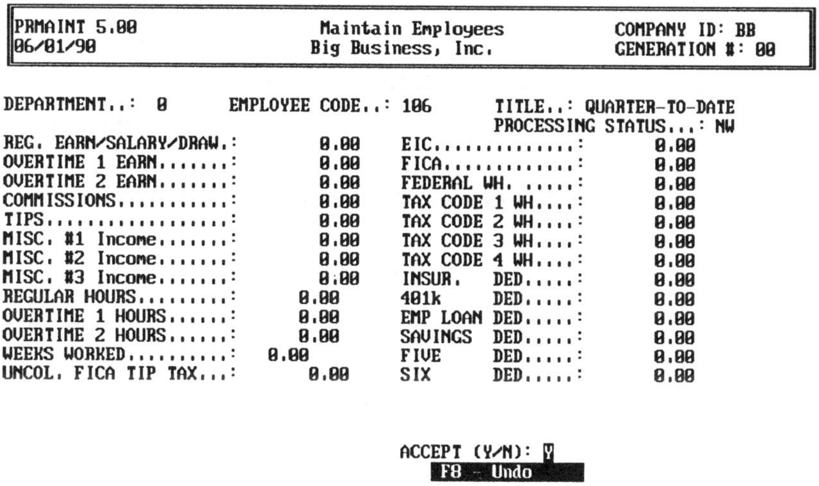

```
PRMAINT 5.00                    Maintain Employees          COMPANY ID: BB
06/01/90                        Big Business, Inc.          GENERATION #: 00


DEPARTMENT..:  0      EMPLOYEE CODE..: 106      TITLE..: QUARTER-TO-DATE
                                                PROCESSING STATUS...: NW
REG. EARN/SALARY/DRAW.:       0.00   EIC.............:        0.00
OVERTIME 1 EARN.......:       0.00   FICA............:        0.00
OVERTIME 2 EARN.......:       0.00   FEDERAL WH. ....:        0.00
COMMISSIONS...........:       0.00   TAX CODE 1 WH...:        0.00
TIPS.................:        0.00   TAX CODE 2 WH...:        0.00
MISC. #1 Income......:        0.00   TAX CODE 3 WH...:        0.00
MISC. #2 Income......:        0.00   TAX CODE 4 WH...:        0.00
MISC. #3 Income......:        0.00   INSUR.  DED.....:        0.00
REGULAR HOURS........:        0.00   401k    DED.....:        0.00
OVERTIME 1 HOURS.....:        0.00   EMP LOAN DED....:        0.00
OVERTIME 2 HOURS.....:        0.00   SAVINGS DED.....:        0.00
WEEKS WORKED.........:    0.00       FIVE    DED.....:        0.00
UNCOL. FICA TIP TAX..:        0.00   SIX     DED.....:        0.00


                              ACCEPT (Y/N): Y
                              F8 - Undo
```

FIGURE 8-12 The Quarter-to-Date screen

not used. You may have other reasons for setting a date on which accrued but unused sick and vacation hours are erased. In either case, enter the appropriate date in the Union Contract Ending Date field. When generating a payroll, Peachtree Complete III will look to see if the date falls within the current pay period. If it does, the program will set accrued sick hours and accrued vacation hours to zero.

QUARTER-TO-DATE AND YEAR-TO-DATE

Peachtree Complete III automatically keeps track of quarter-to-date (QTD) and year-to-date (YTD) information on each employee. You can see this information on the QTD and YTD screens. If you are adding new employees to the system, you don't need to enter any values in these screens. If you are adding a current employee, you will have to enter correct QTD and YTD information to get them started.

Figure 8-12 shows a typical quarter-to-date screen for a new employee. The screen displays all relevant payroll information including regular earnings, overtime earnings (broken out by type), commissions and tips, miscellaneous income, FICA, EIC, and federal withholding. In short, you have a snapshot work record for every employee in your firm.

chapter **9**

GENERATING PAYROLL

By now, you have set up Peachtree Complete III's Payroll module and entered information on all of your employees. Now it's time to generate a payroll. It may seem as though you've been doing a lot of work, but the payoff is near. Peachtree Complete III is ready to generate accurate and timely payrolls, week after week, with only minor work for you.

THE PAYROLL PROCESS

Generating a payroll is easy as long as you follow a step-by-step approach. If you have been doing your payroll manually, the process will probably make a lot of sense. If not, it's easy to learn.

To create a payroll, Peachtree Complete III needs to know who worked and how much they worked. The employee records that you entered indicate who worked. To find out how much each employee worked, Peachtree Complete III must get information from a number of sources, including the Job Cost module. Finally, you need to enter any exceptions, verify that everything is okay, and print the checks.

UPDATE EMPLOYEE INFORMATION

Keeping employee information up to date is crucial to creating an accurate payroll. While this is an important task, it is not one that you will do every day or even every week. The Payroll module will be affected when new employees are hired, existing employees are terminated, employees receive raises, or employees are assigned to different departments. It's also affected by changes in filing status and exemptions, or changes of address.

Maintaining employee information is not particularly difficult, especially if your company is small. Whether your company is large or small, however, be sure to make all updates to employee information before generating a payroll.

UPDATE FROM JOB COST

If you are using the Peachtree Complete III Job Cost module to keep track of workers' hours, you can transfer that information directly into Payroll. If you do not use the Job Cost module, you might want to consider doing so. Using Job Cost will help you track a project's cost against budgeted costs. This is an invaluable management tool that protects you against cost overruns. Transferring information directly from Job Cost to Payroll also eliminates errors. The information in Payroll will match the information in Job Cost exactly.

If you are using Peachtree Complete III's Job Cost module, you must do two things before generating a payroll. First, you must go into Job Cost and run Update To Payroll, which stores current Job Cost payroll information in a temporary file. Next, in Payroll, use Update From Job Cost to read the information from the temporary file.

ENTER TIME CARD HOURS

Many companies employ workers who are paid by the hour. Hourly employees typically punch a time clock when they arrive and when they leave work. You then must collect the cards and compute the hours from the time stamps. Fortunately, Peachtree Complete III eliminates this drudgery and ensures complete accuracy.

To record an employee's hours, select the Paymaster Worksheet/Time Card option from the Payroll Processing Menu (Figure 9-1) and then select Calculate Time Card Hours (Figure 9-2).

To record employee time information, you need to enter two items of information: the time the employee clocked in and the time he or she clocked out. If the employee clocks out for lunch, you have to make two entries for that day. Figure 9-3 shows the hours worked by an employee of Big Business, Inc. The first entry shows the employee punching in at 9:00 A.M. and punching out at 12:00 P.M. for lunch. Peachtree Complete III computes the elapsed time of three hours. After lunch, the employee clocked in at 13.00 and clocked out at the end of the day at 17.00. The Payroll options

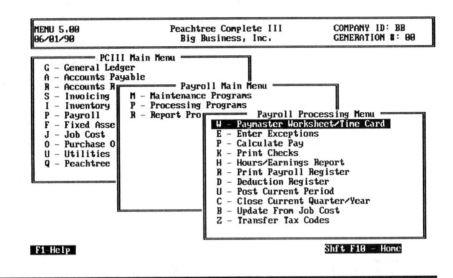

FIGURE 9-1 Selecting Paymaster Worksheet/Time Card

FIGURE 9-2 Selecting Calculate Time Card Hours

were set up to accept military time with fractions of an hour. Therefore, the entry 16.50 on line 4 translates to 4:30 P.M. At the right, Peachtree Complete III keeps a running total of the number of regular and overtime hours worked. The employee in the example worked 30.75 hours for the week.

As you enter an employee's hours, you must identify the type of hours worked: Regular pay is denoted by an R while first and second shift hours are denoted by a 1 or 2 respectively. In the example, all hours are regular hours. If the employee worked any overtime, you must enter those hours on separate lines.

ENTER HOURS DIRECTLY

Many hourly employees keep track of their hours without a punch clock—they simply record the number of hours worked. You can

```
┌─────────────────────────────────────────────────────────────────────────┐
│ PRPROC1 5.00          Paymaster Worksheet/Time Card     COMPANY ID: BB    │
│ 06/01/90                    Big Business, Inc.          GENERATION #: 00   │
└─────────────────────────────────────────────────────────────────────────┘

 DEPARTMENT...:  0  EMPLOYEE...: 104
 EMPLOYEE NAME...: Nancy Billings              TIME CARD HOURS ON FILE
                                               REGULAR    OUT1    OUT2
                                                 0.00     0.00    0.00
 TIME ENTRIES
 NO.....IN.....OUT.....HOURS.....TYPE (R/1/2).....TOTAL HOURS...
  1.    9.00  12.00     3.00       R             REGULAR.......:   30.75
  2.   13.00  17.00     4.00       R             OUT. 1........:    0.00
  3.    9.00  12.00     3.00       R             OUT. 2........:    0.00
  4.   13.00  16.50     3.50       R
  5.    9.00  12.00     3.00       R
  6.   13.00  17.00     4.00       R
  7.    9.00  12.00     3.00       R
  8.   13.00  17.00     4.00       R
  9.    9.00  12.25     3.25       R
 10.   13.00  17.00     4.00       R

   F1-Help                        F10 - Done
```

FIGURE 9-3 An employee's time card

enter this information by using either Calculate Time Card Hours or Enter Exceptions. To use Calculate Time Card Hours, simply leave the IN field blank and enter the number of hours worked in the OUT field. To enter hours directly you must have the Use 24 Hour Time Clock option set to **Y**.

ENTER PAYROLL EXCEPTIONS

Generating payroll is not a neat business. Exceptions can crop up for any number of reasons, including employees who work non-standard hours or earn nonstandard overtime pay rates, commissions, tips, and take vacation or sick hours. The Enter Exceptions option lets you change, add, or override payroll information that deviates from the norm.

Enter Exceptions

You will use Enter Exceptions when you want to alter or add data concerning an employee's pay. Entering pay information as exceptions overrides the information that you entered in Maintain Payroll Options, Maintain Employees, and Calculate Time Card Hours. Entering erroneous exceptions could wreak havoc on your accounting process, so take special care that all of your entries are correct.

To enter exceptions, select Enter Exceptions from the Payroll Processing Menu (Figure 9-4). Peachtree Complete III will present you with two choices: Enter Exceptions or List Transaction File. Select Enter Exceptions.

Next, you will be asked to identify the pay cycles and pay types for which you want to enter exceptions (Figure 9-5). Change the **N** to **Y** for each type you will be using. You can select all of them if you are not sure which to select. Finally, Peachtree Complete III

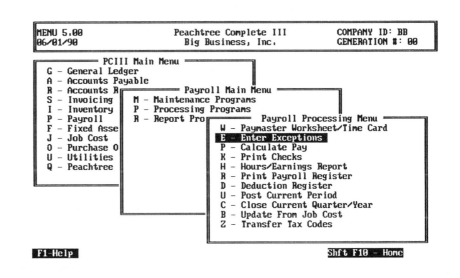

```
MENU 5.00                      Peachtree Complete III          COMPANY ID: BB
06/01/90                         Big Business, Inc.            GENERATION #: 00

         ═══ PCIII Main Menu ═══
    G - General Ledger
    A - Accounts Payable
    R - Accounts R ┌──── Payroll Main Menu ────┐
    S - Invoicing  │ M - Maintenance Programs   │
    I - Inventory  │ P - Processing Programs     │
    P - Payroll    │ R - Report Pro ┌──── Payroll Processing Menu ────┐
    F - Fixed Asse │              │ W - Paymaster Worksheet/Time Card │
    J - Job Cost   │              │ █E - Enter Exceptions█             │
    O - Purchase O │              │ P - Calculate Pay                  │
    U - Utilities  │              │ K - Print Checks                   │
    Q - Peachtree  │              │ H - Hours/Earnings Report          │
                   │              │ R - Print Payroll Register         │
                   │              │ D - Deduction Register             │
                   │              │ U - Post Current Period            │
                   │              │ C - Close Current Quarter/Year     │
                   │              │ B - Update From Job Cost           │
                   │              │ Z - Transfer Tax Codes             │

 F1-Help                                                Shft F10 - Home
```

══ **FIGURE 9-4** Selecting Enter Exceptions

```
PRPROC1 5.00                       Enter Exceptions            COMPANY ID: BB
06/01/90                         Big Business, Inc.            GENERATION #: 00




   INCLUDE PAY CYCLES:   WEEKLY.......: Y
                         BI-WEEKLY...: N
                         SEMI-MONTHLY: N
                         MONTHLY.....: N


   INCLUDE PAY TYPES.:   HOURLY......: N
                         SALARIED....: N
                         DRAW........: N
                         COMMISSION..: N




 F1-Help                              F10 - Done
```

══ **FIGURE 9-5** Selecting Pay Cycles and Pay Types

will ask you to identify the departments for which you will be entering exceptions. You can select all departments or a range of departments. You can also select individual employees manually.

You are now ready to begin entering exceptions. Peachtree Complete III will call up the first employee for the first department selected (Figure 9-6). If you have no exceptions for this individual, type **N** and press **(ENTER)**. If you do wish to make some exception entries, simply press **(ENTER)**. Notice that you can also type an asterisk at this point to exclude this employee from the current pay period.

The employee, whose information is shown in Figure 9-7, is salaried. For salaried employees, exceptions you can enter include a different salary amount and different General Ledger accounts for posting (along with the amount of pay to be allocated to each account).

```
PRPROC1 5.00                Enter Exceptions           COMPANY ID: BB
06/01/90                    Big Business, Inc.          GENERATION #: 00

DEPT:  0                                       PAY PERIOD: MONTHLY
EMPLOYEE: 106    NAME: Bill T. Jones           PAY TYPE: SALARY




ACCEPT (Y/N): Y  ('*' TO EXCLUDE FROM CURRENT PAY RUN)
                         F8 - Undo
```

FIGURE 9-6 Selecting an employee

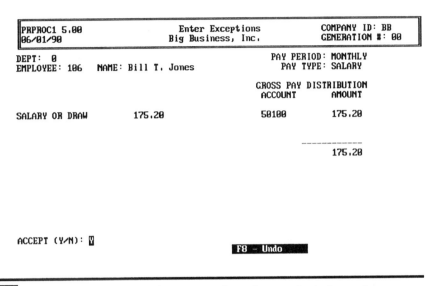

```
┌────────────────────────────────────────────────────────────────────────┐
│ PRPROC1 5.00              Enter Exceptions           COMPANY ID: BB      │
│ 06/01/90                  Big Business, Inc.          GENERATION #: 00    │
└────────────────────────────────────────────────────────────────────────┘
DEPT:  0                                     PAY PERIOD: MONTHLY
EMPLOYEE: 106   NAME: Bill T. Jones            PAY TYPE: SALARY

                                           GROSS PAY DISTRIBUTION
                                           ACCOUNT       AMOUNT

SALARY OR DRAW           175.20             50100        175.20


                                                        ------------
                                                        175.20




ACCEPT (Y/N): Y
                                    ┌──────────────┐
                                    │ F8 -- Undo   │
                                    └──────────────┘
```

FIGURE 9-7   Entering exceptions for a salaried employee

Hourly employees are treated differently from salaried employees. Figure 9-8 shows the exception screen for an hourly employee. You can enter the hours worked, the hourly pay rate, the type of hours worked (regular or overtime), shift differentials, and the General Ledger account used for posting employee pay. In Figure 9-8, a single line was entered showing that the employee worked 40 hours, that the pay rate is $5.00 per hour, and that the hours were regular but were worked on the second shift, resulting in an effective hourly rate of $5.50 per hour. The employee's pay will be posted to General Ledger account 50100. Notice that this differs from the number of hours entered on the time card in Figure 9-3. This conflicts with the 40 hours entered as an exception. In a case such as this, the exception will override the information contained on the time card.

If you have employees who are paid a draw or a commission, you use Enter Exceptions to enter their sales, which will be used

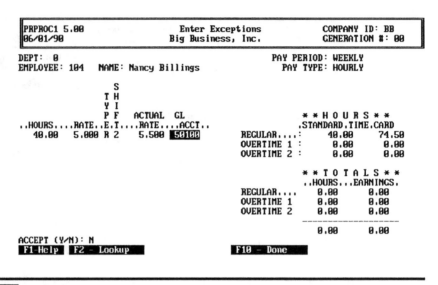

```
┌─────────────────────────────────────────────────────────────────────────┐
│PRPROC1 5.00              Enter Exceptions           COMPANY ID: BB        │
│06/01/90                  Big Business, Inc.         GENERATION #: 00       │
└─────────────────────────────────────────────────────────────────────────┘
DEPT:  0                                    PAY PERIOD: WEEKLY
EMPLOYEE: 104   NAME: Nancy Billings          PAY TYPE: HOURLY

               S
             T H
             Y I
             P F    ACTUAL  GL                    * * H O U R S * *
  ..HOURS....RATE..E.T....RATE....ACCT..        .STANDARD.TIME.CARD
    40.00   5.000 R 2    5.500 50100      REGULAR....:    40.00    74.50
                                          OVERTIME 1 :     0.00     0.00
                                          OVERTIME 2 :     0.00     0.00

                                                  * * T O T A L S * *
                                                 ..HOURS...EARNINGS.
                                          REGULAR....     0.00     0.00
                                          OVERTIME 1      0.00     0.00
                                          OVERTIME 2      0.00     0.00
                                                         ──────────────────
                                                          0.00     0.00

ACCEPT (Y/N): N
 F1-Help   F2 - Lookup              F10 - Done
```

FIGURE 9-8   Entering exceptions for an hourly employee

to compute the commission. For each sale, you can also specify a commission rate.

After you have entered your payroll exceptions, Peachtree Complete III lets you choose from five other types of exceptions: Miscellaneous Income, Change Deductions, Vacation or Sick Hours, Enter Taxes, and FICA on Group Term Life (Figure 9-9).

Miscellaneous Income

Miscellaneous income exceptions include tips, earned income credits, and other types of miscellaneous income. Figure 9-10 shows the screen you will use to enter these types of transactions. You simply enter the amount of the miscellaneous income. As always, the amounts you enter here will override the standard amounts you entered in Maintain Employees. A zero in any field

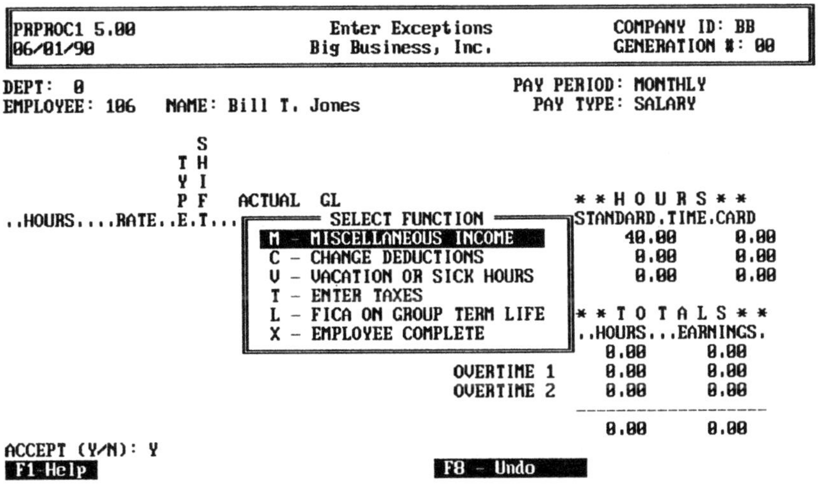

```
┌─────────────────────────────────────────────────────────────────────┐
│ PRPROC1 5.00              Enter Exceptions          COMPANY ID: BB    │
│ 06/01/90                  Big Business, Inc.         GENERATION #: 00  │
└─────────────────────────────────────────────────────────────────────┘

DEPT:  0                                    PAY PERIOD: MONTHLY
EMPLOYEE: 106    NAME: Bill T. Jones        PAY TYPE: SALARY

                    S
                    T H
                    Y I
                    P F   ACTUAL  GL                   * * H O U R S * *
  ..HOURS....RATE..E.T... ┌──────── SELECT FUNCTION ────────┐ STANDARD.TIME.CARD
                          │ M - MISCELLANEOUS INCOME          │   40.00      0.00
                          │ C - CHANGE DEDUCTIONS             │    0.00      0.00
                          │ V - VACATION OR SICK HOURS        │    0.00      0.00
                          │ T - ENTER TAXES                  │
                          │ L - FICA ON GROUP TERM LIFE      │ * * T O T A L S * *
                          │ X - EMPLOYEE COMPLETE            │ ..HOURS...EARNINGS.
                          └─────────────────────────────────┘    0.00      0.00
                                          OVERTIME 1            0.00      0.00
                                          OVERTIME 2            0.00      0.00
                                                             ─────────────────────
                                                                0.00      0.00

ACCEPT (Y/N): Y
 F1-Help                              F8 - Undo
```

FIGURE 9-9 Exception menu

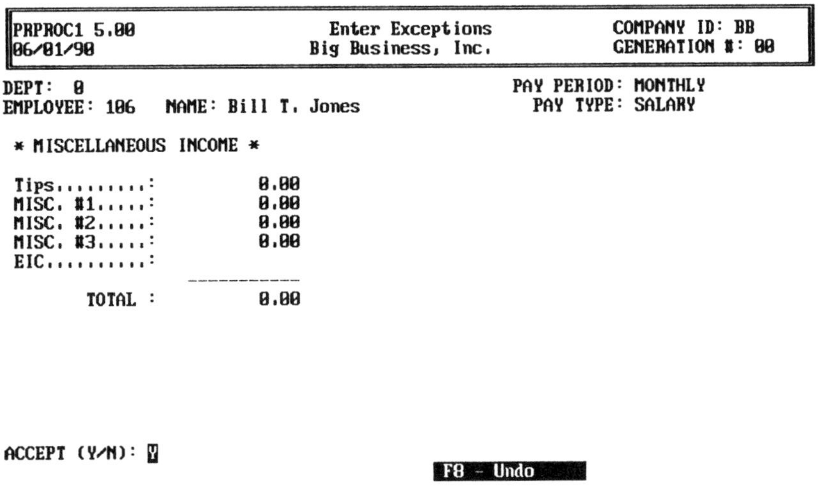

```
┌─────────────────────────────────────────────────────────────────────┐
│ PRPROC1 5.00              Enter Exceptions          COMPANY ID: BB    │
│ 06/01/90                  Big Business, Inc.         GENERATION #: 00  │
└─────────────────────────────────────────────────────────────────────┘

DEPT:  0                                    PAY PERIOD: MONTHLY
EMPLOYEE: 106    NAME: Bill T. Jones        PAY TYPE: SALARY

 * MISCELLANEOUS INCOME *

Tips.........:        0.00
MISC. #1.....:        0.00
MISC. #2.....:        0.00
MISC. #3.....:        0.00
EIC..........:
                   ───────────
        TOTAL :        0.00




ACCEPT (Y/N): Y                       F8 - Undo
```

FIGURE 9-10 Miscellaneous income exceptions

tells Peachtree Complete III to pay the employee the standard amount. If you enter a **–1** in a field, the program will not pay the employee anything for that type of miscellaneous income.

Change Deductions

Peachtree Complete III lets you change miscellaneous deductions for an employee (Figure 9-11). While you can change the amount of the deduction, you cannot change the withholding calculation method here (you would do that in Maintain Payroll Options). As with miscellaneous income, entering a zero causes the standard deduction amount to be used and entering a **–1** eliminates the deduction for the current pay period.

```
┌─────────────────────────────────────────────────────────────────────┐
│ PRPROC1 5.00                Enter Exceptions         COMPANY ID: BB   │
│ 06/01/90                    Big Business, Inc.       GENERATION #: 00 │
└─────────────────────────────────────────────────────────────────────┘
DEPT:  0                                      PAY PERIOD: MONTHLY
EMPLOYEE: 106    NAME: Bill T. Jones          PAY TYPE: SALARY
**DEDUCTIONS**
                      BEFORE      AMOUNT
.DESCRIPTION.....AFTER.TAX../PCT.....AMOUNT..
INSUR.........:     A          A        0.00
COFFEE........:     A          A        0.00
PENSION.......:     A          A        0.00
SAVINGS.......:     A          P        0.00
FIVE..........:     A          P        0.00
SIX...........:     A          P        0.00




ACCEPT (Y/N): Y
                                      ▉ F8 - Undo ▉
```

═══════ **FIGURE 9-11**   Changing deductions

Vacation or Sick Hours

You must enter your employees' vacation and sick days into Peachtree Complete III as exception entries. Using the screen shown in Figure 9-12, you simply enter the number of vacation or sick hours the employee has taken. At the same time, the program displays the number of vacation and sick hours used and accrued.

Enter Taxes

You can make tax exceptions for FICA, federal, state, and customized tax codes. For each, you can select either **C** or **R**. Selecting **C** tells Peachtree Complete III to compute the payroll tax for you, while selecting **R** forces the program to use an amount that you enter here. If you select **R**, be careful about the amount you enter.

```
PRPROC1 5.00                    Enter Exceptions          COMPANY ID: BB
06/01/90                       Big Business, Inc,         GENERATION #: 00

DEPT:  0                                          PAY PERIOD: MONTHLY
EMPLOYEE: 106   NAME: Bill T, Jones               PAY TYPE: SALARY
* * D E D U C T I O N S * *
* * SICK - VACATION   HOURS * *

               , ,HOURS,USED, , ,HRS,ACCRUED, , , ,HOURS,TAKEN, ,
     SICK,,,,,:       0,00          0,00          0,00
     VACATION,:       0,00          0,00          0,00




ACCEPT (Y/N): Y
                                        F8 - Undo
```

══ **FIGURE 9-12**   Vacation or sick hours

If you enter zero, Peachtree Complete III will compute the payroll tax as it normally would. If you enter a negative number, however, the program treats the amount as a tax refund.

FICA on Group Term Life

If your company pays for group term life insurance for an employee and the coverage exceeds $50,000, the employee must pay tax on the cost of the insurance for the amount that exceeds $50,000. This calculation is performed just once a year. If you wish to perform this calculation, enter a **Y** in the field shown in Figure 9-13.

When you have finished entering exceptions for an employee and you are sure that the entries are correct, type **X** at the Select Function Menu to save the changes. If, however, you want to clear the changes you made, use the (F8) key: This resets all exception information you have entered. After you have made all of your exceptions, you should run List Transaction File, which lists all of the exceptions you have made and lets you verify that you have entered all information correctly.

CALCULATE PAY AND VERIFY

Once you have entered all employee pay information, including time card entries and exceptions, you must run Calculate Pay. You can calculate pay for a single employee, selected departments, or all departments.

Calculate Pay is an intermediate step that calculates the figures that will be used to generate your payroll. Before actually printing the paychecks, you should verify that all the information is correct. You do this by using Hours/Earnings Report, Print Payroll Register, and Deduction Register.

```
┌──────────────────────────────────────────────────────────────────┐
│ PRPROC1 5.00              Enter Exceptions         COMPANY ID: BB  │
│ 06/01/90                  Big Business, Inc.        GENERATION #: 00│
└──────────────────────────────────────────────────────────────────┘
DEPT: 0                                     PAY PERIOD: MONTHLY
EMPLOYEE: 106   NAME: Bill T. Jones           PAY TYPE: SALARY
     * * F I C A   O N   G R O U P   T E R M   L I F E * *



TAKE FICA ON GROUP TERM LIFE (Y/N): ▯




  ▆▆▆▆▆▆▆▆
  F1 Help
```

═══ **FIGURE 9-13**   FICA on group term life

Hours/Earnings Report

The Hours/Earnings Report presents detailed information about each employee to be paid. The information in this report includes the employee's

- Code

- Name

- Pay cycle, type, and shift

- Regular earnings and hours

- Overtime earnings and hours

- Sick and vacation hours used

- Tips

- Commission and allocated prior year draw

- Miscellaneous income

- Earned Income Credit (EIC)

Data are presented by department and company. By reviewing the information in the Hours/Earnings Report, you should be able to verify if errors exist in the information you entered. Figure 9-14 shows an example of an Hours/Earnings Report.

Deduction Register

You use the Deduction Register to verify the amounts deducted from an employee's pay during the current pay period. For each employee, the report shows the amounts deducted for

- Federal withholding

- FICA

- State, local, and customized tax codes

- Insurance

- 401k plans

- Savings plans   } Miscellaneous deductions

- Payment of employee loan

- Deferred deductions

The report also shows deductions by current period and year-to-date. An example Deduction Register is shown in Figure 9-15.

RUN DATE: 06/01/90
RUN TIME: 3:42 PM

Big Business,
Payroll
HOURS/EARNINGS REPORT

PAGE 1

PERIOD ENDING 06/30/90

CODE	NAME	CYCLE TYPE SHIFT	REGULAR EARNINGS -HOURS	OVT1. EARNINGS -HOURS	OVT2. EARNINGS -HOURS	SICK/ VAC. HOURS	TIPS	COMM. /PR.YR. DRAW	MISC.#1	MISC.#2	MISC.#3	EIC
00106	Bill T. Jones	M/S/1	175.20	0.00	0.00	0.00	0.00	0.00	0.00	0.00	0.00	0.00
			0.00	0.00	0.00	0.00		0.00				
00104	Nancy Billings	W/H/1	220.00	0.00	0.00	0.00	0.00	0.00	0.00	0.00	0.00	0.00
			40.00	0.00	0.00	0.00		0.00				
DEPARTMENT TOTALS			395.20	0.00	0.00	0.00	0.00	0.00	0.00	0.00	0.00	0.00
			40.00	0.00	0.00	0.00		0.00				
COMPANY TOTALS			395.20	0.00	0.00	0.00	0.00	0.00	0.00	0.00	0.00	0.00
			40.00	0.00	0.00	0.00		0.00				

CODES LEGEND:

CYCLE	TYPE	SHIFT
W - WEEKLY	H - HOURLY	1 - NORMAL - NO DIFFERENTIAL
B - BI-WEEKLY	S - SALARIED	2 - TYPE 1 DIFFERENTIAL
S - SEMI-MONTHLY	D - DRAW	3 - TYPE 2 DIFFERENTIAL
M - MONTHLY	C - COMMISSION	

FIGURE 9-14 Hours/Earnings report

```
RUN DATE:  06/01/90          Big Business,              PAGE   1
RUN TIME:    3:44 PM            Payroll
                             DEDUCTION REGISTER
------------------------------------------------------------------
                                        PERIOD ENDING 06/30/90


EMPLOYEE CODE : 00106          EMPLOYEE CODE : 00104
NAME          : Bill T. Jones  NAME          : Nancy Billings
CHECK NUMBER  :     0          CHECK NUMBER  :      0
PAY PERIOD    : MONTHLY        PAY PERIOD    : WEEKLY
PAY TYPE      : SALARY         PAY TYPE      : HOURLY

             -CURRENT PERIOD DEDUCTIONS

FEDERAL WITH. :      0.00      FEDERAL WITH. :        18.00
FICA          :     13.16      FICA          :        16.52
TAX #1        :      0.00      TAX #1        :         0.00
TAX #2        :      0.00      TAX #2        :         0.00
TAX #3        :      0.00      TAX #3        :         0.00
TAX #4        :      0.00      TAX #4        :         0.00
INSUR.   DED. :      0.00      INSUR.   DED. :         0.00
401k     DED. :      0.00      401k     DED. :         0.00
EMP LOAN DED. :      0.00      EMP LOAN DED. :         0.00
SAVINGS  DED. :      0.00      SAVINGS  DED. :         0.00
FIVE     DED. :      0.00      FIVE     DED. :         0.00
SIX      DED. :      0.00      SIX      DED. :         0.00

DEFER. DED.   :      0.00      DEFER. DED.   :         0.00
   TOTAL CURR. :    13.16         TOTAL CURR. :       34.52

             -YEAR TO DATE DEDUCTIONS

FEDERAL WITH. :      0.00      FEDERAL WITH. :         0.00
FICA          :      0.00      FICA          :         0.00
TAX #1        :      0.00      TAX #1        :         0.00
TAX #2        :      0.00      TAX #2        :         0.00
TAX #3        :      0.00      TAX #3        :         0.00
TAX #4        :      0.00      TAX #4        :         0.00
INSUR.   DED. :      0.00      INSUR.   DED. :         0.00
401k     DED. :      0.00      401k     DED. :         0.00
EMP LOAN DED. :      0.00      EMP LOAN DED. :         0.00
SAVINGS  DED. :      0.00      SAVINGS  DED. :         0.00
FIVE     DED. :      0.00      FIVE     DED. :         0.00
SIX      DED. :      0.00      SIX      DED. :         0.00

DEFER. DED.   :      0.00      DEFER. DED.   :         0.00
   TOTAL YTD. :      0.00         TOTAL YTD. :         0.00
```

FIGURE 9-15   A Deduction Register

Print Payroll Register

The Payroll Register report contains much of the information that will appear on an employee's paycheck including the employee's

- Code

- Name

- Regular earnings

- Disbursed miscellaneous income

- Nondisbursed miscellaneous income

- Voluntary deductions

- Federal withholding

- FICA

- Other taxes

- Check number

- Net pay

Figure 9-16 shows what a typical payroll pre-check register looks like. This report is another way to verify your company's payroll information. At the very least, you should scan it before printing checks to make sure that nothing unusual comes up.

You can run the Payroll Register in three ways: as a pre-check register, as a post-check register, and as a final register. You run the pre-check register prior to printing paychecks. Instead of check numbers, the pre-check register prints warning codes when unusual conditions occur (Table 9-1). If you find warning codes in

```
RUN DATE:  06/01/90                        Big Business,                              PAGE 1
RUN TIME:  3:43 PM                           Payroll
                                          PAYROLL REGISTER
                                                              PERIOD ENDING 06/30/90

                  REGULAR   DISB.    NON-DISB   VOL.                                         CHECK
CODE    NAME      EARNINGS  MISC.INC MISC.INC  DEDUCT.  FED.WH.  FICA  TAX#1 TAX#2 TAX#3 TAX#4 NUMB  NET PAY

00106  Bill T. Jones  175.20   0.00    0.00    0.00     0.00   13.16  0.00  0.00  0.00  0.00        162.04
00104  Nancy Billings 220.00   0.00    0.00    0.00    18.00   16.52  0.00  0.00  0.00  0.00        185.48
               ------            ----    ----    ----    -----   -----  ----  ----  ----  ----       ------
               395.20   0.00    0.00    0.00    18.00   29.68  0.00  0.00  0.00  0.00        347.52

BREAKDOWN OF MISCELLANEOUS INCOME AND TAX CODES FOR DEPARTMENT 00

DRAW         0.00                    CURRENT DEF. DEDUCT.     0.00
COMMISSION   0.00                    CURRENT ALLOC. DEDUCT.   0.00
Tips         0.00
MISC. #1     0.00
MISC. #2     0.00
MISC. #3     0.00
EIC          0.00

WARNING CODES LEGEND

CODE 0 = NET PAY OVER CHECK LIMIT
CODE 1 = DEDUCTIONS EQUAL OR EXCEED EARNINGS
CODE 2 = PAY MAY BE BELOW MINIMUM WAGE
CODE 3 = DRAW EXCEEDS COMMISSION
```

≡≡ **FIGURE 9-16   A Payroll Register**

Code	Meaning
0	Net pay for employee exceeds check limit
1	Deductions equal or exceed earnings
2	Employee's pay may be below minimum wage
3	Draw exceeds commission

TABLE 9-1   Pre-Check Warning Codes

your pre-check register, make sure that they don't indicate a serious error.

The post-check register is exactly like the pre-check register except that check numbers appear on the report. If you are using the pre-check register, you probably won't need to run a post-check register, but it does provide another way of verifying your payroll calculations.

Running the final register is an important step in your payroll process; You must do this before you close the current period. The final register looks just like the post-check register. However, when you run the final register, the program updates the processing status codes of the employees so that you cannot enter exceptions, calculate pay, or print checks. In effect, the final register closes out employees for the current pay period.

PRINT PAYCHECKS

Once you have verified your payroll calculations, you are ready to print the checks. Put your check stock in the printer and select Print Checks from the Payroll Processing Menu. The program asks if you want to print a check mask (Figure 9-17). A *check mask* is a dummy check that you print to make sure that your forms are correctly aligned. You can print as many check masks as you need. When your checks are correctly aligned, type **N**.

Before printing the checks, Peachtree Complete III will want to know the starting check number, the period ending date, and the check date. Enter all of this information, taking special care to make sure that the starting check number matches the number of the next check in your printer. When you are done, enter **Y** to accept the information as shown in Figure 9-18. The program will also ask you if you want to print checks for all departments, for selected departments, or for individual employees. Choose the selection you want and your checks will begin to print.

Figure 9-19 shows what a typical paycheck looks like. The top portion is the stub, which contains information like current and year-to-date earnings, overtime, sick hours, vacation hours, FICA,

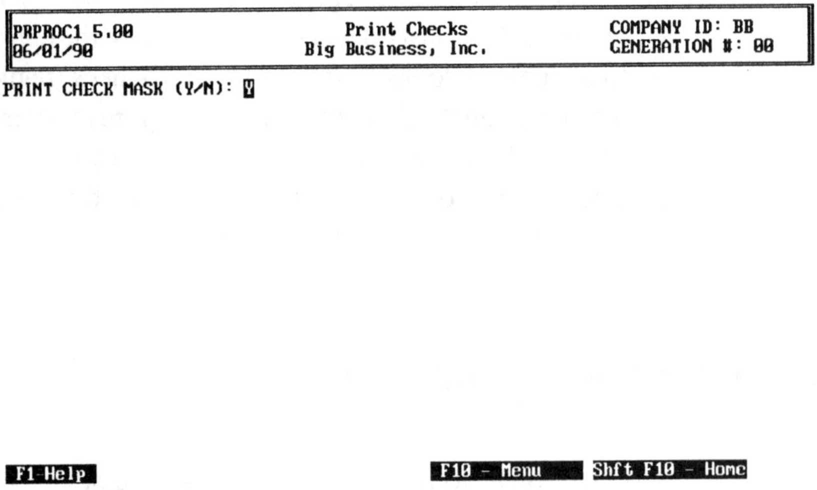

```
PRPROC1 5.00                    Print Checks            COMPANY ID: BB
06/01/90                     Big Business, Inc.         GENERATION #: 00

PRINT CHECK MASK (Y/N): Y
```

```
F1-Help                         F10 - Menu    Shft F10 - Home
```

FIGURE 9-17 Print check masks

```
┌────────────────────────────────────────────────────────────────────┐
│ PRPROC1 5.00                    Print Checks        COMPANY ID: BB   │
│ 06/01/90                    Big Business, Inc.       GENERATION #: 00 │
└────────────────────────────────────────────────────────────────────┘
PRINT CHECK MASK (Y/N): N              STARTING CHECK NUMBER:    1

PERIOD ENDING DATE: 06/01/90      CHECK DATE: 06/01/90



ACCEPT (Y/N): Y
```

FIGURE 9-18   Check printing information

```
106 00 Bill T. Jones       111-22-3333 05/02/90 06/01/90      2

EARNINGS        HRS.  CURR AMT     Y.T.D.  DEDUCTIONS    CURR AMT     Y.T.D.
SALARY                175.20       175.20  FICA            13.16      13.16
OVERTIME 1              0.00         0.00  FEDERAL WH.      0.00       0.00
OVERTIME 2              0.00         0.00
SICK HOURS              3.33         3.33
VACATION HOURS          6.67         6.67

  2102.340    175.20      13.16    162.04     175.20      13.16     162.04
 PAY RATE  CURR EARN  CURR DED    NET PAY   YTD EARN   YTD DED  YTD NET PAY

   Big Business, Inc.                                    2
   123 Main Street
   Anytown, USA

   **** ONE HUNDRED SIXTY TWO & 04 /100 DOLLARS

                                       06/01/90 ******$162.04

   Bill T. Jones
   4 Cherry Lane

   Endwell, NY          13760
```

FIGURE 9-19   Paycheck with stub

and federal and state withholding. The lower part is the actual check, which includes the company name, the amount of the check, and the employee's name and address.

Despite all your best efforts, you might discover an error after you have printed your checks. Don't worry. You can correct the error and reprint the checks *as long as you have not run the final Payroll Register*. Start by making your corrections through Enter Exceptions. Then rerun Calculate Pay and print your checks again. Be sure to destroy the first checks that you printed.

CLOSE THE PAY PERIOD

Once you have printed and verified the payroll checks and run the final Payroll Register, it's time to close out the pay period. You do this by selecting Post Current Period from the Payroll Processing Menu. Besides closing the current pay period, Post Current Period updates employees' earnings, deductions, and sick and vacation hours. It also prints a General Ledger Transaction Register and creates a file that contains the information needed for posting to the General Ledger.

When you run Post Current Period, Peachtree Complete III asks you if this is the last posting for the month. If it is, enter **Y**—this tells Peachtree Complete III to increment the current fiscal period. You also need to tell the program whether you want to post detailed or summary transactions. If you select Detail, Payroll will transfer one journal entry for each payroll transaction; if you select Summary, Payroll will transfer one summary journal entry for each General Ledger account number used in payroll processing.

If you use Peachtree Complete III's General Ledger, you must take one more step to complete the payroll cycle: Run Transfer Summary Journal from the General Ledger Processing Menu. This routine reads in the file of payroll journal entries and posts them to the General Ledger.

As you can see, maintaining employees and generating a payroll is a difficult task, full of details and opportunities to make errors. Peachtree Complete III helps by automating the most mundane of these tasks, making updates and changes easier, and helping you spot errors before they become a problem. It may take some time to get used to the system, but in the end you will save countless hours.

chapter 10

FIXED ASSETS

Setting Up Fixed Assets
Adding and Disposing of Fixed Assets
Using The Fixed Assets Module
Reporting Fixed Assets

This chapter introduces you to the Peachtree Complete III Fixed Assets module. This module requires only that the main program is installed. There is also an optional interface that allows information about fixed assets to be shared with the General Ledger.

Fixed assets are items that your business owns but that are not used for resale. This includes such articles as machinery, equipment, automobiles, buildings, and land. Fixed assets accounting handles the tracking and depreciation of these items, information that is used by the General Ledger and in tax calculations.

Because of the complicated nature of fixed assets accounting and taxation, you may wish to consult a professional accountant to set up this module. This will enable you to make the best use of fixed assets accounting, and to receive the best tax benefits for your business.

SETTING UP FIXED ASSETS

Before you use the Fixed Assets module, you must install it. If you select Fixed Assets for the first time from the Peachtree Complete III Main Menu (as shown in Figure 10-1) you will be reminded that the module is not yet installed. To install the module, type **Y** and then press (ENTER). First you are shown a data path. Then you will see the Fixed Assets Program Options Menu (Figure 10-2). Type **O** and then press (ENTER) to start entering the Fixed Assets module options.

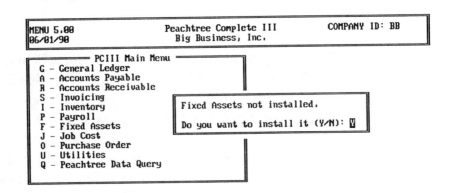

```
MENU 5.00                Peachtree Complete III        COMPANY ID: BB
06/01/90                    Big Business, Inc.
           ══════ PCIII Main Menu ══════
    G - General Ledger
    A - Accounts Payable
    R - Accounts Receivable
    S - Invoicing
    I - Inventory            ┌─────────────────────────────────┐
    P - Payroll              │ Fixed Assets not installed.     │
    F - Fixed Assets         │                                 │
    J - Job Cost             │ Do you want to install it (Y/N): █│
    O - Purchase Order       └─────────────────────────────────┘
    U - Utilities
    Q - Peachtree Data Query
```

══ **FIGURE 10-1**   Installing Fixed Assets

Entering Fixed Assets Options

Because of the complexity of Fixed Assets accounting, there are four setup screens for installing this module: General Module Options, Class Definitions, the General Ledger Interface, and Depreciation Methods. These setup screens will be discussed in the sections that follow.

GENERAL MODULE OPTIONS You enter the General Module Options on the screen shown in Figure 10-3. The Controller Password, Operator Password, and Use Menus options are handled as in other modules. (Refer to Chapter 2 if you have any questions.)

Allow Changes/Deletions When you answer **N** to the Allow Changes/Deletions option, Peachtree Complete III won't allow

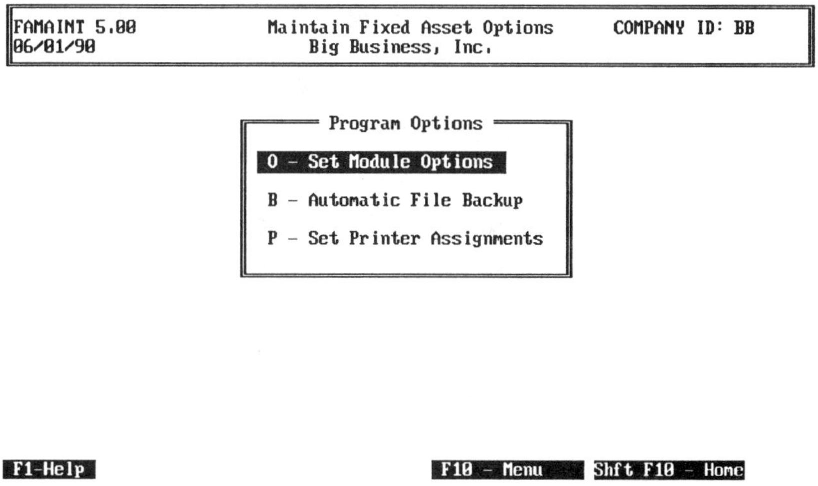

```
FAMAINT 5.00          Maintain Fixed Asset Options    COMPANY ID: BB
06/01/90                   Big Business, Inc.


                    ┌──────── Program Options ────────┐
                    │  O – Set Module Options          │
                    │                                  │
                    │  B – Automatic File Backup       │
                    │                                  │
                    │  P – Set Printer Assignments     │
                    └──────────────────────────────────┘



 F1-Help                            F10 – Menu    Shft F10 – Home
```

FIGURE 10-2 Fixed Assets Program Options Menu

```
┌─────────────────────────────────────────────────────────────────────┐
│ FAMAINT 5.00              Maintain Fixed Asset Options   COMPANY ID: BB │
│ 06/01/90                      Big Business, Inc.                        │
└─────────────────────────────────────────────────────────────────────┘

   General Module Options
      Controller Password......:            Transfer Tax (Y/N).........: N
      Operator Password........:            Last Month of Fiscal Year..: 12
      Use Menus................: Y          Section 179 - Financial....: Y
      Allow Changes/Deletions..: Y          Use Optional Tax (Y/N).....: Y
      Force Control Reports....: N          Depreciation Convention....: 1
   Other Module Options                     First Business Month.......:  1
      Report to G/L............: Y          First Accounting Year......: 75
      Current G/L Period.......:  1         Last Depreciation Year.....: 85
      Use Dept Code in G/L.....: N          Incorporated...............: Y
      Tax/Financial the Same...: N          GL Transfer Ending Date....: 12/31/85

              Accept (Y/N)...: Y



                              ▇▇F8 - Undo▇▇
```

═══════ **FIGURE 10-3**   First Maintain Fixed Asset Options screen

you to make changes or deletions while entering fixed asset information. You will still be able to add new fixed assets, however. This option defaults to **Y**, which makes the program much easier to use, especially when you are setting up your business for the first time. Once your assets are completely entered, you might want to change this option to **N**.

Force Control Reports   Peachtree Complete III generates control reports to provide an audit trail of all changes to fixed asset information. If you answer **Y** to this option, the control reports will be printed automatically when changes are made. If you answer **N** to this option, Peachtree Complete III will ask you each time before printing control reports.

Report to G/L   Answering **Y** to the Report to G/L option causes the depreciation information to be entered into the General Ledger as it is generated. If you answer **N**, the Fixed Assets module will run as a stand-alone unit, and you can manually enter information into your General Ledger later if you want.

Current G/L Period If you choose to have the fixed assets information transferred into the General Ledger, you must specify which period the General Ledger is currently in. Each time the fixed assets information is transferred, this period will be incremented automatically.

Use Dept Code in G/L If your General Ledger is departmentalized, you must answer **Y** to the Use Dept Code in G/L option. If your General Ledger is not departmentalized, or if you are not interfacing the Fixed Assets module with the General Ledger, answer **N**.

Tax/Financial the Same Peachtree Complete III allows you to depreciate your fixed assets by different methods for financial and tax record keeping purposes. If you answer **Y** to Tax/Financial the Same, the same method will be used for each calculation. If you answer **N**, you may select two different methods.

Transfer Tax (Y/N) Even though you may select the same methods for reporting tax and financial numbers, you may wind up with different final amounts. This is because the tax numbers are determined using the current tax laws, while the financial numbers follow accepted standards of determination. If you responded **Y** to Tax/Financial the Same, the Transfer Tax option allows you to specify whether the tax number (Y) or the financial number (N) should be transferred to the General Ledger.

Last Month of Fiscal Year This option requires that you enter the last month of your company's fiscal year. In most cases, this will be 12 (December).

Section 179 - Financial Enter **Y** if you want to include Section 179 depreciation in your financial records. Enter **N** if you want to exclude Section 179 depreciation from your financial records.

 You can answer **N** even if you answered **Y** to the option Tax/Financial the Same.

Use Optional Tax (Y/N) Enter **Y** if your state's depreciation laws are different from federal depreciation laws and you want to maintain separate state depreciation records; otherwise, enter **N**.

Depreciation Convention This option allows you to choose when depreciation will take place. There are three possible options:

1   The depreciation in the year an asset is acquired is calculated for the number of months the asset was owned in that year. The same calculation is used in the year the asset is disposed of.

2   The depreciation is split, so that six months of depreciation are allowed in the year the asset was acquired, and six months are allowed in the year in which it was disposed of.

3   The depreciation is taken as 12 months in the year the asset was acquired, and no depreciation is taken in the year in which it is disposed of.

First Business Month This option requires that you enter the month in which your business starts its year. For instance, if your business year starts in January, you enter **1** as the First Business Month.

First Accounting Year and Last Depreciation Year For the next two options, you enter the year in which your business was started and the year in which depreciation was last taken. For instance, if you started your business in 1982, and this is the year 1991, you would answer the first option with **82** and the second with **90**.

If this is your first year of business, you should enter the previous year as the last depreciation year, so that you can accrue depreciation for the current year. If your business opens its doors in 1991, enter **91** as the First Accounting Year, and **90** as the Last Depreciation Year.

Incorporated   To aid in certain tax calculations, Peachtree Complete III needs to know if your business is incorporated. Answer **Y** or **N** based on whether or not your business is incorporated.

CLASS DEFINITIONS   The second Peachtree Complete III Fixed Assets setup screen (Figure 10-4), allows you to determine

```
┌─────────────────────────────────────────────────────────────────────┐
│FAMAINT 5.00          Maintain Fixed Asset Options    COMPANY ID: BB   │
│06/01/90                  Big Business, Inc.                           │
└─────────────────────────────────────────────────────────────────────┘

                         CLASS DEFINITIONS

        CLASS                              PROPERTY
        .CODE.      .......DESCRIPTION.......   TYPE
        AUTOS     COMPANY AUTOMOBILES          A
        BUILD     BUILDINGS                    R
        EQUIP     MACHINERY & EQUIPMENT        P
        FURN      OFFICE FURNITURE             P
        LAND      LAND                         L
        TRUCKS    TRUCKS                       P


     Accept (Y/N)..: Y



                                        ▐ F8 - Undo ▌
```

FIGURE 10-4   Fixed Asset Class Definitions screen

the classes of fixed assets that will be tracked. Six classes are supplied; these classes may be changed and two additional classes may be included. All assets in a class will be depreciated using the same property type.

For each class, you must enter the code (a six-letter mnemonic for the class), the description of the class, and the property type. The property type may be one of the following:

A   Automobiles

L   Land

N   Low income housing

P   Personal property

R   Commercial real estate

T   Residential real estate

GENERAL LEDGER INTERFACE   Once the classes have been described (as shown), you must define the interface with the Peachtree Complete III General Ledger module. You do this on a screen that follows the Class Definitions screen (Figure 10-5).

For each class that you will use, you must outline how the depreciation expenses will be entered into the General Ledger. You may supply up to three accounts for each class, and a percentage of the total that will be posted to that account.

Next, you supply the account numbers for the accounts that contain the accumulated depreciation (in the column marked ACCUM), the accounts that receive losses generated by the disposition of assets (in the column marked LOSS), and the accounts that receive gains achieved when disposing of the assets (in the column marked GAIN).

For Land, no entries are needed since you cannot depreciate land—it does not lose value.

```
┌────────────────────────────────────────────────────────────────────────┐
│FAMAINT 5.00              Maintain Fixed Asset Options    COMPANY ID: BB  │
│06/01/90                     Big Business, Inc.                           │
└────────────────────────────────────────────────────────────────────────┘

                        GENERAL LEDGER INTERFACE

CLASS:

CLASS    ......GL EXPENSE ACCOUNT DISTRIBUTION.....    ...GL CREDIT ACCOUNTS...
.CODE.    .%.    ACCOUNT   .%.    ACCOUNT   .%.    ACCOUNT   .ACCUM   .LOSS.   .GAIN.
AUTOS    100     55500      0        0       0        0      16000    81000    72000
BUILD    100     55500      0        0       0        0      16000    81000    72000
EQUIP    100     55500      0        0       0        0      16000    81000    72000
FURN     100     55500      0        0       0        0      16000    81000    72000
LAND       0         0      0        0       0        0          0        0        0
TRUCKS   100     55500      0        0       0        0      16000    81000    72000
           0         0      0        0       0        0          0        0        0
           0         0      0        0       0        0          0        0        0

Accept (Y/N)..: Y


                                    ┌──────────────┐
                                    │ F8 - Undo     │
                                    └──────────────┘
```

══════ **FIGURE 10-5**   Fixed Asset General Ledger Interface screen

DEPRECIATION METHODS   Most of the depreciation methods are preassigned by the Peachtree Complete III program, but
you may supply five declining balance percentages in options 9-13
on the next screen (Figure 10-6). These depreciation methods are
then available for all assets entered into the system.

After you accept the information on the Depreciation Methods
screen, Fixed Assets displays the Depreciation Limitations for
Luxury Automobiles screen (shown in Figure 10-7). This is for
your information only; you do not need to make any entries on this
screen. Press (ENTER) to continue. Fixed Assets will return you to
the Program Options Menu screen. Press (F10) and then enter **Y** at
the prompt to create the Fixed Assets files. Fixed Assets will then
return you to the Main Menu.

```
┌─────────────────────────────────────────────────────────────────────┐
│FAMAINT 5.00            Maintain Fixed Asset Options   COMPANY ID: BB  │
│06/01/90                    Big Business, Inc.                         │
└─────────────────────────────────────────────────────────────────────┘

                         DEPRECIATION METHODS

METHOD  ..............DESCRIPTION.............
   1     STRAIGHT LINE  (ST-L)
   2     SUM-OF-THE-YEARS-DIGITS  (SYD)
   3     ACCELERATED COST RECOVERY SYSTEM (ACRS)
   4     ACRS STRAIGHT LINE   (AST-L)

                                           DB%
   5     DECLINING BALANCE   (DBA)         200
   6     DECLINING BALANCE   (DBB)         175
   7     DECLINING BALANCE   (DBC)         150
   8     DECLINING BALANCE   (DBD)         125
   9     DECLINING BALANCE   (DBE)         100
  10     DECLINING BALANCE   (DBF)         100
  11     DECLINING BALANCE   (DBG)         100
  12     DECLINING BALANCE   (DBH)         100
  13     DECLINING BALANCE   (DBI)         100
Accept (Y/N)..: Y
                                      ┌────────────┐
                                      │  F8 – Undo │
                                      └────────────┘
```

FIGURE 10-6   Depreciation Methods screen

```
┌─────────────────────────────────────────────────────────────────────┐
│FAMAINT 5.00            Maintain Fixed Asset Options   COMPANY ID: BB  │
│06/01/90                    Big Business, Inc.                         │
└─────────────────────────────────────────────────────────────────────┘

            DEPRECIATION LIMITATIONS FOR LUXURY AUTOMOBILES

  EFFECTIVE        FIRST YEAR      REMAINING YEARS         ITC
    DATE          DEPRECIATION      DEPRECIATION        LIMITATION

  06/19/84          4000.00           6000.00            1000.00
  04/03/85          3200.00           4800.00             675.00

             FIRST YEAR       SECOND YEAR      THIRD YEAR      REMAINING

  08/01/86     2560.00          4100.00          2450.00        1475.00



PRESS 'ENTER' TO CONTINUE     ▮
```

FIGURE 10-7   The Depreciation Limitations for Luxury
Automobiles screen

ADDING AND DISPOSING OF FIXED ASSETS

Once you have installed the Fixed Assets module, you are ready to add Fixed Assets information. Select Maintain Asset File from the Fixed Assets Main Menu, as shown in Figure 10-8.

You will be prompted for the asset code. Enter the asset code to retrieve an existing asset or to create a new asset (asset codes will be described later). Once an asset is entered, press **Y** or **N** to confirm the changes/additions made. To dispose of an asset, enter **D** instead of **Y** or **N**. Then enter the date of disposal and the sales price.

When you are done adding, changing, or disposing of the asset, press (F10) to complete the transaction. Then either acknowledge the change by pressing **Y**, or cancel it by pressing **N**.

General Asset Information

You enter fixed assets on a screen like the one shown in Figure 10-9. You must answer the following general questions about the asset in the first column.

Asset Code   The asset code is a name you are giving to the fixed asset. You will use this name to look up the information later. This field is case sensitive—PC, Pc, pc, and pC are all different asset codes.

Class Code   The class code is the class into which the fixed asset falls. You can press (F2) to review these classes if you forget their names. Once you select a class code, its description is displayed on the screen.

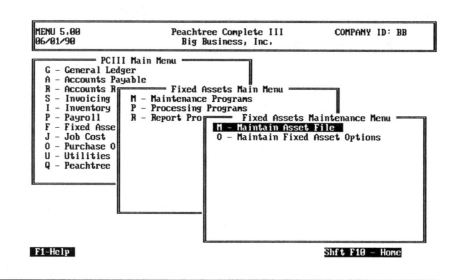

FIGURE 10-8   Select Maintain Asset File

```
┌─────────────────────────────────────────────────────────────────────┐
│ FAMAINT 5.00              Maintain Asset File         COMPANY ID: BB  │
│ 06/01/90                  Big Business, Inc.                          │
└─────────────────────────────────────────────────────────────────────┘


 ASSET CODE.......: PC                Asset code not found - Add (Y/N): Y
 CLASS CODE.......: EQUIP  MACHINERY & EQUIPMENT

 ASSET DESCRIPTION: Personal Computer
 SERIAL NUMBER....: 1234567890     **************FINANCIAL**************
 ACQUISITION DATE.: 06/01/90       ITC RATE...............:    0
 NEW OR USED.(N/U): N              TEFRA CODE (0-3).......: 0
 GL DEPARTMENT....:  0             SECTION 179............:          0.00
 LOCATION.........: Office         ORIGINAL COST..........:       4540.00
 VENDOR NAME......: Clone          SALVAGE VALUE..........:       2200.00
 DISPOSITION DATE.:                TEFRA BASIS ADJUSTMENT:           0.00
 SALES PRICE......:                METHOD (1-13)..........:    1   ST-L
                                   LIFE...................:    5.00
                                   ACCUM DEPRECIATION.....:          0.00
                                   OPT RECOVERY PERIOD....:    0
                                   AUTO SW TO ST-L (Y/N).: N
                                   YEAR OF SW TO ST-L....:    0
 ACCEPT (Y/N):Y     D=DISPOSE OF ASSET   MID-QUARTER CONV.(Y/N): N
                                           F8 - Undo
```

FIGURE 10-9   Asset entry screen

Asset Description   The Asset Description field more fully describes the asset in question. For instance, in Figure 10-9, the code of PC is more fully described as a Personal Computer.

Serial Number   This field contains the serial number assigned to the asset. This number will help you track the asset if your company owns several similar items—for example, several personal computers, typewriters, or calculators.

Acquisition Date   This field contains the date that the asset was acquired. This information is important, since it is the date when Peachtree Complete III will begin to collect depreciation for the fixed asset.

GL Department   If you are using departmentalized General Ledger accounts with Peachtree Complete III, use this field to specify the department to which the asset belongs.

Location   Store the location of the asset in this field. This information will help you track the items that are alike. This information is also useful for insurance purposes.

Vendor Name   The name of the vendor that supplied the fixed asset is kept in this field for future reference.

Disposition Date/Sales Price   You use these two fields to record when the asset was disposed of and what its final selling price was. This information is used to determine the final depreciation value, and possible loss or gain generated by the disposition of the asset.

Asset Financial Information

The second column of stored information about an asset deals with
the financial details. You must answer the following questions in
the second column.

ITC Rate   Enter the Investment Tax Credit rate for this asset. This
can be a percentage from 0 to 100. If you do not want Fixed Assets
to calculate the Investment Tax Credit for this asset, press (ENTER)
to accept the default of 0.

TEFRA Code (0-3)   If you depreciate an asset under ACRS, you
may reduce either the depreciable basis of the asset or the amount
of Investment Tax Credit you take. Enter **0** if you acquired the asset
before January 1, 1983 or are depreciating the asset with any
method other than ACRS Method 3 or 4.

Enter **1** if you acquired the asset between January 1, 1983 and
December 31, 1986, if you are using ACRS Method 3 or 4 to
depreciate the asset, and if you want to reduce the depreciable basis
of the asset by 50% of the tax credit amount.

Enter **2** if you acquired the asset between January 1, 1983 and
December 31, 1986, if you are using ACRS Method 3 or 4 to
depreciate the asset, and if you want to reduce the basic tax credit
amount. Furthermore, the depreciation basis will also be reduced
by 50% of the remaining tax credits above the basic tax credits if
the Investment Tax Credit rate is more than 10%.

Enter **3** if you are taking a rehabilitation credit on this asset.

Section 179   Enter part or all of the cost of this asset as a currently
deductible expense under the Section 179 limits. Press (ENTER) to
accept the default if you do not want to take Section 179 bonus
depreciation.

Original Cost   The Original Cost field records the original cost of the fixed asset. This field, along with the Salvage Value and the Life fields, allows Peachtree Complete III to determine the amount of annual depreciation on the asset.

Salvage Value/Life   The Salvage Value is the value that the fixed asset will have after the life of the asset has expired. The Life is the number of years that the asset is expected to be used and useful. For instance, in Figure 10-9, the personal computer was purchased for $4,540 and was expected to have a value of $2,200 after a life of five years.

TEFRA Basis Adjustment   If you entered **3** in the TEFRA code earlier, enter the basis adjustment that takes into consideration your rehabilitation credit for this asset; otherwise, press (ENTER) to accept the default 0.

Method (1-13)   This field indicates the depreciation method that will be used for the particular asset. If you forget the names of the 13 depreciation methods, you can press (F2) to bring up the list and then select one of the methods. Just press the arrow keys to highlight the method you wish to use and then press (ENTER).

Accum Depreciation   Enter the accumulated depreciation for this asset through the last accounting period. If you bought the asset in the current fiscal year, enter **0**.

Opt Recovery Period   Enter an optional recovery period for this asset if you are using Method 4 depreciation, as follows:

Asset Life	Recovery Period
3	5 or 12
5	12 or 15

10	25 or 35
15	35 or 45
18	35 or 45
19	35 or 45

Auto Sw to ST-L (Y/N)   Enter **Y** if you want Fixed Assets to switch from double declining depreciation to straight-line depreciation for an asset. Otherwise, enter **N**.

Year of Sw to ST-L   If you entered **N** in the previous field, enter the year in which you want to switch the asset to straight-line depreciation.

Mid-Quarter Conv. (Y/N)   Enter **Y** to apply a Mid-Quarter Convention to the depreciation calculations for this asset.

USING THE FIXED ASSETS MODULE

Using the Peachtree Complete III Fixed Assets module is fairly straightforward once you have installed the system and assets. Simply select Fixed Assets from the Peachtree Complete III Main Menu and then select Processing Programs from the Fixed Assets Main Menu; this takes you to the Fixed Assets Processing Menu (see Figure 10-10).

Fixed Asset Inquiries

The first two options in the Fixed Assets Processing Menu are inquiries. The first option is a depreciation inquiry used to determine the current amount of depreciation that has accumulated on a fixed asset.

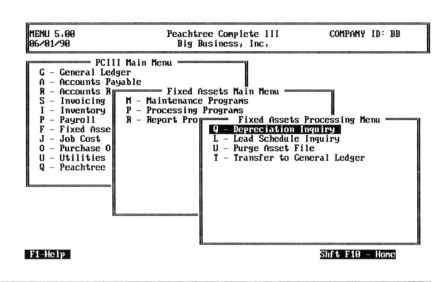

```
┌──────────────────────────────────────────────────────────────────┐
│MENU 5.00              Peachtree Complete III        COMPANY ID: BB │
│06/01/90                   Big Business, Inc.                       │
└──────────────────────────────────────────────────────────────────┘
     ┌──────── PCIII Main Menu ──────┐
     │ G - General Ledger            │
     │ A - Accounts Payable          │
     │ R - Accounts R┌──── Fixed Assets Main Menu ────┐
     │ S - Invoicing │ M - Maintenance Programs       │
     │ I - Inventory │ P - Processing Programs        │
     │ P - Payroll   │ R - Report Pro┌───── Fixed Assets Processing Menu ─────┐
     │ F - Fixed Asse│               │ Q - Depreciation Inquiry              │
     │ J - Job Cost  │               │ L - Lead Schedule Inquiry             │
     │ O - Purchase O│               │ U - Purge Asset File                  │
     │ U - Utilities │               │ T - Transfer to General Ledger        │
     │ Q - Peachtree │               │                                        │
     └───────────────┘               │                                        │
                                      └────────────────────────────────────────┘
   ▐F1-Help▌                                            Shft F10 - Home
```

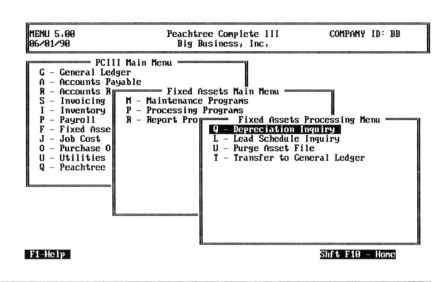
FIGURE 10-10   Fixed Assets Processing Menu

First, enter the asset code for the asset you are interested in. Then, choose whether to show the tax or financial basis report. These two methods may give slightly different results since the tax method is based on the current tax laws, while the financial basis is based on financial accounting methods.

Next, specify whether the report should be displayed on the screen or on the printer. The report will then be displayed. This report includes the original value of the fixed asset, its salvage value, depreciation method, amount of depreciation accumulated, and the amount depreciated each year of its existence.

The second inquiry option is the Lead Schedule Inquiry option. This inquiry displays the information about assets acquired and disposed of during a specific period of time, and the depreciation accumulated during that time.

To use this option, first decide whether to use the tax or financial method of depreciation. Then select the year you wish to view, and the number of months of that year to view. Again, you may send this report to the screen or to the printer.

For each of the asset classes, this report shows the beginning balance, acquisitions, dispositions, final balance, and depreciation expense.

Transferring to the General Ledger

From the Fixed Assets Processing Menu, you may also decide to transfer the fixed assets depreciation information to the General Ledger. You should perform this at the end of each accounting period.

First, specify the ending date of the period to transfer. A control report is printed, showing the actions that were performed. The General Ledger accounts are then updated to show the depreciation expenses incurred during the period.

REPORTING FIXED ASSETS

You can select several reports from the Peachtree Complete III Fixed Assets Reports Menu (see Figure 10-11). These include Depreciation Schedules, Supporting Schedules, Individual Disposition Schedule, and List Asset File. You can also process the end-of-year reports.

Depreciation Schedules

There are several depreciation schedules available from the Depreciation Schedules Menu. These include the Interim Depreciation Schedule, Pro Forma Schedule, and Expanded Depreciation

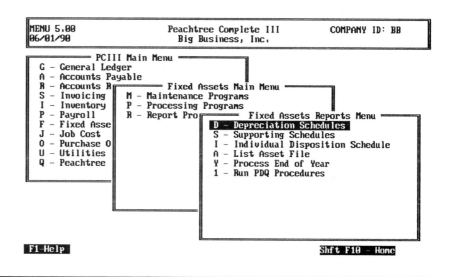

FIGURE 10-11   Fixed Assets Reports Menu

Schedule. These reports differ mostly in the information they give about each fixed asset listed. The Interim Schedule reports the depreciation incurred for a portion of a year. The Pro Forma Schedule breaks down the information into annual, quarterly, monthly, and weekly units of time. The Expanded Schedule shows the depreciation for the entire year.

All three reports are run in a similar manner. First, you select whether to run the reports using the tax or financial method of calculating depreciation. Then, select which year to run the report for. Finally, specify whether the report should cover all classes (A), or just a specific range of classes (R).

You can have the reports sent to a printer, to a disk file, or to the screen. Simply press (F7) when the report is about to start. You can then specify your output destination.

Supporting Schedules

To summarize the transactions that occur in the Fixed Assets module, there are series of supporting schedules to list what has occurred. These reports include the following:

- The Asset Acquisition Schedule lists assets that were acquired (by class code).

- The Asset Disposition Schedule lists assets that have been disposed of (by class code).

- The Schedule of Cumulative Timing Differences compares the tax and financial methods of depreciation calculation.

- The Investment Tax Credit Schedule shows the amount of investment tax credit that may be taken in the year an asset was acquired.

- The Investment Tax Credit Recapture Schedule shows the dispositions, and the necessary investment tax credit that must be recaptured.

- The Property Control Report reports the actual location of all your assets, as found in the Fixed Assets file.

- The Individual Disposition Schedule depicts the lifetime of an asset, when it was acquired and disposed of, and any gain or loss (for one or all assets).

Lists of Assets

Any time you make changes to your Fixed Assets files, you may wish to run the List Asset File Report from the Fixed Assets Reports Menu. This report details all items that are currently in the Fixed Assets file, showing class code, description, serial number, acquisition and disposition dates, location, life, salvage value, and depreciation (for tax and financial calculations). This report also shows the number of classes and assets that you have on file.

End-of-Year Processing

To run the end-of-year processing, select Process End of Year from the Fixed Assets Report Menu. This selection accumulates the depreciation on each fixed asset, reporting this information to the General Ledger module.

Several reports are generated by the end-of-year processing. These include an End of Year Depreciation Schedule (similar to the Interim Depreciation Schedule), an Individual Disposition Schedule (detailing items that were disposed of during the year), a Lead Schedule Inquiry (describing the life of the current fixed assets), an Investment Tax Credit Schedule (for new and used assets acquired during the year), and an Investment Tax Credit Recapture Schedule (for items that were disposed of during the year).

The Peachtree Complete III Fixed Assets module is fairly straightforward. However, the depreciation methods used and whether Tax or Financial records are kept are important decisions that can affect how your business reports depreciation expenses for tax purposes. For these reasons, it is a good idea to consult with your accountant when determining how you should enter fixed assets into the system.

chapter 11

INVENTORY

Many businesses, from shoe stores to ship builders, carry inventory. In some cases, inventory is the single largest asset the company owns, and managing inventory well can mean the difference between profit and loss. Many pitfalls lurk in the stock room: employee theft, shipping errors, miscalculations, incomplete records, slipshod billing. Add to that the complexity of calculating the cost of goods sold, tracking sales by item, and measuring profitability. However, with Peachtree Complete III you can keep tabs on every item in your shop as never before.

KEEPING TABS ON INVENTORY

First you need to understand some of the terms and concepts that underlie inventory. Consider Big Business, which has expanded into the assembly and sale of personal computers. Before Big Business sells a computer, however, it has to buy and assemble the parts. In the language of Peachtree Complete III Inventory, parts are called *components* and the finished product is called an *assembly*. The Inventory module's main task is to keep track of components and assemblies in order to track sales, returns, purchases, and costs.

As components are purchased, they are added to the parts inventory and their quantity and cost is recorded in the computer. As components are assembled into finished products, the parts inventory is reduced and the finished product inventory is increased. In addition, as the finished products are sold, the finished product inventory is decreased.

The fundamental unit in Peachtree Complete III Inventory is the *item,* which can be either a component or an assembly. Each item is identified by a code that consists of an item type, a departmental code, and an item number.

INVENTORY COSTING METHODS

Before you can sell something, you need to know how much it cost you. There are a number of ways to calculate a product's cost. Peachtree Complete III Inventory lets you select from five costing methods: standard cost, average cost, FIFO, LIFO, and specific unit costing. The method you choose will have an important impact on the profitability of your business.

Standard Cost

The standard costing method is the simplest. You just tell Peachtree Complete III what each item costs. Clearly, this method will not do if your inventory consists of a large number of low-cost items. On the other hand, if your inventory consists of a few expensive items, you may want to choose this method.

Average Cost

Under the average cost method, the cost of an item is calculated as the average cost of all items of the same type. In other words, if your inventory of widgets contains ten items that cost $10 each and ten that cost $12 each, the cost of each item would be $11. Note that item cost is recomputed only when stock is added to the inventory, not when it is removed.

The average cost method tends to smooth out price fluctuations over time. The cost of goods sold resulting from this method will be higher than with FIFO but lower than with LIFO.

FIFO

FIFO stands for "first in first out." In the FIFO method, components taken out of inventory are costed at the price of the oldest (first in) items. For example, suppose a company buys ten widgets at $10 each and later buys another ten at $12 each. The company now has 20 widgets in inventory. When the company takes a widget out of inventory, its recorded cost is $10, since that was the cost of the "first in" widgets. When the first ten widgets are used up, the item cost will jump to $12 a widget. Because prices generally move upward over time, the FIFO method, which uses the oldest cost first, tends to produce the lowest cost of goods sold.

LIFO

LIFO stands for "last in first out," and works just the opposite of FIFO. Consider the previous example, where a company buys $10 widgets and then buys $12 widgets. When a widget is taken from inventory, its recorded cost is $12 because that was the cost of the widgets that were most recently added to inventory. When the $12 widgets are used up, the unit price will drop to $10 per widget (unless new widgets are added to inventory at a higher price). Keep in mind that the widget taken from inventory may have been actually purchased for $10, yet LIFO assigns a $12 cost to the item.

Because prices tend to go up over time, the LIFO inventory method tends to maximize the cost of goods sold. It also tends to minimize the value of inventory and reduce income.

Specific Unit Costing

Specific unit costing is, in some ways, the most accurate method of inventory costing. Under this system, the cost of each item is tracked along with the item's serial number. When an item is removed from inventory, its serial number is recorded and its original cost is used to calculate the cost of goods sold. Thus, if you use a widget that originally cost $10, that amount is added to the cost of goods sold. As you can see, using specific unit cost requires that you keep more detailed information about every item in your inventory.

Choosing a Costing Method

Given the alternatives, what is the best costing method for you? In one sense, it doesn't matter because your company's cash flow from earnings will be the same regardless of the costing method that you choose. For example, if you buy ten widgets for $10 and another ten for $12, you've laid out $220 no matter what costing method you use. When you consider income taxes, however, the costing method you use makes quite a difference.

Income taxes are based on net income, which, in simple terms, is revenues minus costs. The higher your costs, the lower your net income, and the lower your taxes. That is, the inventory method that maximizes costs will reduce your income tax burden. For this reason, many companys choose the LIFO costing method, especially during times of rapid price inflation.

On the downside, LIFO tends to distort your company's true value because inventory will always be recorded at its lowest possible value. You can gain a more realistic valuation by using either the FIFO or the specific cost method. Consult your accountant to determine the best method for you.

THE INVENTORY PROCESS

Setting up your inventory on Peachtree Complete III requires organization and preparation. For each item in your stock, you have to identify a department, an item number, a product code, and a costing method, among other things. You also need to distinguish between components and assemblies and to specify reorder levels and reorder amounts. The good news is that once you have your inventory set up on Peachtree Complete III, nearly everything is automated. Given the investment your business has made in its inventory, the time spent setting up your inventory on Peachtree Complete III is well worth the effort.

Daily Inventory Tasks

Inventory is a dynamic part of your company—it's always there but it's different from day to day. The task of the Inventory module is to keep track of these changes so that you can always get up-to-the-minute data on your stock.

Imagine that it's a typical work day at the Big Business warehouse. At 9:00 A.M. sharp a truck arrives with a shipment of computer parts to be added to inventory. As you are unpacking the shipment, an order comes through that the company's prices are increasing 10% across the board, effective immediately. On your desk sits a report of the number of computers that were assembled last week and the number that were sold. These are the daily tasks that face any inventory manager, and usually fill an eight-hour day. Peachtree Complete III Inventory can handle all of this work with ease before your coffee break.

SETTING UP YOUR INVENTORY

Before you can use Peachtree Complete III Inventory, you must enter all of your inventory information by using the Maintain Inventory Items option on the Inventory Maintenance Menu (Figure 11-1). The Inventory module tracks information on every item you stock, providing a detailed level of control over your entire inventory.

To add an item to the Inventory module, you need to identify the item's type (product or service), its departmental number, and its item number (Figure 11-2). The item being entered in Figure 11-2 is a product, so a **P** was entered in the Item Type field. In most cases, inventories consist of products rather than services, but the two are treated in a similar fashion.

The second field in Figure 11-2 defines the department to which the item belongs. You must enter something here, so if you don't

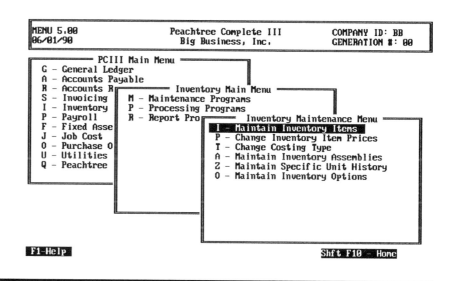

FIGURE 11-1 Select Maintain Inventory Items

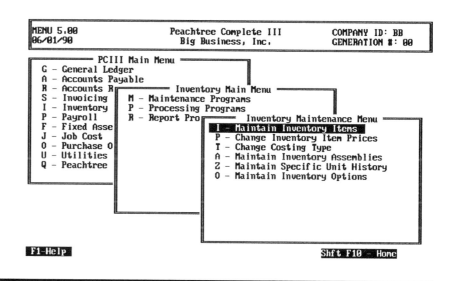

FIGURE 11-2 Adding an inventory item

plan to departmentalize your inventory, simply enter a zero. If you use departments in your business, you should use departments in your inventory, and the department numbers should match to simplify cost tracking.

The third field in Figure 11-2 is the item number, a code that uniquely identifies that particular item in your inventory. You can enter up to 15 characters in any combination of numbers and letters, but it is a good idea to assign some sort of meaning to the item number. For example, the first digit of the code might identify the item as a suit, a shirt, a blouse, or a pair of shoes. The second digit might represent a color or style. In no time, you will have the coding scheme memorized and be able to identify any inventory item just from its item number.

Having entered the item type, departmental code, and item number, Inventory pops up an entry screen for detailed item information. Figure 11-3 shows how this screen looks with infor-

```
┌──────────────┐
│INMAINT 5.00  │          Maintain Inventory Items      COMPANY ID: BB
│06/01/90      │             Big Business, Inc.         GENERATION #: 00
└──────────────┘

ITEM TYPE (P/S): P        DEPARTMENT : 0        ITEM NUMBER : 10101
─────────────────────────────────────────────────────────────────────
   ITEM DESCRIPTION..: 286 Motherboard
   EXT DESCRIPTION...: N
   PRODUCT CODE......: A
   LOCATION..........: 2-23-101
   RECEIVING UNIT....: EACH
   SELLING UNIT......: EACH
   CONVERSION FACTOR.:        1.00
   VENDOR ID.........: ACME            REORDER LEVEL.........:      15.00
   VENDOR ITEM #.....: 30A111          REORDER QUANTITY......:      20.00
   NEG QUANTITY......: N               ON REORDER RPT DATE...:   /   /
   COSTING TYPE......: L
   COMPONENT ITEM....: C               SELLING PRICES
   CURRENT COST......:   150.0000000      PRICE A...........:     257.4000
   LAST COST/UNIT....:   150.0000000      PRICE B...........:     317.9000
   ITEM TAX STATUS...: T                  PRICE C...........:     331.1000

ACCEPT (Y/N) : Y
                       ▐ F8 - Undo ▌
```

FIGURE 11-3   Inventory item data entry

mation on an item in Big Business's inventory. Here is where you enter all the information Peachtree Complete III needs to keep track of this inventory item. While not all the fields are required, you should use all that make sense for you.

Item Description

In the Item Description field, you can enter an item description of up to 20 characters. The description not only appears on reports and screens, but is printed on invoices that your customers receive. The description should be clear and unambiguous so that your customers can understand what item the invoice refers to.

Extended Description

If the 20-character item description is not enough to identify this item adequately, you can enter an extended description of up to 160 characters. However, if you use an extended description for service items, it will replace the item description on invoices. Therefore, be sure that the extended description contains all the information in the item description.

To use an extended description, type **Y** and press (ENTER). Peachtree Complete III will display a pop-up window in which you can enter your extended description.

Product Code

The product code is a single letter or number that you can use to group similar products when posting inventory transactions to the General Ledger. Both the Accounts Receivable and Invoicing module use product codes. If you use Accounts Receivable and Invoicing, the product codes you assign to inventory items must match those that you set up for invoicing. If you plan to use Invoicing and have not yet installed it, do so before proceeding with Inventory. See Chapter 6 for more on how inventory product codes are used by Accounts Receivable and Invoicing.

Location

If you store your inventory items in particular locations (such as numbered bins), you can enter the location identifier here. This information is optional, but can help you keep track of your inventory.

Receiving Unit and Selling Unit

To keep accurate track of inventory levels, Peachtree Complete III Inventory needs to know how items are delivered—individually or in groups. For example, you may sell boxes of disks that are delivered in cases containing 24 boxes. Yet, your inventory keeps track of the number of individual boxes, not the number of cases. In this example, the receiving unit is a case and the selling unit is a box. In the Receiving Unit and Selling Unit fields, you can enter any description that accurately represents how the item is delivered and sold.

Conversion Factor

The conversion factor indicates the number of selling units contained in one receiving unit. In the previous example, the conversion factor is 24 because each case contains 24 boxes of disks. As you receive a case of disks, Inventory increases the inventory by 24 units. Inventory also divides the cost of the receiving unit by the conversion factor to derive the cost per selling unit. Thus, if the case of disks costs $122.88, the recorded cost per selling unit would be $5.12.

Vendor ID

Peachtree Complete III Inventory keeps track not only of the items in stock but the vendor from whom you purchased them. The vendor ID is a code that you create to identify a particular vendor. If you receive the same item from different vendors, you have to add the item to inventory for each vendor.

The Peachtree Complete III Accounts Payable module also uses the vendor ID. If you intend to use Accounts Payable, you should install that module and define your vendor IDs there before continuing with inventory.

Vendor Item Number

The vendor item number is the code that the vendor uses to identify the inventory item in question. While this information is optional, it can be helpful when it is time to reorder, because the vendor will be able to refer to the ordered items by their codes.

Negative Quantity

Businesses occasionally take orders for more items than they have in stock. This creates a negative amount in inventory—a condition that ideally should never exist. For example, if you take orders for ten disk drives but have only five in stock, your inventory will show –5 units on hand. That is, you need to receive five units just to meet your current commitments.

If you want Peachtree Complete III to allow negative inventory amounts, enter **Y** in this field; otherwise, enter **N**.

Costing Type

The different inventory costing methods—standard cost, average cost, LIFO, FIFO, and specific unit costing—were described earlier in this chapter. You must identify the type of costing you wish to use for the current item. Enter the code (Table 11-1) for the desired costing method.

While you are allowed to use different costing methods for different items, doing so can complicate your accounting tremendously. To keep things simple, use the default costing method you set up in the Inventory options module and apply that to all items in your inventory.

Component Item

Peachtree Complete III Inventory distinguishes between three types of inventory items: stand-alone items (S), nonsalable components (N), and salable components (C). *Stand-alone* items are sold individually and are not used as components of an assembly.

Code	Meaning
S	Standard cost
A	Average cost
L	LIFO
F	FIFO
U	Specific unit costing

TABLE 11-1   Inventory Costing Codes

Nonsalable components are sold only as components of an assembly and are never sold individually. *Salable* components are used as components in assemblies and are also sold individually.

Big Business stocks computer monitors, boxes of disks, and surge suppressers. For example, if the monitors are sold only as part of complete computer systems, they are nonsalable components. If the disks, on the other hand, are only sold individually, this will make them stand-alone items. The surge suppressers are sold individually, but are also included with every computer system sold, making them salable components.

In the Component Item field, you can enter **C** for a salable component, **S** for a stand-alone component, or **N** for a nonsalable component. Note that if you selected the specific item costing method, you must define the item as a stand-alone item.

Current Cost

In the Current Cost field, you will enter the current item cost for the items already in inventory. If you have no items in inventory, you can leave this field blank—Peachtree Complete III will update it for you when you add items to inventory. If you do have items in inventory, you must enter a correct value. If you are using the average cost method, enter the average cost of the items in inventory. For standard cost items, enter the fixed cost that will be assigned to all items. For FIFO and LIFO items, enter the cost of the item that will next be drawn from inventory. For specific unit cost items, enter the cost of the units last added to inventory.

Last Cost Per Unit

In the Last Cost/Unit field, enter the amount you paid for the items you received most recently. This field is for your information only; you can leave it blank if you like. Peachtree Complete III will update it when you receive your next shipment of this item.

Item Tax Status

Inventory items can be either exempt from tax or taxable. Enter **E** for tax exempt items or **T** for taxable items.

Reorder Information

Peachtree Complete III Inventory can generate reorder information automatically. You just specify a reorder level (in terms of number of items) and a reorder quantity. As you sell items or use items in assemblies, the inventory level will be drawn down. When it reaches the reorder level, Peachtree Complete III will include that item on the Reorder Items Report and specify the quantity to reorder.

REORDER LEVEL   In the Reorder Level field, enter the inventory level at which you want to reorder additional items. The level you choose should reflect the amount of time it takes to receive the shipment as well as a safety margin to protect you against delays in shipment.

Big Business sells 100 boxes of disks a week. It usually takes two weeks to get a new shipment, but sometimes takes as long as three weeks. In any case, they always want at least 50 boxes of disks in stock. To be safe, Big Business sets their reorder level at 550 (100 boxes per week times 5 weeks plus 50 for margin of error). If the shipment takes four weeks, they will have 150 boxes in stock, but if it takes five weeks, they will still have at least 50 left.

REORDER QUANTITY   The reorder quantity is the number of units to be ordered when the reorder level is reached. The amount should reflect both the rate at which the items are drawn from inventory and the time it takes to receive an order. Using the preceding example, Big Business would order 500 boxes of disks, which is equal to the reorder level minus the margin for error.

ON REORDER REPORT DATE   From time to time, you will run the Reorder Items Report to find out what you need to reorder. When an item is included in the report, Peachtree Complete III Inventory puts the report date in the Reorder Report Date field. This lets you know when an item was last ordered so you can track the promptness of delivery. For now, just leave this field blank.

Selling Prices

Peachtree Complete III Inventory keeps track of selling prices as well as item costs. You can specify up to three different selling prices. Price A is the default price and should contain the price at which the item is most often sold. Prices B and C are alternative prices and can reflect discounts given to special customers or for bulk orders.

Additional Inventory Information

Once you have entered the base information on your inventory item, you can enter additional information such as the number of items in stock and statistics for the year (Figure 11-4). The information on this screen, which is updated for you by Peachtree Complete III, is a powerful tool for determining which items are moving well, which are generating excess returns, and which are the most profitable.

QUANTITY-ON-HAND In the Quantity-On-Hand field, you simply enter the number of items currently in stock. If you enter an amount that you then find is incorrect, you must enter the correction as an adjustment by using Enter Inventory Transactions.

YEAR-THROUGH-LAST-PERIOD INFORMATION No matter how many products your company sells, you will want to know which ones are selling best and generating the most profits. You will often want to discontinue a product if it fails to meet your minimum goals. The Year-Through-Last-Period information is just what you need to keep track of items on an ongoing basis.

The information consists of sales, cost of goods sold, and the number of items sold, received, returned, adjusted, or used as

```
INMAINT 5.00              Maintain Inventory Items      COMPANY ID: BB
06/01/90                    Big Business, Inc.           GENERATION #: 00


ITEM TYPE (P/S): P      DEPARTMENT : 0        ITEM NUMBER : 10101

          QUANTITY-ON-HAND.........:        0.00

          YEAR-THROUGH-LAST-PERIOD INFORMATION:

          PROFITABILITY:
              SALES..................:       0.00
              COST OF SALES..........:       0.00

          QUANTITY FIGURES:
              NUMBER SOLD............:       0.00
              NUMBER RECEIVED........:       0.00
              NUMBER RETURNED........:       0.00
              NUMBER ADJUSTED........:       0.00
              NUMBER AS COMPONENTS..:        0.00


   F1-Help               F8 - Undo     F10 - Done
```

FIGURE 11-4 Additional inventory information

components. You don't have to enter information in these fields now—Peachtree Complete III updates the fields for you when you run Close Current Period. (At year end, the fields are reset to zero.) However, if you have current information to enter, feel free to do so.

The time it takes to set up your inventory depends largely on the number of items you stock and the amount of information you maintain in your current inventory records. If your company stocks many items, you will need several days to enter item information. Once this task is done, however, you don't have to do it again. Moreover, the economies you will gain by automating your inventory will more than make up for the time and effort you expend setting up Peachtree Complete III.

ASSEMBLIES

As mentioned, assemblies are combinations of components, and they play a special role in the inventory process. When you create an assembly, you increase the assembly inventory and decrease the component inventory. When you sell an assembly, the cost is the sum of the costs of each component included in it.

As you can see, tracking assemblies and the components they use can be complicated. Fortunately, Peachtree Complete III makes it a lot easier. Managing assemblies can be divided into three phases: entering the assembly description into the Inventory module, defining the components that go into an assembly, and combining the components to construct the assembly.

Enter Assembly in Inventory

Assemblies are treated like any other inventory item—you have to add them to the Inventory module by using Maintain Inventory Items.

You can also add assemblies in the Maintain Assemblies program. You will assign the assembly an item number, description, product code, and location, just like a component (Figure 11-5).

However, with assemblies you must treat some of the input fields a bit differently. For example, the conversion factor for assemblies is always 1. The vendor ID and vendor item number make little sense; it's best to enter a code that refers to your own company and item number. Of course, you will never order assemblies since you construct them yourself, but you can still use the reorder level and quantity to determine when the stock of assemblies runs low.

Defining Assembly Item

Before you can construct an assembly, you must tell the Inventory module which components go into it. To do this, select Maintain

```
INMAINT 5.00              Maintain Inventory Assemblies     COMPANY ID: BB
06/01/90                      Big Business, Inc.             GENERATION #: 00

═══════════════════════ Add New Inventory Item ═══════════════════════
ITEM TYPE (P/S):P     DEPARTMENT : 0     ITEM NUMBER : 100

  ITEM DESCRIPTION..: PC KIT
  EXT DESCRIPTION...: N
  PRODUCT CODE.....: B
  LOCATION.........: S100
  RECEIVING UNIT...: EACH
  SELLING UNIT.....: EACH              ITEM TAX STATUS.......: T
  CONVERSION FACTOR.:       1.00       REORDER LEVEL.........:        0.00
  VENDOR ID.........: MIXED            REORDER QUANTITY......:        0.00
  VENDOR ITEM #.....:                  ON REORDER RPT DATE...:    /  /
  NEG QUANTITY......: N
  COSTING TYPE......: L                SELLING PRICES
  COMPONENT ITEM....: S                    PRICE A..........:        0.0000
  CURRENT COST......:        0.0000000     PRICE B..........:        0.0000
  LAST COST/UNIT....:        0.0000000     PRICE C..........:        0.0000

ACCEPT (Y/N) : Y

                           ▐ F8 – Undo ▌
```

═══════ **FIGURE 11-5**   Adding an inventory assembly

Inventory Assemblies from the Inventory Maintenance Menu (Figure 11-6).

Peachtree Complete III will ask you to enter the item type (P for product or S for service), the departmental code, and the item number. As Figure 11-7 shows, if you do not remember the item number for the assembly you wish to define, you can simply press (ENTER) and select from a list of inventory items. Notice that the list contains one assembly item (PC KIT) and three component items. Be sure you select an assembly item.

Once you have selected the assembly item to define, the Inventory module displays a screen with room to enter the components of the assembly. Figure 11-8 shows the definition of the PC KIT assembly. For each component, you must enter the item type, departmental code, item number, and number of components required for each assembly (once you have defined the item, the

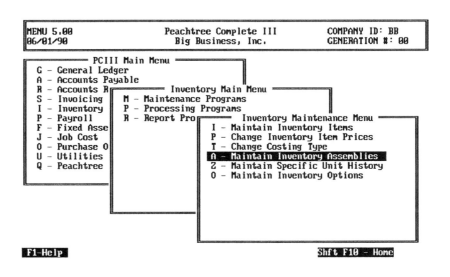

FIGURE 11-6 Select Maintain Inventory Assemblies

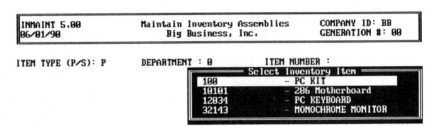

```
INMAINT 5.00          Maintain Inventory Assemblies    COMPANY ID: BB
06/01/90                  Big Business, Inc.            GENERATION #: 00


ITEM TYPE (P/S): P      DEPARTMENT : 0        ITEM NUMBER :
                                         ══ Select Inventory Item ══
                                         100       - PC KIT
                                         10101     - 286 Motherboard
                                         12034     - PC KEYBOARD
                                         32143     - MONOCHROME MONITOR
```

FIGURE 11-7   Select the assembly from a list

```
INMAINT 5.00          Maintain Inventory Assemblies    COMPANY ID: BB
06/01/90                  Big Business, Inc.            GENERATION #: 00


ITEM TYPE (P/S): P      DEPARTMENT : 0        ITEM NUMBER : 100

     Screen #1              Component Information        LIST MODE

     Item Type    Dept      Item #        Description    # Required

1.      P          0        10101      286 Motherboard      1.00
2.      P          0        32143      MONOCHROME MONITOR    1.00
3.      P          0        12034      PC KEYBOARD          1.00




     F1-Help    F6 - Add      F7 - Edit     F8 - Delete    F10 - Done
```

FIGURE 11-8   Defining the assembly components

program displays the description for you). Simply keep adding components until your assembly is completely defined.

Some assemblies are more complicated then others. You might, for example, want to construct an assembly that uses other assemblies (called *subassemblies*) as components. Or you might want to add an overhead component. To do this, you need to add an overhead component to your inventory. Of course, you don't stock overhead components, but you can assign to them a standard cost that can be added to an assembly. Any component that you add to inventory can be used as a component to an assembly.

Constructing Assemblies

As you use components from inventory to construct assemblies for sale, you must inform the Inventory module so that your inventory data are up-to-date. Fortunately, assembling a product using Peachtree Complete III is much easier than putting together the actual product. You can even disassemble existing components, in which case the components are added back to inventory.

To assemble an item, select Assemble/Disassemble Items from the Inventory Processing Menu. The program asks if you want to assemble or disassemble an item (Figure 11-9); the example will assemble an item.

Next, you must specify which item you want to assemble. As you have seen, you select an item by entering the item type, departmental code, and item number. Last, you need to enter the number of items you wish to assemble (Figure 11-10). Once you enter this number, Peachtree Complete III removes the components from inventory and adds the assembled units. Assuming that you have actually assembled these units, your inventory now accurately reflects the number of available components and units.

```
┌──────────────────────────────────────────────────────────────────┐
│ INPROC  5.00            Assemble/Disassemble Items    COMPANY ID: BB │
│ 06/01/90                  Big Business, Inc.          GENERATION #: 00 │
└──────────────────────────────────────────────────────────────────┘

ITEM TYPE (P/S): P      DEPARTMENT : 0        ITEM NUMBER : 100
```

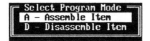

```
F1-Help
```

≡≡≡≡ **FIGURE 11-9**   Select program mode

```
┌──────────────────────────────────────────────────────────────────┐
│ INPROC  5.00            Assemble/Disassemble Items    COMPANY ID: BB │
│ 06/01/90                  Big Business, Inc.          GENERATION #: 00 │
└──────────────────────────────────────────────────────────────────┘

ITEM TYPE (P/S): P      DEPARTMENT : 0        ITEM NUMBER : 100

                   ┌─────────────────────┐
                   │ ASSEMBLE ITEMS MODE │
                   └─────────────────────┘

   Please Enter The Number Of Units That You Wish To Assemble: ███████2
```

≡≡≡≡ **FIGURE 11-10**   Assembling an item

RECORDING A SALE IN INVENTORY

There are four types of inventory transactions: receipts, returns, sales, and adjustments. They all operate in the same way, but sales will be your most common transaction. This section demonstrates how to enter a sale into the Inventory module.

To record a sale in inventory, select Enter Inventory Transactions from the Inventory Processing Menu. You will be asked to enter the date of the transaction and then the program will display the transaction entry screen. Figure 11-11 shows what the screen looks like to record the sale of a 286 motherboard. You record the sale by entering the item sold, the quantity, and the price as detailed next.

Transaction

In the Transaction field, you enter one of four transaction codes: SAL for a sale, RET for a return, REC for a receipt, and ADJ for an adjustment.

Item Type, Department, Item Number

The item you sold is identified, as always, by its type (P for a product or S for a service), its departmental code, and its item number. When you enter these three codes, the program displays the item description and quantity available.

Quantity

In the Quantity field, you enter the number of items sold. Normally, you cannot sell more items than you have available. You can override this protection feature, however, by allowing negative

```
┌────────────────────────────────────────────────────────────────────┐
│ INPROC  5.00              Enter Inventory Transactions    COMPANY ID: BB │
│ 06/01/90                      Big Business, Inc.          GENERATION #: 00 │
└────────────────────────────────────────────────────────────────────┘

 TRANSACTION DATE: 06/01/90

 TRANSACTION.: SAL

 ITEM TYPE...: P
 DEPARTMENT..: 0
 ITEM NUMBER.: 10101
 DESCRIPTION.: 286 Motherboard
 QTY AVAIL...:       23.00

 QUANTITY....:        1.00
 UNIT PRICE..:      257.4000 (PRICE A)   TOTAL PRICE.:      257.4000
 UNIT COST...: (LIFO Costing)            TOTAL COST..:
 COMMENT.....:


 ACCEPT? (Y/N): Y
```

═══════ **FIGURE 11-11**   Entering a sales transaction

amounts for the item you are selling. Note that specific unit cost items can be sold only in quantities of one.

Unit Price

You must also enter the unit price of the item you sold. Peachtree Complete III fills in the default price (Price A) for you, but you can enter another price manually. To select Price B or Price C, simply press (F2) and select the price you want from the list. When you enter this amount, the program calculates and displays the unit cost, total price, and total cost (if known) for you. Since in Figure 11-11 the unit cost is determined by LIFO and is therefore is not known immediately, the total cost is not displayed.

Comment

Finally, you are allowed to add a comment to the sale. The comment is optional but can help if you need to track sales of specific inventory items.

INVENTORY REPORTS

The Peachtree Complete III Inventory module provides a wealth of reports that give you all the information you need to manage your inventory effectively. While you will probably use all of the reports occasionally, the most important for day-to-day management are the Transaction Register Report, the Reorder Items Report, and the Inventory Status Report.

The Transaction Register Report

The Transaction Register Report provides a detailed accounting for everything that happens to your inventory. While most of the items on the report are easily understood, the transaction codes (Table 11-2) are a bit cryptic. Notice, however, that some of the transaction codes listed are generated not by the Inventory module but by the Invoicing and Purchase Orders modules. Peachtree Complete III modules are highly integrated, allowing inventory to be updated by other modules.

Figure 11-12 shows a Transaction Register Report for Big Business. As you can see, the report shows two sales, three item types used as components in an assembly, and the assembly of two items. Notice that sales and components used in assemblies generate negative costs while assembled items generate positive costs. The report provides totals by generation and department, and concludes with a grand total.

Code	Meaning
ADJ	Adjustment
ASM	Assembly of item
ACM	Component used in an assembly
DIS	Disassembly of item
DCM	Component returned to stock
SAI	Sale generated by invoicing
SAL	Sale generated from inventory
REC	Receipt
REI	Return generated by invoicing
RET	Return generated by inventory
RCP	Receipt generated by purchase orders

TABLE 11-2   Transaction Codes

The Reorder Items Report

Keeping inventory in stock is a crucial part of any inventory manager's job. Lack of inventory means lost sales. The Reorder Items Report provides an easy way to keep track of items you need to reorder.

The Reorder Items Report (Figure 11-13) lists your item number, the item's description, the vendor's name and item number, the product code, the quantity available, the reorder level, the number of weeks that the item has been under the reorder level, the reorder quantity, the date the item was initially ordered (if available), and whether this is the first time the item is being reordered. The listing is sorted by vendor ID, which makes it easy to place orders efficiently.

```
RUN DATE: 06/01/90                        Big Business, Inc.                              PAGE   1
RUN TIME: 5:57 PM                          Inventory Control
                                      Transaction Register Report
-----------------------------------------------------------------------------------------------
ITEM TYPE: P

DEPT  GEN #   DATE      TRAN   ITEM #              UNIT         UNIT         TOTAL       TOTAL
                                       QUANTITY    PRICE        COST         PRICE       COST
----  -----  --------   ----   ------  --------   -------   ------------   -------     -------

 0     00    06/01/90   SAL    10101       1.00    257.40   150.0000000    257.40      150.00-
             06/01/90   ACM    10101       2.00-     0.00   300.0000000      0.00      600.00-
             06/01/90   ACM    12034       2.00-     0.00   114.0000000      0.00      228.00-
             06/01/90   ACM    32143       2.00-     0.00   196.0000000      0.00      392.00-
             06/01/90   ASM    100         2.00      0.00   305.0000000      0.00      610.00
             06/01/90   SAL    10101       1.00    257.40   150.0000000    257.40      150.00-

             GENERATION TOTALS:                                            514.80      910.00-
                                                                          -------     -------
             DEPARTMENT TOTALS:                                            514.80      910.00-
                                                                          -------     -------
             GRAND TOTALS......:                                           514.80      910.00-
                                                                          =======     =======


*** End of the Transaction Register Report ***
```

FIGURE 11-12 The Reorder Items Report

```
RUN DATE: 06/01/90                          Big Business, Inc.                                      PAGE  1
RUN TIME: 5:57 PM                            Inventory Control
                                            Reorder Items Report
-------------------------------------------------------------------------------------------------------------
  YOUR                                    VENDOR  P            REORDER  WEEKS BELOW  REORDER   DATE     FIRST
  ITEM ID    DESCRIPTION        VENDOR    ITEM #  C  QTY AVAIL  LEVEL   R/O LEVEL   QUANTITY  ORDERED  TIME?
---------   --------------     -------    ------  -  ---------  -------  ----------  --------  -------  -----
0 -12034    PC KEYBOARD        ACME       K102    A     3.00    10.00       0         15.00   _____   *YES*
0 -32143    MONOCHROME MONITOR ACME       M120    A    10.00    10.00       0         15.00   _____   *YES*

TOTAL ITEMS BELOW REORDER LEVEL = 2


                              *** End of Reorder Items Report ***
```

≡ FIGURE 11-13 The Reorder Items Report

```
RUN DATE: 06/01/90                        Big Business, Inc.                              PAGE   1
RUN TIME: 5:56 PM                          Inventory Control
                                        Inventory Status Report

DEPARTMENT: 0

                               BEGINNING                                              UNITS      UNITS
ITEM NUMBER   DESCRIPTION       BALANCE    SALES   RETURNS   RECEIPTS   ADJMTS.   COMPNTS   PENDING   AVAILABLE
-----------   -----------      ---------   -----   -------   --------   -------   -------   -------   ---------
100           PC KIT              0.00     0.00     0.00       2.00      0.00      0.00      0.00        2.00
10101         286 Motherboard    23.00     2.00     0.00       0.00      0.00      2.00      0.00       19.00
12034         PC KEYBOARD         5.00     0.00     0.00       0.00      0.00      2.00      0.00        3.00
32143         MONOCHROME MONITOR 12.00     0.00     0.00       0.00      0.00      2.00      0.00       10.00
                                                                                           -------   ---------
DEPARTMENT TOTALS:                                                                           0.00       34.00
    NUMBER OF ITEMS:     4.00                                                               =======   =========

GRAND TOTALS:                                                                                0.00       34.00
    NUMBER OF ITEMS:     4.00                                                               =======   =========


                                  *** End of Inventory Status Report ***
```

FIGURE 11-14 Inventory Status Report

You can run the Reorder Items Report as often as you like, but you should run it at least once a week. While the reorder quantity is provided, you should view this only as a recommendation. The exact amount you reorder should reflect seasonal sales patterns and other factors that affect the rate at which an item sells.

The Inventory Status Report

Because inventory involves so many details, you need a report that summarizes your overall situation simply and effectively. The Inventory Status Report (Figure 11-14) provides a snapshot of your inventory by item type. For each item type, you see the item description, the beginning balance, sales, returns, receipts, adjustments, the number used as components, the number of units pending (those committed to entered but unposted invoices), and the number of units available. Totals are provided by department and grand total.

chapter 12

JOB COST

This chapter discusses Peachtree Complete III's Job Cost module. *Job costing* is the process of tracking the costs and receipts for a job, the largest individual unit of cost in Job Cost. A *job* is usually composed of a number of subtasks known as *phases*.

Accurate job costing is fairly complex. To use Job Cost, you must identify each job and each step in completing a job. It may take you some research to find out how jobs are currently being handled in your company. For example, you may discover that you have never allocated certain costs, or that the job estimates are not being accurately incorporated in your bids. When you start using Job Cost, you can obtain precise information about the profitability of each job your company does. This, in turn, lets you pinpoint areas where you can improve your time or cost estimates.

INSTALLING JOB COST

Job Cost can interface with three other Peachtree Complete III modules: Accounts Receivable, Accounts Payable, and Payroll. If you want to use Job Cost with any of these modules, you should install them first. See the preceding chapters on these modules for more information.

To install Job Cost, select Job Cost from the PCIII Main Menu (Figure 12-1). Peachtree Complete III will ask you whether you want to install the Job Cost module. Type **Y** and press (ENTER) to continue.

Tell Peachtree Complete III where to store your company's Job Cost files (Figure 12-2). The default directory is \PEACH\JCDATA. You can change this to any directory you like. If the directory you select does not exist, Peachtree Complete III will ask if you wish to create it. Type **Y** and press (ENTER).

You will need to set up options for the Job Cost module. Select Set Module Options from the Program Options Menu. The Maintain Job Cost Options screen appears (shown in Figure 12-3).

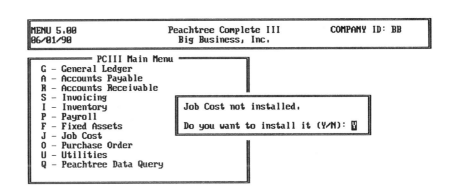

FIGURE 12-1 Installing Job Cost

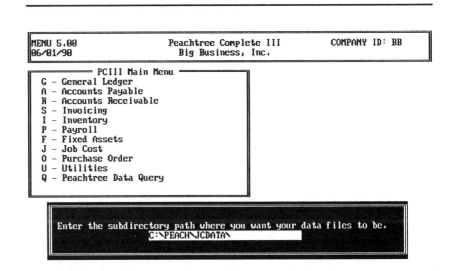

FIGURE 12-2 Selecting the Job Cost directory

```
┌─────────────────────────────────────────────────────────────────────┐
│ JCMAINT 5.00              Maintain Job Cost Options      COMPANY ID: BB │
│ 06/01/90                     Big Business, Inc.                         │
└─────────────────────────────────────────────────────────────────────┘

                              Set Module Options


 JOB COST PASSWORDS:
      CONTROLLER PASSWORD....:              OVERTIME 1 RATE........:       1.50
      OPERATOR PASSWORD......:              OVERTIME 2 RATE........:       2.00
 USE MENU...................: Y            DIFFERENTIAL - $ OR %..:   P
 ALLOW CHANGES/DELETIONS....: Y            SHIFT 2 DIFFERENTIAL...:      10.000
 PAYROLL INTERFACE..........: N            SHIFT 3 DIFFERENTIAL...:      20.000
 PAYABLES INTERFACE.........: N            HOURS/SALARY PERIOD....:      40.00
 RECEIVABLES INTERFACE......: N            PAYROLL OVERHEAD RATE..:       0.00
 CONSOLIDATE PAYROLL........: N
 CONSOLIDATE PAYABLES.......: N
 ALLOCATE COSTS.............: N



 Accept (Y/N): ▓
```

FIGURE 12-3   Options for Job Cost

Entering Job Cost Module Options

The Controller Password, Operator Password, and Use Menu options work the same for Job Cost as for the General Ledger. See Chapter 2 if you need to refresh your memory on how these options work.

Allow Changes/Deletions   When you respond **N** to the Allow Changes/Deletions option, you cannot change or delete Job Cost information. However, you can still add new Job Cost transactions and information.

Payroll Interface   Enter **Y** in the Payroll Interface field if you want to interface Job Cost with the Payroll module. You can then apply Job Cost employee hours and earnings directly to Payroll, rather than having to enter them as time card hours or exceptions. Enter **N** in this field if you do not want to interface Job Cost with Payroll, or if you are not using Peachtree Complete III's Payroll module.

Payables Interface   Enter **Y** in the Payables Interface field if you want to interface Job Cost with the Accounts Payable module. This will let you transfer costs from Accounts Payable directly to jobs in Job Cost, instead of having to enter Accounts Payable invoices into Job Cost as miscellaneous costs. Enter **N** in this field if you do not want to interface Job Cost with Accounts Payable, or if you are not using Peachtree Complete III's Accounts Payable module.

Receivables Interface   Enter **Y** in the Receivables Interface field if you want to interface Job Cost with the Accounts Receivable module. You can then transfer customer billings and payments directly from Accounts Receivable to Job Cost. Enter **N** in this field if you do not want to interface Job Cost with Accounts Receivable, or if you are not using Peachtree Complete III's Accounts Receivable module. You will then have to enter billings and payments as part of the job master information.

Consolidate Payroll   Enter **Y** if you want to consolidate payroll transactions on the Job Cost Detail report. Enter **N** if you want to see the payroll detail. This option does not affect Payroll information in any way. It is only for Job Cost reporting purposes.

Consolidate Payables   Enter **Y** if you want to consolidate Accounts Payable transactions on the Job Cost Detail report. Enter **N** if you want to see the Accounts Payable detail. This option does not affect Accounts Payable information in any way. It is only for Job Cost reporting purposes.

Allocate Costs   Enter **Y** if you want to allocate additional cost amounts and/or percentages. This feature is helpful for distributing miscellaneous overhead costs. Enter **N** if you don't want to allocate additional costs.

Overtime 1 Rate   Enter a multiplier for your company's base overtime rate. The default is 1.5 (time-and-a-half). You can enter a multiplier of up to 3.2. Enter **0** to suppress calculation of overtime.

Overtime 2 Rate   Enter a multiplier for your company's extended overtime rate. The default is 2.0 (double-time). You can enter a multiplier of up to 3.2. Enter **0** to suppress calculation of overtime.

Differential - $ or %   Enter **A** if you want Job Cost to calculate the shift differential pay as a standard dollar amount, or if your company does not have standard shift differentials. Enter **P** to calculate the shift differentials based on a percentage of the employee's hourly pay. You must use the same method for calculating a shift differential for second and third shifts; you can't have a percentage for one and an amount for the other.

Shift 2 Differential and Shift 3 Differential   Enter the shift differentials in these fields, either as a dollar amount (if you selected **A** in the Differential field) or as a percentage (if you selected **P** in the Differential field).

Hours/Salary Period   Enter the number of hours an employee works for straight pay in a pay period, or press (**ENTER**) to accept the default of 40.00. An employee must work more than this number of hours in a pay period in order to receive overtime pay as specified in the overtime rate fields earlier.

Payroll Overhead Rate   Enter a percentage for allocating over-head costs to payroll. For example, you may want to add employee overhead expenses such as FICA, FUTA, and insurance benefits to the employee costs on a job. This option only affects the labor costs on a job, and is independent of the Allocate Costs option.

After you accept the information on this screen, Job Cost returns you to the Program Options screen. When you press (F10), Job Cost asks whether you want to create the Job Cost files. Press (ENTER). Job Cost will create the various files needed to run Job Cost and return you to the Main Menu.

SETTING UP PHASE AND COST CODES

Once you have set up the general Job Cost options, you need to enter the phase codes you want to use. A *phase* is a single task within a job. You use phases to break a job into smaller pieces that are easier to examine and identify. A job can have one or many phases, depending on the size of the job and the nature of the work. Each cost you assign to the job relates to a phase, identified by a phase code.

For example, some of the phases involved in designing and producing software are design and analysis of the projected software, coding (writing the programs), testing, and documenting the product. You could also set up phases for specific divisions of labor or activities. For example, you might have software analysis, coding, and testing as part of a development phase, and writing the manuals and online help as part of a documentation phase. You could even set up phases for materials, such as buying the computers on which to write the software and printing the manuals.

When you set up Job Cost, you need to create phase codes for all phases in your jobs. If you have different phases from one job to another, you need to enter all of them. You should do some planning to identify all of your phases and to set up a system for identifying them. For example, Big Business assembles and installs computers. These two major categories can be broken into smaller phases, as shown in Table 12-1.

In-house Phases

I1	Computer design and specification
I2	Checking and ordering inventory
I3	Component subassembly
I4	Main assembly
I5	Initial testing and configuration
I6	Burn-in
I7	Final testing and configuration
I8	Software installation and configuration
I9	Packing
I0	Shipping

On-site Phases

O1	Customer site preparation
O2	On-site testing
O3	Configuring computer on-site
O4	Installing software
O5	Customizing software
O6	On-site training

TABLE 12-1   Phase Codes for Big Business

As you identify phases in your business, you may discover that phases from one job overlap phases from another job, or contain two or three smaller phases. Not every job will have all of these phases. For example, you might want to specify very small phases on a large job, or just a few phases on a small job.

A *cost* is any expenditure relating to a job. A *cost type* is just a way of identifying and tracking related costs. There are five different cost types:

Labor	Work done by your employees or temporaries (subcontractors have their own category)
Materials	Inventory and supplies used in part of a job
Equipment	Any special equipment used in the job, such as heavy moving equipment or special testing and manufacturing facilities
Subcontractors	Contract labor (as opposed to employees and temporary help)
Other	Overhead and miscellaneous costs that don't fit in the other four cost types

A *cost code* describes a specific type of cost that occurs within a phase. There can be many cost codes within a cost type. For example, the cost type labor can include temporary shipping help, line workers, secretarial overload workers, and regular employees. Each of these costs would have a different cost code, although they are all part of the same cost type. Cost codes may not be necessary on jobs that only have one or two phases.

Entering Phase Codes

Once you have made a list of all phases in your jobs, you are ready to enter phases. Start by selecting Maintain Phase Code File from the Job Cost Maintenance Menu. The Maintain Phase Code File screen appears (Figure 12-4). Enter the information in the fields as described here.

Phase Code   Enter two characters for the phase code. You should assign a logical, consistent system of phase codes to your phases. If Job Cost cannot find the phase code, type **Y** and press (**ENTER**) at the prompt to add it. Press (**F2**) to list the existing phase codes.

Description   Enter up to 25 characters describing the phase. Make this information as unambiguous as possible. This field is required.

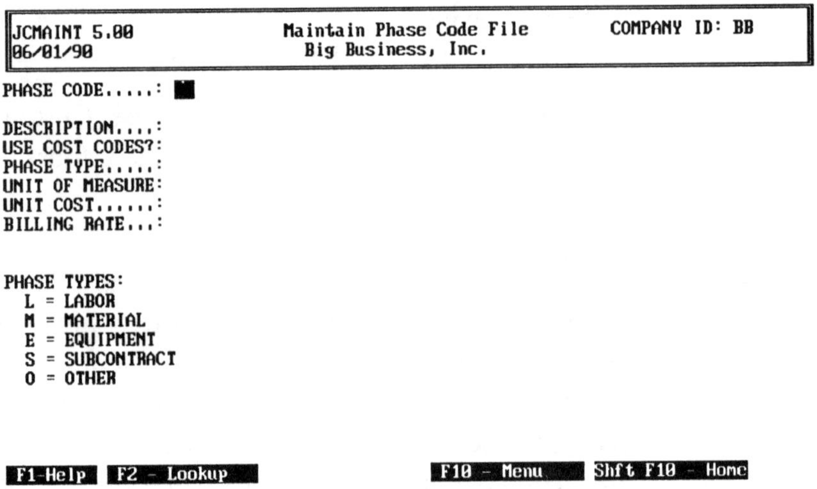

```
┌────────────────────────────────────────────────────────────────────┐
│JCMAINT 5.00              Maintain Phase Code File     COMPANY ID: BB │
│06/01/90                    Big Business, Inc.                        │
├────────────────────────────────────────────────────────────────────┤
 PHASE CODE.....: ■

 DESCRIPTION....:
 USE COST CODES?:
 PHASE TYPE.....:
 UNIT OF MEASURE:
 UNIT COST......:
 BILLING RATE...:


 PHASE TYPES:
   L = LABOR
   M = MATERIAL
   E = EQUIPMENT
   S = SUBCONTRACT
   O = OTHER



    F1-Help   F2 - Lookup              F10 - Menu     Shft F10 - Home
```

FIGURE 12-4   Maintain Phase Code File screen

Use Cost Codes   Enter **Y** if you want to enter different cost codes for this phase code. This allows you to be even more specific when tracking your costs. Enter **N** if this phase code will have no related cost code. Job Cost will automatically enter ALL as the cost code for any phase code that doesn't use cost codes. This cost code is predefined in the cost code file.

 If you have not done much job cost analysis before, you may not be sure which phases to allow cost codes for. A good rule of thumb is to use cost codes for any phase that has more than one cost type or billing rate.

Phase Type   Enter the letter for the appropriate phase type:

L   Labor

M   Material

E   Equipment

S   Subcontract

O   Other

The phase type is a cost type assigned to this phase code. You only need to make an entry in this field if you answered **N** to the prompt "Use Cost Codes?"

Unit of Measure   Enter up to four characters for the unit of measure. For labor, this is likely to be something like Hour, Day, or Week; for material, it might be Case, Box, or Ton. You only need to make an entry in this field if you answered **N** to the prompt "Use Cost Codes?"

Unit Cost   Enter the cost for one unit of the item, service, or activity that this phase represents. You only need to make an entry in this field if you answered **N** to the prompt "Use Cost Codes?"

Billing Rate   Enter the amount you bill your customers for one unit of this item, service, or activity. You only need to make an entry in this field if you answered **N** to the prompt "Use Cost Codes?"

When you press (F10), you can accept the phase code information. If you want to browse through the entries, enter **B** in this field and press (ENTER). Each time you press (ENTER), you will see the next phase code. To delete a phase code, select the phase code and then enter **D** in the acceptance field.

You can check your entries at any time by printing a list of phase codes. Select List Phase Code File from the Job Cost File List Menu, as shown in Figure 12-5. Specify where you want Job Cost

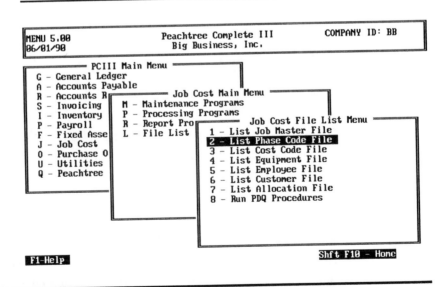

```
MENU 5.00              Peachtree Complete III        COMPANY ID: BB
06/01/90               Big Business, Inc.
          ═══ PCIII Main Menu ═══
    G - General Ledger
    A - Accounts Payable
    R - Accounts R┌═══════ Job Cost Main Menu ═══════
    S - Invoicing │ M - Maintenance Programs
    I - Inventory │ P - Processing Programs
    P - Payroll   │ R - Report Pro┌═══ Job Cost File List Menu ═══
    F - Fixed Asse│ L - File List  │ 1 - List Job Master File
    J - Job Cost  │               │ ▐2 - List Phase Code File▌
    O - Purchase O│               │ 3 - List Cost Code File
    U - Utilities │               │ 4 - List Equipment File
    Q - Peachtree │               │ 5 - List Employee File
                  │               │ 6 - List Customer File
                  │               │ 7 - List Allocation File
                  │               │ 8 - Run PDQ Procedures

   F1-Help                                     Shft F10 - Home
```

═══ **FIGURE 12-5**   Select List Phase Code File

to print the list, and specify the range of phase codes you want to print. Figure 12-6 is a list of phase codes entered for Big Business.

Entering Cost Codes

Once you have set up phase codes, you can set up cost codes for your costs. You should include cost codes for every item, service, and activity you might pay for in the course of a job. Table 12-2 lists a number of cost codes for Big Business.

The easiest way to plan your cost codes is to go through each of the five cost types and list all the costs that you can think of for

```
PHASE CODES FOR BIG BUSINESS

RUN DATE: 06/01/90              Big Business, Inc.               PAGE  1
RUN TIME: 10:26 PM                   Job Cost
                                PHASE CODE FILE LIST
------------------------------------------------------------------------
PHASE CODE RANGE ALL TO END

----------PHASE------------  -USE-   --PHASE--  ------UNIT------  --BILLING-
CODE       DESCRIPTION       COSTS     TYPE     MEAS     COST        RATE
--  -----------------------  -----   --------   ----  ----------  ----------

I0  Shipping                  NO     LABOR      Each     22.40       22.40
I1  Computer design and spec. NO     LABOR      Hour     15.00       25.00
I2  Preparing inventory       YES                         0.00        0.00
I3  Component sub-assembly    YES                         0.00        0.00
I4  Main assembly             YES                         0.00        0.00
I5  Initial testing & config. NO     LABOR      Hour     12.50       25.00
I6  Burn-in                   NO     LABOR      Each     30.00       50.00
I7  Final testing & config.   NO     LABOR      Hour     12.50       25.00
I8  S/W installation & config YES    LABOR      Hour     12.50       30.00
I9  Packing                   NO     LABOR      Each      8.20       15.00
O1  Customer site preparation YES                         0.00        0.00
O2  On-site testing           YES                         0.00        0.00
O3  Configuring cmptr on-site NO     LABOR      Hour     20.00       35.00
O4  Installing software       NO     LABOR      Hour     20.00       35.00
O5  Customizing software      NO     LABOR      Hour     20.00       35.00
O6  On-site training          NO     LABOR      Hour     25.00       40.00

    TOTAL PHASE CODES    16

        *** END OF PHASE CODE FILE LIST ***
```

FIGURE 12-6 Phase Code File List

Cost Code	Cost Description
HOLDAY	Holiday - all
EQUIP1	Styro shipping peanuts
EQUIP2	Shrink wrap film
LAB001	Labor - assembly line
LAB002	Labor - h/w installation
LAB003	Labor - s/w installation
LAB004	Labor - shipping
LAB005	Labor - on-site prep
LAB006	Labor - on-site wiring
LAB007	Labor - on-site testing
LAB008	Labor - on-site h/w cnfig
LAB009	Labor - on-site s/w cnfig
LAB010	Labor - on-site training
MAT001	Cost of chassis
MAT002	Cost of power supplies
MAT003	Cost of 286 motherboard
MAT004	Cost of RAM chips
MAT005	Cost of mono monitor
MAT006	Cost of VGA monitor
MAT007	Cost of MDA card
MAT008	Cost of VGA card
MAT009	Cost of keyboard
MAT010	Cost of disk drives
MAT011	Cost of hard drives

TABLE 12-2 Cost Codes for Big Business

Cost Code	Cost Description
MEAL	Meal break - all
MISCL	Miscellaneous labor
MISCM	Miscellaneous materials
PSNL	Personal time - all
SICK	Sick leave - all
VAC	Vacation - all

TABLE 12-2 Cost Codes for Big Business (*continued*)

each of the categories. You can look through previous accounts payable invoices for possible costs. Make a list of each cost you incur as part of doing a job. Don't worry if you can't think of all the possible costs: You can always add a cost code later if you need one.

Don't set up several different cost codes for the same cost. You can apply the same cost code to different phases. For example, the LAB001 cost code could be applied to phases I2 through I7. You don't need a different cost code for each phase.

When you have made a list of all potential cost codes, create a simple, coding system for them. This system should be reasonably logical and consistent. When this is done, you are ready to enter cost codes in Job Cost. Select Maintain Cost Code File from the Job Cost Maintenance Menu. The Maintain Phase Code File screen appears (Figure 12-7). Fill in the fields as described next.

Cost Code   Enter a cost code of up to six characters. The ALL cost code (the default) is already set up. If Job Cost cannot find the cost code you enter in this field, type **Y** and press (**ENTER**) at the prompt to add it. Press (**F2**) to list the existing cost codes.

```
┌─────────────────────────────────────────────────────────────────────┐
│JCMAINT 5.00                Maintain Cost Code File      COMPANY ID: BB│
│06/01/90                      Big Business, Inc.                       │
│COST CODE......: ▓LL▓▓                                                 │
│                                                                       │
│DESCRIPTION....: COST DOES NOT APPLY                                   │
│COST TYPE......: O                                                     │
│UNIT OF MEASURE:                                                       │
│UNIT COST......:         0.00                                          │
│BILLING RATE...:         0.00                                          │
│                                                                       │
│                                                                       │
│COST TYPES:                                                            │
│  L = LABOR                                                            │
│  M = MATERIAL                                                         │
│  E = EQUIPMENT                                                        │
│  S = SUBCONTRACT                                                      │
│  O = OTHER                                                            │
│                                                                       │
│                                                                       │
│                                                                       │
│   F1-Help   F2 - Lookup            F10 - Menu    Shft F10 - Home      │
└─────────────────────────────────────────────────────────────────────┘
```

FIGURE 12-7 Maintain Cost Code File screen

Description   Enter up to 25 characters describing the phase.

Cost Type   Enter the letter for the appropriate cost type:

L   Labor

M   Material

E   Equipment

S   Subcontract

O   Other

The cost type is a general category for this cost code.

Unit of Measure   Enter up to four characters for the unit of measure. For labor, this is likely to be something like Hour, Day, or Week; for material, it might be Case, Box, or Ton.

Unit Cost   Enter the cost for one unit of the item, service, or activity that this cost code represents.

Billing Rate   Enter the amount you bill your customers for one unit of this item, service, or activity.

When you press (F10), you can accept the cost code information. You can browse and delete cost codes as you did with phase codes.

After you enter your cost codes, print a cost code list by selecting List Cost Code File from the Job Cost File List Menu and specifying the range of cost codes and where the list should be printed. Figure 12-8 is a list of cost codes entered for Big Business.

Entering Equipment

After setting up your phase codes and cost codes, you need to tell Job Cost which pieces of equipment you will be using. Big Business only has four large pieces of equipment that are used in jobs: an EPROM programmer/blaster, a test rack for motherboards, and two delivery vans. To enter the equipment, select Maintain Equipment File from the Job Cost Maintenance Menu and enter the equipment on the Maintain Equipment File screen shown in Figure 12-9.

Equipment Code   Enter a code of up to four characters that uniquely identifies this piece of equipment.

Phase Code   Enter the phase code for the default phase in which you use this equipment. If you use the equipment in more than one phase, you can change this default when you assign the equipment to a job. Press (F2) for a list of the available phase codes.

```
COST CODES FOR BIG BUSINESS

RUN DATE: 06/01/90            Big Business, Inc.              PAGE  1
RUN TIME: 11:34 AM               Job Cost
                          COST CODE FILE LIST
-----------------------------------------------------------------------
COST CODE RANGE ALL TO END

---------------COST--------------   ---COST---   ------UNIT------   --BILLING-
  CODE          DESCRIPTION           TYPE       MEAS      COST        RATE
------   ------------------------   ---------   ----------------   ----------

ALL      COST DOES NOT APPLY        OTHER                   0.00        0.00
BREAK    Coffee break - all         LABOR       Hour       12.50       20.00
EQUIP1   Styro shipping peanuts     EQUIPMENT   Bag         7.84        0.00
EQUIP2   Shrink wrap film           EQUIPMENT   Roll       15.25        0.00
HOLDAY   Holiday - all              LABOR       Day        12.50      200.00
LAB001   Labor - assembly line      LABOR       Hour       12.50       25.00
LAB002   Labor - h/w installation   LABOR       Hour       12.50       25.00
LAB003   Labor - s/w installation   LABOR       Hour       15.00       30.00
LAB004   Labor - shipping           LABOR       Hour        8.00       15.00
LAB005   Labor - on-site prep       LABOR       Hour       20.00       35.00
LAB006   Labor - on-site wiring     LABOR       Hour       20.00       35.00
LAB007   Labor - on-site testing    LABOR       Hour       20.00       35.00
LAB008   Labor - on-site h/w cnfig  LABOR       Hour       20.00       35.00
LAB009   Labor - on-site s/w cnfig  LABOR       Hour       20.00       35.00
LAB010   Labor - on-site training   LABOR       Hour       35.00       50.00
MAT001   Cost of chassis            MATERIAL    Each       43.20       57.90
MAT002   Cost of power supplies     MATERIAL    Each       54.00       73.00
MAT003   Cost of 286 motherboard    MATERIAL    Each      257.40      299.95
MAT004   Cost of RAM chips          MATERIAL    Each        3.25        6.50
MAT005   Cost of mono monitor       MATERIAL    Each       37.50       51.00
MAT006   Cost of VGA monitor        MATERIAL    Each      262.33      499.00
MAT007   Cost of MDA card           MATERIAL    Each        8.97       35.00
MAT008   Cost of VGA card           MATERIAL    Each      174.95      275.00
MAT009   Cost of keyboard           MATERIAL    Each       25.15       56.00
MAT010   Cost of disk drives        MATERIAL    Each       68.00       99.00
MAT011   Cost of hard drives        MATERIAL    Each      225.00      299.00
MEAL     Meal break - all           LABOR       Hour       12.50       20.00
MISCL    Miscellaneous labor        LABOR       Hour       15.00       25.00
MISCM    Miscellaneous materials    MATERIAL    Each       36.00       50.00
PSNL     Personal time              LABOR       Hour       12.50        0.00
SICK     Sick time                  LABOR       Hour       12.50       20.00
VAC      Vacation time              LABOR       Hour       12.50        0.00

         TOTAL COST CODES    32

              *** END OF COST CODE FILE LIST ***
```

═══ **FIGURE 12-8**   Cost Code File List

Cost Code   Enter the cost code representing this piece of equipment. As with phase codes, you can change this default to another cost code.

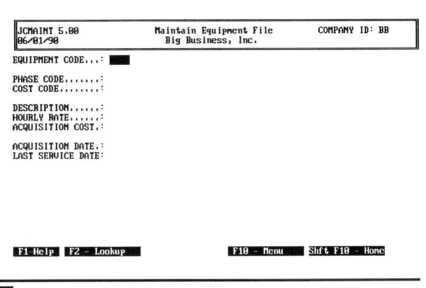

FIGURE 12-9   Maintain Equipment File screen

Description   Enter a description of up to 25 characters.

Hourly Rate   Enter an amount for the hourly rate you charge your customers for the use of the equipment.

Acquisition Cost   Enter the cost of the equipment, including upkeep and insurance.

Acquisition Date   Enter the date the equipment went into service.

Last Service Date   Enter the date the equipment was last serviced.

You can check your entries by printing an equipment list. Select List Equipment File from the Job Cost File List Menu, and specify where Job Cost should print the list and the range of equipment to be printed. Figure 12-10 is a list of equipment entered for Big Business.

```
EQUIPMENT FOR BIG BUSINESS

RUN DATE: 06/01/90                    Big Business, Inc.                              PAGE   1
RUN TIME: 12:09 PM                         Job Cost
                                      EQUIPMENT FILE LIST
-------------------------------------------------------------------------------------------------
EQUIPMENT RANGE ALL TO END
-------------------------------------------------------------------------------------------------
------------EQUIPMENT-------   ------PHASE------   ------COST------  -HOURLY-  ---ACQUISITION---  -SERVICE
CODE     DESCRIPTION           CODE  DESCRIPTION   CODE  DESCRIPTION  RATE      COST      DATE      DATE
------   ------------------   ----  ------------   ----  -----------  ------    -------   -------   -------

CHIP EPROM programmer/blaster  I3  Component sub-assembly  LAB001 Labor - assembly line      25.00   2495.00  03/21/90   /  /
TEST Test rack for motherboard I3  Component sub-assembly  LAB001 Labor - assembly line      25.00   4500.00    /  /     /  /
VAN1 Delivery van 1            O1  Customer site preparation LAB006 Labor - on-site wiring    35.00   7856.43  01/17/89 04/15/90
VAN2 Delivery van 2            O1  Customer site preparation ALL    COST DOES NOT APPLY       35.00   9422.00  10/16/87   /  /
                                                                                                    ========
TOTAL EQUIPMENT    4                                                                                24273.43


                              *** END OF EQUIPMENT FILE LIST ***
```

═ FIGURE 12-10 Equipment File List

Entering Employees

You use Job Cost to assign labor costs for every job. To do this, you need to know which of your employees are working on each job. If you are interfacing Job Cost with Payroll, you won't need to enter your employees as part of the Job Cost setup procedures, since Job Cost will be able to use all employees listed in Payroll. However, if you do not use Peachtree Complete III's Payroll module, you will need to enter employee information into Job Cost.

 If you have not already done so when setting up Payroll, you will need to establish an employee numbering system (see Chapter 8).

To enter employees directly into Job Cost, select Maintain Employee File from the Job Cost Maintenance Menu. The Maintain Employee File screen appears (Figure 12-11). Enter the employee information as described here.

Employee Code   Enter an employee code of up to six characters. You will use this code when you enter the employee's time card information.

Employee Name   Enter up to 25 characters for the employee's name.

Social Security Num   Enter the employee's social security number.

Employee Type   Enter **S** if the employee is salaried or **H** if the employee is hourly.

Shift (1/2/3)   Enter **1**, **2**, or **3**, depending on which shift the employee normally works.

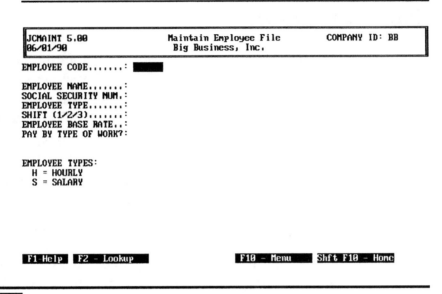

```
JCMAINT 5.00                Maintain Employee File        COMPANY ID: BB
06/01/90                      Big Business, Inc.

EMPLOYEE CODE.......: ▮▮▮▮▮

EMPLOYEE NAME.......:
SOCIAL SECURITY NUM.:
EMPLOYEE TYPE.......:
SHIFT (1/2/3).......:
EMPLOYEE BASE RATE..:
PAY BY TYPE OF WORK?:


EMPLOYEE TYPES:
  H = HOURLY
  S = SALARY




    F1-Help   F2 - Lookup              F10 - Menu    Shft F10 - Home
```

FIGURE 12-11   Maintain Employee File screen

Employee Base Rate   Enter the base pay rate for the employee. If the pay is hourly, enter the hourly rate; otherwise, enter the employee's annual salary.

Pay by Type of Work   Enter **Y** if you want the information in the phase and cost codes to determine the default rate. Enter **N** if Job Cost should use the employee's base pay rate as the default pay rate in Enter Employee Time Cards. If you answer **Y** to Payroll Interface on the Maintain Job Cost Options screen, you cannot pay by type of work.

You can print a list of employees, regardless of how you entered them, by selecting List Employee File from the Job Cost File List Menu, and specifying where Job Cost should print the list and the range of employees to be printed. Figure 12-12 is a list of employees entered for Big Business.

Entering Customers

The next type of general information you need to set up in Job Cost is your customers. Job Cost will use the customer information when you are posting receivables against jobs. If you are interfacing Job Cost with Accounts Receivable, you won't need to enter your customers as part of the Job Cost setup procedures. Job Cost

```
EMPLOYEES FOR BIG BUSINESS

RUN DATE: 06/01/90          Big Business, Inc.                PAGE  1
RUN TIME:  1:30 PM               Job Cost
                            EMPLOYEE FILE LIST
-----------------------------------------------------------------------
EMPLOYEE RANGE ALL TO END

----------------EMPLOYEE------------    -    ---BASE---  --PAY--  --SOC SEC--
  CODE             NAME        TYPE  SHIFT     RATE      BY WORK    NUMBER
 ------   --------------------  ------   -   ----------  -------  ----------

 00102   James K. Habbakuk    HOURLY   1       6.750      NO      222-33-4444
 00106   Bill T. Jones        SALARY   1   21500.000      NO      777-88-9999
 00144   Eric Gross           HOURLY   1       8.210      NO      325-21-5575
 00235   Janice Broxon        HOURLY   1       6.750      NO      082-51-3211
 00391   Chuck Reynolds       HOURLY   1       8.200      NO      144-01-1088
 00540   Bill Burgess         HOURLY   1      10.420      NO      243-76-9874
 00666   Bill Austin          HOURLY   1       6.750      NO      282-65-8980
 00701   Tom Palmer           SALARY   1   25400.000      NO      602-32-6110
 00800   Larry Cobb           HOURLY   1       6.750      NO      343-55-0022
 00934   Mel Carlton          HOURLY   1       6.750      NO      340-34-6781

         TOTAL EMPLOYEES    10

             *** END OF EMPLOYEE FILE LIST ***
```

FIGURE 12-12 Employee File List

will be able to use all customers listed in Accounts Receivable. However, if you do not use Peachtree Complete III's Accounts Receivable module, you will need to enter customer information into Job Cost.

 If you have not already done so for Accounts Receivable, you need to establish a customer numbering system. See Chapter 6, "Accounts Receivable and Invoicing," for more information.

To enter customers directly into Job Cost, select Maintain Customer File from the Job Cost Maintenance Menu. The Maintain Customer File screen appears (Figure 12-13). Enter the customer information as described next.

```
┌──────────────────────────────────────────────────────────────────┐
│ JCMAINT 5.00            Maintain Customer File      COMPANY ID: BB │
│ 06/01/90                  Big Business, Inc.                       │
└──────────────────────────────────────────────────────────────────┘
 CUSTOMER NUMBER: ████████

 CUSTOMER NAME..:




    F1-Help   F2 - Lookup              F10 - Menu    Shft F10 - Home
```

FIGURE 12-13   Maintain Customer File screen

Customer Number Enter a customer code of up to six characters.

Customer Name Enter a customer name of up to 25 characters.

You can print a list of customers, regardless of how you entered them, by selecting List Customer File from the Job Cost File List Menu, and specifying where Job Cost should print the list and the range of customers to be printed. Figure 12-14 is a list of customers entered for Big Business.

SETTING UP A NEW JOB

After you have set up the general information, you are ready to enter information for a specific job. Because Job Cost, unlike

```
CUSTOMERS FOR BIG BUSINESS

RUN DATE: 06/01/90          Big Business, Inc.              PAGE  1
RUN TIME:  1:42 PM                 Job Cost
                               CUSTOMER FILE LIST
-----------------------------------------------------------------------
CUSTOMER RANGE ALL TO END

-----------CUSTOMER-------------
NUMBER          NAME
------   ----------------------

GILMAN   Joel Gilman, Attorney
KRELL    Krell Office Systems
LIL001   Lily Pod Systems
SANTOS   Santos, Harley, and Jones

         TOTAL CUSTOMERS     4

              *** END OF CUSTOMER FILE LIST ***
```

FIGURE 12-14 Customer File List

Accounts Receivable and Payroll, does not have periods, you can enter a job at any time.

Remember, Big Business assembles and sells computers. This chapter tracks one of Big Business's jobs—building and installing a number of computers in the office of a prominent attorney.

Before you enter the information for a new job, you should answer the following questions:

- Who is this job for?

- What is the nature of this job?

- How much will this job cost?

- How many phases are there in this job and what are they?

- Which employees will be performing the work?

- What equipment will I need for this job?

- What are my overhead costs?

- Which costs do I want to track?

- Which costs do I want to pass on to the customer?

Armed with these answers, you are ready to set up and track a new job in Job Cost.

Entering Job Master Information

To set up a new job, you first need to enter job master information. This is information such as the customer name, the project supervisor, and so on. To enter job master information, select Maintain Job Master File from the Job Cost Maintenance Menu (Figure 12-15). The Maintain Job Master File screen then appears (Figure 12-16). Enter a job number in the first field.

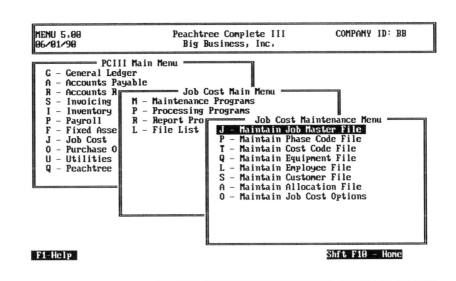

FIGURE 12-15 Select Maintain Job Master File

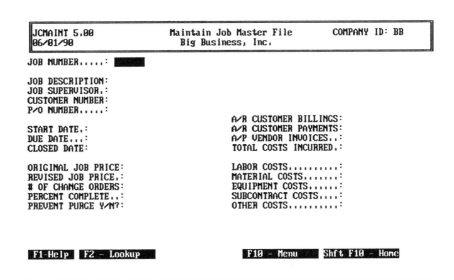

FIGURE 12-16 Maintain Job Master File screen

The job number is a six-character ID code that uniquely identifies each job. Like vendor and customer ID's, job numbers are case sensitive. That is, Job Cost treats GILJOB and giljob differently. You may wish to set a policy that all letters in job numbers be entered as capital letters.

All the transactions you enter for a job are keyed to the job number. Once you set up a job, you cannot change the job number. Also remember that Job Cost sorts jobs on reports in order of the job number. If you are just using the next available six-digit number for each job, you may have to look through pages to find a particular customer. You cannot change a job number once you have entered it. If you enter the wrong job number, you must use the Purge Jobs program.

After you have entered the job number, Job Cost will ask if you want to add the job. Type **Y** and press (ENTER). Job Cost will fill in some of the fields on the screen with default entries. You can accept the defaults or change them as described here.

Job Description   Enter a description of up to 25 characters in this field.

Job Supervisor   Enter up to 25 characters to identify the job's supervisor or project manager.

Customer Number   Enter the ID of the customer who ordered the job. Press (F2) for a list of the customers you can enter. You can leave this field blank if you wish.

P/O Number   Enter up to 15 characters to list the customer's purchase order number.

Start Date and Due Date   Enter the estimated starting and ending dates.

Closed Date   Enter the date the job was actually completed. If the job is not complete, leave it blank. Once you enter a date in this field, Job Cost will assume that the job is closed.

Original Job Price   Enter the original contracted price for this job.

Revised Job Price   If the price changed during the course of the job, Job Cost will enter the revised price in this field based on the change orders you enter.

# of Change Orders   Job Cost will update the number in this field each time you add or delete a change order.

Percent Complete   Enter a percentage for job completion. This is for your information only.

Prevent Purge   Enter **Y** if you don't want this job purged when it is completed. You can use unpurged jobs as templates for new jobs by typing new information over the existing information. Enter **N** if you want to be able to purge this job.

A/R Customer Billings and A/R Customer Payments   If you are setting up a new job, you need not make an entry in these fields. If you are setting up a job in progress, enter the total customer billings and payments made to date.

A/P Vendor Invoices   If you are setting up a new job, you need not make an entry in this field. If you are setting up a job in progress, enter the total of the accounts payable invoices and credits made to date.

The remaining cost fields are updated automatically by Job Cost. You don't need to make an entry in any of them.

When you are done, press (F10) and then enter **Y** to accept the information. You can continue entering information on jobs, or press (F10) to return to the Main Menu. To print a list of the jobs in Job Cost, select List Job Master File from the Job Cost File List Menu, and tell Job Cost where to print the list. Job Cost will ask you if you want to print a listing for open jobs, closed jobs, or both, and will then ask you to select the range of jobs. Figure 12-17 is a list of the jobs entered for Big Business in Job Cost.

Allocating Costs

You can add costs over and above the costs set up for a phase or a cost code by allocating costs. You use this option to allocate costs for overhead, wasted or defective materials, and miscellaneous un-trackable costs. You can allocate costs to reflect temporary or anticipated price changes in materials, and to allow for labor overhead.

 You must have entered **Y** in the Allocate Costs field on the Maintain Job Cost Options screen to allocate costs. If you don't want to allocate additional costs, you can skip this section.

To allocate additional costs, select Maintain Allocations File from the Job Cost Maintenance Menu. The Maintain Allocation File screen appears (Figure 12-18).

Phase Code and Cost Code Enter the phase and cost code you want to allocate costs from. You can allocate costs from this phase and cost code combination to one or more other phase or cost codes, or to this phase and cost code. Press (F2) in each field for a list of the available codes.

Est or Act Enter **E** if you want this allocated cost to apply to estimated job costs. Enter **A** if you want this allocated cost to apply

```
JOB MASTER INFORMATION AS OF 6/1/90

RUN DATE: 06/01/90                    Big Business, Inc.                                    PAGE  1
RUN TIME: 2:23 PM                         Job Cost
                                     JOB MASTER FILE LIST

JOB RANGE ALL TO END
```

NUMBER	DESCRIPTION/SUPERVISOR	CUSTOMER NUMBER / PURCHASE ORDER	START	DUE	CLOSE	ORIGINAL	REVISED	CHG ORD	% COM
GILJOB	Install 10 cptr network. Michael Dispater	GILMAN per contract, Joel Gilman, Attorney	06/01/90	09/01/90	/ /	23475.00	23475.00	0	0
KRELL1	15 PC kits - Krell Office, Michael Dispater	KRELL 2232, Krell Office Systems	06/01/90	07/01/90	/ /	10400.00	10400.00	0	0
KRELL2	Computer w/ Peachtree S/W, Michael Dispater	KRELL see salesperson, Krell Office Systems	06/01/90	06/20/90	/ /	1875.00	1875.00	0	0
SHJJOB	Assemble 2 computers, Michael Dispater	SANTOS PO# 1542, Santos, Harley, and Jones	06/01/90	06/15/90	/ /	2400.00	2400.00	0	0

```
        TOTAL JOBS    4

                          *** END OF JOB MASTER FILE LIST ***
```

FIGURE 12-17 Job Master File List

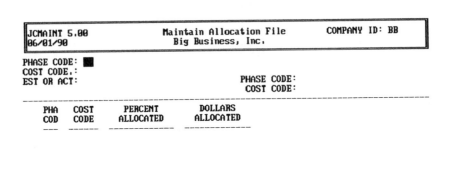

```
JCMAINT 5.00              Maintain Allocation File        COMPANY ID: BB
06/01/90                     Big Business, Inc.

PHASE CODE: ■
COST CODE.:
EST OR ACT:                                    PHASE CODE:
                                                COST CODE:
_____
     PHA    COST     PERCENT        DOLLARS
     COD    CODE    ALLOCATED      ALLOCATED
     ___    ____    _____      _____



  F1-Help  F2 - Lookup              F10 - Menu     Shft F10 - Home
```

═══════ **FIGURE 12-18**   Maintain Allocation File screen

to actual job costs. If this phase and cost code combination has not been entered before, type **Y** and press (ENTER). You can then enter specific allocations in the lower portion of the screen.

Pha Cod and Cost Code   Enter the phase and cost code you want to allocate costs to. These can be the same as the phase and cost code you entered earlier, or they can be different. Press (F2) in each field for a list of the phase and cost codes.

Percent Allocated   Enter the percent of the cost you would like to allocate in additional costs. If you want to allocate 2%, enter **2.00**.

Dollars Allocated   Enter the dollars you want to allocate in additional costs. If you enter a percentage and a dollar amount, Job Cost will allocate both costs.

You can continue entering allocations until you press (ENTER). You can then accept or reject the information on the screen. You can also enter **M** if you want to add more allocations. Figure 12-19 shows a sample list of allocations based on the estimated failure rates of RAM chips during various phases of assembly and testing.

You can print a list of the allocations. Select List Allocations from the Job Cost File List Menu, and tell Job Cost where to print the list. Job Cost will ask if you want to print a listing for estimates, actuals, or both, and will then ask you to select the range of allocations. Figure 12-20 lists the allocations entered for Big Business.

Entering Job Estimates

An *estimate* is the amount of time and money you think it will take to do a job. Estimates provide valuable history. By tracking your

```
┌─────────────────────────────────────────────────────────────────────┐
│ JCMAINT 5.00              Maintain Allocation File     COMPANY ID: BB │
│ 06/01/90                     Big Business, Inc.                       │
└─────────────────────────────────────────────────────────────────────┘
  PHASE CODE: I2        Preparing inventory
  COST CODE.: MAT004    Cost of RAM chips
  EST OR ACT: E                              PHASE CODE: Final testing & config.
  ALLOCATION ENTRY NOT FOUND - ADD (Y/N): Y   COST CODE: COST DOES NOT APPLY

     PHA   COST    PERCENT      DOLLARS
     COD   CODE   ALLOCATED    ALLOCATED

     I3   MAT004   1.0000        0.00
     I4   MAT004   1.0000        0.00
     I5   ALL      1.0000        0.00
     I6   ALL      1.0000        0.00
     I7   ALL      0.5000        0.00
     █

  ▐F1-Help▌ ▐F2 - Lookup▌            ▐F8 - Undo▌ ▐F10 - Done▌
```

FIGURE 12-19 Sample allocations

```
ALLOCATIONS

RUN DATE: 06/01/90                    Big Business, Inc.                                      PAGE  1
RUN TIME: 3:01 PM                          Job Cost
                                      ALLOCATION FILE LIST

PHASE CODE RANGE ALL TO END

EST -------------FROM PHASE/COST-------------  -------------TO PHASE/COST-------------
    -----PHASE-----      ------COST------      -----PHASE-----      ------COST------      -PERCENT-  -DOLLARS-
ACT CODE DESCRIPTION     CODE   DESCRIPTION     CODE DESCRIPTION     CODE   DESCRIPTION     ADDED      ADDED
--- ---- -----------     ------ -----------     ---- -----------     ------ -----------     --------   --------

 E  I2 Preparing inventory MAT004 Cost of RAM chips I3 Component sub-assemb MAT004 Cost of RAM chips    1.0000     0.00
 E  I2 Preparing inventory MAT004 Cost of RAM chips I4 Main assembly        MAT004 Cost of RAM chips    1.0000     0.00
 E  I2 Preparing inventory MAT004 Cost of RAM chips I5 Initial testing & co ALL    COST DOES NOT APPLY  1.0000     0.00
 E  I2 Preparing inventory MAT004 Cost of RAM chips I6 Burn-in              ALL    COST DOES NOT APPLY  1.0000     0.00
 E  I2 Preparing inventory MAT004 Cost of RAM chips I7 Final testing & conf ALL    COST DOES NOT APPLY  0.5000     0.00

    TOTAL ALLOCATION RECORDS    5

                              *** END OF ALLOCATION FILE LIST ***
```

FIGURE 12-20 Allocations list

actual costs against your original estimates, you can see where you can improve your production techniques. Comparing actual costs against estimates will also make you a better estimator, and better able to provide an accurate bid on your next job.

Before you enter an estimate, you must

- Plan the job and identify its phases

- Identify the number of people who will be working on the job

- Specify the quantities and types of materials necessary

- Identify the equipment you will use in each phase

- Determine how many subcontractors you will need and how much they will cost

- Identify any other miscellaneous job costs, such as insurance or a performance bond

You enter job estimates against the job's phase and cost codes. To start entering estimates, select Enter Cost Estimates from the Job Cost Processing Menu, as shown in Figure 12-21. Enter **M** at the first prompt that appears (shown in Figure 12-22) to maintain job estimates. (If you enter **S**, Job Cost will use an old job as a template for creating a new job.) The Enter Cost Estimates screen appears (Figure 12-23).

The first time you enter the job number, Job Cost will ask if you want to add a cost estimate. Type **Y** and press (**ENTER**). You can then enter cost estimate information in the lower portion of the screen.

Ph Cd   Enter the phase code for the estimate. Press (**F2**) to see a list of the phase codes.

Cost Code   If the phase code allows cost codes, you can enter a cost code in this field. Press (**F2**) to see a list of the cost codes.

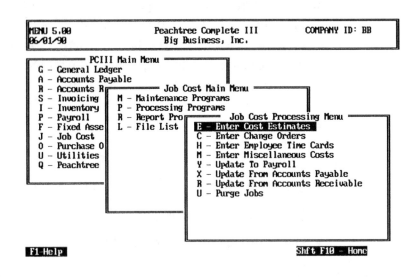

FIGURE 12-21   Select Enter Cost Estimates

```
JCPROC1 5.00              Enter Cost Estimates        COMPANY ID: BB
06/01/90                  Big Business, Inc.

START A NEW JOB WITH AN OLD ESTIMATE
OR MAINTAIN JOB ESTIMATES (S/M): ▯
```

F1-Help   F10 - Menu   Shft F10 - Home

FIGURE 12-22   Enter Cost Estimates prompt

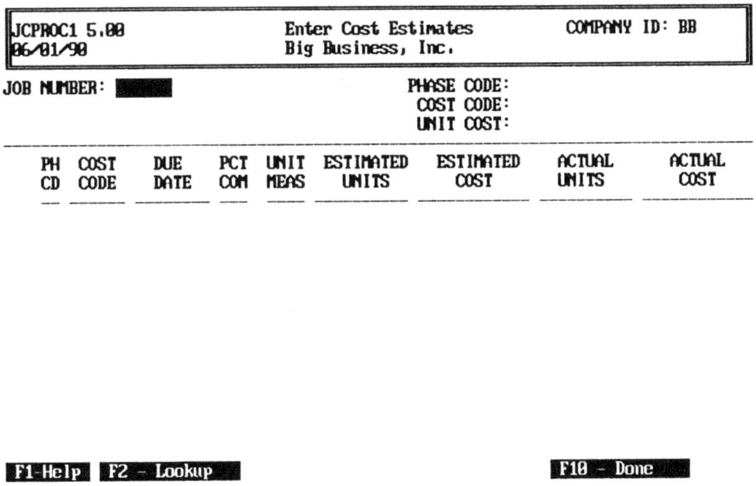

```
┌─────────────────────────────────────────────────────────────────────┐
│ JCPROC1 5.00              Enter Cost Estimates        COMPANY ID: BB  │
│ 06/01/90                  Big Business, Inc.                          │
└─────────────────────────────────────────────────────────────────────┘
 JOB NUMBER: ▓▓▓▓▓▓                    PHASE CODE:
                                       COST CODE:
                                       UNIT COST:
 ───────────────────────────────────────────────────────────────────────

   PH   COST    DUE    PCT  UNIT  ESTIMATED   ESTIMATED    ACTUAL    ACTUAL
   CD   CODE    DATE   COM  MEAS    UNITS        COST       UNITS     COST
   ──   ────    ────   ───  ────  ─────────   ─────────    ──────    ──────



       F1-Help   F2 - Lookup                          F10 - Done
```

FIGURE 12-23 Enter Cost Estimates screen

Due Date   Enter the estimated date this phase ends.

Pct Com   Enter the percent complete of this phase and cost code.

Unit Meas   Job Cost fills in this information for you automatically from the phase and cost code combination.

Estimated Units   Enter the estimated number of units for this phase and cost code.

Estimated Cost   Enter the estimated cost for this phase and cost code, or press (ENTER) to accept the default.

Actual Units and Actual Cost   These fields track the actual units and cost for this phase and cost code combination. Job Cost will automatically update this information. Make entries only if you are setting up a job already in progress.

When you press (ENTER) at the end of the line, Job Cost will take you to the next line to enter another estimate. You can continue entering estimates, or press (F10) to go to the Accept prompt. You can edit estimates by entering **N** at the acceptance prompt and then telling Job Cost which line you want to edit. Figure 12-24 shows several estimates entered for a job.

Printing a Job Cost Estimate Report

When you have finished entering estimates for a job, you can print the Job Cost Estimate report. Select Job Cost Estimate Report from the Job Cost Reports Menu and tell Job Cost where to print the

```
JCPROC1 5.00                 Enter Cost Estimates        COMPANY ID: BB
06/01/90                     Big Business, Inc.

JOB NUMBER: CILJOB                          PHASE CODE:
            Install 10 cptr network.        COST CODE:
                                            UNIT COST:

   PH  COST   DUE     PCT  UNIT  ESTIMATED   ESTIMATED   ACTUAL    ACTUAL
   CD  CODE   DATE    COM  MEAS  UNITS       COST        UNITS     COST
 1 I0 ALL    08/15/90  0  Each    10.00       224.00      0.00      0.00
 2 I1 ALL    06/05/90  0  Hour     8.00       120.00      0.00      0.00
 3 I2 ALL    06/10/90  0          10.00       125.00      0.00      0.00
 4 I3 LAB001 06/15/90  0  Hour    35.00       437.50      0.00      0.00
 5 I3 LAB002 06/30/90  0  Hour    30.00       375.00      0.00      0.00
 6 I3 MAT001 06/15/90  0  Each    10.00       432.00      0.00      0.00
 7 I3 MAT002 06/15/90  0  Each    10.00       540.00      0.00      0.00
 8 I3 MAT003 06/15/90  0  Each    10.00      2574.00      0.00      0.00
 9 I3 MAT004 06/15/90  0  Each   400.00      1300.00      0.00      0.00
10 I4 LAB001 06/30/90  0  Hour    20.00       250.00      0.00      0.00
11 I4 LAB002 06/30/90  0  Hour    40.00       500.00      0.00      0.00

  F1-Help  F2 - Lookup                        F10 - Done
```

FIGURE 12-24 Sample estimates

report and whether to print it for open jobs, closed jobs, or both. You can print this report in two versions: an in-house version, which shows all the information about the estimate, and a customer version, which uses the customer billing amounts. Figure 12-25 shows an in-house Job Cost Estimate report. Figure 12-26 shows the customer version of the same report.

Entering Change Orders

After a job has been in progress for a while, you may need to issue a change order. A *change order* is an adjustment you make to a job. This adjustment can be a change in the type or quantity of items or services delivered, a change in the price, or both. Change orders can result from many things, such as a change in the cost of materials above an allocation you may have made for normal inflation, adding more equipment or personnel to a job, or an increase or decrease in the scope of the project.

To enter a change order, select Enter Change Orders from the Job Cost Processing Menu. The Enter Change Orders screen appears, as shown in Figure 12-27.

Job Number   Enter the job number you are entering a change order for, or press (F2) for a list of jobs.

C/O Number   Enter the number for the change order. It is a good idea to enter sequential numbers for change orders. If the change order number is new, type **Y** and press (ENTER) to add it.

C/O Date   Enter the date of the change order.

C/O Amount   Enter the amount of the change order. This is the difference between the price of the work specified in the change

```
RUN DATE: 06/01/90                          Big Business, Inc.                                              PAGE  1
RUN TIME: 3:48 PM                                Job Cost
                                            JOB COST ESTIMATE REPORT

JOB RANGE ALL TO END

JOB NUMBER GILJOB  Install 10 cptr network.        START 06/01/90    0% COMPLETE
SUPERVISOR  Michael Dispater                       DUE   09/01/90
CUSTOMER # GILMAN  Joel Gilman, Attorney           CLOSE   /  /
```

PHASE/COST CODE	DESCRIPTION	DUE DATE	MEAS	UNIT COST	ESTIMATED UNITS	ESTIMATED DOLLARS	COST ESTIMATE CALCULATED	COST ESTIMATE DIFFERENCE	BILLING ESTIMATE RATE	BILLING ESTIMATE AMOUNT
	PHASE CODE 01 TOTAL				80.00	1600.00	1600.00	0.00		2800.00
02	On-site testing									
ALL	COST DOES NOT APPLY	08/15/90		0.00	50.00	0.00	0.00	0.00	0.00	0.00
03	Configuring cmptr on-site	08/25/90	Hour	20.00	5.00	100.00	100.00	0.00	35.00	175.00
05	Customizing software	/ /	Hour	20.00	10.00	200.00	200.00	0.00	35.00	350.00
06	On-site training	09/01/90	Hour	25.00	24.00	600.00	600.00	0.00	40.00	960.00
	LABOR				422.00	6863.50	6863.50	0.00		12534.00
	MATERIAL				482.00	10111.25	10111.25	0.00		15346.50
	EQUIPMENT				0.00	0.00	0.00	0.00		0.00
	SUBCONTRACT				0.00	0.00	0.00	0.00		0.00
	OTHER				60.00	125.00	0.00	125.00-		0.00
	JOB GILJOB TOTAL				964.00	17099.75	16974.75	125.00-		27880.50

FIGURE 12-25 In-house Job Cost Estimate report

```
RUN DATE: 06/01/90                          Big Business, Inc.                                    PAGE  1
RUN TIME:  3:49 PM                               Job Cost
                                          JOB COST ESTIMATE REPORT

JOB RANGE ALL TO END

JOB NUMBER GILJOB   Install 10 cptr network.          START 06/01/90        0% COMPLETE
SUPERVISOR    Michael Dispater                        DUE   09/01/90
CUSTOMER # GILMAN   Joel Gilman, Attorney             CLOSE   /  /

-------PHASE/COST--------    --DUE--  UNIT  -----ESTIMATED-----
  CODE       DESCRIPTION     DATE     MEAS  UNITS     BILLING
  ----   ---------------     -----    ----  -----     -------

        PHASE CODE 01 TOTAL                           80.00     2800.00

 02   On-site testing
 ALL  COST DOES NOT APPLY    08/15/90                 50.00        0.00

 03   Configuring cmptr on-site 08/25/90 Hour          5.00      175.00

 05   Customizing software       /  /    Hour         10.00      350.00

 06   On-site training        09/01/90   Hour         24.00      960.00

        LABOR                                        422.00    12534.00
        MATERIAL                                     482.00    15346.50
        EQUIPMENT                                      0.00        0.00
        SUBCONTRACT                                    0.00        0.00
        OTHER                                         60.00        0.00
                                                    =======   ==========
        JOB GILJOB TOTAL                             964.00    27880.50
```

FIGURE 12-26 Customer Job Cost Estimate report

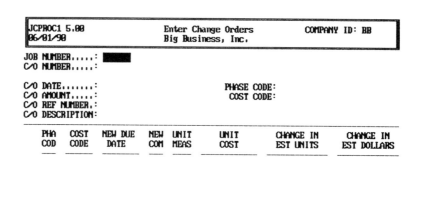

FIGURE 12-27 Enter Change Orders screen

order and the previous cost of the job, rather than the total cost of the new job.

C/O Ref Number   Enter a purchase order number or other information describing the source for the change order.

C/O Description   Enter up to 25 characters describing the change order.

When you have entered the information in the top portion of the screen, press (F10). Enter changes to the job on the lower portion of the screen with the appropriate phase and cost codes. You enter the information in the format in which you entered job estimates. Figure 12-28 shows a change order ready to be accepted. The

```
┌─────────────────────────────────────────────────────────────────────┐
│ JCPROC1 5.00              Enter Change Orders        COMPANY ID: BB   │
│ 06/01/90                  Big Business, Inc.                          │
└─────────────────────────────────────────────────────────────────────┘
  JOB NUMBER.....: GILJOB      Install 10 cptr network.
  C/O NUMBER.....: 000001      CHANGE ORDER ENTRY NOT FOUND - ADD (Y/N): Y

  C/O DATE.......: 06/01/90              PHASE CODE:
  C/O AMOUNT.....:      2240.00          COST CODE:
  C/O REF NUMBER.: per salesperson
  C/O DESCRIPTION: Chg all monitors to VGA

  PHA    COST    NEW DUE   NEW  UNIT      UNIT      CHANGE IN     CHANGE IN
  COD    CODE    DATE      COM  MEAS      COST      EST UNITS     EST DOLLARS
  ───    ────    ───────   ───  ────      ────      ─────────     ───────────
  I4     MAT006  06/15/90   0   Each      262.33       5.00          1311.65


  ACCEPT (Y/N/M): Y
```

════ **FIGURE 12-28**   Sample change order

Change Order Report option, available on the Job Cost Reports Menu, shows you the change orders issued against each job.

UPDATING PAYROLL INFORMATION

If you are interfacing Job Cost with Payroll, you will need to transfer employee time card information from Job Cost to Payroll at the close of your pay period. You will also need to post employee time to the job and update your job costs even if you are not using Job Cost with Payroll.

Updating the payroll information is a three-part process. First, you enter the time card hours for each employee. Next, you print a Time Card Edit List and check your information. Finally, you use the Update to Payroll option to update the payroll information in Job Cost and Payroll.

Entering Time Card Hours

You enter time card hours as part of your end-of-period payroll activities. Start by selecting Enter Time Card Hours from the Job Cost Processing Menu. The Enter Employee Time Cards screen appears (Figure 12-29).

Time Card Date Enter the date of the time card or the ending date of the pay period.

Employee Code Enter the employee's code number. Press (F2) for a list of employees and employee codes. If you are making an entry for equipment usage, enter **EQPT** in this field.

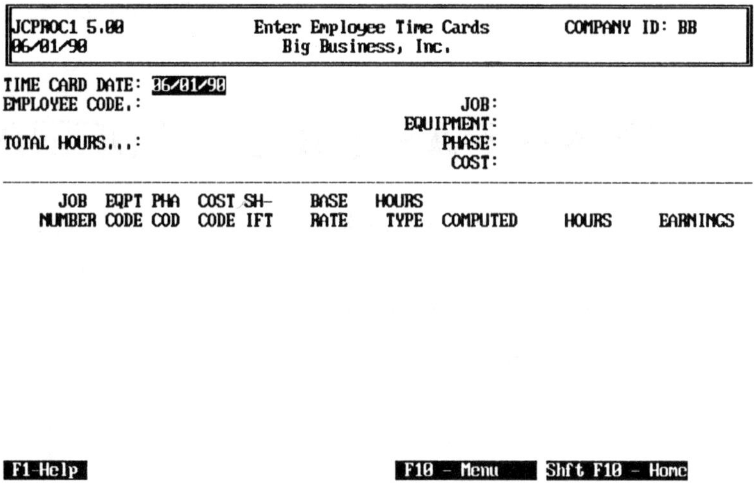

```
┌─────────────────────────────────────────────────────────────────┐
│ JCPROC1 5.00          Enter Employee Time Cards    COMPANY ID: BB │
│ 06/01/90                Big Business, Inc.                        │
└─────────────────────────────────────────────────────────────────┘
 TIME CARD DATE: 06/01/90
 EMPLOYEE CODE.:                            JOB:
                                      EQUIPMENT:
 TOTAL HOURS...:                           PHASE:
                                           COST:
─────────────────────────────────────────────────────────────────────
     JOB   EQPT PHA  COST SH-   BASE  HOURS
   NUMBER  CODE COD  CODE IFT   RATE  TYPE  COMPUTED   HOURS    EARNINGS


  [ F1-Help ]                    [ F10 - Menu ]  [ Shft F10 - Home ]
```

FIGURE 12-29 Enter Employee Time Cards screen

If there is no time entry for this employee on this date, type **Y** and press (ENTER).

Total Hours   Enter the total number of hours the employee worked in this period, or press (ENTER) to accept the default.

Job Cost moves the cursor to the lower portion of the screen. You enter the time card hours for each job the employee worked on during the period here.

Job Number   Enter a job number, or press (F2) to see a list of jobs and job numbers.

Eqpt Code   Enter the code for the equipment an employee may have used if the equipment used is also billable. If you are making an entry for equipment, you must make an entry in this field. Press (F2) for a list of equipment codes.

Pha Cod and Cost Code   Enter the phase and cost code the employee hours should be billed to. Press (F2) in each field for a list of the phase and cost codes.

Shift   Enter the shift the employee worked. If you are making an entry for equipment, enter **1**.

Base Rate   Job Cost will display the default base rate for the employee. (If the employee is hourly, the base rate will be the employee's annual salary expressed as an hourly wage.) Press (ENTER) to accept the default or enter another rate.

Hours Type   Enter **R** if this is regular (straight) time. Enter **1** to bill this at overtime rate 1, and **2** to bill this at overtime rate 2. If you are making an entry for equipment, leave this field blank.

Computed This is the base rate times the type of time. If you have a nonstandard pay rate, you can change the entry in this field; otherwise, press (ENTER).

Hours Enter the total hours the employee worked in this phase and cost code.

Earnings Job Cost will display the calculated employee earnings for this entry. Press (ENTER) to accept the default, or change the entry as necessary.

When you press (ENTER), Job Cost lets you enter another line of time card information. The total number of hours on the individual items must equal the total employee hours at the top of the screen. You can continue entering information, or press (F10). Figure 12-30 shows a completed time card screen.

```
JCPROC1 5.00                Enter Employee Time Cards       COMPANY ID: BB
06/01/90                         Big Business, Inc.

TIME CARD DATE: 06/01/90
EMPLOYEE CODE.: 00102                          JOB:
           James K. Habbakuk             EQUIPMENT:
TOTAL HOURS...:    40.00                      PHASE:
TIME CARD ENTRY NOT FOUND - ADD (Y/N): Y       COST:


    JOB  EQPT PHA  COST SH-  BASE   HOURS
  NUMBER CODE COD  CODE IFT  RATE   TYPE  COMPUTED    HOURS      EARNINGS
  GILJOB      I3  LAB001 1   6.750   R      6.750     40.00       270.00




ACCEPT (Y/N/H): Y
```

FIGURE 12-30 Sample Enter Employee Time Cards hours screen

Printing the Time Card Edit List

When you have entered the time card information, print a Time Card Edit List by selecting Time Card Edit List from the Job Cost Reports Menu. Tell Job Cost where to print the list and the range of dates. Check your time card information against the entries on the report to make sure that it is complete and correct. A sample report appears in Figure 12-31.

Updating Payroll

Once the employee time card information is entered and verified, you are ready to update the payroll. Select Update to Payroll from the Job Cost Processing Menu. Job Cost asks you for the run date and then makes sure that you have run the Time Card Edit List (Figure 12-32). When you type **Y** and press (**ENTER**), Job Cost will create a temporary file to hold the time card hours. You then can select a date range for the transfer. If you enter **N**, Job Cost will transfer all time card hours in the time card file.

To complete the transfer, you must go to the Payroll module and select Update from Job Cost from the Payroll Processing Menu. After you tell Payroll where to print the control report, it will read the information from the temporary file and update the employee records in Payroll.

ENTERING MISCELLANEOUS COSTS

You will occasionally have miscellanous costs that will not come from time cards or Accounts Payable. For example, there may be minor additional costs that you don't want to enter in Accounts Payable. You may have to pay for shipping a product, for renting equipment, or a one-time materials or labor cost. You'll also want

```
TIME CARDS AS OF 6/1/90

RUN DATE: 06/01/90                    Big Business, Inc.                         PAGE  1
RUN TIME: 8:51 AM                         Job Cost
                                      TIME CARD EDIT LIST
```

TIME CARD DATE	NUMBER	EMPLOYEE/JOB DESCRIPTION	EQPT CODE	PHASE CODE	COST CODE	SH-IFT	BASE RATE	HOURS TYPE	COMPUTED-RATE	HOURS	EARNINGS
06/01/90	00144	Eric Gross									
	GILJOB	Install 10 cptr network.		I3	LAB001	1	8.210	R	8.210	10.00	82.10
06/01/90	00235	Janice Broxon									
	GILJOB	Install 10 cptr network.		I1	ALL	1	6.750	R	6.750	15.00	101.25
06/01/90	00391	Chuck Reynolds									
	GILJOB	Install 10 cptr network.		I2	MISCL	1	8.200	R	8.200	5.00	41.00
		WARNING - ESTIMATE DOES NOT EXIST FOR THIS ENTRY									
06/01/90	00540	Bill Burgess									
	GILJOB	Install 10 cptr network.		I3	LAB001	1	10.420	R	10.420	13.40	139.63
06/01/90	00666	Bill Austin									
	GILJOB	Install 10 cptr network.		I2	LAB001	1	6.750	R	6.750	6.00	40.50
		WARNING - ESTIMATE DOES NOT EXIST FOR THIS ENTRY									
		LABOR TOTAL								49.40	404.48

FIGURE 12-31   Time Card Edit List

```
┌─────────────────────────────────────────────────────────────────┐
│ JCPROC2 5.00              Update To Payroll         COMPANY ID: BB │
│ 06/01/90                  Big Business, Inc.                       │
└─────────────────────────────────────────────────────────────────┘


   RUN DATE: 06/01/90




   ** WARNING ** THE TIME CARD EDIT LIST MUST BE RUN BEFORE
                 TIME CARD ENTRIES CAN BE TRANSFERRED TO OTHER FILES.
                 HAVE YOU RUN TIME CARD EDIT LIST (Y/N): Y
```

═══════ **FIGURE 12-32** Update To Payroll warning screen

to enter miscellaneous costs for a job if you aren't interfacing Accounts Payable with Job Cost.

Select Enter Miscellaneous Costs from the Job Cost Processing Menu. The Miscellaneous Costs screen appears (shown in Figure 12-33). Enter the date you are entering the miscellaneous cost and the job number. If this miscellaneous entry is new, type **Y** and press (ENTER).

Pha Cod and Cost Code Enter the phase and cost code the miscellaneous cost should be billed to. Press (F2) in each field for a list of the phase and cost codes.

Src Job Cost will enter the source of the cost for you, as follows:

M	Miscellaneous cost	Enter Miscellaneous Costs screen

T	Time cost (personnel)	Enter Employee Time Cards
E	Equipment cost	Enter Employee Time Cards
P	Accounts Payable	Accounts Payable module
R	Accounts Receivable	Accounts Receivable module

Unit Meas and Unit Cost   Job Cost enters the unit of measurement and the unit cost from the phase or cost code information.

Unit Quantity   Enter the number of units you are adding.

Extended Cost   Job Cost multiplies the unit cost by the quantity to create the extended cost. Press (**ENTER**) to accept this or enter a different amount.

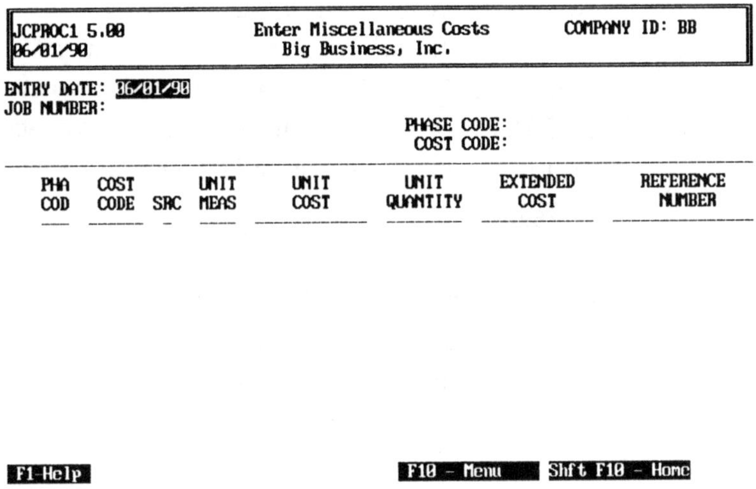

```
JCPROC1 5.00                 Enter Miscellaneous Costs      COMPANY ID: BB
06/01/90                        Big Business, Inc.

ENTRY DATE: 06/01/90
JOB NUMBER:
                                              PHASE CODE:
                                              COST CODE:

   PHA   COST         UNIT   UNIT    UNIT    EXTENDED      REFERENCE
   COD   CODE  SRC    MEAS   COST   QUANTITY   COST         NUMBER
```

```
 F1-Help                          F10 - Menu    Shft F10 - Home
```

FIGURE 12-33   Enter Miscellaneous Costs screen

Reference Number   Enter up to 15 characters of reference information.

When you press (ENTER), Job Cost lets you enter another line of costs. You can continue entering information, or press (F10). The information you enter on the Enter Miscellaneous Costs screen appears on the Job Cost Detail report.

INTERFACING WITH ACCOUNTS PAYABLE

In Accounts Payable, you will need to distribute costs to Job Cost after you enter the invoice information. A sample distribution to a job appears in Figure 12-34.

When you want to transfer information from Accounts Payable, select Update from Accounts Payable on the Job Cost Processing Menu and tell Job Cost where to print the report. Job Cost will then apply the Accounts Payable transactions to your jobs. The Accounts Payable transactions will show up on the Accounts Payable Update report (from the Accounts Payable module) and on several of the Job Cost reports.

INTERFACING WITH ACCOUNTS RECEIVABLE

To enter a Job Cost transaction in Accounts Receivable, enter an exclamation point followed by the job number in the Comment field of the Enter Transactions screen (shown in Figure 12-35), or in the Reference field of the Apply Payments screen. This tells Accounts Receivable that this transaction is to be transferred to Job

```
┌─────────────────────────────────────────────────────────────────────┐
│ APPROC1 5.00              Enter Invoices         COMPANY ID: BB       │
│ 06/01/90                  Big Business, Inc.      GENERATION #: 00     │
└─────────────────────────────────────────────────────────────────────┘

  Vendor ID..............: SHA001    Sharma Software
  Invoice Number.........: 1493

  Amount To Distribute To Job Cost:      445.00

              Job Number   Phase Code   Cost Code    Amount
              ──────────   ──────────   ─────────    ──────
               GILJOB         I2         MAT007       445.00
               ███                                      0.00


                                                  ===============
                                                       445.00



      ┌─────────┐ ┌──────────────┐        ┌───────────┐ ┌───────────┐
      │ F1-Help │ │ F2 - Lookup  │        │ F8 - Undo │ │ F10 - Done│
      └─────────┘ └──────────────┘        └───────────┘ └───────────┘
```

FIGURE 12-34   Sample Accounts Payable distribution

```
┌─────────────────────────────────────────────────────────────────────┐
│ ARPROC 5.00             Enter Transactions       COMPANY ID: BB       │
│ 06/01/90                Big Business, Inc.        GENERATION #: 01     │
└─────────────────────────────────────────────────────────────────────┘

  Customer ID.: GILMAN     Joel Gilman, Attorney      Balance:      301.24
  Trans. Type.: PA  Payment                          Credit Limit: 5000.00
  Product Code:     Payment

  Invoice Terms    Terms      Trans.   Due    Discount   Trans.              T
  Number  Code  Description   Date     Date   Date       Amount    Comment   E
  ─────── ───── ───────────   ──────   ────   ────────   ──────    ───────   ─
  0                           06/01/90                    4000.00  *GILJOB   T

                                     State Tax.:            0.00
                                     County Tax:            0.00
                                     City Tax..:            0.00
                                                         ───────
                                     Invoice Total:       4000.00


                                          Accept (Y/N)  Y
                                     ┌────────────┐
                                     │ F8 - Cancel│
                                     └────────────┘
```

FIGURE 12-35   Enter Transactions screen in Accounts
Receivable

Cost. When you want to transfer information from Accounts Receivable, select Update from Accounts Receivable on the Job Cost Processing Menu and tell Job Cost where to print the report. Job Cost will then apply the Accounts Receivable transactions to your jobs. The Accounts Receivable transactions will show up on the Accounts Receivable Update report (from the Accounts Receivable module) and on several of the Job Cost reports.

Accounts Receivable transactions only affect the job cost totals in the Job Master file.

PURGING JOBS

You can purge jobs and their associated detail information from Job Cost with the Purge Jobs option. Select Purge Jobs from the Job Cost Processing Menu and tell Job Cost where you want to print the report.

If you have not done so, print a Job Cost Detail report before purging jobs as a permanent record of the job activity. This report is described in the next section.

To continue, you must answer **Y** to the "Have you backed up your files" warning. You can select closed jobs only (those that do not have **Y** in the Prevent Purge field), or purge details for all open and closed jobs. You can also select a range of dates and jobs. When the purge process is done, Job Cost returns you to the Main Menu.

OTHER REPORTS

Most of the work you encounter with Job Cost involves setting up the Job Cost module and then setting up phase and cost codes for each job. After that, you can transfer information directly between Job Cost and the other Peachtree Complete III modules. There are a number of reports that you can run during and after the job costing process that will give you valuable information about a job's progress.

The reports have a number of things in common. All of these reports are options on the Job Cost Reports Menu. You must tell Job Cost where to print the information: on the printer, to a disk file, or on your screen. Jobs are sorted by job number, phase code, and cost code. You can also select a range of phases, jobs, employees, or equipment rather than printing all selections on the report. Where applicable, reports will also give subtotals for the five phase/cost code categories: labor, material, equipment, subcontractors, and other. Finally, you can select information from open jobs, closed jobs, or both. The following report descriptions will only list variations from this pattern.

Job Cost Inquiry Report

The Job Cost Inquiry report gives you detailed information about a specific job. Select Job Cost Inquiry Report from the Job Cost Reports Menu. The Job Cost Inquiry Report screen appears (Figure 12-36).

You can select a job by making an entry in the Job Number field. Job Cost will ask you if you want to print the totals only. Enter **Y** for a summary report or **N** for a detail report. Enter **B** to browse through the jobs on file. Job Cost then asks you to specify the output device. When the report is through printing, you can select another job and print a Job Cost Inquiry report for it as well. A sample Job Cost Inquiry report appears in Figure 12-37.

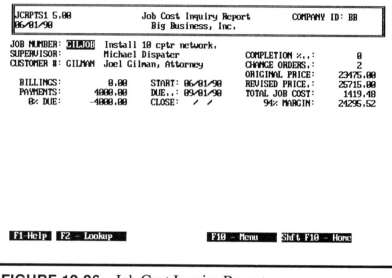

FIGURE 12-36 Job Cost Inquiry Report screen

Job Cost Estimate Report

The Job Cost Estimate report lists estimates for a specific job. Select Job Cost Estimate Report from the Job Cost Reports Menu. You can select a range of jobs and print this report in in-house and customer versions. The in-house version uses estimates based on actual costs, and the customer version uses billable rates. Figure 12-38 shows an in-house version of this report.

Job Cost Summary Report

The Job Cost Summary report gives a summary of information for all or selected jobs. Select Job Cost Summary Report from the Job Cost Reports Menu. Figure 12-39 shows a sample Job Cost Summary report.

```
INQUIRY 6/1/90

RUN DATE: 06/01/90          Big Business, Inc.          PAGE  1
RUN TIME: 10:11 AM              Job Cost
                            JOB INQUIRY REPORT
-----------------------------------------------------------------------
JOB NUMBER GILJOB  Install 10 cptr network.
SUPERVISOR         Michael Dispater           COMPLETION %         0
CUSTOMER # GILMAN  Joel Gilman, Attorney       CHANGE ORDERS        2
                                               ORIGINAL PRICE   23475.00
   BILLINGS        0.00      START 06/01/90    REVISED PRICE    25715.00
   PAYMENTS     4000.00      DUE   09/01/90    TOTAL JOB COST    1419.48
   0 % DUE      4000.00-     CLOSE   /  /      94 % MARGIN      24295.52

PHASE COST   ESTIMATED  ACTUAL   %    ESTIMATED    ACTUAL
CODE  CODE     UNITS    UNITS   DIF    DOLLARS     DOLLARS   DIFFERENCE   %
--    -----  --------- -------- ---  ------------ ---------- ---------- ---

  I0  ALL        10.00    0.00 100-       224.00       0.00   224.00-100-
  I1  ALL         8.00   15.00  88        120.00     101.25    18.75- 16-
  I2  ALL        10.00    0.00 100-       125.00       0.00   125.00-100-
  I2  LAB001      0.00    6.00   0          0.00      40.50    40.50   0
  I2  MAT007      0.00    0.00   0          0.00     445.00   445.00   0
  I2  MISCL       0.00    5.00   0          0.00      41.00    41.00   0
  I3  LAB001     35.00   75.40 115        437.50     791.73   354.23  81
  I3  LAB002     30.00    0.00 100-       375.00       0.00   375.00-100-
  I3  MAT001     10.00    0.00 100-       432.00       0.00   432.00-100-
  I3  MAT002     10.00    0.00 100-       540.00       0.00   540.00-100-
  I3  MAT003     10.00    0.00 100-      2574.00       0.00  2574.00-100-
  I3  MAT004    400.00    0.00 100-      1300.00       0.00  1300.00-100-
  I4  LAB001     20.00    0.00 100-       250.00       0.00   250.00-100-
  I4  LAB002     40.00    0.00 100-       500.00       0.00   500.00-100-
  I4  MAT005      5.00    0.00 100-       187.50       0.00   187.50-100-
  I4  MAT006     10.00    0.00 100-      2623.30       0.00  2623.30-100-
  I4  MAT007      5.00    0.00 100-        44.85       0.00    44.85-100-
  I4  MAT008      5.00    0.00 100-       874.75       0.00   874.75-100-
  I4  MAT009     10.00    0.00 100-       251.50       0.00   251.50-100-
  I4  MAT010     15.00    0.00 100-      1020.00       0.00  1020.00-100-
  I4  MAT011      7.00    0.00 100-      1575.00       0.00  1575.00-100-
  I5  ALL        30.00    0.00 100-       375.00       0.00   375.00-100-
  I6  ALL        20.00    0.00 100-       600.00       0.00   600.00-100-
  I7  ALL        40.00    0.00 100-       500.00       0.00   500.00-100-
  I8  LAB003     60.00    0.00 100-       900.00       0.00   900.00-100-
  I9  ALL        10.00    0.00 100-        82.00       0.00    82.00-100-
  O1  LAB005     40.00    0.00 100-       800.00       0.00   800.00-100-
  O1  LAB006     40.00    0.00 100-       800.00       0.00   800.00-100-
  O2  ALL        50.00    0.00 100-         0.00       0.00     0.00   0
  O3  ALL         5.00    0.00 100-       100.00       0.00   100.00-100-
  O5  ALL        10.00    0.00 100-       200.00       0.00   200.00-100-
  O6  ALL        24.00    0.00 100-       600.00       0.00   600.00-100-

LABOR          422.00   101.40  76-      6863.50     974.48  5889.02- 86-
MATERIAL       487.00     0.00 100-     11422.90     445.00 10977.90- 96-
EQUIPMENT        0.00     0.00   0          0.00       0.00     0.00   0
SUBCONTRACT      0.00     0.00   0          0.00       0.00     0.00   0
OTHER           60.00     0.00 100-       125.00       0.00   125.00-100-
             ========= ========      ============ ========== ==========
JOB TOTAL      969.00   101.40  90-     18411.40    1419.48 16991.92- 92-

           *** END OF JOB INQUIRY REPORT ***
```

FIGURE 12-37   Job Cost Inquiry report

```
RUN DATE: 06/01/90                        Big Business, Inc.                              PAGE   1
RUN TIME: 10:12 AM                             Job Cost
                                        JOB COST ESTIMATE REPORT

JOB RANGE ALL TO END

JOB NUMBER GILJOB  Install 10 cptr network.    START 06/01/90    0% COMPLETE
SUPERVISOR         Michael Dispater            DUE   09/01/90
CUSTOMER # GILMAN  Joel Gilman, Attorney       CLOSE   /  /
```

PHASE/COST CODE	DESCRIPTION	DUE DATE	UNIT MEAS	UNIT COST	ESTIMATED UNITS	ESTIMATED DOLLARS	COST ESTIMATE CALCULATED	COST ESTIMATE DIFFERENCE	BILLING ESTIMATE RATE	BILLING ESTIMATE AMOUNT
19	Packing	08/10/90	Each	8.20	10.00	82.00	82.00	0.00	15.00	150.00
01	Customer site preparation									
LAB005	Labor - on-site prep	08/10/90	Hour	20.00	40.00	800.00	800.00	0.00	35.00	1400.00
LAB006	Labor - on-site wiring	08/12/90	Hour	20.00	40.00	800.00	800.00	0.00	35.00	1400.00
	PHASE CODE 01 TOTAL				80.00	1600.00	1600.00	0.00		2800.00
02	On-site testing									
ALL	COST DOES NOT APPLY	08/15/90		0.00	50.00	0.00	0.00	0.00	0.00	0.00
03	Configuring cmptr on-site	08/25/90	Hour	20.00	5.00	100.00	100.00	0.00	35.00	175.00
05	Customizing software	/ /	Hour	20.00	10.00	200.00	200.00	0.00	35.00	350.00
06	On-site training	09/01/90	Hour	25.00	24.00	600.00	600.00	0.00	40.00	960.00
	LABOR				422.00	6863.50	6863.50	0.00		12534.00
	MATERIAL				487.00	11422.90	11422.90	0.00		17841.50
	EQUIPMENT				0.00	0.00	0.00	0.00		0.00
	SUBCONTRACT				0.00	0.00	0.00	0.00		0.00
	OTHER				60.00	125.00	0.00	125.00-		0.00
	JOB GILJOB TOTAL				969.00	18411.40	18286.40	125.00-		30375.50

FIGURE 12-38 In-house version of Job Cost Estimate report

SUMMARY 6/1/90

RUN DATE: 06/01/90
RUN TIME: 10:12 AM

Big Business, Inc.
Job Cost
JOB COST SUMMARY REPORT

PAGE 1

JOB RANGE ALL TO END

NUMBER	DESCRIPTION	REVISED PRICE	% COM	DUE DATE	BILLINGS TOTAL	%	PAYMENTS TOTAL	%	COSTS TOTAL	%	MARGIN TOTAL	%
GILJOB	Install 10 cptr network.	25715.00	0	09/01/90	0.00	0	4000.00	16	1419.48	6	24295.52	94
KRELL1	15 PC kits - Krell Office	10400.00	0	07/01/90	0.00	0	0.00	0	0.00	0	10400.00	100
KRELL2	Computer w/ Peachtree S/W	1875.00	0	06/20/90	0.00	0	0.00	0	864.00	46	1011.00	54
SHJJOB	Assemble 2 computers	2400.00	0	06/15/90	0.00	0	0.00	0	0.00	0	2400.00	100
	REPORT TOTAL	40390.00			0.00	0	4000.00	10	2283.48	6	38106.52	94

*** END OF JOB COST SUMMARY REPORT ***

FIGURE 12-39 Job Cost Summary report

Job Cost Totals Report

The Job Cost Totals report compares the estimated units and costs to the actual units and costs. You can list the totals by job number, by phase code, or by cost code. Select Job Cost Totals Reports from the Job Cost Reports Menu and select a report option from the options menu (Figure 12-40). Figure 12-41 shows a sample Job Cost Totals report listed by phase code.

Job Cost Detail Report

The Job Cost Detail report lists all job transactions by job, phase code, and cost code. You should print a Job Cost Detail report as a permanent record immediately before purging job detail or closed jobs. Select Job Cost Detail Report from the Job Cost

```
┌──────────────────────────────────────────────────────────────────┐
│ JCRPTS1 5.00            Job Cost Totals Reports      COMPANY ID: BB │
│ 06/01/90                  Big Business, Inc.                        │
└──────────────────────────────────────────────────────────────────┘

Program Loading...Please Wait

              ┌══════ Select Report ══════┐
              │ J - TOTALS BY JOB NUMBER   │
              │ P - TOTALS BY PHASE CODE   │
              │ C - TOTALS BY COST CODE    │
              └────────────────────────────┘
```

FIGURE 12-40   Job Cost Totals Reports Options Menu

RUN DATE: 06/01/90
RUN TIME: 10:13 AM

Big Business, Inc.
Job Cost
TOTALS BY PHASE CODE

PAGE 1

PHASE CODE RANGE ALL TO END

| PHASE/COST | | | | -JOB- | --UNITS-- | | | | -DOLLARS- | | | |
CODE DESCRIPTION	DUE	COM%	NUMBER		ESTIMATE	ACTUAL	DIFF.	DIF%	ESTIMATE	ACTUAL	DIFFERENCE	DIF%
MAT011 Cost of hard drives	06/15/90	0	GILJOB		7.00	0.00	7.00-100-		1575.00	0.00	1575.00-100-	
PHASE CODE I4 TOTAL					117.00	0.00	117.00-100-		7326.90	0.00	7326.90-100-	
I5 Initial testing & config	07/12/90	0	GILJOB		30.00	0.00	30.00-100-		375.00	0.00	375.00-100-	
I6 Burn-in	07/15/90	0	GILJOB		20.00	0.00	20.00-100-		600.00	0.00	600.00-100-	
I7 Final testing & config.	07/31/90	0	GILJOB		40.00	0.00	40.00-100-		500.00	0.00	500.00-100-	
I8 S/W installation & confi												
LAB003 Labor - s/w installation	08/08/90	0	GILJOB		60.00	0.00	60.00-100-		900.00	0.00	900.00-100-	
I9 Packing	08/10/90	0	GILJOB		10.00	0.00	10.00-100-		82.00	0.00	82.00-100-	
O1 Customer site preparatio												
LAB005 Labor - on-site prep	08/10/90	0	GILJOB		40.00	0.00	40.00-100-		800.00	0.00	800.00-100-	
LAB006 Labor - on-site wiring	08/12/90	0	GILJOB		40.00	0.00	40.00-100-		800.00	0.00	800.00-100-	
PHASE CODE O1 TOTAL					80.00	0.00	80.00-100-		1600.00	0.00	1600.00-100-	
O2 On-site testing												
ALL COST DOES NOT APPLY	08/15/90	0	GILJOB		50.00	0.00	50.00-100-		0.00	0.00	0	
O3 Configuring cmptr on-sit	08/25/90	0	GILJOB		5.00	0.00	5.00-100-		100.00	0.00	100.00-100-	
O5 Customizing software	/ /	0	GILJOB		10.00	0.00	10.00-100-		200.00	0.00	200.00-100-	
O6 On-site training	09/01/90	0	GILJOB		24.00	0.00	24.00-100-		600.00	0.00	600.00-100-	

FIGURE 12-41 Job Cost Totals report by phase code

Reports Menu. You can select a range of dates for detail transactions. You can also specify the source of the transactions or enter C for all transactions. In addition, you can condense the transaction detail. Enter **C** for a condensed version, which will show a summary for each transaction source code; otherwise, enter **D** to show every transaction. Figure 12-42 is a sample Job Cost Detail report.

Employees by Job Report

The Employees by Job report lists the employees that worked on each phase of a job, the hours they worked, and their earnings. To ensure the most accurate information, you should enter all employee time card and updated payroll information before printing this report. Select Employees by Job Report from the Job Cost Reports Menu. You can specify a date range if you wish. A sample Employees by Job report appears in Figure 12-43.

Equipment by Job Report

The Equipment by Job report lists the equipment used on each phase of a job. Equipment hours are entered along with employee hours, so you should enter all employee time card and updated payroll information before printing this report. Select Equipment by Job Report from the Job Cost Reports Menu. You can specify a date range if you wish. This report is very similar to the Employees by Job report. A sample Equipment by Job report is shown in Figure 12-44.

Pre-Billing Worksheet

The Pre-Billing Worksheet gives you a list of proposed billing amounts for the costs and phases of a job. It also projects the amount and percentage of profit or loss based on actual versus estimated costs. Select Pre-Billing Worksheet from the Job Cost Reports Menu. You can specify a date range if you wish. A sample Pre-Billing Worksheet appears in Figure 12-45.

```
RUN DATE: 06/01/90                                    Big Business, Inc.                                        PAGE  1
RUN TIME: 10:14 AM                                        Job Cost
                                                     JOB COST DETAIL REPORT

JOB RANGE ALL TO END

JOB NUMBER KRELL2  Computer w/ Peachtree S/W     START 06/01/90      0% COMPLETE
SUPERVISOR    Michael Dispater                   DUE   06/20/90
CUSTOMER # KRELL  Krell Office Systems           CLOSE   /  /

----PHASE/COST--------          ------TRANSACTION-------        ---UNITS----    ----COST----       -----UNIT COSTS-----
CODE        DESCRIPTION      DATE   SOURCE  REFERENCE       MEAS QUANTITY    DOLLARS  % TOT      STANDARD   ACTUAL

I3     Component sub-assembly
MAT001    Cost of chassis    06/01/90 MISC  Out of stock    Each  20.00    864.00  100.0        43.20      43.20

                                                                          ------  -----
          LABOR                                                             0.00    0.0
          MATERIAL                                                        864.00  100.0
          EQUIPMENT                                                         0.00    0.0
          SUBCONTRACT                                                       0.00    0.0
          OTHER                                                             0.00    0.0
                                                                          ------  -----
          JOB KRELL2 TOTAL                                                864.00  100.0
```

FIGURE 12-42 Job Cost Detail report

```
EMPLOYEES 6/1/90                                                                        PAGE  1

RUN DATE: 06/01/90                           Big Business, Inc.
RUN TIME: 10:14 AM                               Job Cost
                                           EMPLOYEES BY JOB REPORT

JOB RANGE ALL TO END

JOB NUMBER GILJOB  Install 10 cptr network.      START 06/01/90      0% COMPLETE
SUPERVISOR    Michael Dispater                   DUE   09/01/90
CUSTOMER # GILMAN  Joel Gilman, Attorney         CLOSE   /  /

-------PHASE/COST-------    --ENTRY-    -------EMPLOYEE--------
CODE       DESCRIPTION        DATE      CODE       NAME            HOURS       AMOUNT
------  ----------------    --------    -----  -----------------  --------   --------

I1      Computer design and spec.  06/01/90   00235  Janice Broxon     15.00      101.25

I2      Preparing inventory
LAB001  Labor - assembly line     06/01/90    00666  Bill Austin        6.00       40.50

MISCL   Miscellaneous labor       06/01/90    00391  Chuck Reynolds     5.00       41.00

        PHASE CODE I2 TOTAL                                            11.00       81.50

I3      Component sub-assembly
LAB001  Labor - assembly line     06/01/90    00102  James K. Habbakuk  40.00      270.00
                                  06/01/90    00144  Eric Gross         10.00       82.10
                                  06/01/90    00540  Bill Burgess       13.40       39.63
                                                                      --------   --------
        COST CODE LAB001 TOTAL                                         63.40      491.73
                                                                      --------   --------
        PHASE CODE I3 TOTAL                                            63.40      491.73
                                                                      ========   ========
        JOB GILJOB TOTAL                                               89.40      674.48
```

FIGURE 12-43 Employees by Job Report

```
EQUIPMENT 6/1/90

RUN DATE: 06/01/90                        Big Business, Inc.                                    PAGE  1
RUN TIME: 10:15 AM                            Job Cost
                                        EQUIPMENT BY JOB REPORT

JOB RANGE ALL TO END

JOB NUMBER GILJOB   Install 10 cptr network.        START 06/01/90        0% COMPLETE
SUPERVISOR    Michael Dispater                      DUE   09/01/90
CUSTOMER # GILMAN  Joel Gilman, Attorney            CLOSE   /  /

       --------PHASE/COST---------     --ENTRY-          ------EQUIPMENT-----------      --------  --------
       CODE      DESCRIPTION            DATE      CODE      DESCRIPTION                    HOURS     AMOUNT
       ----      -----------           -------    ----      -----------                  --------  --------

       I3      Component sub-assembly
       LAB001  Labor - assembly line   06/01/90   CHIP   EPROM programmer/blaster         12.00     300.00
                                                                                         ========  ========
               JOB GILJOB TOTAL                                                           12.00     300.00
```

FIGURE 12-44 Equipment by Job Report

```
RUN DATE: 06/01/90                              Big Business, Inc.                                                    PAGE  1
RUN TIME: 10:16 AM                                  Job Cost
                                              PRE-BILLING WORKSHEET

JOB RANGE ALL TO END

JOB NUMBER KRELL2  Computer w/ Peachtree S/W    START 06/01/90    0% COMPLETE      CURRENT PRICE      1875.00
SUPERVISOR         Michael Dispater             DUE   06/20/90                     TOTAL BILLINGS        0.00
CUSTOMER # KRELL   Krell Office Systems          CLOSE   /  /                      TOTAL PAYMENTS        0.00

--------PHASE/COST---------  --TRANSACTION-  UNIT  --BILLING-  -ACTUAL-  -BILLABLE-  -ACTUAL-  -------MARGIN-------
 CODE      DESCRIPTION        DATE   SOURCE  MEAS    RATE       UNITS     DOLLARS     COST      DOLLARS       %

I3      Component sub-assembly
MAT001  Cost of chassis       06/01/90 MISC   Each   57.90      20.00     1158.00     864.00     294.00      34.0


                                                               0.00         0.00       0.00       0.00       0.0
        LABOR                                                 20.00      1158.00     864.00     294.00      34.0
        MATERIAL                                               0.00         0.00       0.00       0.00       0.0
        EQUIPMENT                                              0.00         0.00       0.00       0.00       0.0
        SUBCONTRACT                                            0.00         0.00       0.00       0.00       0.0
        OTHER
                                                      =======  ========  =========  ========  =========  ======
        JOB KRELL2 TOTAL                             20.00      1158.00     864.00     294.00      34.0
```

FIGURE 12-45 Pre-Billing Worksheet

INDEX